Understanding Islam

By the Same Author

- Illegal Migration from Bangladesh
- India and Central Asia: A Shared Past
- India and Central Asia: Classical to Contemporary Periods
- India: Caste, Culture and Traditions
- Naga Identity
- Problems of Ethnicity in the North-East India
- Rashtriya Samasyaen: Chinta Avem Chintan (Hindi)
- Re-Organization of North-East India: Facts and Documents
- Small State Syndrome in India

ABOUT THE AUTHORS

B.B. Kumar, (b. 1941), M.Sc. (Chemistry), M.Sc. (Anthropology), M.A. (Hindi), Ph.D. (Authro.), an educationist and social activist, is former Principal, Sao Chang Government College, Tuensang (Nagaland), and Science College, Kohima. He was member, Executive Council, Academic Council, University Court, College Development Council, Examination Committee, School Board of Physical Sciences and other numerous committees of the North-Eastern Hill University, Shillong (India). He was Chairman, Hindi Board of Studies, and member, Board of Studies, of 'Science for Rural Development; Gandhigram Rural University, Tamilandu. He remained associated with a large number of NGOs as President, Vice-President, Secretary and founding member. He was founder secretary of Nagaland Bhasha Parishad and Thinkers Forum, Nagaland and Governing Body member of the Nagaland Peace Centre, the organization founded by Jai Prakash Narayan. Presently, he is Secretary, Astha Bharati, New Delhi and member, Governing Body of India Central Asia Foundation, New Delhi.

Dr. Kumar has written/edited/co-authored 135 books; he has written more than 100 papers. Presently, he is editing quarterly journals, Dialogue (English) and Chintan-Srijan (Hindi), both published from Delhi, and Quest (bi-annual journal of the Vivekanand Kendra Institute of Culture, Guwahati). His publication include India: Caste, Culture and Traditions, Small States Syndrome in India, Tension and Conflict in North-East India, Naga Identity, Macro-Perception of Indian Tribal Societies India and Central Asia: A Shared Past and Illegal Migration from Bangladesh (edited). He has written/edited 64 dictionaries/vocabularies, 14 outline grammars, 15 self-teachers and folk tales of 4 tribal languages of North-East and Eastern India.

Understanding Islam

B.B. Kumar

CONCEPT PUBLISHING COMPANY PVT. LTD.
NEW DELHI-110059

ISBN-13: 978-93-86682-19-2

First Published 2018

Published and Printed by

Concept Publishing Company Pvt. Ltd.
A/15-16, Commercial Block, Mohan Garden,
New Delhi-110059 (INDIA)
Phones : 25351460, 25351794
E-mail : publishing@conceptpub.com
Website: www.conceptpub.com

Cataloging in Publication Data—DK Courtesy: D.K. Agencies (P) Ltd. <docinfo@dkagencies.com>

Kumāra, Braja Bihārī, 1941- **author.**
Understanding Islam / B.B. Kumar.
pages cm
Includes bibliographical references and index.
ISBN 9789386682192

1. Islam--Doctrines. I. Title.

LCC BP166.K86 2017 | DDC 297.2 23

Contents

Preface

This book is the outcome of an endeavour to have an emic view of Islam by an outsider, utilizing traditional Islamic sources of study. It is not a polemical study, and therefore, there is conscious avoidance of the value judgment. India has a large number of intellectuals, who believe that 'all the religions say the same truth.' The author, after the study of Islam, has no such illusion; and, therefore, there is no exercise for searching similitude in the book.

An average Indian, especially the Hindu, has tremendous perceptional haziness about Islam, and there are reasons for the same. The present day Hindu suffers from intellectual passivity and laziness; there is serious lack of endeavour to understand and explicate Islam as explicitly as possible. As a result, and to cover-up, a Hindu often talks about Islam by placing it in Hindu spiritual framework/parameter. On the contrary, what is necessary, is to place everything Islamic into Islamic context, as Hinduism and Islam greatly differ. The two totally differ in their spiritual equipage, framework and content; they have different value-systems as well. God of Semitic persuasion—Allah and Yahweh—and the Hindu *Ishwara* are not the same. Wholly otherness of Semitic God and in-dwellingness of Hindu God, have no meeting ground. Like other Semitic religions, Islam has one God and at least two humanities; Hinduism, on the other hand, has multiple Gods and one humanity. Here it needs mention that even Islam and Christianity differ in many ways, although the spiritual equipage of both—Islam and Christianity—is similar, their spiritual content, both in quality and quantity, are about the same.

In Qur'an, the voice and tenor of the Meccan and Medinan *Suras* differ. In fact, Quran accepts its changing voice, when it says: "Whatever verses We cancel, or cause thee to forget, We give thee better in their stead, or the like thereof" (Qur'an 2:100). In reality, Qur'an may not contain certain passages once revealed and subsequently cancelled. It is a recognized fact that the Qur'an contains no fewer than 225 verses cancelled by latter ones (Muir, *The Life of*

Mahomet, p. xxvi, note 1). A section of the Muslims quote Qur'an (*La ikrah fi'l din;* there is no compulsion in religion); *Sura* 2:256). On the other hand, the radical Jihadists rely on numerous other *Suras* (Qur'an 2:191, 2:154, 2:216; 4:91-92; 8:12, 8:39; 9:5, 9:14, 9:15, 9:23, 9:29, 9:39, 9:73, 9:123; 25:52; 48:29; 49:15; 61:4; 66:9; 69:30-31). The compulsion to deny the existence of other religions is very much inherent in Medinan *Suras,* and is the dominant voice of Qur'an.

Prophet Muhammad begged Allah to grant three things, according to *Hadis*, and the two of them were granted. The one, which was not granted, was that there should be no bloodshed among the people of his *Ummah*, i.e., the Muslims (*Sahih Muslim, Hadis* 6906). The Islamic history attests to the same.

This book is not the product of a critiquing endeavour, but that of understanding Islam. Therefore, the approach to the subject has been without bias, condescension and sentimentality.

The author has not tried to place Islam in spiritual framework/map as a member of the Hindu faith community. There may, however, be inadequacies in the book due to my limitations.

Sarvashri J.N. Roy, Utpal Kumar, and my son, have gone through the manuscript on my request. They made some valuable suggestions, for which I heartily thank them.

B.B. Kumar

Background

The Birthplace of Islam

Arabia: the Geographical Features

Arabia, the south-western peninsular part of Asia, called 'the Arabian Peninsula' or 'Gazirat el Arab' is the birthplace of Islam. It is bounded on the west by the Red Sea. On the east by the Persian Gulf and the Gulf of Oman; on the south by the Indian Ocean; and in the north, extending to the confines of Babylonia and Syria. The peninsula slopes eastward, towards the Persian Gulf, from a mountain range running parallel to the western Red Sea coast. The highest points of the range are 9000 feet at Midian in the north, and 12000 feet in the south at Yemen (al-Yemen). As an exception to the eastward slope decline, the height of al-Jabal ai-Akhdar (the Green Mountain) in south-east Oman (Uman) reaches 9900 feet above the sea level. Arabia, usually described as a triangle with right angle at the Strait of Bab al-Mandeb, is rather of the oblong shape with the sides bounded by the Red Sea on one hand and the Persian Gulf and Euphrates on the other as the longest ones.

Apart from mountains and highlands, the surface area consists mainly of desert and steppe. Largely covered by a tract, 80 to 160 kms wide, of white or red sand, the northern part of the peninsula, called al-Nufud, receives enough rain during certain occasions in winter to produce grass for the camels and sheep of nomadic Bedouins. Another tract, some 1000 kms towards the south of al-Nufud, called al-Dahna, extends up to the great sandy desert of 'Rubal-Khali' (the Empty Quarters), which is one of the most forbidden and least known areas on the surface of the earth. Harrah, the tract to the central and western part, another variety of desert land, consists of the surface of fissured lava overlaying sandstone. A plain, called Tihamah, extends, from five to forty feet inland, along the entire Red Sea shoreline. The peninsula, from very early days, was inhabited by the sedentary town dwellers and the nomadic Bedouin tribes. The nomads lived in tents made of hair or woolen cloth; their principal wealth consisted of the camels, horses, sheep, and male and female slaves.

Terra Incognita: Western Explorers

Hijaz (al-Hijaz; Hejaz, the holy land of Islam) is the western region of Arabia on the eastern side of the Red Sea. It has the two holy cities of Islam – Mecca and Medina – within its limits. Most of the region has been a forbidden territory to non-Muslims through the centuries after the acceptance of Islam by the Arabs. With the exception of the seaboard, even the southern part of the peninsula remained *terra incognita* during the medieval periods. Thus the only sources of knowledge about Arabia until the mid-eighteenth century were the antiquated sources, such as, Herodotus, Strabo, Pliny, Ptolemy, al-Hamdani, al-Bakri, Yakut, and a few others. One of the earliest Christian born Europeans to visit to the holy places of Mecca (Makkah; Makka) and Medina (Yathrib, al-Madinah; Madina) during 1814-15 was Johann Ludwig Burckhardt, a Swiss, under the name of Ibrahim ibn-Abdullah. Richard Burton, translator of the *Arabian Nights,* visited these cities as a pilgrim, al-Haji ‘Abdullah. Charles M. Doughty, an Englishman, the author of *Travels in Arabia Deserta,* traversed Hejaz and Nejd in 1875, but did not visit Mecca and Medina, as he did not profess Islam. Carsten Niebuhr, a Dane, who was sent to Yemen in 1761 on a scientific mission, was the first among the modern scholars to describe the region. The other two scholars – Joseph Halevy, a Frenchman, and Eduard Glaser, an Austrian – visited the same region a century later. Halevy, in the guise of a Jewish beggar from Jerusalem, explored the region, as far inland as Ma’rib, during 1869-70; he copied many south Arabic inscriptions. His work, together with that of Glaser in 1882, provided first hand information about the pre-Islamic south Arabians. This is important as the only source of information about Pagan Arabia of the pre-Islamic days. The works of two English explorers – H. St. John Philby (his Muslim name is al-Haji ‘Abdullah), who explored most of the peninsula during 1917, and crossed Rub al-Khali from east to west in 90 days, beginning his journey on 7 January, 1932; another Englishman, Bertram Thomas, crossing the same in fifty-eight days from south to the north-east – need special mention.

The Early History

Arabia, except the extreme northern and southern confines, remained largely an unknown country till the Muslim conquest in the seventh century; this was especially true in the case of the Central Arabia. The notices of Arabia, in ancient times, are few and meagre. There is mention of the Arab traders carrying the spiceries of Gilead on their camels down to Egypt; a naval station was formed at Elath, the modern Acaba, during the reign of Solomon; ‘the kings of

Arabia' and its merchants supplied Judaea with the rarities of the East; the queen of Sheba came from the far south to visit the widely famed Jewish monarch; Aelius Gallus, during the reign of Augustus, penetrated from the northern shores of the Red Sea to the south with a Roman army, but was forced to return due to treachery and scarcity of water. However, the Arabs carried their caravan trade since the remote past in limited scale.[1]

Arabian Peninsula, supposedly the original home of the Semites, was the region from which they migrated outside into the valley of the Tigris and Euphrates to form the Assyro-Babylonians (*c* 3500 BC), and then into Syria and Lebanon to form Amorites and Canaanites (*c* 2500 BC), and finally (*c* 1500 BC) into the Aramaeans of Damascus and Hebrews of Palestine. The migration also took place from the southern region of the Yemen into Abyssinia across the Red Sea. It needs mention that Abyssinian, like Hebrew and Arabic is a Semitic language, and the outside migration from the peninsula was necessitated due to dearth of fertile land, except in the peripheral regions, to support the growing population. The Old Testament repeatedly makes it clear that the Hebrews, like Arabs, had their origin in the deserts. Many early names in Bible may be identified as Arabic. The Semitic god, Yahveh or Jehovah, is supposed to be a North Arabian deity; Moses was introduced into the cult of Yahveh in Sinai by his Midianite wife. Ophir, from where the navy of Hiram and Solomon brought gold, algum and precious stones, is identified by the scholars with Zafar in Oman. It is probable that Queen Sheba belonged to a Sabaean colony of North Arabia, and the Arabians of the Pentacost[2] were also the North Arabians, especially, Nabataeans. The Sumerians, who preceded Babylonians, discovered and used copper in Oman, before Egyptians did it in Sinai. The Greeks and Romans acknowledged Arabs as traders.

The Assyrian king Shalmaneser III led an expedition in 854 BC, against an Armaean king of Damascus. An Arab Sheikh (sheik, shaikh), named Jundub was one of the latter's allies, whose name occurs in the Assyrian king's inscriptions. Zabibi, a queen of "Aribi" land paid tribute to another Assyrian king Tiglath-pileser III, who later defeated another queen of "Aribi," called Samsi *(Shams,* sun); Sabaeans sent him tribute of gold, camels and spices. The Persians, the predecessors of Muslim rule, replaced Assyrians and neo-Babylonians in the region. In South Arabia, Minaean (about 1200 to 650 BC), Sabaean (930-115 BC) and Himyarite kingdoms (115 BC to 525 AD) were prominent, apart from the brief period of Abyssinian sway. The Roman expedition, during 20 BC, was brief and unsuccessful. Some petty kingdoms ruled in the northern part of the Arabian Peninsula, apart from the brief period of Persian sway, which succumbed to Islam in 633 AD just a year after the death of Prophet Muhammad.

The limited caravan trade between al-Yemen in the south – al-Yemen means the 'South Land' – to Syria in the north along the western route near the Red Sea coast continued for centuries. Such trade, however, suffered when the Roman enterprise, early in the Christian era, established a maritime traffic from Egypt direct to the Yemen. Two routes in the north linked Syria with the Indian Ocean. Central Arabia remained almost the empty land with little nomadic population. The peninsula has no river.[3]

During the period of the Muhammad's successors, the four orthodox caliphs *(trashidun,* 632-661 AD), Hejaz remained politically and religiously important. But the seat of the caliphate shifted from Medina in Arabia to Damascus in Syria when Mu'awiyah became caliph in 661 AD and continued to be there during the entire Umayyad caliphate period (661-750 AD). The centre of Islamic power, the caliphate, shifted further east to Baghdad during Abbasid caliphate (750-1258 AD) However, the importance of Hejaz continued due to the location of twin pilgrimage centres – Mecca and Medina – within its limit. Mecca, with its holy temple, Ka'ba (also written as Kaaba, Kaba), lies within the great mountain range skirting the Red Sea, and midway between the Yemen and the Syrian border.

Hijaz

The forbiddingly jagged mountain chain in which Mecca is located is called al-Hijaz (the Hijaz; the barrier). There is no such thing as the gentle rain in the harsh Hijaz landscape of rock and dust. Lesley Hazleton has given a graphic picture of the same: "It comes instead in rare spasms, violent downpours as capable of wreaking havoc as the most malevolent of *jinns.* With a kind of warped vengeance, water turns from blessing into curse, and the stuff of life becomes the agent of death. The sky might be clear with no cloud in sight, so that the first sign of rain cascading off rock miles away could be nothing more than a barely perceptible scent carried on a passing breeze. If humans don't notice it, animals do. They stand still, ears alert, vaguely aware of something different. Minutes pass, even an hour, when the sand underfoot begins to dampen. It might be the merest trickle at first, as though someone has emptied a pail on the ground, then the trickle builds, tugging gently at your ankles as a faint rumble echoes through the mountains. Before you quite know what is happening, you find you are stumbling in a current that seems to have come from nowhere." She further writes: "Thrown off balance, you flail and fall, trying to pick yourself up only to be knocked down again by the gathering weight of tumbling sand laden water sweeping down through the wadi, hammering at your shins. The roar of it is on you now, the terrible sound of large stones grinding against rock. Branches of broom and acacia and saltbush and then whole bushes come hurtling at you, and there's the flailing bulk of a drowning animal, legs akimbo, and you can't hear your own voice crying for help as you fall again and again, caught up in the chaotic momentum of water and debris, If a stone hits your head and you lose consciousness, you can drown in a few inches." Prophet Muhammad was caught up in such a situation in 605 AD, while returning from Mount Hira. Although most floods happened to be relatively shallow, but that particular flood was not so; the torrent during that flood raced on into the sacred temple of Kaaba leading to its collapse. Here, it needs mention that the temple is located at the lowest point of Mecca, where all the wadis met.[4] Prophet Muhammad played an important role in the restoration/reconstruction of the temple, as discussed elsewhere, before the start of his Prophetic career.[5]

Approach to Mecca

The sacred valley of Mecca, the birthplace of Prophet Muhammad and the city where Ka'ba (also written Kaaba; Ka'bah) is located, may be approached by a traveller from the seashore by an almost imperceptible rise of about fifty miles, chiefly through sandy plains and defiles hemmed in by low hills of gneiss and quartz, reaching in some places up to the height of 400-500 feet. In the immediate vicinity of the sacred valley, about two miles in length, the hills are formed of the quartz and gneiss. However, moving a little towards the east, grey strata of granite appears, and within one or two miles of the city, lofty and rugged peaks shoot upwards in grand masses. The general direction and slope are from north to south, but the upper or northern extremity on the way to Arafat bends eastwards; on the other hand, at the lower end, where three roads from the Yemen, Jidda, and, Syria meet, there is a still more decided curve to the west. Pursuing an eastward course from Mecca, one proceeds with the same gentle rise between hills of granite through the valley of Mina, and then arrives at the Mount Arafat.

Further east, the hills ascend to a great height; granite peaks of Jebel Kora crowns the range; and thirty miles across there is the fertile and the lovely valley, where At-Taif – the city, the centre of Thakif tribe, about which we may discuss elsewhere also, is visible.[6] The old name of the city was Bajj; Al-Lat was their deity.[7]

With pleasant greenery and large shady trees, numerous rivulets descending from the hills, At-Taif is famous for large and delicious flavoured grapes; varieties of peaches, pomegranates, apples, almonds, figs, apricots and quinces grow in abundance. Situated in an oasis of sweet water and fertile soil on a plain surrounded by mountains in a horseshoe form, with an opening facing the east, Taif, a walled town, as perhaps its name signifies, was located some thirty-six hours' journey from Mecca. Tamisier, who visited the city, counted fourteen kinds of fruit trees in the orchards, surrounding the city. It was famous for the cultivation of vine; the raisins made from the same looked like flasks of purified honey. It was well-known even for the cultivation of various kinds of grain, and for brick-making and the art of building. The frowning hills and barren valleys around Mecca, on the other hand, present an entirely different scenario. Mecca, the birthplace of the Prophet Muhammad, unlike Medina and At-Taif, or even unlike Aden, from where the Meccans were forced to migrate after the destruction of the irrigation dam there, was not a suitable area for agriculture. Of course, Mecca, though within the tropics, does not have the advantage of tropical showers; rainy season begins in about December, but the rain is irregular, and even in summer, rain is not infrequent. Calamities of occasional drought and flood are the well-known phenomena in the narrow valley. The heat, especially during autumn, is oppressive.[8] Mecca had, from the ancient days, the trade and pilgrimage-centric economy.[9] It was also a craft centre; fairs used to be organized all around Mecca.

Yemen: Collapse of Marib Dam

Quraysh (also written as Quraish, Kuraish, and Kuraysh), the dominant community of Mecca, migrated there only five generations earlier than Prophet Muhammad. It was the collapse of the giant Marib Dam of Yemen, which forced them to migrate towards the north. The dam, whose ruins can still be seen in the hills outside Sana, the biblical Sheba, irrigated a quarter million acres of fields. The dam collapsed due to negligence, caused by the chaos of warfare. Lesley Hazleton writes: "Along with irrigation came a vibrant civilization, funded in large part by the cultivation of the native spindly thorn trees that looked utterly negligible to anyone who failed to realize the value of their sap: myrrh. But with wealth, as always, came greed. And with greed 'instability. Control of Yemen shifted from Byzantine-backed Christian Ethiopia to Zoroastrian Persia to independent kings (one of them, in the fifth century, Jewish) and then through the whole cycle again, each shift accomplished by force of arms. The chaos of warfare took its inevitable toll, and the upkeep of the Marib dam was neglected. In the end, its collapse was due to something ridiculously simple; moles had burrowed so deep into its huge clayey base that it gave way, and the land reverted to high desert."[10]

Migration of Quraysh; Settling in Mecca

The overall result of the collapse of Marib Dam was the northwards exodus of the people from Yemen; it included several clans migrating under the leadership of legendary Qussay, the great-grandfather of Abd al-Muttalib, the grandfather of Prophet Muhammad. These clans formed a single tribe, adopting the nomenclature 'Quraysh,' meaning 'those gathered together.' They abandoned agriculture, as there was less scope for the same in Mecca.[11] The control of Kaaba, by defeating the Zurhum tribe, opened up new avenues of livelihood for the Quraysh. Ibn Ishaq writes about Jurhum: "Afterwards Jurhum behaved high-handedly in Mecca and made lawful that which was a taboo. Those who entered the town, who were not of their tribe, they treated them badly and they appropriated gifts which had been made to the Ka'ba so that their authority weakened. When B. Bakr b. 'Abdu Manat b. Kinan and Ghubshan of Khuza'a perceived that, they came together to do battle and drive them out of Mecca. War was declared and in the fighting B. Bakr and Ghubshan got the upper hand and expelled them from Mecca."[12]

Ibn Ishaq further writes: "Now in the time of paganism Mecca did not tolerate injustice and wrong within its borders and if anyone did wrong therein it expelled him; therefore it was called 'the Scorcher' and any king who came to profane its sanctity died on the spot. It is said that it was called Bakka because it used to break the necks of tyrants when they introduced innovations therein."[13]

Meccan Economy

D.S. Margoliouth provided the glimpse of the Meccan economy, which is given below:

"For the economic basis of the community we have some data though little in the way of statistics. The possession of a popular sanctuary ensured a certain revenue from strangers; taking the form partly of a visitors' tax, partly of fees paid to the worker of oracle (said to be 100 dirhems and a camel for each consultation), and partly of remuneration for entertainment and garments furnished to visitors; for by a lucrative rule the pilgrims might not use food or clothes brought by themselves. Secondly, the sanctity which attached to the neighbourhood of the temple rendered it a suitable place for the pursuit of the arts of peace. Hence our authorities enumerate a number of trades that were practiced at Mecca: such as those of carpenter, smith, sword-maker, wine-merchant, oil merchant, leather merchant, tailor, weaver, arrow-maker, stationer, and money-lender. On the goods which were imported from the Byzantine Empire, partly for use in those industries, the Meccans levied a tax of ten per cent. If a Bedouin wished to purchase an idol for his tent he would come to

Meccah to procure it. But in the third place the sacred character which attached to "God's neighbours" gave them a great advantage for the prosecution of the carrying trade. By wearing certain badges merchants could in many places secure themselves from attack."[14]

Whereas the caravan trade with Syria towards the north and Aden towards the south brought ample wealth, the leading men of Mecca remained engaged locally also in commercial activities; hospitality to the pilgrims, providing pilgrims' dresses on payment, etc. generated money. Muhammad's grandfather supplied water to the pilgrims from the well of Zemzem. The commercial pursuits of some of the contemporaries of the Prophet Muhammad is on record. Abdallah, son of Jud'an, dealt in slaves; he was a leading man when the Prophet was a boy. Abu Sufyan, Muhammad's opponent, sold oil and leather; the keeper of the key of Ka'ba was a tailor. Abu Bakr was a trader; Muhammad himself was the agent of his wealthy wife, Khadija. The records revealing the price tag of some of the commodities is interesting, and worth quoting.

Four hundred dinars, or about £150 was the price of a dwelling at Mecca before it was taken by Muhammad. A Meccan paid fifty dinars, or about £20, for an antique robe; an excellent war horse cost about 300 dirhems, or about £12.[15]

There is no doubt that Mecca's economy was in good shape. Hind, daughter of Abdal-Muttalib, and wife of Abu Sufyan, manumitted forty slaves in one day. There were persons who could pay 4000 dinars, £500 for ransom after the battle of Badr. The gifts lavished on the Ka'ba, which was covered with fine fabrics and silks, brought from Iraq and Yemen, and luxurious life style of many, confirmed the same. Apart from the wealth coming due to trade and commerce, pilgrimage economy and earnings from crafts, the gold dug out of mines in the country of the Sulaim was also some times brought to Mecca and profitably utilized. Many Meccans hoarded coins, but the preferred practice was to have their wealth in live stock or in some form of goods. Many wealthy Meccans possessed estates or villas in the neighbouring oasis of Taif.[16] Meccan aristocrats owned estates in Egypt, mansions in Damascus, farms in Palestine, and date orchards in Iraq.[17]

The Meccan Caravan Trade

It was the number of traders joining the caravan, which provided safety to the traders. Otherwise, there was always the danger of bandits or of rogue Beduin raiders tempted by the drawn-out line of heavily laden beasts. Besides sickness and accident, guarding a caravan during the night against the predators like wolves, hyenas, and mountain lions, sharing "sheer arduousness of travel in the scorching heat and light, magnified by the stone and packed dust of the desert pavement, which was seared to a crust, were the problems which the members of the caravan shared and thereby reduced each others difficulties."[18] Lesley Hezleton writes: "The caravan provided the safety of numbers. The lone traveler may have been a staple of the great Beduin odes, taking his pleasures where he could and stoically enduring the dangers of the road even as he boasted of them, but that was poetry, and this was real life, and only the young and inordinately idealistic would be so rash as to confuse the two. Any caravan consisted of at least a dozen camels, but twice a year the Meccan merchants organized huge camel trains up to two thousand strong, one heading north to Damascus in the spring, the other south to Yemen in the fall."[19] Occasionally, Meccan caravans also visited Egypt, Abyssinia and Persia.[20]

Although, caravans were skillfully conducted; the local chiefs provided protection, and water facilities, as they were negotiated and suitably paid. Nevertheless, the arduous journey was not always a happy-ending affair. After all, Muhammad's father never returned from such a journey. "It's a measure of how much they risked that of the four ancestors who had given their names to the main clans of the Quraysh, only one had died at home in Mecca; the other three, including Muhammad's forebear Hashim, had ended their lives far away in Gaza, in Iraq, and in Yemen.[21]

The caravan trade of the Meccans was organized as a cartel and run by a syndicate. As Lesley Hazleton writes: "This financial system redounded to the benefit of all, or at least all who were allowed in. In the years Muhammad worked for abu-Talib, the largest shares were held by the four main clans of the Quraysh, but many others had minority shares, including individuals. Tolls, protection money, customs duties, and sales taxes were all paid by the syndicate and factored in, with a share of each member's profits deducted to cover the cost of administration. Here too diplomacy was needed to defuse the inevitable arguments about the distribution of profits, ..."[22] On the northbound caravan route from Mecca to Damascus, there were oases with permanent settlements at Medina, Khybar, Tayma and Tabuk with spring-fed plantations stretching for miles long, looking like long ribbons of green hidden in deep valleys.

Muhammad's Exposure to the World Outside Mecca

Muhammad was a highly experienced person. He was also a highly exposed person with the knowledge of the world outside Mecca. The eloquence in expression, fluent and correct delivery, familiarity with Bedouin life, deeper knowledge about camels and sheep were acquired in early life while staying with the foster mother; the love of horses which characterised Muhammad at a latter time is likely to have been imbibed in early age.[23] Muhammad accompanied his uncle in the northwards caravan journey, and here too he learned quickly, becoming as skilled at calming ruffled egos as he was at negotiating differences. "By the time he was in his early twenties, he'd become abu-Talib's trusted lieutenant on the long caravan journeys, and had risen in his uncle's estimation that he was treated almost as a son. But only almost."[24] Here, it needs mention that abu-Talib, his own uncle, the father of Ali, who became the son-in-law of Muhammad, gave lifelong protection to Muhammad, but declined the hand of his daughter, Fakhita to him.

He visited Syria several times as part of the caravan journey, and even Egypt and other places. His writings reveal his exposure of the sea journey also;[25] he was certainly a person of wider experience and knowledge about the culture and religion of the people he visited before the start of his Prophetic career.

Medina

The original name of Medina, situated about 200 miles to the north of Mecca, was Yathrib. It is equidistant from Mecca and Damascus on the road linking the two cities. The present name, Medina (the City) is the abbreviation of 'Medinan un-Nabi,' i.e., 'the City of the Prophet.' Unlike Mecca, Medina lies in a fruitful plain. As Keane wrote: "Walled habitations! green fields, running water; every blessing, the Eastern mind can desire, are there."[26] Muhammad's triple link with Medina is a well-known phenomenon. His great-grandmother, and again his own mother, belonged to Medina. It was Medina, where Muhammad migrated; laid solid foundation of the Islamic Empire. Muhammad's father, his great-grandmother, and he himself died and was buried in Medina. When Muhammad's mother was returning from Medina to Mecca with her young son, she died halfway in between and was buried there. The continuing civil war situation in Medina at the time of his migration, and the way he resolved it is yet another story discussed in the book.[27]

"Makka had been the birthplace of Islam, but its cradle, the place where it would grow and thrive, would be Medina," as Lesley Hazleton rightly observes: "it was from Muhammad's arrival in Medina that the Muslim era – After the Hijra, or AH – would eventually be dated."[28]

Language and Literature

The language of Islam, in which Qur'an is written, is Arabic. It is akin to Aramaic, which used to be the lingua franca of the region. Arabic was rich in oral literature. There is mention of many poets and poetesses in the Islamic literature. Even Muhammad had to deal with them during his lifetime. Max Mueller writes about the language thus:

"The Arabs made use of a rhymed and rhythmical prose, the origin of which is not difficult to imagine. The Arabic language consists for the most part of triliteral roots, i.e. the single words expressing individual ideas consist generally of three consonants each, and the derivative forms expressing modifications of the original ideas are not made by affixes and terminations alone, but also by the insertion of letters in the root. Thus **zaraba** means 'he struck,' and **qatala,** 'he killed,' **mazrub** and *maqtal* signify 'one struck' and 'one killed.' A sentence, therefore, consists of a series of words which would each required to be expressed in clauses of several words in other languages, and it is easy to see how a next following sentence, explanatory of or completing the first, would be much more clear and forcible if it consisted of words of a similar shape and implying similar modifications of other ideas. It follows then that the two sentences would be necessarily symmetrical, and the presence of rhythm would not only please the ear but contribute to the better understanding of the same, while the rhyme would mark the pause in the sense and emphasize the proposition."[29]

Max Mueller further writes about the rhetorical style of writings of Qur'an: "in which the clauses are rhythmical though not symmetrically so, and for the most part end in the same rhyme throughout the chapter." His observation, about the different ways of using Arabic language, is worth noting: "The Arabic language lends itself very readily to this species of composition, and the Arabs of the desert in the present day employ it to a great extent in their more formal orations, while the literary men of the towns adopt it as the recognized correct style, deliberately imitating the Qur'an."[30]

The Importance of Arabia and the Arabic Language

The importance of Arabia, as the birthplace of Islam, and the Arabic language, as the language of Qur'an, is self-evident. As mentioned in the Hadith, Prophet Muhammad said:

"Love the Arabs for three reasons because (1) I am an Arab, (2) the Holy Qur'an is in Arabic, and (3) the tongue of the dwellers of paradise shall also be Arabic."[31] Again, Kaaba in Mecca is the *qibla,* the direction of the Muslim prayer. Initially, it was the direction of the Jerusalem; but it changed after the expulsion of the Qaynuqa from Medina. The Qur'an declared: "We are turning you in a prayer direction that pleases you. Turn your face in the direction of the Sacred Mosque."[32]

The Arabia is important for every Muslim, as the pilgrimage centre of Mecca is situated there, and every Muslim must visit that at least once in his lifetime for *hajj,* if he has the means to do so. A Muslim must not defecate facing the direction of Mecca. The body of a Muslim, on his death, must be buried facing Mecca. The Model of Islamic behavioural pattern, in anyway, comes from Arabia.

Notes and References:

1. Muir, Sir William; *The Life of Mahomet: From Original Sources,* Voice of India, New Delhi, Reprint, 2002; p. lxxxix. (Hereafter, Muir).
2. Bible Acts 2: 11.
3. Muir, op. cit., p. xci.
4. Lesley Hazleton, *The First Muslim,* pp. 72-73. (Hereafter, Hazleton).
5. Hazleton, p. 72.
6. Margoliouth, D.S.; *Mohammed and the Rise of Islam,* Voice of India, New Delhi, Reprint, 1985, pp. 402-06. (Hereafter, Margoliouth).
7. Ibid, pp. 428-29.
8. Muir, pp. 1-2.
9. Ibid.
10. Hazleton, 38-39.
11. Ibid, p. 39.
12. Ibn Ishaq, *Sirat Rasul Allah,* pp. 46-47 (Hereafter – Ibn-Ishaq).
13. Ibid, p. 47; the Arabic term for 'the Scorcher is *al-Nissa;* the name Bakka is derived from the Arabic verb *bakka,* he broke.
14. Margoliouth, pp. 13-14.
15. Ibid, pp. 14-15.
16. Ibid.
17. Hazleton, pp. 55.
18. Ibid, pp. 49-50.
19. Ibid, p. 50.
20. Ibid, p. 57.
21. Ibid, p. 49; Ibn-Ishaq, p. 60.
22. Ibid, p. 60.
23. Margoliouth, pp. 51-53.

24. Hazleton, p. 60.
25. Margoliouth, p. 56.
26. Margoliouth, op. cit., p.185; quotes Keane, p. 219.
27. Hazleton, p. 49.
28. Ibid, p.164.
29. Max Mueller, *The Sacred Books of the East: The Qur'an,* Vol. VI, Part I, Reprint, Delhi, 2006; pp. I-Ii.
30. Ibid, p. Ii.
31. Mishkat-ul-Masabih, Vol. 3, hadith no. 5751.
32. Qur'an 2:144.

Glimpses of the Pre-Islamic Pagan Culture of Arabia

Dominance of Paganism in Pre-Islamic Arabia

The pre-Islamic Arabia was a pagan country. Except for few Jewish and Christian settlements, the people of Arabia adhered to the traditional religion of the land till the advent of Islam. There were Jewish settlements around Medina and in some other places, which is discussed elsewhere in the book. Christians, though not very numerous, were also scattered in Arabia. Even in Mecca, Waraqa, the aged cousin of Khadija, the wife of Prophet Muhammad, professed Christianity.[1] However, pre-Islamic Arabia was, by and large, pagan.

As Qur'an says, the Meccans had no previous revelation, no Prophet, no books, no guidance,[2] and thus, according to Semitic belief system, they lacked true knowledge. This led to the Quranic concept of *jahiliya*, which was variously translated as 'darkness,' 'ignorance,' 'idolatry' and, 'barbarism.' The word 'pagan' (Latin: *pagus*; meaning a rural district) is also used in the same sense as that of *jahiliya*, and is synonymously used. The word 'pagan' is derived from the same root as the English word 'peasant.' A pagan, for a Roman aristocrat, was a peasant. The word 'pagan' gradually acquired derogatory meaning.[3] Paganism, as Margoliouth writes: "is called by the Qur'an the period of Ignorance—a phrase in the opinion of some, borrowed from the New Testament."[4]

The picture of *jahiliya* or paganism, as emerged from the writings of Semitic writers or historians, be it Hebrew prophets, such as Isaiah, Jeremiah, or Ezekiel, describing Jerusalem or Israel, in terms of 'harlotry', or Islamic historians writing about pre-Islamic Mecca, present the image of godlessness, total lack of morals and values, erotically charged lasciviousness, chaotic infinity of false deities, primitive and barbaric rituals and soullessness.[5] The fact remains that all ancient great thinkers of the world, including Greek ones, who laid the foundations of profound and deep thought processes, were pagans. They lacked neither the soul, nor the sacred.[6]

Pagans: Advanced in Commercial Civilization

Margoliouth opines in this respect, thus:

"Of respect for property and loyalty and honour, pagan Arabia shows no exalted standard. The institution of private property would appear to have existed, and indeed to have been fairly developed at Meccah, in spite of its apparent contradiction to the doctrine of the blood-feud. Thus the Meccan heads of houses are represented as forming a joint-stock company for the purpose of foreign trade, the profits of each occasion being divided proportionately among the investors, and by them expended or hoarded, or invested in fresh speculations. Sales of various sorts between individuals are recorded for the period before taking of Meccah. Probably, therefore, this community was somewhat further advanced in commercial civilization than the Crows or Blackfeet of Beckwourth's time."[7]

A Highly Exposed Society

Being highly exposed, the pagans (pre-Islamic Arabs), especially the Meccans, did not lack knowledge about outside world. They regularly used to visit, Damascus and Yemen, and occasionally, Egypt, Abyssinia and other places. At Damascus, they used to meet people of different nationalities, following diverse religions. Thus Arabian pagans, especially the Meccans, were not ignorant about the outside world; their society was not a closed society. The adventures of Alexander[8] were certainly known to them, and the familiarity might have been due to social converse.[9] The name finds mention in Qur'an.[10] Numerous mentions of 'Indian sword' in Islamic literature,[11] personal names, such as 'Hind,'[12] apart from other facts[13] point towards Indian linkages.

Perceptional Haziness About the Pagan Society

There is considerable perceptional haziness in our understanding of the pagan society, wherever the Semitic religions prevailed. This happened, mainly, due to two reasons: (i) No spokes-person of the pagan society was left to tell the tale about them after their conversion to a Semitic religion; (ii) the distortions were inherent in the dominant scholarship of the day.

No Spokesperson of Pagan Arabia Left in Islamic Arabia

It is difficult to have a clear picture of the pre-Islamic Arabic traditions, as none among the pagans was left there to tell their tale. The Qur'an[14] mentions about Noah's prayer: 'My Lord! Leave not any one of the disbelievers in the land.' The prophet advised against following even the Jewish and Christian traditions. Writing about the society, culture, and religion of pagan Arabia is, therefore, difficult, as we do not have access to their spokes-persons, as Islam did not allow its adverseries to survive.

The perusal of Islamic traditions, Qur'an and the *Hadis*, however, bring out certain facts to our notice, which provide glimpses of the Arabian pagan culture. Another factor was the "Emerging monotheism's need to claim the higher moral ground," which no doubt had the blurring effect on our perception, if not outright distortion.[15] The fact that the spokespersons of the Meccan side were also their adversaries can not be ignored. The opinion of Margoliouth in this case is worth quoting. He writes: "Thus then the years of the Meccan controversy rolled on; in which the parties increased in vehemence and antagonism, and in which successful polemics of the Meccans on the new religion were met by ridicule and refutation of the religious notions current among the pagans. As has been said, the Meccan side is known only from the statements of their adversary, whose acquaintance with the Meccan religion may not have been deep."[16]

Distortions Inherent in Orientalism

Distortions were inherent in the writings of the early Islamic historians, as was the case with the writings of the nineteenth century colonial scholars. Lesley Hazleton ably sums up the weaknesses of those scholars:

"The irony is that early Islamic historians, like the Hebrew prophets before them, thus proved themselves as Orientalist as any of the nineteenth–century scholars and writers so effectively dissected by Edward Said in his classic critique *Orientalism*. Orientalism, that is, began in the Middle East itself, long before European imperialism, and for the same reason: intellectual snobbery. These supremely urban eighth- and ninth century took understandable pride in the cultural and intellectual achievements of the Muslim empire, from the splendor of Jerusalem's Dome of the Rock to the academies laying the foundation of modern medicine and science. They contrasted their own sophistication with the presumed primitivism of what had gone before, painting an Islamic picture of pre - and post-enlightenment."[17]

Drawing a parallel with the Western scholarly pursuits, she further writes: "As we tend to do in the West today, they nurtured the fond idea that they and their contemporaries were at the peak of civilization, the sophisticated heirs who have come so far from the days of darkness. Like us, they couldn't help seeing the past through the lens of their own accomplishments and thus distorting it in the process, as though looking through the wrong end of the telescope."[18]

A Case of Wrong Interpretation

Lesley Hazleton has cited a case of misinterpretation, which needs to be quoted. She writes: "This is how they could come to interpret a single Quranic reference to "abominations" at the Kaaba to mean nakedness, which was exactly what they would expect of unenlightened pagans. But like those who read the Hebrew prophets' condemnation of harlotry literally, they grasped the image but missed the point."[19]

She further writes: "Pilgrims would indeed cast aside everyday clothes in acknowledgement of the presence of the sacred, but then they'd don the two seamless lengths of homespun unbleached linen, still worn on the *hajj* today known as *ihram*. By comparison with the usual billowing robes covering everything but the hands and feet, this was nakedness."[20] Their attitude towards the divine was also responsible for the same. Lesley Hazleton writes: "The pilgrims made themselves deliberately vulnerable, assuming the simplest and humblest possible covering in order to allow no distinction of status or tribe, emphasizing that all were equal in presence of the divine. All, that is, except those who supplied the homespun garments, the people who ran the business of pilgrimage, the Quraysh."[21]

Sources for the Study of Arabic Pagan Culture

As the spokespersons of pagan Arabia did not survive after Islam came to power, the only sources for the appraisal, though scant, of the pre-Islamic Arabian pagan culture and ethos are: (i) the residual cultural traits among the Muslims, and (ii) tangential and scant references of the same in the Islamic literature.

Residual Cultural Traits

After the conquest of Mecca by Muhammad, the entry of pagans in Kaaba was prohibited.[22] Therefore, it is difficult to know precisely about the rituals followed by the pagan pilgrims. As is discussed elsewhere, the Prophet made numerous changes in religious, cultural and other parameters, but many remained unchanged. As for example, the Muslims, like their pagan forefathers, shave their hair, use unstitched pair of cloth during pilgrimage, circumambulate deity and the shrine seven times; and use water for purification; these are the examples of some of the residual pre-conversion pagan traditional practices. The Muslims, like pagans, wash the dead body before burial.[23]

Tangential and Scant References and Statements

Certain conclusions about the pre-Islamic cultural traits and the pagan ethos and the belief system of Arabia may be drawn from tangential and scant references and statements scattered in the Islamic literature. The *ahadis* are full of the statements, such as, "The Jews and the Christians, or the pagans, do like this, therefore do the opposite", which indirectly inform about the practice of the adversaries of Islam. Take the case of the *hadis*, which says: "Act against the polytheists, trim closely the moustache and grow beard."[24] It clearly informs that the pagans of Arabia used to keep their moustache and shave the beard. The translator, however, provides the rational for the same; he writes: "Islam created a new brotherhood on the basis of belief and good conduct. … For the identification of faces, the Muslims have been ordered to trim the moustache and wear the beard, so that they may be distinguished from the non-Muslims who grow a moustache and shave beard."[25]

Pre-Islamic Religious Scenario

Regarding the Arabian concept of Supreme deity, Margoliouth points out, that even traditional Arabic concept does not differ from the Islamic concept of the same. The only difference lies in case of the local tribal deities, who were accepted as the minor ones. Margoliouth, referring to the above mentioned statement writes: "If his statements were to be trusted, we should fancy the Meccans to have been very near monotheism. We should infer that Allah was the national God, to whom they appealed in any trouble, whereas in times of comfort and quiet they slid back into polytheism. We should suppose that they recognized Allah as the creator of heaven and earth, and assigned the other deities quite subordinate functions. "How many deities do you worship?" Muhammad is supposed to have asked a Khuza'ite (Hasim, son of 'Ubaid), sent by the Kurashites. To reason with him "Seven on earth and one in heaven," was the reply, and further conversation elicited the confession that in all serious troubles the God of heaven (Allah) only was invoked.[26]

The Arabs, like people of the rest of the world, worshipped many gods; they were polytheists. Their society, rather than being godless, had an over-abundance of them. Some of the deities worshipped by them during pre-Islamic period were the following:

Allah ta'alah, the God, most high, was their supreme deity; the other deities were Hubal, Wadd, Suwa'h, Yaghuth, Yauq, Nasr, El-Huzza, Al-Lat (Allat), Manat, etc. The chief of the minor deities was Hubal. He was in the human form; he who was brought from Syria, and was supposed to procure rain.

Wadd was also worshipped in human form; it is said to have represented the heaven. Suwa'h, an idol in the form of a woman, was believed to be a relic of antediluvian times. Yaghuth's idol used to be in the shape of a lion; Yauq was worshipped under the figure of a horse; Nasr was worshipped in the shape of an eagle. El 'Huzza, Allat and Manat find mention in Qur'an.[27] Pre-Islamic Arabs supposed them to be the daughters of Allah. Identified with Venus, El-Huzza used to be worshipped under the form of an acacia tree. Allat used to be the chief idol of the tribe of Thaqif at at-Taif. Huddheil, and many other tribes, worshipped Manat in the form of a large sacrificial stone. Duwar was a favourite idol with the young women, who used to go in procession round it. Camels were slaughtered upon a large stone called Hab'hab.[28]

Isaf, an idol on Mount Zafa, and Naila, an image on Mount Marva "were such favourite objects of worship that, although Mohammed ordered them to be destroyed, he was not able entirely to divert the popular regard from them, and the visitation of Zafa and Marwa are still an important part of the Hajj rites. Kaabah, the chief shrine of worship, contained 365 idols including the above ones, and the celebrated black stone inserted in the wall of the shrine. It also had images representing Abraham and Ishmael, each with divining arrow in his hand, and a statue or picture representing the virgin and child." The black stone of Kaabah "is supposed to have been one of the stones of Paradise, originally white, though since blackened by the kisses of sinful but believing lips."[29]

Originally, Allah was the tribal god of the Quraish. It was believed that there was some connection between Allah and Hubal, and also between Allah and Al-Lat.[30] The Quraish, and their co-religionists, used to say at the ceremonies of Muzdalifah: "We are the family of Allah," and "by this name they were known in Arabia."[31] According to the ancient custom, as Margoliouth writes, the Quraish, "when they became supreme, gave their deity a place beside the deities of older tribes, such as Al-'Uzza, Al-Lat, Manat, and others; a process described in the Qur'an by the commercial term "associating" or "taking into partnership," which probably had no underlying theological speculation."[32] Margoliouth further writes: "That association did not lead to a distinction of functions between different gods and goddesses, which was only found in Arabia by those who had been schooled in the theology of Egypt or Greece. In Arabia each tribe had its god or patron, from whom it expected everything, and where tribes were confederate the relation between the gods was a friendly one, whence a man might call different sons after different gods; as indeed was done by Prophet Muhammad's grandfather."[33] It may be interesting to note in this case that in India also, the different communities, apart from pan-Indian gods, had community and local deities (*kul-devata, gram/sthan devata*), as well as the household ones (*griha devata*).

About the worship of the goddesses, the remarks of Margoliouth is worth quoting: "The fact, moreover, that several of the chief objects of worship were goddesses suggests that the Arabs of Central Arabia were not wanting in piety, since the cult of goddesses all over the world appears to be conducted with fervour, and calls into play sentiments which male cult is not capable of exciting."[34]

The use of the 'fire worshippers' for 'polytheists' in *Hadis* points towards prevalence of fire worship in pre-Islamic Arabia.[35] The name, such as 'Abd-al-Shams' (slave, or servant, of the Sun-God), similarly, points towards the practice of sun worship. Abd al-Uza (slave of goddess Uzza) was one of the ancestors of Prophet Muhammad. Prophet's own father was Abd al-lah (slave of Allah). Proplet Muhammad, however, brought a change in the names pointing towards pre-Islamic beliefs and deities.[36]

Pre-Islamic Traditions

As we have discussed fully in the chapter on *Islamic Identity Formation*, Prophet Muhammad reversed a large number of pre-Islamic traditions. The perusal of *Hadis* may bring many more of them to our notice. Of course, a large number of the pre-Islamic traditions continued to have currency even after the conversion of the Arab pagans to Islam.

Environmental Protection

Muhammad ordered the destruction of the date orchards of the Jewish tribe, Nadir of Medina.[37] In a similar way, the destruction, by cutting down and burning to their roots, the vineyards of At-Taif was ordered.[38] In Arabia, trees of any kind, especially date palm trees were treasured. The palm date, it needs mention, "needed generations of tending and work, so that to destroy the palms was to destroy not only property but history."[39] The protection of trees/plantation, as elsewhere among the pagans, was an accepted norm. By protecting the trees, the Arabs ensured environmental conservation. Naturally, "recourse to an expedient, unusual, if not unwarranted, by the laws of Arab warfare"[40] was a shocking experience for the people. Nadirs even pointed out that it was specially forbidden by the law of Moses.[41] Muhammad justified the act by divine command. It said, "Whatever you believers have done to their trees, whether cutting them down or uprooting them, was done by God's leave, so that he might disgrace those who defied him."[42]

Pagan Ethos

While going through the Islamic literature, we find numerous insightful statements, pointing towards Arabian pagan ethos. Some of such statements/phrases, needing mention, are: "Paganism did not tolerate injustice,"[43] "No ill-gotten gains in temple building,"[44] "betrayal is not good,"[45] "Hesitation to tell lies,"[46] "Giving food during draught;"[47] "tears for slain/poetry," "Getting killed for prestige/ prestige precious than life."[48] Evidently, these statements convey much and need no elaboration.

Sahih Muslim mentions about the virtuous work of Hakim b. Hizam (Hakim, the son of Hizam) done during his pre-Islamic days. He did many deeds of religious purification while he was still a non-believer.[49] According to another *Hadis*[50], he freed one hundred slaves and donated one hundred camels. When Hakim became Muslim, Muhammad assured him: "you have accepted Islam with all the previous virtues that you have practiced."[51] This indicates that freeing slaves and donating camels were considered to be virtuous during the pagan days and very much so for a man getting converted to Islam.[52]

Positives of Human Behaviour

Going through the Islamic literature, we occasionally find some episodes which clearly bring forth the positive side of the behaviour of certain persons – both Muslims and non-Muslims. One such character was Abu'l As, the son-in-law of Prophet Muhammad, and husband of his daughter Zainab. The couple, following different religions, lived together. Despite pressure, they did not divorce each other. The couple stayed in Mecca after the Prophet migrated to Medina. Abu'l As, being a non-Muslim, participated in the battle of Badr, and was captured among the prisoners and remained at Medina with the apostle. But when the Meccans sent to ransom their prisoners, Zainab sent money for Abul As; with it she sent a necklace which Khadija had given her on her marriage to Abu'l As. When the apostle saw it his feelings overcame him and he said: "If you would like to let her have her captive husband back and return her money to her, do so." The people at once agreed to let him go and sent her money back.[53] Now, as Ibn Ishaq writes, the apostle had imposed a condition on Abu'l As, or the latter had undertaken it voluntarily—the facts were never clearly established—that he should let Zainab come to him. Abu'l As, after coming to Mecca, 'told Zainab to rejoin her father, and she went out to make her preparations.' Muhammad, on the other hand, instructed Zayd b. Haritha and one of the Ansars to go and stay in the valley of Yajaj, and accompany her back. They reached there for the same about a month or so after Badr.[54]

Zainab, the daughter of Prophet Muhammad, was going from Mecca to Medina to stay with her father. Her husband, Abu'l As, keeping his promise, arranged to send her away mounted on camel litter, under the charge of his brother Kinan. "Certain of the baser sort, however, from among Quraysh went in pursuit, determined to bring her back. The first that appeared was Habbar, who struck the camel with his spear, and so affrighted Zainab as to bring on a miscarriage. But the cruelty against even one's enemy's daughter was not liked in Mecca; the cruelty of Habbar was scouted as unmanly." Even Hind, the wife of Abu Sufyan, the main adversary of Muhammad, chastised Hebbar for his cruelty. She gave vent to her indignation; meeting the party as it returned, she extemporized some severe verses against them.[55] Ibn Ishaq details Hind's and Kinan's reactions against undue behaviour of Habbar towards Zainab. Hind's verse criticizing Habbar's action is worth quoting:

> In peace are you wild asses –rough and course.
> And in war like women in their courses.[56]

While Zainab was preparing for going to Medina, 'she was met by Hind, daughter of Utba, who inquired whether she was going off to rejoin Muhammad. When she said that she did not wish to go, Hind offered to give her anything she needed for the journey. She need not be shy of her, for women stay closer together than men. However, though she thought she was sincere, she was afraid of her and denied that she had any intention of going But she went on with her preparation.'[57]

Kinana expressed his reaction on what happened to Zainab in the following verse:

> I am astonished at Habbar and the paltry ones of his people
> Who wish me to break my word with Muhammad's daughter.
> I care not for their numbers as long as I live
> And as long as my hand can grasp my trusty blade.[58]

And, really, Kinan considered his words dearer than even his life. When Habbar threatened Zainab with his lance as she sat in the howdah, she became frightened and had abortion. Kinan knelt and emptied his quiver (in front of him) and said, 'By God, if one of you comes near me, I will put an arrow through him.' So the men fell back.[59] Then Abu Sufyan came with some Quraish leaders and asked him to unbend his bow, so that they would discuss the matter. After that, he came up to him and said: 'You have not done the right thing. You have taken the women out publicly over the heads of the people when you know of our misfortune and disaster which Muhammad has brought on us. The people will think, if you take his daughter publicly over the heads of everyone, that that is a sign of our humiliation after the disaster that has happened and an exhibition of utter weakness.' He further said that 'we don't want to keep her from her father and that is not our way of seeking revenge. But take the women back, and when chatter has died down and people say that we have brought her back you can take her away secretly to rejoin her father.' This is exactly what happened and one night he took her off and delivered her to Zayd b. Harith and his companion, and they took her to the apostle.[60]

The fact, that many prominent Meccans died in the battle of Badr, but the attitude of Hind, Abu Sufyan and Kinan was helpful, rather than revengeful, towards the daughter of their main enemy, Muhammad, clearly indicates the evolved status of the society in Mecca.

As Abu'! As persisted in polytheism, Muhammad declared that Zainab was not lawful for him. The Quraish wanted him to divorce Zainab, and offered him the choice of marrying any women of Mecca, he liked. As the couple deeply and truly loved each other, they lived together, ignoring the barrier of religion. But after Abu'l As, keeping his word sent her to Medina, the two lived separately. Abu'l As, just before the conquest of Mecca by Prophet Muhammad, went to Syria trading with his own money; as he was a trustworthy man, Quraish also entrusted to him their money. During his return journey, one of the apostle's raiding parties fell in with him and took all he had. Abu'l As, however, managed to escape them. After the raiders went off with their plunder, he went into Zainab's house under the cover of night and asked for her protection, which she readily gave. He came to her to ask for his property. Next day, when Prophet Muhammad went out to morning prayer, Zainab cried from the place where the women sat, 'O you men, I have given protection to Abu'l As, son of al-Rabi. The apostle, after the prayer was over, turned round to face the men and asked them whether they had heard what he had heard. After they affirmed, he swore that he knew nothing about the matter until Zainab made the declaration. He further said that 'the meanest Muslim can give protection on their behalf.' After that, the Prophet 'went off to see his daughter and told her to honour her guest but not to allow him to approach her for she was not lawful to him' Then he called the raiding party and said: "This man is related to us as you know and you have taken property of his. If you think well to restore it to him we should like that; but if you will not, it is booty which Allah has given you and you have the better right to it." The raiders agreed, and scrupulously returned everything to Abu'l As.[61]

Abu'l As came back to Mecca, 'paid everything what was due, including those who had given him money to lay out on their behalf, and asked them if anyone of them had any further claim on him.' 'No,' they said, 'Allah reward you; we have found you both trustworthy and generous.' Then he expressed his faith in Islam, and said, 'I feared that you would think that I only wanted to rob you of your property; and now that Allah has restored it to you, and I am clear of it, I submit myself to Allah.' Saying so, he went to Medina to join the Prophet.[62]

Clearly, Abu'l As, was not only honest, he also conveyed his honesty by proper action. Abu Sufyan, while joining the battle of Uhud, said to the Medinans, "you men of Aus and Khazraj, leave me to deal with my cousin and we will depart from you, for we have no need to fight you." But they gave him a rude answer.[63] While leaving the battlefield, he called out: "There are some mutilated bodies among your dead. By Allah, it gives me no satisfaction, and no anger." Evidently, these expressions with such a mental detachment tell a lot.[64]

Pagan Life and Belief-Systems

A Companion of Prophet Muhammad wanted to live celibate life; another Companion said: "I will not marry women;" one another said: "I will not eat meat;" and yet another said: "I will not lie down in bed." Although observed by few only, and forbidden by the Prophet when Islam came, these statements clearly indicate that life of celibacy and self-denial, as in India, was part of the Arabian life-system.[65] This was the same as ascribed by Indian *yoga* under *yama* and *niyama*. A statement: "To be born and killed again for God's cause" clearly shows that there were Arabs who believed in re-birth.[66] Numerous other references clearly show that seclusion, hermitage and celibacy[67]; ascetic life, monkery, and non-use of wine[68] were not something which the Arabs did not know, or did not practice. Bahira, a monk, lived a secluded life;[69] Arabs used to have *hanifs*. It was Islam, which prohibited hermitage, monkery, celibacy and asceticism for the Muslims. Its verdict was also against austerity.[70] Again, according to a tradition, Muhammad said: "In my *ummah*, he is the best who has the largest number of wives.[71]

Islam tabooed wine, when Hamza, the uncle of Prophet Muhammad, was overdrunk, and during his drunkenness, he killed and feasted on the camel of Ali; and when Prophet Muhammad approached and began to reprimand him, Hamza's eyes were red. He cast a glance at Allah's messenger and then looked towards his knees, and then lifted his eyes and cast a glance at his waist and then lifted his eye and saw his face. And then Hamza said: 'Are you anything but the slave of my father?' The Allah's Messenger came to know that he was intoxicated, and he thus turned upon his heels, and came out.[72] Liquor was forbidden in Islam. It was, however, not new for the Arabs. As Margoliouth writes: "Abstention from wine—as a form of religious asceticism—is said to have been practiced by several of the pagan Kuraysh."[73] About monasticism, the Prophet said a firm 'no.'[74]

Acts of Charity

There are numerous mentions of the persons giving food to the hungry, especially during draught and famine. An ode says:

They gave their food when rain failed
When all was dry and no cloud could be seen.[75]

Another ode mentions about generous feasting, and giving milch camels to the guests:

Men of eminence, successful in enterprise,
Who say and do and order what is right,
Who feed their guests on fat meat
Served on bread white as a lamb's stomach;
Who offer dishes and yet more dishes
As large as water pools
The hungry finds them not empty
Nor wide without depth,
To guest after guest they send them
With broad open hand,[76]

It further says:

Givers of hundreds from hundreds of milch camels
To hundreds of their guests,[77]

Respect for the Knowledge of the Book

Although Arabian pagans were less literate; they followed the path of their fathers[78] but they had respect for the knowledge of the book.[79] An Arab, like Waraqa, even translated a Gospel in Arabic.[80] They were a tolerant lot, and lived side by side with the people of the book in different parts of Arabia.

Relaxed Way of Living

The songs were the essential part of the pagan life. Even ordinary persons composed poems, and used them in their conversations. Of course, allowing poetry of pagan era was possible only when Arabia was totally converted to Islam.[81] Music, however, remained a taboo. Whistling and clapping during prayer was a normal pagan practice in Arabia.[82] Making pictures was a usual practice for the pagans, which Islam prohibited. Prophet Muhammad said: "Those who make these pictures will be punished on the Day of Resurrection, and it will be said to them, 'Make alive what you have created'"[83] Pagans used to wish 'good' to each other; they said 'Good Morning.'[84] The Muslims wished 'peace' (*Salaam Alaikum*), which was natural, as the last ten years of the Prophet were spent in conducting raids and fighting wars. It was normal for any one to weep after the death of a near and dear one; 'Sa'd, son of Mu'adh, compelled the Medinese women to forego weeping over their own dead in order to weep for Hamzah; and the custom remained among them when any death occurred in a family, of weeping for Hamzah before they mourned their own dead.'[85]

Status of Women

The status of women in Arabia varied from tribe to tribe, but by and large, it was considerably high. In some tribes, the birth of a daughter was the occasion for special felicitation, containing an allusion to the dowry or purchase money she would bring her parents; on the other hand Qur'an asserts that the birth of a daughter was regarded as a misfortune, and that burying girls alive was common, and such occurrences are attested for the period with which Prophet Muhammad's early life coincided. Institution of marriage was an ancient practice, the wife usually joined the tribe and the home of the husband; divorce was the prerogative of wife; concubinage was considered improper in some tribes.[86]

Though 'deprived of the custom of the right of inheritance, women not infrequently accumulated and disposed of wealth;'[87] Hisham, the great-grandfather of Prophet Muhammad, was himself attracted by a Medinian lady seeing her entrepreneurship.[88] Singing girls were the parts of the tradition;[89] women used to sing war songs, and they encouraged warriors;[90] as poetesses, they acted as war equipments.[91] They practiced no veil (*purdah*).[92] Women, during Islamic period, participated in Jihad.[93] Margoliouth writes about their role in war as poetesses and prophetesses:

"As poetesses, they could fan the embers of feuds into flame, and as prophetesses direct the movements of their tribes. Following the men into the battlefield, they could encourage the fighters by savage music, or could themselves (like Beckwourth's "Pine Leaf") deal wounds and death; or, more often, strip and mutilate the slain. The institution (if that term may be used) of paganism were not unfavourable to the prominence of those women who had the requisite gifts of courage or insight. And the ensuing narrative will show examples of women acting with originality and resolution, when there was room for the display of these qualities."[94]

As women participating in the war, they also received due protection. There is mention in an ode about Indian sword protecting women. A poet says:

"A party deserted them, while they protected
Their women from disgrace,
Men who smote the front ranks of the enemy
With broad-bladed Indian swords;"[95]

The women, as usual, used to be pious and kind-hearted. Among the people of Medina, Margoliouth writes: "some pious women, as might be expected, placed large portions of their possessions at the Prophet's disposal.[96] Zainab, widow of the Prophet's cousin Obeida, killed at Badr, whom the Prophet married, was famous for her charity, and was known as the 'mother of the poor.'

Women: The Value-Keepers

Women in Mecca were considered to be the value-keepers of the society. The story goes that Prophet forbade the killing of Abu'l Bakhtari, 'because he had kept back the people in Mecca from the Apostle; he never insulted him or did anything offensive; and he took a prominent part in the cancelling of the boycott which Quraish had written against B. Hashim and B. al-Muttalib.' When Mujadhdhar, a Muslim, met Abu'l Bakhtari in the war field, and told him that the Prophet had forbidden his killing, the latter was accompanied by his fellow rider Junada. Abu'l Bakhtari asked, 'And what about my friend here?' 'No, by Allah,' said al-Mujadhdhar, 'we are not going to spare your friend. The apostle gave us orders about you only.' 'In this case,' he said: 'I will die with him. The women of Mecca shall not say that I forsook my friend to save my own life.' As Ibn Ishaq writes:[97] 'He utterered this *rajaz* as al-Mujadhdhar came at him and he insisted on fighting, and was killed.'

A son of the free betrays not his friend
Till he's dead, or sees him safe on his way.[98]

Thus, 'what the women of Mecca shall say' was not less important; it cost a life. Many Arab women undoubtedly had immense inner strength, which the following two episodes related to Sauda, the wife of the Prophet, and Hind, the wife of Abu-Sufyan, the Prophet's main Quraish rival. Hind, managed the killing of Hamza, the uncle of Muhammad, disfigured his dead body, took out his liver, chewed and threw it. It may be mentioned that Hind's son, Muawiyah, became the fifth caliph of Islam.

When the prisoners of Badr were brought to the house of Prophet Muhammad, Sauda saw Abu Yazid Suhayl, son of Amr, in a corner of the room with his hand tied to his neck. Seeing him in that state, she could hardly contain herself and said: "O Abu Yazid, you surrendered too readily. You ought to have died a noble death!" Suddenly the Prophet's voice startled her: "Sauda, would you stir up trouble against Allah and his apostle?" She said: "By Allah, I could hardly contain myself when I sawAbu Yazid in this state and that is why I said what I did." Incidently, it may be mentioned that veil was yet to be introduced for the Muslim women by then.[99]

The remark of Margoliouth in the above mentioned case is worth quoting. He wrote: "The slain whom the conquerors have left on the field were their fathers and brothers; those whom they were bringing back with their hands bound and tied to their camels were their nearest kin. This short of triumph shocked those in whom the old humanity had not been killed by the new religion. Even the Prophet's wife, Saudah, asked the Kurashite Sulaim, when he was brought in, tied and bound, why he could not have died like a man?" It needs mention that such sentiments might have been re-echoed[100], and to tame such sentiments a warning was revealed against them, with a request, however, not to punish them too severely.[101]

After the conquest of Mecca by Prophet Muhammad, men and then women came to him for seeking apology. Hind came veiled and disguised because she was afraid for what she did to Hamza. When they approached him, he asked if they gave their word not to associate anything with Allah; then Hind replied: 'by Allah, you lay on us something that you have not laid on men and we will carry it out.' He said: 'And you shall not steal.' She said: 'By Allah, I used to take a little of Abu Sufyan's money and I do not know whether that is lawful for me or not.' Abu Sufyan, who was present there, told her that so far as the past was concerned it was lawful. The apostle said, 'Then you are Hind, daughter of Utba? She replied: 'I am; forgive me what is past and Allah will forgive you.' He said: 'And do not commit adultery.' She replied: 'Does a free woman commit adultery, O apostle of Allah?' He said: 'And you shall not kill your children.' She said: I brought them up when they were little and you killed them on the day of Badr when they were grown up, so you are the one to know about them!' Umar laughed immoderately at her reply, and said: 'You shall not invent slanderous tales.' She said: By Allah, slander is disgraceful, but it is sometimes better to ignore it.' He said: 'You shall not disobey me in carrying out orders to do good.' She said: 'We should not have sat all this time, if we wanted to disobey you in such orders.'[102] The dialogue, undoubtedly, tells a lot about the inner strength of Hind, and the pagan women in general; it reflects her wisdom.

Keeping the Flag High

The importance of keeping one's flag high was as important for the Arabian pagans, as it is for any nation of the world today. Uthman, son of Abu Talha, was carrying the flag of the polytheists in a war. He said:

> "It is the duty of standardbearers
> To blood their spears until they are broken."[103]

Su'ab, an Abyssinian, a slave of the son of Abu Talha, was the last, who held the flag of the Quraish in a war. 'He fought until his hands were cut off; then he knelt upon it and held the flag between his breast and throat until he was killed over it, saying the while 'O Allah, have I done my duty?' He could not pronounce the *dhal*.[104]

Peace Mechanism

The Arabs, especially the Meccans, had well established mechanism to maintain peace, or at least to contain violence. During certain sacred period of the year and at certain places, violence was tabooed. The four sacred months included three consecutive—the last two of the old year, and the first of the new—and one separate, which was the seventh month *Rejeb*. At least during two months of the year, even enemies were not to be killed. The sacred tract, or the *Haram*, several miles around Mecca, was regarded to be hallowed and inviolable since time immemorial. So far as it concerned the sacred months, greater accuracy may be attributed to the statement about the piety of the Arabs.[105] Margoliouth writes:

"For three autumn months and one spring month a truce of God was observed by many tribes, who therein laid down their arms and shed no blood. This institution in the fixed form which it had assumed by the commencement of Islam, must have been the result of many stages of development, and was itself fruitful in effects."[106]

Counting the benefits of this institution, Margoliouth further writes: "It can not be severed from the desire to visit a sanctuary and celebrate a feast, and indeed the two seasons correspond with those of the birth of domestic animals and the harvesting of fruit. The month before and the month after that in which the more important visit was paid, may have been included in the time for the benefit of distant visitors, who thereby were enabled to arrive and return in safety. For those who had no great distance to traverse the truce provided a period in which they could recover from the ravages of constant warfare, and by secure communication interchange ideas as well as produce."[107] The people attended fairs, such as at Ukaz, which provided opportunity to meet and evolve the idea of a common nationality.[108]

Clan solidarity and protection of an individual by the head or members of the clan was also a factor diminishing violence in the society. In Mecca, even the head of the other clan was capable of providing protection to an individual, as Al-Mul'im did to Prophet Muhammad after the death of Abu-Talib, when Abu-Lahab, head of his own clan, refused to do so.[109] As we know, Abu Talib, head of the Hashim clan, gave protection to Prophet Muhammad, and during that period none dared to attack him due to fear of revenge. The blood of an individual used to become licid, and he faced danger, only when he lost such protection. One way of containing tension in the society was social boycott or outcasting an individual or a community, which like elsewhere, was in use in Arabia also.

Before ending the discourse on this topic, it is necessary to point out two things: (i) The raids on the settlements or on moving parties were not new for the pagan Arabs, but the same were usually conducted for goods, and not for life, and were not so widespread, and (ii) The Islamic and Western historians usually exaggerated the prevailing violence situation in pagan Arabia. Lesley Hazleton writes: "Both early Islamic historians and modern Western ones tend to paint a picture of seventh century Arabia as mired in ceaseless inter-tribal warfare fuelled by blood-feuds in which every violent death demanded retaliation by other members of the clan or tribe, resulting in a self-perpetuating spiral of violence. It's a picture that might well lead one to ask how any such society could survive for very long."[110]

As Lesley Hazleton rightly points out, the root cause of conflict in Arabia was the competition for power, the fear of revenge worked to deter one from the same. She writes: "In fact the root cause of inter-tribal conflict, throughout history and into the modern era, was the competition not for revenge but for power. In Arabia this meant control of water sources, territorial grazing rights, and the authority to levy taxes and tolls on those living in and passing through tribal territory. If anything the principle of blood vengeance worked to keep the peace more than to break it; in the absence of a strong control authority, it was a rough-and-ready but effective way of ensuring security. Rather than perpetuating violence, it served to deter it.[111] In Pagan society, the fear of civil strife and its consequences led to an extraordinary amount of mutual forbearance.[112]

Functioning of Society and Governance

Various clans in Mecca had their heads, who had considerable influence on their clan members. In Mecca, during peace time, there was little governance, but in time of war, the fighters subjected themselves, in some degree, to a leader.

Some matters were settled in the committees in which heads of the tribes, free citizens, and in some cases, even strangers participated. Wealth, oratorical ability, personal courage and personal dignity counted, but even poor could become the chief of the clan/community.[113]

References:

1. Muir; Sir William, *The Life of Mahomet*, p. 56. (Hereafter, Muir).
2. Qur'an 34:43; 36:5.
3. Lesley Hazleton, *The First Muslim*, pp. 42-43. (Hereafter, Hazleton).
4. Margoliouth, D.S., *Mohammed and the Rise of Islam*, p.21. (Hereafter Margoliouth).
5. Hazleton, p. 43.
6. Margoliouth, pp. 30-31.
7 Margoliouth, pp. 30-31.
8. Alexander refereed as 'Dhu'l Karnein' in Qur'an.
9. Muir, p. lx n; Anwar Sheikh, *Islam: Sex and Violence*, p. 88.
10. Qur'an 6:82 ff.
11. Ibn Ishaq, *Sirat Rasul Allah*, English translation, *The Life of Muhammad*, by A. Guillaume, p.354; numerous odes quoted by Ibn Ishaq, in his *Sirat Rasul Allah*, mention about Indian sword. Hereafter, Ibn Ishaq.
12. The name of the wife of Abu Sufyan, and the mother of Muawiya, the 5th caliph.
13. See, *India's Contribution to the Arab Civilization*, by W.H. Siddiqi; in India's Contribution to World Thought and Culture, Lokesh Chandra, *et al*, Vivekanand Rock Memorial Committee, Madras, 1970.
14. Qur'an 71.26.
15. Hazleton, pp. 43, 44, 79-80.
16. Margoliouth, p. 141.
17. Hazleton, pp. 43-44.
18. Ibid, p.44.
19. Ibid.
20. Ibid.
21. Ibid.
22. Ram Swarup, *Understanding Islam through Hadis*, pp. 55-56; hereafter Ram Swarup.
23. Ibn Ishaq, p. 311.
24. *Sahih Muslim, Hadis* no. 500.

25. Ibid, translator's note 471.
26. Margoliouth, p. 142.
27. Qur'an LIII.19-20.
28. Pamer, Qur'an, English translation by Palmer; edited by Max Mueller; Sacred books of the East, Vol.VI:I; pp. viii-ix.
29. Ibid, pp. ix.
30. Margoliout, p. 19.
31. Ibid.
32. Ibid, pp. 19-20.
33. Ibid, p. 20.
34. Margoliouth, p. 26.
35. *Sahih Muslim*, Hadis no. 500.
36. Ibid, p. 110.
37. Muir, p. 282; Hazleton, p. 211.
38. Muir, p. 419.
39. Hazleton, p. 211.
40. Muir, p. 282.
41. Bible, Deut. XX.19.
42. Ibn Hisham, p. 653 vide Muir, p. 283.
43. Ibn Ishaq, p. 47.
44. Ibid, p. 84.
45. IbnI pp. 366-370.
46. Ibn Ishaq, p. 367.
47. Ibid, p. 355.
48. Ibn Ishaq, pp. 301-2.
49. *Sahih Muslim*, Hadis 222.
50. Ibid, Hadis 225.
51. Ibid, Hadis 223.
52. Ram Swarup, p. 5.
53. Ibn Ishaq, p. 314.
54. Ibid, p. 314.
55. Muir, pp. 345-46, note 1.
56. Ibn Ishaq, p. 316.
57. Ibid, pp. 514-15.
58. Ibid.
59. Ibid.
60. Ibid, p. 315.
61. Ibid, pp. 316-17.

62. Ibid, p. 317.
63. Ibid, p. 374.
64. Ibid, p. 386.
65. *Sahih Muslim*, *ahadis* no. 3239, 3236.
66. Ibn Ishaq, p. 400.
67. Muir, p. 180; *Sahih Bukhari, Hadis* no. 1432; pp. 677-98.
68. Muir, p. 59; Margoliouth, pp. 43, 151.
69. Margoliouth, p. 50-1.
70. Mishkat, *Hadis* 181.
71. Ram Swarup, p. 57 note; *Tabaqat*, Vol. II, p. 146.
72. *Sahih Muslim*, *Hadis* no. 4881.
73. Margo 43.
74. MuM 724
75. Ibn Ishaq, p. 355.
76. Ibid, p. 354.
77. Ibid.
78. Ibn Ishaq, p. 259.
79. Margoliouth, p. 41.
80. Ibid, p. 42.
81. Ibn Ishaq, p. 355 note1.
82. Ibid, p. 324.
83. Ibid, ch 18; *Sahih Bukhari, Hadis* -7:835.
84. Ibn Ishaq, p. 319.
85. Margoliouth, p. 306.
86. Ibid, pp. 28-29.
87. Ibid, p. 30.
88. Muir, p. cxii.
89. Ibid, p. cxii.
90. Ibid, p. 259.
91. Margoliouth, p. 411.
92. Muir, p. 259.
93. *Sahih Muslim, Hadis* no. 4453-4456.
94. Margoliouth, p. 30.
95. Ibn Ishaq, p. 354.
96. Margoliouth, p. 237.
97. Ibn Ishaq, pp. 301-302.
98. Ibid, p. 302.
99. Ibid, p. 309.

100. Margoliouth, p. 276.
101. Qur'an lxiv:14.
102. Ibn Ishaq, p. 553.
103. Ibid, p. 377.
104. Ibid, p. 379.
105. Margoliouth's observation on the authority of Greek writers; p. 5.
106. Ibid.
107. Ibid, pp. 5-6.
108. Ibid, pp. 5-6.
109. Muir, p. 112 notes.
110. Hazleton, p. 109.
111. Ibid, pp.109-110.
112. Margoliouth, p. 19.
113. Margoliouth, pp. 16-17.

The Prophet's Ancestors

Family Background: The Ancestors

Ibn Ishaq,[1] in the biography of Muhammad, *Sirat Rasul Allah,*[2] traces Prophet Muhammad's family link to Abraham, and further to Adam.[3] In the long list of generations, it is difficult to ascertain as to where the history ends, and the mythology starts. But Ibn Ishaq, himself, uses the phrases – "according to what they allege" and "God knows best" – to express his doubts about the authencity of the parts of the statements. As A. Guillaume, an English translator of *Sirat Rasul Allah,* notes – "The phrase employed indicates that the writer doubts the statement. There is a saying in Arabic: "There is a euphemism for everything and polite way of saying "It's a lie" is "they allege" (za 'amu)."[4] The Meccans linking their ancestry to Abraham, through Isma'il and his mother, Hagar, shows the overlapping of the Arabic and Jewish mythologies.

As discussed elsewhere in the book, the ancestors of Muhammad migrated from Yemen after the collapse of Marib Dam, and settled in Mecca. Earlier the Jurhum tribe controlled the temple, Ka'ba. As they behaved high-handedly in Mecca, Kinan and Khuza'a tribes took possession of the temple and expelled them from Mecca.[5] Ibn Ishaq had noted: "Mecca did not tolerate injustice and wrong within its borders in the time of paganism, and if anyone did wrong therein it expelled him; this was the reason that Mecca was called the scorcher, and any king who came to profane its sanctity died on the spot."[6] The Quraish became more important and strong, and they predominated Mecca after Kusayy b. Kilab, the ancestor of Prophet Muhammad, gained power there.[7]

Power of the Chiefs of Mecca and the Change Brought by Kosai

In Mecca, like the rest of Arabia, the system of administration was like the one run by the nomadic Bedouins. Under that system, a chief possessed no shadow of authority. In reality, the real change was brought by the Islam. However, as William Muir writes: there was some difference between the two systems. He writes about the power of the Chief of Mecca: "But in reality his powers, though vague and undefined, were large and effective. The position of the Chief always secured an important share in forming and giving expression to public opinion; so that, except in rare and unusual cases, he swayed the councils and the movements of his tribe. It was mainly by the influence derived from the offices attaching to the Ka'ba and the pilgrimage that the Chiefs of Mecca differed from the Sheikhs of the nomad tribes, and exercised a more regular and permanent rule."[8]

Kosai and his Descendants

Kosai emerged in Meccan scene in 440 AD. About the middle of the fifth century, as Muir observes: "he had concentrated the chief of these offices in his own person. When he became old and infirm, he resigned them into the hands of his eldest son, 'Abd ed-Dar. From him they descended to his sons and grandsons, but the latter, who succeeded to the inheritance in the beginning of the 6th century, were too young effectually to maintain their rights. 'Abd Menaf, another son of Kosai, whose name was al-Mughira,[9] had been the powerful rival of his brother; and the sons of 'Abd Menaf inherited their father's influence. The chief were Al-Muttalib and 'Abd Shams, Naufal and Hashim." It needs mention that Prophet Muhammad descended from Hashim, who was his great-grandfather. Abu Sufyan, one time rival of Muhammad and his chief enemy at Badr, descended from 'Abd Shams, the eldest brother of Hashim. Abu Sufyan's son, Mu'awiya became the fifth caliph after Ali. The other two brothers of Hashim were Naufal and Al-Muttalib. Here, it needs mention that Khadija, the first wife of Muhammad, was the daughter of Khuweilid, who was the grandson of 'Abd al-Ozza, the third son of Kosai.[10]

Hashim Gathers Strength

As a result of the discord between the descendants of Kosai, his other sons, under the lead of Hashim, conspired to wrest hereditary offices bequeathed by Kosai from the descendants of 'Abd ed-Dar. Hashim claimed superior dignity of the family of 'Abd Menaf. The rival party refused to concede. Kuraysh were divided; one party siding with the claimants, others with the actual possessors of the office. The situation was tense, as the respective factions, having bound themselves by the most stringent oaths, were already marshalled in hostile array; however, truce was, unexpectedly, called; the agreed conditions were to give Hashim and his party the office of providing food and water for the pilgrims, while the descendants of 'Abd ed-Dar retained custody of the Ka'ba and the

Council-hall, and the right of mounting the banner on its staff in war. The agreement on these terms led to restoration of peace.[11]

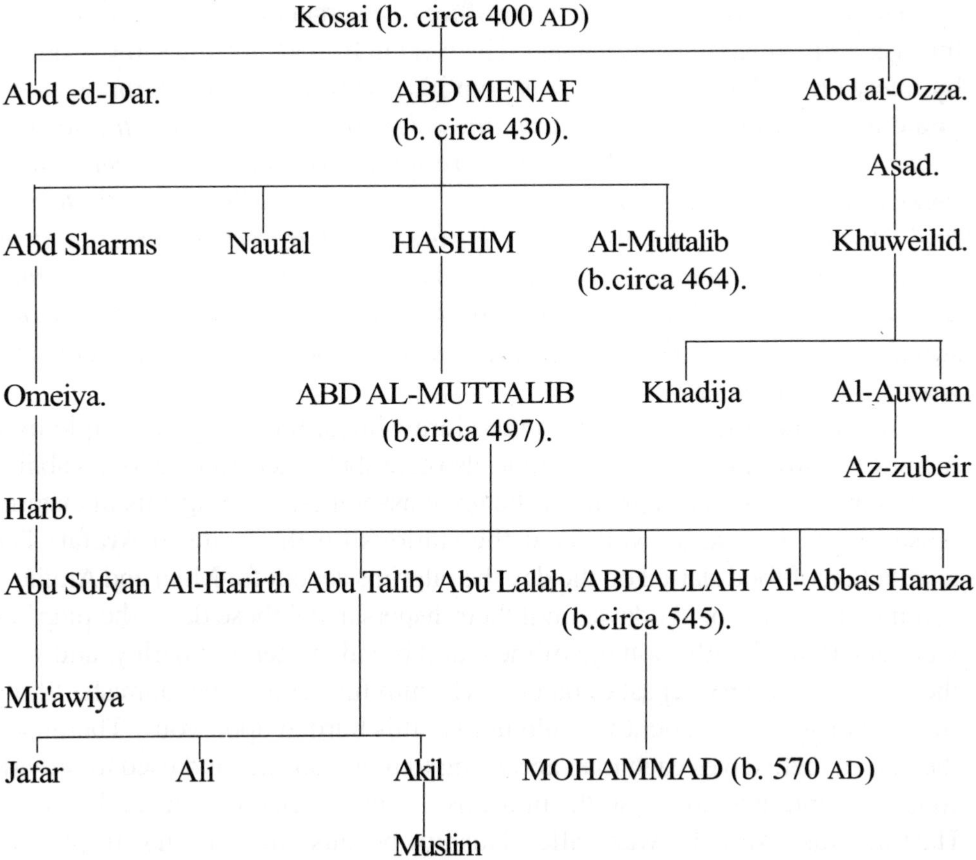

Hashim brought qualitative change in the acts of entertainment of the pilgrims. He supported the credit of Mecca; and became more renowned for feeding the people of Mecca during a famine. Hashim and his brothers conducted the foreign relations of the Kuraysh. In this case, Hashim himself concluded a treaty with the Roman authorities and the Ghasanid prince, and as such, he is said to have received from the Emperor a rescript authorizing Quraysh to travel through Syria in security. His brother, 'Abd Shams made a treaty with the Negus in pursuance of which Quraysh traded with Abyssinia. Two other brothers, Naufal and Al-Muttalib entered into an alliance with the king of Persia, who allowed the merchants of Mecca to trade in Al-'Irak and Fars, as well as with the kings of Himyar, who encouraged their commercial operations in Yemen. Hashim is also credited for establishing upon a uniform footing the mercantile expeditions of his people, enabling them to conduct caravan trade with Yemen and Abyssinia during winter and a second during summer visiting Gaza, Ancyra, and other Syrian marts. Thus, Quraish prospered in every direction due to his endeavour.[12]

Hashim, after being installed in the office of entertaining the pilgrims, fulfilled the task with princely magnificence. The wealth, he had, and the same acquired by many Quraish due to trade, was helpful. Hashim appealed to them, as his grandfather Kusai did earlier: "*Ye are the neighbours of Allah, and the keepers of his house. Pilgrims to the temple are his guests; and it is meet that ye entertain them above all other guests. Ye are especially chosen unto this high dignity; wherefore honour His guests and refresh them. For, from distant cities, on their lean and jaded camels, they come unto you fatigued and harassed, with hair disheveled and bodies covered with the dust and squalor of the way. Then invite them hospitably, and furnish them with water in abundance.*"[13]

Hashim, not only appealed to the Qurayshites, but set the example by a munificent provision. Every Qurayshite also contributed according to one's ability. Sufficient water was provided for the great assemblage of pilgrims in cisterns close by the Ka'ba, as well as at the stations on the route to Arafat. The distribution of food started on the day the pilgrims set out for Mina and Arafat; it continued, for five or six days, until their dispersal. All these days, the pilgrims were entertained with 'pottage of meat and bread, butter and barley, and with the favourite national repast of dates.'[14] Hashim further told the Quraish: "If my own means were sufficient I would not lay this burden upon you." Thereupon they taxed themselves each man according to their capacity and used to provide food, as mentioned above, to the pilgrims.[15] It needs mention that real name of Hashim was 'Amr; he was called Hashim because he was first to provide *tharid* (broth in which bread is broken up) to the people of Mecca during a famine. A Quraish poet, or one of the Arabs, remembered this, and the fact that he was the first to start two caravan journeys. The poem said:

'Amr who made bread-and-broth for his people,
A people in Mecca who suffered lean years,
He it was who started the two journeys,
The winter's caravan and the summer's train.[16]

Hashim died in Ghaza in Syria while travelling with his merchandise; his place was taken by his brother, al-Muttalib, who assumed the right of feeding and watering the pilgrims. An Arab poet mourned him when he died in Radman in the Yaman:

Thirsty are the pilgrims now al-Muttalib is gone,
No more bowls with overflowing brims.

Now that he is gone would that Quraysh were in torment![17]

The elegy, written by an Arab poet, Matrud b. Ka'b al-Khuza'i, after the death of Naufal, the brother of Hashim, remembering the death of all four brothers, is given bellow:

O night! Most miserable night,
Disturbing all other nights,
With thoughts of what I suffer
From sorrow and blows of fate.
When I remember my brother Naufal,
He reminds me of days gone by,
He reminds me of the red waist-sashes,
The fine new yellow robes.
There were four of them, everyone a prince,
Sons and grandsons of princes.
One dead in Radman, one in Salman,
A third lies near Ghaza,
A fourth lies in a grave by the Ka'ba
To the east of the sacred buildings.
'Abdu Manaf brought them up virtuously
Safe from reproof of all men.
Yea there are none like Mughira's children
Among the living or dead.[18]

As the poem indicates, al-Mughira was the real name of 'Abdu Manaf. A point, needing mention here, is that instant poetry was in the very nature of the Arabs, and Ibn Ishaq's book, *Sirat Rasul Allah*, is full of poetry. As detailed elsewhere, the Prophet had also to deal with the poets during his prophetic career.

Intra-Familial Discord

The success, glory and popularity of Hashim generated envy of his nephew, Omeiya, the son of his eldest brother 'Abd Shams. As Muir informs, "Omeiya was opulent and he expended his riches in vain attempt to rival the splendour of his kinsman's munificence. The Qurayshites perceived the endeavour, and turned it into ridicule. Omeiya was enraged, *Who*, said he, *is Hashim?* And he defied him to a trial of superiority. Hashim would willingly have avoided a contest with one so much his inferior both in years and dignity; but the Qurayshites, who loved such exhibitions, would not excuse him; he consented, therefore, but with the stipulation that the vanquished party should lose fifty black-eyed camels, and be ten years exiled from Mecca. A Khoza'ite soothsayer was appointed umpire; and, having heard the pretensions of both, pronounced Hashim to be the victor. Hashim took the fifty camels, slaughtered them in the vale of Mecca, and fed with them all the people present. Omeiya set out for Syria, and remained there the period of his exile. The circumstance is carefully noted by Mohammadan writers as the first trace of that rivalry between the Hashimits and Omeiyad factions, which in after ages shook the caliphate."[19]

Muhammad's grandfather, Abdu'l Muttalib was born in Medina; he remained there till his uncle, al-Muttalib brought him to Mecca.

Muhammad's Grandfather

Hashim, the great-grandfather of Muhammad, went to Yathrib, and married Salma, daughter of Amr, who, on account of her high position among her people, used to marry only on the condition that she should retain control of her own affairs. Naturally, if she disliked a person, she left him. Salma bore a son to Hashim, and called him Shayba, who was later known as Abdu'l Muttalib. Salma was married twice before her marriage to Hashim. She had a son, named Amr from her second husband.[20]

Hashim left his son with his mother in Yathrib when Shayba was very young. Later on his uncle, al-Muttalib came to Yathrib to take his nephew away to Mecca and bring him up among his people, but Salma declined to let him go. Al-Muttalib argued, as Ibn Ishaq writes: "that his nephew was now old enough to travel and was as an exile away from his own tribe who were the people of the temple, of great local reputation, holding much of the government in their hands. Therefore, it was better for the boy that he should be among his own family, and therefore he refused to go without him. It is popularly asserted that Shayba refused to leave his mother without her consent; and this she ultimately gave. So his uncle took him away to Mecca, riding behind him on his camel, and the people cried: 'It's al-Muttalib's slave whom he has bought and that is how he got the name of Abdu'l Muttalib. His uncle called out: 'Rubbish! This is my nephew whom I have brought from Medina.'" Thus, Shayba, the grandfather of Prophet Muhammad, got the new name Abdu'l Muttalib, i.e., the 'Slave of Muttalib (Abd = slave, in Arabic).[21]

Al-Muttalib installed his nephew in possession of his father's property, but it was not a smooth affair. His other uncle, Naufal interposed, and violently deprived him of the same. When Abdu'l Muttalib's appeal, for help to his tribe, failed, then he wrote to his maternal relatives at Medina for help; eighty mounted men of his mother's clan started for Mecca, as soon as they received the intelligence, and with their help Abdu'l Muttalib succeeded in getting his due. Muir writes: "'Abd al-Muttalib went forth to meet them, and invite them to his house; but their chief refused to alight until he had called Naufal to account. Proceeding straightway to the holy house, he found him seated there among the chiefs of Quraysh. Naufal arose to offer welcome; but the stranger refused his welcome, and drawing his sword declared that he would plunge it into him unless he forthwith reinstated the orphan in his rights. The oppressor was daunted, and agreed to the concession, which was then ratified by oath before the assembled Quraysh." 'Abd al-Muttalib succeded al-Muttalib to the office of entertaining the pilgrims after some years after the death of the latter.[22]

Abd al-Muttalib, for long time, was destitute of power and influence; as he had only one son, Al-Harith, to assist him in assertion of his claims; he was finding it difficult to cope with the opposing faction of Quraysh. As his family was small, bringing water from the distant wells for the pilgrims was a tiresome act. But, before centuries, there used to be a well, named Zemzem, in the temple premises; its memory was almost forgotten, even the site was unknown. In a period of the decline of Meccan trade and commerce, the well was neglected; it got choked. Abdu'l Muttalib and his son undertook the task of digging and searching the well. After digging deeper and deeper, they got two golden gazelles, with swords and suits of armour buried by the Jurhumite king three centuries earlier. This aroused the envy of the Quraysh; they demanded a share, as well as their right to the well itself, being the possession, as they claimed, of their common ancestor Ishmael. Abdu'l Muttalib finding himself weak to resist their claim, agreed to refer it to the arrows of god Hubal, who spoke through his arrow. As a result, lots were cast; Gazelles fell to the share of Ka'ba, swords and suits of armour to Abdu'l Muttalib. The Quraysh relinquished their pretensions to the well. Abdu'l Muttalib, during his early troubles, as he had only one son, and had to contend with the large influential families, developed bitterness for his opponents, and vowed that, if providence should ever grant him ten sons, he would devote one of them to the Deity. Gradually his family increased, he had ten sons. Ultimately, he had to decide to sacrifice one of his sons; the lot fell on the youngest, and the most loved, Abdullah, the father of Prophet Muhammad. Lots were caste, and Abdullah was ransomed from sacrifice for one hundred camels.[23]

The digging of the well Zemzem in the precincts of the sacred area of Mecca made Abdu'l Muttalib more important and influential. It generated envy and invited opposition of the house of Omeiya. Harb b. Omeiya challenged him to a trial of their respective merits. The judgment was committed to a Qurayshite, as the Abyssinian king declined to be the umpire. Abdu'l Muttalib was declared to be superior in every respect.[24]

Abdu'l Muttalib had ten sons and six daughters, out of which four sons and two daughters played important roles. His all the sons were of massive built and dark colour. The names of some of his sons, such as Abdallah (Abd-al-Lah; slave of Allah), Abdal-Manat (slave of the Manat), Abd-al-Uzza (slave of the Uzza), indicate that he was piously disposed towards the deities Allah, Manat and Al-Uzza.[25] His sons engaged themselves in trade and commerce. Abbas inherited the business of money-lending and watering; he also imported spices from Yemen and sold during feasts. Abu Talib traded in cloth and perfume. Zubair was also a trader; Hamzah was a hunter. Abdallah, father of the Prophet, was absent from Mecca during his birth; this might have been due to business journey outside Mecca.[26]

As Muhammad was born after the death of his father, Abdullah, his grandfather, Abdu'l Muttalib was his guardian. After the death of the grandfather, his uncle Abu Talib remained his guardian and protector.

Notes and References

1. The author of *Sirat Rasul Allah* is Ibn Ishaque (Son of Ishaq; *ibn* = bin = b. = son); his real name is Muhammad. He was born in Medina about AH 85 and died in Baghdad in 151. He associated with the second generation of traditionalists.
2. *The Life of Muhammad*, English translation of *Sirat Rasul Allah* of Ibn Ishaq, by A. Guillaume, Oxford University Press, Karachi, 1996; (hereafter, Ibn Ishaq).
3. The genealogy, given in Ibn Ishaq's biography (*Sirat Rasul Allah*, p. 3) is: "Muhammad was the son of Abdullah, b. 'Abd'l Muttalib (whose name was Shayba)), b. Hashim (whose name was 'Amr), b. Abd Manaf (whose name was al-Mughira), b.Qussay (whose name was Zayd), b. Kilab, b.Murra, b. Ka'b, b. Lu'ayy, b. Ghalib, b. Fihr, b. Malik, b. al-Nadr, b. Kinan, b. Khuzayma, b. Mudrika (whose name was 'Amir), b. Ilyas, b. Mudar, b. Nizar, b. Ma'add, b. 'Adnan, b. Udd (or Udad). b. Muqawwam, b. Nahur, b. Tayra, b. Ya'rub, b. Yashjun, b. Nabit, b. Isma'il, b. Ibrahim, the friend if the Compassionate, b. Tarin (who is Azar), b. Nahur, b. Surugh, b. Ra'u, b. Falikh, b. 'Aybar, b. Shalikh, b. Arfakhshadh, b. Sam, b. Nuh, Lamk, b. Mattushalakh, b.Akhnukh, who is the prophet Idris according to what they allege, but God knows best (he was the first of the sons of Adam to whom

prophecy and writing with a pen were given), b. Yard, b. Mahlil, b. Qaynan, Yanish, b. Shith, b. Adam".

4. Ibn Ishaq, p. 3, Note 2.
5. Ibid, pp. 46-47.
6. Ibid, p. 47.
7. Ibid, pp. 52-53.
8. Muir, Sir William, *The Life of Mahomet*, p. cix; hereafter, Muir.
9. Ibn Ishaq, p. 60.
10. Muir, pp. cix-cx.
11. Ibid, p. cx.
12. Ibid, pp. cxi-cxii.
13. Ibid, pp. cx-cxi.
14. Ibid, p. cxi.
15. Ibid, p. cxii.
16. Ibn Ishaq, p. 58.
17. Ibid, p. 59.
18. Ibid, pp. 59-60.
19. Ibid, pp. 59-60.
20. Ibid, p. 59.
21. Ibid.
22. Muir, p. cxiii.
23. Ibid, pp. cxv.
24. Ibid, pp. cxv-cxvi.
25. Margoliouth, D.S.; *Mohammed and the Rise of Islam,* p. 49.
26. Ibid.

Source Material for the Study of Islam

The Qur'an

The Quran, the sacred text of Islam – variously written as Quran, Qur'an, Koran, Kor'an – is the supreme authority in religious, as well as legal matters of the Muslim community. It is the fundamental and paramount source of the creed, rituals, ethics, and laws of Islamic religion. Its supreme status stems from the belief that the Quran is the word of Allah, revealed to the Prophet Muhammad via the archangel Gabriel; it is intended for all times and all places. Apart from its supreme importance and status as the Holy Book of Islam, it has immensely rich material for the sociological study also.

The Revelation of the Qur'an

Quran is an Arabic word, meaning 'recitation;' the name 'Quran' is derived from the Gabriel's command to Muhammad to 'recite.' 'Recitation,' it needs mention, was an established Arabic method for preserving poetry; the first followers of the Prophet used to memorize his recitation, so that to recite it to others. The Quran is, as Muslims believe, the flawless record of the Angel Gabriel's revelations to Muhammad starting from 610 AD until his death in 632 AD.

As is well-known, Muhammad used to visit Mount Hira, in the neighbourhood of Mecca, regularly, for solitary contemplation. In one such occasion in the month of Ramadan in 610 AD, when he was forty years old, the angel Gabriel came, and Muhammad had the first revelation. The account of the same by the Prophet Muhammad himself, credited to his wife, Ayesha, is worth knowing: "He said: 'When the angel came to me, I had been standing, but I fell to my knees and crawled away, my shoulders trembling…I thought of hurling myself down from a mountain crag, but he appeared to me as I was thinking this and said, Muhammad, I am Gabriel and you are the messenger of God.' Then he said, 'Recite!' I said: 'What shall I recite?' He took me and pressed me tightly three times until I was nearly stifled and thought that I should die, and then he said, 'Recite in the name of thy Lord who created, created man from a clot of blood, that thy Lord is the most munificent, who teaches by the word, teaches man what he knew not.'"[1]

Mills writes about the traditional account of the revelation given by Al-Wakidi:

"The first beginnings of Mohammad's inspiration were *real visions*. Every vision that he saw was clear as the morning dawn. These again provoked the love for solitude. He would repair to a cave on mount Hira, and there pass whole days and nights. Then drawn by affection for Khadija, he would return to his home. This went on till the truth burst upon him in the cave. It happened on this wise. Wandering in the hills around, an angel from the sky cried to him, 'O Muhammad, I am Gabriel!' He was terrified, for as often as he raised his head, there was the appearance of the angel. He hurried home to tell his wife. 'Oh, Khadija,' he said, I have never abhorred anything as I do these idols and soothsayers; and now verily I fear lest I should become a soothsayer myself.' 'Never,' replied his faithful wife; "the Lord will never suffer it thus to be,'—and she went on to speak of his many virtues, upon which she founded the assurance. Then she repaired to her cousin Waraka, and told him all. 'By the Lord,' cried the aged man, he speaketh truth! Doubtless it is the beginning of the prophecy, and there shall come upon him the *Great Namus*, like as it came upon Moses."[2]

Thus, what happened was not only the beginning of the Prophetic career of Muhammad, but also the beginning of Qur'an. The first Sura revealed to him was the Sura 96, verses 1-5 of the Qur'an. Anyway, he remained highly terrified for some time, and even meditated suicide. Even there was stoppage of inspirations for some time. Then, it continued till the end of his life.[3]

The Structure of the Qur'an: Suras and Ayats

The Quran has 114 chapters (*sura*, *surahs*) of widely varying length, which, except for the opening one (*Fatihah, al-Fatiha*), which is an essential part of Muslim ritual prayer, is learnt and read in Arabic by the Muslims throughout the world, are generally arranged from longest to the shortest. Chronologically, this is in the reverse order, or at least, they are not chronologically arranged, as the shortest chapters seem to date from the earlier period of Muhammad's revelations. In the earlier shortest verses, the form closely resembles the rhymed prose of the seers (*kahins*) of that time; the verses of latter days are more detailed and less poetic. The second sura is the longest one, whereas numbers 108 and 112 are the shortest ones with only one line in Arabic in each of them. The Quran has 6236 verses (*ayats*, signs).

The Suras are not Chronologically Arranged

The *ahadis* provide ample proof that Quranic suras are not arranged chronologically. Here, it needs mention that the ninth Sura (*Al-Tawba*,, also called *Baraat*) is chronologically one of the last, and according to Muir the very last one.[4] This *Sura*, according to *Sahih Muslim*, was meant to humiliate the non-believers and the hypocrites.[5]

The Contents

Bulk of the material in Quran deal with the Islamic beliefs and morals; about 100 verses deal with ritual practices, 70 verses discuss personal laws, 70 verses civil laws, 30 penal laws, and 20 judiciary matters and testimony.[6] "Out of the total of 6236 verses in the Quran, some 3900 are directly or indirectly related to *Kafirs, Mushriks, Munkirs, Munafiquins* or non-believers in Allah and the apostle. These include the rewards for the believers and punishment for the unbelievers in this as well as afterlife."[7]

Stylistic and other Features

Each *surah* of the Quran has a heading, which usually incorporates the following elements:

i. The title *Suras*, such as 'The Cow,' 'The Bee,' is taken from a prominent word of the Surah; it does not, however, necessarily represent its overall contents.

ii. The *Bismillah*, a formula prayer, such as, "In the name of Allah the merciful, the Compassionate; *Bismillah-ir-Rahman-ir-Rahim,*" except in *Sura* 9.

iii. The indication as to whether the revelation descended at Mecca or Medina.

iv. The number of verses in the Chapter (*Surah*).

v. In 29 *Suras*, there are *fawatih* or 'detached letters of unclear significance, such as '*Alif Lam Mim*' or '*Alif Lam Ra,*' which may be abbreviations, initials of the owners of early manuscripts, or have some esoteric meaning.

Most of the Quran is written in the first person plural, with Allah as the speaker. Muhammad's words are introduced by "Say," when he himself speaks, so that to clarify that he was commanded by Allah to do so. Except for some borrowed Hebrew or Syriac terms, such as *injil* (gospel), *taurat* (law, Torah), *iblis* (Devil), *amana* (to believe) and *salat* (prayer), the vocabulary of Quran is overwhelmingly Arabic.

The Quranic revelations did not come to Muhammad at a time; it came to him gradually, piece by piece, over a period of 23 years. The different Quranic verses were revealed on different occasions. They often relate to incidents in the life of the Prophet, external events and the individual men and women. As discussed earlier, the verses are not arranged according to the chronology of the revelation.

The Quranic material revealed to the Prophet at Mecca, and those revealed at Medina after the Hijra (migration) differ considerably. The Quran, during the Meccan period, was mainly concerned with the basic Islamic beliefs – the unity of God,[8] the Prophethood of Muhammad, Resurrection and the Final Judgment.[9] The frequent use of 'partnership (*shirk*) and 'associate' throughout the Quran refers to worship of multiple Gods, the polytheism. It also refers to earlier prophets, including Biblical prophets – Noah, Abraham, Jacob, Joseph, Moses and Jesus.[10] Quran states that Muslims should believe in all these prophets without making any distinction between them.[11]

The Suras of the Medinan period introduced laws regarding marriage, commerce, finance, war and peace, etc.[12] The Suras of this period frequently refer to the new class of the hypocrites (*munafiqun*; the group pretending to be Muslims, but actually working against the Islamic state). There are numerous verses dealing with retaliation against the *kafirs*, hypocrites and the Jews in the Medinan verses. As Muhammad gains strength, the tone of Quranic voice begins to change; it becomes especially against the 'People of the Book,' the Jews.[13] Numerous Ayats of Qur'an express anger against the hypocrites

Compilation of the Qur'an in the Present Form

The Quran was committed to memory by early Muslims. The recital of passages formed essential part of the private and public prayers. There were persons who were capable of reciting the entire Qur'an. Such persons were highly honoured while living or dead. Among the Muslims killed in a war, he who had been most versed in Qur'an was honoured with the first burial. The one who in any company could most faithfully repeat the Quran was of right entitled to be the *Imam,* or conductor of the public prayers. The post of Imam also implied military command. After the spoils taken on the field in Al-Kadisiya in AH 14 were distributed, the residue was divided among those who knew most of the Quran.[14] Apart from committing to memory, the verses of Quran were also written down by an inner circle of the followers of the Prophet. After the battle of Tamama, a year after the death of the Prophet, in which a number of persons who knew the Quran by heart died, it was feared that with the gradual passing away of such men there was danger of some Quranic material being lost. This prompted Abu Bakr, the first caliph, to order that a written copy of the whole body of the Quranic material, as arranged by the Prophet and memorized by the Muslims, be made and safely stored with him.

According to Muir, "It was not till the overthrow of Museilima, when great carnage took place amongst the Muslims at Al-Yemama, and a large number of the best reciters of the Kur'an were slain, that a misgiving arose in 'Omar's mind as to the uncertainty which would be experienced regarding the text, when all those who had stored it in their memories should have passed away. 'I fear,' said he, addressing the Caliph Abu Bakr, that slaughter may again wax hot amongst the reciters of the Qur'an, in other fields of battle; and that much may be lost therefrom. Now, therefore, my advice is, that thou shouldest give speedy orders for the collection of the Qur'an. Abu Bakr, agreed, and thus made known his wishes to Zeid ibn Thabit (Zeid, the son of Thabit), the Prophet's chief amanuensis: 'Thou art a young man and wise; against whom no one amongst us can cast an imputation; and thou wast wont to write down the inspired revelations of the Prophet of the Lord. Wherefore now search out the Qur'an and bring it together.' So new and unexpected was the enterprise that Zeid at first shrank from it and doubted the propriety, or even lawfulness, of attempting that which Muhammad had neither himself done nor commanded to be done. At last yielding to the joint entreaties of Abu Bakr and 'Omer, he sought out the Suras and fragments from every quarter, and gathered them together, from date-leaves, and tablets of white stone, and from the breasts of men."[15] According to some other traditions, the material collected included the fragments written on parchment or paper, pieces of leather, and the shoulder and rib bones of camels and goats also. It needs mention here that leather was frequently used for writing those days, and many of Muhammad's treaties and letters were recorded on the same.[16]

Zeid laboured hard; within 2-3 years, the scattered and confused materials were reduced to the order and sequence, which we find now, and in which it is said that Zeid used to repeat the Quran in presence of Muhammad. The original copy prepared by Zeid was committed by 'Omar to the custody of Hafsa, his daughter and Prophet's widow. About twelve years after that, the third caliph, Uthman ordered that a number of copies should be made from the same to be distributed to different parts of the Muslim world as the official copy of the Qur'an. The need of distribution of that text, which became known as the Uthman Codex, was felt as variety of expressions either prevailed in the previous transcripts and modes of recitation, or soon crept into the copies made from Zeid's edition. Hodheifa had warred in Armenia and Adherbaijan, and had observed the different readings of the Syrians and of Ar-'Irak; he was alarmed at the number and extent of the variations. These differences scandalized the Muslims; the revelation as sent down from heaven was one, but where was now its unity? Hodheifa warned the third caliph, 'Othman; he was convinced, and to remedy the evil had recourse again to Zeid, with whom he associated a syndicate of three of Kureish. Zeid's original copy from Hafsa's depository was obtained; various readings from throughout the empire were sought; a careful recension of the whole was set on foot. In case, there was difference between Zeid and his coadjutors, as Muir says: "the voice of the latter, as conclusive of the Koreishite idiom was to be followed, and collation thus assimilated exclusively to the Meccan dialect. Transcripts were multiplied and forwarded to the chief cities in the empire, and previously existing copies were all, by the caliph's command, committed to the flames. The original was returned again to Hafsa's custody. As the Muslims believe, some of the selfsame copies, penned by 'Othman or by his order, are still in existence.[17]

It is alleged that 'Othman left out certain Suras or passages which favoured Ali. It, however, seems to be improbable, because such allegation was made by the Shi'as of later time; no open breach had taken place between Omayyads and 'Alides by that time, and the unity of Islam was still unthreatened. Moreover, there were many such persons alive until then who could recite Qur'an correctly. Even Ali, a person deeply versed in the Qur'an, who said of himself that "There is not a verse in the Koran of which I do not know the matter, the parties to whom it refers, and the place and time of its revelation, whether by night or by day, whether in the plains or upon the mountains," rather than objecting to 'Othman's revision, he multiplied its copies. If the allegations were true, then he was certainly to take corrective measures to rectify the mutilations in the text. The insurgents, anyway, as Muir notes, 'made it one of their complaints against 'Othman that he had caused the revision, and ordered all previous copies of the sacred volume to be burnt. But these proceedings were objected to simply because of being unauthorized and sacrilegious. No hint was, however, dropped of ulterior object or of any alteration or omission.'[18] Muir, in this connection, raises two questions and tries to answer the same. The first one is, "Whether Zeid's collection was itself an authentic and exhaustive collection of Muhammad's revelations?" He gives four reasons to 'warrant the belief that it was authentic and in the main as complete as at the time was possible.' Abu Bakr, under whose direction the revision work was undertaken, 'Omer, under whose Caliphate the revision was completed, Zeid, performing the work, all three, were earnest believers in the divine origin of the Qur'an. The same was the case with the scribes and the humble believers who brought the matter for compilation to

Zeid. In the light of the earnest desire of these persons and the feeling of the believers at large to get the authentic words of the Prophet compiled, and the frequent denunciation in Qur'an itself against those who should presume to 'fabricate anything in the name of the Lord' or conceal any part of that which He has revealed, such action of impiety, as fabricating fact, on their part was unthinkable. Secondly, as the compilation by Zeid was made within 2-3 years of the death of Muhammad, the Qur'an was yet fresh in the memory of Prophet's followers. Thirdly, the compilation must have corresponded with numerous transcripts in daily use of the believers. The fourth point in favour of the authenticity of the compilation was the internal evidence of simplicity and faithfulness of the compilers. Elaborating this point Muir explains about the frequent repetition in Qur'an. He writes:

"The contents and arrangement of the Qur'an speak forcibly for its authenticity. All the fragments have, with artless simplicity, been joined together. The patchwork bears no marks of a designing genius or moulding hand. It testifies to the faith and reverence of the compiler, and proves that he dared not more than simply collect the sacred remains and place them in juxtaposition. Hence the interminable repetition; the wearisome reiteration of the same ideas, truths, and doctrines; scriptural stories and Arab legends, told over and over again, with little or no verbal variation; hence also the pervading want of connection, and the startling chasm between adjacent passages. Even the frailties of the Prophet, as noticed by the Deity, have with evident faithfulness been entered in the Qur'an. Not less undisguised are the many passages contradicted or abrogated by later revelations. Thus, the editor plainly contented himself with compiling and copying in a continuous form, but with scrupulous accuracy, the fragmentary materials within his reach. He neither ventured to select from the repeated versions of the same incident, or to reconcile differences, or by the alteration of a letter to connect abrupt transitions of context, or by tampering with the text to soften discreditable appearances. In fine, we possess every internal guarantee of confidence."[19]

So far, Margoliouth is concerned, he does not explain the repetition in Qur'an, but views it from another angle. He writes: "If, to us, the repetitions in the Qur'an seem intolerable, it must be remembered that the men who have impressed the world most are those who have always been saying the same about the same things."[20]

But, the question was further raised: "If the text of Zeid was pure and universally received, how come it to be so soon deteriorated as to require, in consequence of its variations, an extensive recension?" Muir tries to explain this question. He writes: "Tradition does not afford sufficient light to determine the cause of these discrepancies. They may have been due to various readings in transcripts that remained in the possession of the people, or have originated in the diverse dialects of Arabia, and different modes of pronunciation and orthography; or have sprung up naturally in the already vast domain of Islam, before strict uniformity was officially enforced. It is sufficient for us to know that in 'Othman's revision recourse was had to the *original* exemplar of the first compilation, and that there is otherwise every security, internal and external, that we possess the text which Muhammad himself gave forth and used."[21]

He further writes that the Qur'an may not contain some passages once revealed but subsequently cancelled, as the Qur'an itself recognizes the withdrawal of certain passages, after they have been promulgated as a part of the Revelation: 'Whatever verses We cancel, *or cause thee to forget*, We give thee better in their stead, or the like thereof.'[22] It is, anyway, a recognized fact that the Kor'an contains no fewer than 225 verses cancelled by later ones.[23] It needs mention that the *Satanic Verses* were, likewise, abrogated by the Prophet.

Basing on the tradition (Hadis), he also points out the cases of the careless way of the collection of some revelations.[24]

Verses Related to Real Life

A large number of Quranic verses are related to real life of the Prophet, and the life around him and the prevailing historical and social situations. *Sura* 30 (*Al-Rum*, Byzantines) opening with a reference to the defeat of the Byzantines at the hands of the Persians (613-14 AD), *Sura* 60 (*Al-Mumtahana*; *The Women Tested*), revealed between the treaty of Hudaybiyya and the conquest of Mecca (AH 6-8), *Sura* 105 (*Al-Fil*; *The Elephant*), referring to the events linked to the march of the Christian king, Abraha, said to have happened during 570 AD, have historical linkages. Many, such as *Sura* 106 (*Kuraysh*) and *Sura* 63 (*Al-Munafiqun*, Hypocrites) have the social significance. The revelations related to family life of the Prophet are well-known and many. The study of Hadis becomes helpful in understanding the historicity and linkages of many revelations.

Importance of Hadis in Understanding Qur'an

The books of Hadis include 'The Book of Commentary' (*Kitab al-Tafsir*). In the case of '*Sahih Muslim*', it is the 41st book. It contains only fifty *ahadis*. The commentary helps in deeper understanding of the Qur'anic *ayats*.

Qur'an is very different from other scriptures; it differs in temper, subject matter and the style of expression. The very tone is full of excitation; often agitated; it threatens and promises; it does not elucidate, but lays down and e Hadis provides background information, although very brief, erses of the Qur'an.[25] A Quranic verse says: "This day I have perfected your religion for you, completed favour upon you, and have chosen for you al-Islam for your religion."[26] It does not inform about the time and place of the revelation, but the Hadis does so. In a Hadis, Umar reports: "it was reveled on the night of Friday and we were in 'Arafat with Allah's messenger.[27] Yet another Quranic verse says: "And if a woman fears ill-treatment from her husband or desertion, it is no sin for them twain if they make terms of peace between themselves"[28] Ayesha reported the context of the revelation: "It was revealed in case of a woman who had long association with a person (as his wife) and now he intends to divorce her and she says: Do not divorce me, retain me (as wife in your house) and you are permitted to live with another wife."[29] According to Tirmizi, the characters mentioned in the Hadis by Ayesha were the Prophet himself and his wife Sauda.[30] Katib al-Wakidi has also written in *Tabaqat* that Muhammad wanted to divorce his wife, who was in her forties then, but she went to him and offered to forgo her term for Ayesha and to remain as his wife, as she wanted to remain on the Day of Resurrection among his wives, to which Muhammad agreed.[31]

We get to know from Hadis that *Sura Anfal* ('Spoils of War, 8th Sura) was revealed on the occasion of the Battle of Badr, and 'Sura al-Hashr ('The Gathering' or 'Banishment;' 58th Sura) 'was reveled in connection with the tribe of Banu Nazir.[32] Thus, Hadis helps in understanding of the context of the Quranic verses.

Notes and Rferences

1. Lesley Hezleton, *The First Muslim*, pp. 77-78; quoted from Qur'an; hereafter Hezleton.
2. William Muir, *The Life of Mahomet*, pp. 49-50; hereafter Muir.
3. Ibid, p. 50.
4. Ram Swarup, *Understanding Islam through Hadis*, New Delhi, 2001, p. 245; hereafter Ram Swarup.
5. *Sahih Muslim*, *Hadis* No. 7185.
6. *The Qur'an*, English translation by M.A.S. Abdel Haleem, *Introduction*, p. xix.
7. K.S. Lal, *Muslim State in India*, New Delhi, 1992, pp. 4-5.
8. Qur'an, 25:1-33; 27:59 ff; 30:17 ff; 41:53, etc.
9. Quran 36:76-83; 56: 47-96; 22: 5-10.
10. Quran 2:136; 3:84-85; 6:83-90; 42:13, etc.

11. Quran 2: 285.
12. Quran, Suras 2, 3, 4, 6, 8 and 9.
13. Lesley Hazleton, op. cit., p. 189.
14. Muir, op. cit., p. xvi, note 1.
15. Muir, op. cit., pp. xx-xxi.
16. Ibid, note 1.
17. Ibid, p xxii; note 2.
18. Ibid, p. xxiv, note 1.
19. Ibid, pp. xxvi-xxvii.
20. Margoliouth, *Mohammed and the Rise of Islam*, p. 147; hereafter Margoliouth.
21. Muir, op. cit., p. xxvii.
22. Qur'an, Sura 2:100.
23. Muir, op. cit., p. xxvi, note 1.
24. Margoliouth, op. cit., pp. 217-20.
25. Ram Swarup, op. cit., New Delhi, 2001.
26. Qur'an 5:4.
27. *Sahih Muslim*, *Hadis* No. 7134.
28. Qur'an, 4:128.
29. *Sahih Muslim*, *Hadis* No. 7165.
30. Timizi, Vol. II, *Hadis* 899; quoted by Ram Swarup, op. cit., pp. 244-245.
31. Ram Swarup, op. cit., p. 245; he quotes Katib al-Wakidi from his *Tabaqat*,
32. *Sahih Muslim*, *Ahadi* No. 7185; reported by Sa'ad b. Jubair.

Hadith: The Islamic Traditions

The two most important sources for the study of Islam are the Qur'an and the Hadis. Whereas the Qur'an contains the revelations (*wahy*) of the Prophet, the *Hadis* (*Hadith* singular, saying or tradition, plural, *ahadis*), usually called *Sunnah*, customs, informs about all that the Prophet said or did. Whereas the Quran provides the text, the *Hadis* provides the context for the study of Islam. The *Hadis* consists of the sayings of the companions and followers of the Prophet Muhammad, about all that Prophet did or said, or enjoined, forbade or did not forbid, approved or did not approve. It was handed down by an alleged chain of narrators to the period of their collection, recording and classification. The term, 'Hadis,' is also used collectively for all the traditions taken together.

Subjects Covered

The *Hadis* treats multiple and diverse subjects; it covers the views of the Prophet on Allah, faith (*iman*), prayer (*salat*), fast (*sawm*), pilgrimage (*hajj*), poor-tax (*zakat*), holy war (*jihad*), war booty (*al-anfal*), hell and heaven, life here and hereafter, the Last day of Judgment, the food, drink, clothing, marriage, sex, toilet, ablution, bathing, crime and punishment. Practically every thing related to Islamic law, precepts and practices, comes as the subject matter of *Hadis*. Islamic scholars give equal importance to both Qur'an and *Hadis*; both give equal guidance. For Muslims, both are works of revelation and inspiration.

Muhammad: The Best Model of Behavioural Pattern

As Muhammad is the best model of behavioural pattern, the Muslims were to follow whatever he said and did. The Qur'an said: "Verily in the Apostle of Allah you have the best example for anyone who looks forward towards God and the Day of Judgment."[1] In reality, Qur'an leaves no option than to act as the Prophet decided; it said: "when Allah and his Apostle have decided a matter, the believer does not have his or her own choice in the matter."[2] As Muslims have been ordained to recite not only the Qur'an, but also the 'Wisdom' of the Prophet, the Hadis acquires divine sanctity. The Qur'an says: "And remember that which is recited in your houses of the Messages of Allah and the wisdom."[3] In reality, Allah leaves no scope than to follow the Prophet. The Qur'an says: "And whatsoever the Messenger gives you, accept; and whatsoever he forbids you, avoid."[4] All these make it clear why the Prophet and his tradition, the *Sunna,* are so important for the Muslims. For them, the *Hadis* is 'unread revelation (*wahy ghair matlu*) and the Qur'an is the tradition considered authentic and genuine (*Hadis mutwatir*).

The Qur'an, mentions about the Book and the Wisdom revealed by Allah;[5] whereas the Book is the Quran, by Wisdom, according to Abdul Hameed Siddiqui, a well-known Muslim scholar, is meant 'the elucidations and enunciation of the Will of Allah by the Holy Prophet.'[6]

Text and the Transmission

Every *Hadis* has two parts; it has a text (*matn*) and a chain of transmission (*isnad*). The transmission of the traditions, mostly oral, was, many times, through a long chain. In a large number of cases, the same Hadith had different chain of transmitters. Thus, in many cases, one finds the same text having several chains, but every text must be traced back to a Companion (*as-hab*) of the Prophet, a person, who remained in latter's contact. The *Hadis* gives all sorts of information about the Prophet; even insignificant details about his life, his utterances, his commands; his every word, his every gesture, every nod or shake of head, was remembered, and formed part of the *Hadis*. Naturally, *Hadis* constitutes vast and voluminous literature.

Initially, the traditions were orally transmitted, though some of the Companions must have kept the note of some kind of the same. Anyway, these traditions were remembered and passed on from generation to generation till the need of their collection and compilation was felt and steps were taken to do the same.

The Sources

The most fertile sources of the *ahadis* (traditions) were the persons, who came into greater contact of the Prophet. This naturally includes the names of 'Ayesha, Prophet's wife, Abu Bakr and 'Umer, his fathers in-law and his most intimate followers, Anas b. Malik (Anas, son of Malik, a servant of the Prophet for ten years; he died at the ripe age of 103 in AH 93), Abdullah b. Abbas, his cousin. Abu Huraira, who specialized in collecting traditions from the Companions, is the authority of 3,500 traditions. Jabir, the authority of 1,540 traditions, belonged to Khazraj community of Medina.

The Need of the Sunna

Prophet Muhammad, during his last days, could control almost the entire Arabia. There were ample provisions in the Qur'an for the regulation of the religious, social and the political affairs of the simple and unsophisticated Arabs. After his death, his followers issued forth with a resolve to impose Islam upon all the nations of the world; they conquered a vast region from banks of Oxus to the farthest shores of Northern Africa and the Iberian Peninsula of South-Western Europe; the inhabitants of the vast region were made Muslims. Thus, the diverse people were brought under a single administrative umbrella. The administrative task with multiple nationalities and cities with vast populations, such as Al-Kufa, Cairo and Damascus, became more difficult and complex. Whereas the Qur'an was available to the Islamic State as the standard of theology, politics and law, the Sunna, or sayings and practices of Muhammad, came as supplementary of the same. But the authentic collection of these traditions was not available. In fact, the traditions were not collected as a rule till later part of the first century AH.

Authentic Collection of the Sunna

The attempts to collect Hadis, and to select and compile the authentic ones, were made by many Islamic scholars from time to time. Some of them were Muhammad Ismail al-Bukhari (Real name – Muhammad bin Ismail bin al-Mughira Al-Bukhari; AH 194-256; 810-870 AD), Muslim ibn'l-Hajjaj (Real name – Abu'l-Husain 'Asakir-ud-Din Muslim b. Hajjaj al-Qushayri al-Naisaburi; AH 204-261; 819-875 AD), Abu Isa Muhammad al-Tirmizi (AH 209-279; 824-892 AD), Abu Daud as-Sajistani (AH 202-275; 817-888 AD) and others, such as, Tirmidhi, Ibn Majah, Imam Ahmad b. Hanbal etc. The important *Hadis*, include *Sahih Bukhari*, *Sahih Muslim*, *Sunam* of Abu Daud, Tirmidhi, Ibn Majah, al-Nasa'I, Muwatta of Imam Malik, *Musnad* of Imam Ahmad b. Hanbal, *Musnad* of Abu Dawud al-Tayalisi. Out of all these collections, first six collections, known as *Sihah Sittah*, the six Sahihs, are considered to be genuine and more reliable ones. Out of the six, the two – *Sahih Bukhari* and *Sahih Muslim* – known as the two *Sahihs* (*al-Sahihain*), are recognized as the most authentic ones, and are held in highest esteem. But even among the two, *Sahih Bukhari* occupies a higher position than *Sahih Muslim*.

Abdul Hamid Siddiqi, the English translator of *Sahih Muslim*, who has also given scholarly and valuable notes in his translation of the book, while placing *Sahih Bukhari* at the top among all the *Hadis* collections, has pointed towards the positives of *Sahih Muslim*, which need mention. He writes: "I fully subscribe to the view of the Muhaddithin that after the Holy Qur'an, Bukhari's *Sahih* is the most reliable book of Islamic Shariah. Muslim's *Sahih* comes next to it. However, in certain respects, Siddiqi observes, the latter is considered superior to the former. Imam Muslim strictly observed many principles of the science of hadith, which has been slightly ignored by his great teacher Imam Bukhari."[7] For a tradition to be genuine and authentic, it should have been transmitted by unbroken chain of reliable authorities, and it should be in perfect harmony with other trustworthy narrations. Bukhari, while referring to the chain of narrators, especially in case of the Syrian ones, sometimes gives their *kunya,*[8] and sometimes gives their names. Muslim avoids such confusion. In *Sahih Muslim*, attention is paid on the exact words used by the narrators; even the minutest differences in the wording of the reports are not ignored. Muslim keeps in view the differences between two well-known modes of narration, *Huddathana* (he narrated to us; the teacher narrating and the student listening) and *Akkbarana* (he informed us; student is reading the Hadith before the teacher).[9] Siddiqi further observes:

"Imam Muslim has taken great pain in connecting chain of narrators. He has recorded only that hadith in which, at least, two reliable successors (*tabi'in*) had heard from two Companions and this principle is observed throughout subsequent chain of narrators." Needless to say that only the authentic *ahadis* were included in his collection of *Hadis*, which included only 4000 traditions out of 3,00,000 collected by him from the vast region consisting of Arabia, Egypt, Syria and Iraq.[10] The same is the case with his teacher Bukhari, who collected 6,00,000 traditions, and after ruthless sifting accepted only 7,000 as authentic ones for inclusion in his collection.[11] Although 40,000 names were mentioned in different chains of transmission, Bukhari accepted only 2,000 as genuine ones.[12] (The total number of traditions collected by Bukhari, according to Siddiqi, however, is only 3,00,000 Abu Da'ud included only 4800 traditions in his collection out of the total collection of 5,00,000.[13] This clearly indicates that a large number of spurious traditions were in currency when the collection work started, which got mixed up with the authentic ones, requiring sifting of the same. The Islamic scholars, like Bukhari and Muslim, did the same, making their writings – *Sahih Bukhari* and *Sahih Muslim* – extremely valuable documents for proper understanding of Islam.

It was generally believed that the traditions, in early days, were only committed to memory, and not subjected to writing. This is, however, not true. Sprenger, a scholar, who critically studied the biography of Muhammad, writes:

"It is generally believed that the traditions were preserved during the first century of the Hijrah solely by memory. European scholars, under the erroneous impression that *haddathana* (he informed us) is the term by which the traditions are generally introduced, are of the opinion that none of the traditions contained in the collection of al-Bukhari had been written down before him......This appears to be an error. Ibn 'Amr and other Companions of Muhammad (May peace be upon him) committed his sayings to writing and their example was followed by many of the Tabi'un."[14]

Of course, the Islamic scholars have also written that the utterances of Prophet Muhammad were memorized, and at the same time, it was subjected to writing. A narrative transmitted on the authority of an eminent Companion of the Prophet, given below, makes the point clear:

"It is reported on the authority of Hadrat Anas: So long as we remained in the company of Allah's Apostle (peace and blessings of Allah be upon him), we listened attentively to what he uttered and as we departed we repeated them till these were retained in our memories."[15]

It further said:

"It is reported on the authority of Abu Sa'id Khudri: We were sitting and writing what we were hearing from Allah's Messenger (peace and blessings of Allah be upon him) that he turned his attention to us and said: What is this that you are writing? We said: We are writing that what we are hearing from you. Whereupon he said: Are you writing another Book along with the Book of Allah. Keep the Book of Allah separate and make its text pure so that there may not be confusion in it."[16]

Thus, the Prophet did not prohibit the recording of the traditions; he only wanted the recordings of the Qur'an and the *Hadis* to be made separately. The following tradition makes the point clear:

The famous *Muhaddith* Imam Khattabi writes: "He (the Holy Prophet) prohibited the writing of the words of the Qur'an and those of *ahadith* together lest there should be any intermingling in them and the reader may be confused. The writing of hadith (itself) is in no way prohibited."[17]

Notes and References

1. Qur'an 33.21.
2. Ibid 33.36.
3. Ibid 33.34.
4. Ibid 59.7.
5. Ibid 4.113; 3.163.
6. Abdul Hameed Siddiqui, *Mishkat-ul-Mashabih*, Introduction, p. vi. (Here

after, Mishkat).

7. Abduk Hamid Siddiqi, *Sahih Muslim,* English translation, Vol. I, Introduction, pp. v-vi. (Here after, Muslim).
8. The honorific naming by addressing some one as 'father of so and so' or 'son of so and so.'
9. Muslim, Introduction p. vi.
10. Mishkat, op. cit.
11. Ram Swarup, *Understanding Islam through Hadis*, Introduction, pp. x-xi. (Here after, Ram Swarup).
12. Ibid.
13. Ibid.
14. *Journal of the Asiatic Society of Bengal*, Calcutta, Vol. XXV, p. 303.
15. *Majma al-Zawaid*, Vol. IV, p. 152; quoted in Mishkat, p. ix.
16. Ibid.
17. *Ma'alim Sunan*, Vol. IV, p. 184; quoted in Mishkat, p. ix.

Early Historians of Islam and their Works

The earliest work of Islamic history, available to us, is *Sirat Rasul Allah*, the biography of Prophet Muhammad. It was, of course, preceded by the *Maghazi* books (*Maghazi*, war-chronicles, expedition accounts), most of which have been lost, and known only by the references made in the writings of Ibn Ishaq, Ibn Hisham, Al-Wakidi, and his secretary, Ibn Sa'd, and At-Tabari, the writings which are more or less extant.[1]

Maghazi Books

The name of Aban, the son of caliph 'Uthman, born in AH 20, often appears in the *Isnads* of the canonical collections of Hadith. Al Wakidi, while writing about the work of Ibn al-Mughira, indirectly brings to notice the work of Aban. He writes, "he (Ibn al-Mughira) had nothing written down about hadith except the prophet's maghazis which he has acquired from Aban." Thus, Aban must be either a writer or a narrator of the *Maghazis*. However, it is strange that neither Ibn Ishaq nor al-Wakidi have cited him in their works. It was possibly, as Ibn Ishaq, a follower of Ali preferred to ignore the son of the man the Alids regarded as a usurper.[2] Aban, it needs mention, fought war against the killers of his father. He died at the age of 100.

Urwa (also written 'Orwa; a cousin of Prophet Muhammad) was a recognized authority on the early history of Islam. Though, it is uncertain whether he wrote a book, but, many traditions that are handed down in his name by Ibn Ishaq and other writers justify the assertion that he was the founder of Islamic history. Persons, such as Ummayad caliph 'Abdu'l Malik wanted to have, and received accurate knowledge about the Prophet from him. Much of his material is based on the statements of his aunt Ayesha. Like Ibn Ishaq, and his aunt Ayesha, who uttered verses on every subject, he used to insert poetry in his traditions.[3] Another person Az-Zuhri, who died at the age of 72 during AH 144, had been employed in the task of recording traditions systematically; he worked with his master Urwa. It is stated that both of them composed regular biographies of Muhammad. No writing of Az-Zuhri is extant in independent form, but subsequent biographers have largely quoted him. It is believed that the accounts of Muhammad's military expeditions by the latter writers are probably in great part the reproduction of materials collated by Az-Zuhri.[4]

Shurahbil also wrote a *Maghazi* book. He listed the names of the emigrants and the combatants at Badr and Uhud, and was discredited in his old age, because he blackmailed his visitors by telling them that their fathers were not present at Badr, if they did not pay him anything. Though, persons best qualified to judge regarded him as an authority, he earned a bad name, because poverty and old age made him cantankerous.[5]

Wahb (Wahb b. Munabbih, Wahb, son of Munabbih; AH 34-110), a Yamanite of Persian origin, was probably the son of a Jew. A fragment of his *Maghazi*, written in 228 AH, has been discovered. An opinion about him is worth quoting: "He is notorious for his interest in, and knowledge of, Jewish and Christian scriptures and traditions; and though much that was invented later was fathered on him, his *K. al-Muhtada*' lies behind the Muslim version of the lives of the prophets and other biblical stories. With his book on the legendary history of the Yaman, on aphorisms, on free will, and other matters preserved in part in I.H.'s *K. al-Tijan,* we are not concerned; but the statement of Hajji Khalifa that he collected the *Maghazi* is now confirmed by the discovery of a fragment of a lost work on papyri written in 228. Unfortunately, this fragment tells us little that is new; nevertheless, its importance is great because it proves that at the end of the first century, or some years before AH 100, the main facts about the Prophet's life were written down much as we have them in the later works.[6] The names of some other *Maghazi* writers and/or scholars are Asim b. 'Umar, Muhammad b. Muslim, 'Abdullah b. Abu Bakr, Abu'l-Aswad Muhammad b. 'Abdu'l Rahman b. Naufal, Musa b. 'Uqba (*c* 55-141); the names of most of them appear in the *ahadis* as narrators. *Maghazis* were also written in Iraq, Syria, and the Yaman."[7]

A fragment of the work of Musa b. 'Uqba (Musa, son of 'Uqba), a freed man of the family of al-Zubayr, has survived and was published by Sachau in 1904. Three Islamic scholars –Malik b. Anas, al-Shafi'I, and Ahmad b. Hanbal –'asserted that his book was the most important and trustworthy of all, posterity evidently did not share their opinion or more of his work would have survived.' The book was in circulation up to nineth century AH; but Ibn Ishaq has never taken note of the same. This led A. Guillaume to observe, "One can not escape the conviction that petty professional jealousy was rife in those days as now, and that scholars deliberately refrained from giving their predecessors credit for their achievements."[8] The biographies (*sira*, singular, *siyar*) of Muhammad, written by Musa ibn Uqba (also written 'Okba') and Mashar are not extant, but At-Tabari has extensively referred to that of the latter.[9]

The *Sira*

The earliest biographer, whose work we have, is Muhammad Ibn Ishaq. Of course, no copy of Ibn Ishaq's biography is available in its original form; but its 'materials have been so extensively adopted by Ibn Hisham and wrought into his history in so complete and unaltered a form, that we have probably not lost much by the absence of the work itself.' Ibn Ishaq's statements have been embodied in all subsequent biographies of Muhammad excepting that of Al-Wakidi, who sparingly quotes from him. This proves former's character, authority and fidelity.

Ibn Ishaq's father, and his uncle Musa, were also traditionists. Ibn Ishaq died, some twenty years after the overthrow of the Omayyad dynasty, in 151 AH; his "work was published under the auspices and influence of the 'Abbasid Princes, and was in fact composed 'for the use' of the Caliph Al-Mansur, the second of that line. Its accuracy has been impugned. But the portions that have come down to us, there seems no ground for believing that Ibn Ishaq was less careful than other traditionists; ..."[10]

Ibn Khalikan's biographical dictionary has published glowing testimony of Ibn Ishaq, which needs mention. According to the same, "Muhammad ibn Ishaq is held by the majority of the learned as a sure authority in traditions, and none can be ignorant of the high character born by his work, *the Maghazi* (military expeditions). *Whoever wishes to know the early Muslim conquests*, says Az-Zuhri, *let him refer to Ibn Ishaq*; and Al-Bukhari himself cites him in his history. Ash-Shafi'i said: *Whoever wishes to obtain a complete acquaintance with the early Muslim conquests, must borrow his information from Ibn Ishaq*. Sufyan ibn 'Oyeina declared that he never met any one who cast suspicions on Ibn Ishaq's recitals; and Sho'ba ibn al-Hajjaj, was heard to say, '*Mohammad ibn Ishaq is the Commander of the Faithful*, meaning that he held that rank as a traditionist. ... As-Saji mentions that Az-Zuhri's pupils had recourse to Mohammad ibn Ishaq, whenever they had doubts respecting the exactness of any of the traditions delivered by their master; such was the confidence they placed in his excellent memory. It is stated that Yahya ibn Ma'in Ahmed ibn Hanbal, and Yahya Sa'id al-Kattan, considered Mohammad ibn Ishaq as a trustworthy authority, and quoted his traditions in proof of their legal doctrines. ... It was from Ibn Ishaq's works that Ibn Hisham extracted the materials of his biography of the prophet, and every person who has been obliged to take Ibn Ishaq for his authority and guide."[11] Even Az-Zuhri praised him, when he was in Medina in 123 AH for collection and arrangement of the material on the war expeditions of Prophet Muhammad; Az-Zuhri is reported to have said that Medina would never lack '*ilm* as long as Ibn Ishaq was there.'[12]

But, even Ibn Ishaq was not free from controversy and had to suffer. As Guillaume writes: "Unfortunately Ibn Ishaq excited the enmity of Malik b. Anas (Malik, son of Anas) for whose work he showed his contempt, and it was not long before his own writings and his orthodoxy were called in question. Probably it was our author's lost book of *Sunan* which excited Malik's ire, for it would have been in the field of law based on the practice of the prophet that differences would be most keenly felt. He was accused of being a Qadari and a Shi'i. Another man attacked his veracity: he often quoted Fatima, the wife of Hisham b. 'Urwa, as the authority for some of his traditions. The husband was annoyed and denied that he has ever met his wife; but as she was nearly forty years Ibn Ishaq's senior it was easily credible that they often met without occasioning gossip."[13] Perhaps, Ibn Ishaq left Medina after that controversy.

The book written by Ibn Ishaq had three sections –Ancient Legends, Muhammad's early life and mission, and his wars—rather than the fact that he wrote three separate books. He, and also Al-Wakidi, is the original source for latter historians of Islam, or biographers of Prophet Muhammad, including At-Tabari.

Ibn Hisham edited and annotated *Sirat Rasul Allah* of Ibn Ishaq, and used its material for his own biography of the Prophet, *Sirat ar-Rasul*, or *Biography of the Prophet*. A native of Old Cairo –but his family were from Al-Basra—, he died in 213 (or 218) AH. He had superior information in genealogy and grammar. He was, however, not as trustworthy as Ibn Ishaq. Muir writes: "certainly there is one instance which throws suspicion upon him as a witness, disinclined at least to tell the *whole* truth. We find in At-Tabari *a quotation from Ibn Ishaq*, in which is described the temporary lapse of Mohammad into idolatry; and the same incidents are also given by Al-Wakidi from other original sources. But no notice whatever of the fact appears in the biography of Ibn Hisham, though it is professedly based upon the work of Ibn Ishaq. His having thus studiously omitted all reference to so important an incident, for no other reason apparently than because he fancied it to be discreditable to the Prophet, can not but lessen our confidence generally in this book."[14]

Al-Wakidi (Muhammad ibn 'Omer Al-Wakidi) was born in Medina in about 130 AH, and died in AH 207. A man of vast traditional researches and voluminous contributions, Al-Wakidi worked under the patronage of Abbasid Caliphs, and passed a part of his life in their court. He served as *Kadi* of Baghdad in his later days. 'In judging, therefore, of his learning and prejudices,' as Muir writes, 'we must always bear in mind that the influence of the 'Abbasid dynasty bore strongly and continuously upon him.' Muir, further, quotes the opinion from Ibn Khallikan about him: "Al-Wakidi was a man eminent for learning, and the author of some well-known works on the conquests of the Muslims, and other subjects. His *Kitab ar-Ridda*, a work of no inferior merit, contains an account of apostasy of the Arabs on the death of the Prophet, and of the wars between his followers and Toleiha, Al-Aswad, and Museilima, the false prophets. … His Secretary, Mohammad ibn Sa'd, and a number of other distinguished men, delivered traditional information on his authority. He held the post of Kadi in the eastern quarter of Baghdad, and was appointed by the Caliph Al-Mamun to fill the same office at 'Askar al-Mahdi. Al-Wakidi, have been a follower of the 'Alid sect, it is said, and probably yielded to the prevailing influences of the day, which tended to exalt the Prophet's son-in-law as well as the progenitors of the Abbasid race. The traditions received from him are considered of feeble authority, and doubts have been expressed on the subject of his veracity. Al-Mamun testified a high respect for him, and treated him with marked honour." Although a prolific writer and having extraordinary fertility of pen, his books remained non-extant, except the *Maghazi*, or *History of the Wars of the Prophet*, discovered in Syria, and published in the *Bibliotheca Indica*. But, the results of Al-Wakidi's labour were preserved by his secretary Mohammad ibn Sa'd.[15]

Ibn Khallikan informs about Ibn Sa'd, the Secretary of Al-Wakidi, thus: "Mohammad ibn Sa'd was a man of highest talent, merit, and eminence. He lived for some time with Al-Wakidi in character of a Secretary, and for this reason became known by the appellation "The Secretary of Al-Wakidi." … He composed an excellent work in fifteen volumes on the different classes of Mohammad's Companions and the Successors; it contains also a history of the caliphs, brought down to his own time. He left also a smaller edition of the same. His character as a veracious and trustworthy historian is universally admitted. It is said that the complete collection of Al-Wakidi's works remained in the possession of four persons, the first of whom was his Secretary, Ibn Sa'd. This distinguished writer displayed great acquirements in the sciences, the traditions, and traditional literature; most of his books treat of the traditions and law. The khatib Abu Bekr, author of the 'History of Baghdad,' speaks of him in these terms: 'We consider Mohammad ibn Sa'd as a man of unimpeached integrity, and the traditions which he delivered are a proof of veracity, for, in the greater part of information handed down by him, we find him discussing it passage by passage.' At the age of sixty-two he died at Baghdad, AH 230, and was interned in the cemetery outside the Damascus gate."[16]

Ibn Sa'd is supposed to have embodied the researches of Al-Wakidi, as well as his own, in the fifteen volumes he compiled. The first volume, containing the 'Biography of Mohammed' with the detailed accounts of the learned men of Medina, and all the Companions of the Prophet present at Badr, has been preserved. The treatise, composed entirely of detached traditions, arranged fairly in chronological order, and according to subject, is arranged in chapters.[17] Ibn Sa'd's published book, *Great Book of the Classes* (*Tabakat*) includes biographies of the famous Muslims down to his own time.

At-Tabari, the third historian after Ibn Ishaq and Al-Wakidi as rendered by his Secretary Ibn Sa'd, and a judicious historian, was born at Amul in Tabarestan in 224 AH, and died at Baghdad during AH 310. Sprenger was the first to discover a portion of a long-lost volume from amongst a heap of neglected manuscripts, written by At-Tabari (Abu Ja'far ibn Jarir at-Tabari) in a library in Lucknow during 1857. It began with the birth of Muhammad, and terminated with the siege of Madina, which was five years before the Prophet's death. An interesting point, needing mention, about At-Tabari's writing is that two-thirds of his work "are composed of extracts quoted formally from Ibn Ishaq and Al-Wakidi," which "proves not only that these two biographers were in his day held as trustworthy, but likewise that they were the standard writers and the chief authorities on the subject, upto at least the close of the third century."[18]

The early historians of Islam, in the case of the miracle stories, either make a compromise between his believer and historian, or simply avoid the same. Take the case of the night journey of Prophet Muhammad. The Qur'a says: "Glory be to God, who made his servant go by night from the sacred house to the far house."[19] This refers to the night journey from Sacred house (Kaaba) to far house (Jerusalem). Qur'an does not give the story, but the verse provides the reference. Lesley Hazleton writes as to how Ibn Ishaq sums up the same. She writes: 'In the light of this Qur'anic verse, ibn Ishaq sums up his reportorial dilemma this way: "The matter of the place of the journey and what is said about it is a searching test and a matter of God's power and authority, wherein is a lesson for the intelligent with guidance, mercy, and strengthening for those who believe."[20]

"It's a wisely phrased abstention from certainty. Whether the night journey was a dream, a vision, or lived experience, ibn Ishaq's view is that what matters is not how it happened, but its significance. He steps carefully between his duty as a believer and his obligation as a biographer—a delicate balancing act that he carries out with considerable aplomb, finally threading the needle with this conclusion: "I have heard it said that that the messenger used to say, 'My eyes sleep while my heart is awake.' Only God knows how revelation came and what he saw. But whether he was asleep or awake, it was all true."[21]

Lesley Hazleton further writes; "Not every early Islamic historian would agree. At-Tabari, writing a century later in the new Muslim capital city of Baghdad, was wary as always of miracle tales and far more focused on politics. Despite his repeatedly acknowledged debt to ibn Ishaq, he would omit the episode altogether in his multi-volume history and ignore the much quoted dictum attributed to Ayesha speaking many years after Muhammad's death: "The messengers body remained where it was but God removed his spirit by night."[22]

Dearth of Material for Study in Nineteenth Century

Initially, there was dearth of material for the European scholars. The scholars were not happy to use the biography written by Abu'l Fida, who died in the year 722 AH. The "scholars of the nineteenth century were, naturally not satisfied with so late an authority: and they succeeded bringing to light all the earliest documents preserved by the Muhammedans."[23]

Notes and References

1. Ibn Ishaq, *Sirat Rasul Allah*, English translation, *The Life of Muhammad* by A. Guillaume, Karachi, 1996; Introduction, A. Guillaume, pp. xiv-xvii; (Hereafter, Ibn Ishaq); Sir William Muir, *The Life of Mahomet*, New Delhi, Reprint, 2002; p. lxxvi (Hereafter, Muir).
2. Ibn Ishaq, op. cit, p. xiv.
3. Ibid, pp. xiv-xv.
4. Muir, op. cit, p. lxxvi.
5. Ibn Ishaq, p. xv.
6. Ibid.
7. Ibid, pp. xv-xvii.
8. Ibid, p. xvi.
9. Ibid, p. lxxvi.
10. Muir, pp. lxxvii-lxxviii.
11. Quoted by Muir on p. lxxviii.
12. Ibn Ishaq, Introduction, p. xiii.
13. Ibid.

[14.] Muir, op. cit., pp. lxxix-lxxx.
[15.] ibid, pp. lxxx-lxxxi.
[16.] Ibid, pp. lxxxi-lxxxii.
[17.] Ibid, p. lxxxii.
[18.] Ibid, p. lxxxv.
[19.] Qur'an 17:1, 60.
[20.] Lesley Hazleton, *The First Muslim*. London, 2013; p. 141.
[21.] Ibid.
[22.] Ibid, pp. 141-42.
[23.] Margoliouth, *Muhammad and the rise of Islam*, New Delhi, Reprint, 1985. Preface, p. iii.

Biographies of the Prophet

Islam is so intimately connected with its Prophet that there is practically, no distinction between his biography and the history of that religion. Thus, the early history of Islam, about which we have already discussed, is in reality, the biography of its Prophet; and the material used by the first two –Ibn Ishaq and Al-Wakidi –was so exhaustive that those who followed them, such as At-Tabari, or the modern ones, such as, William Muir, Margoliouth and others, relied mostly on the same.

Considerable number of biographies of Prophet Muhammad has been published during the last one and a half century. The best among them, in comprehensiveness and the wealth of the material, is the one by Sir William Muir; the book is a real classic, and remains unsurpassed by all the biographies published after that. Muir, belonging to the highest rung of British officialdom in India, was an outstanding Arabist and Islamist; he was also a believing Christian. His *The Life of the Mahomet* was published in 1861 in four volumes; it was a pioneering study based entirely on orthodox sources. In 1876, an abridged edition of the book was published, which was followed by the publication of the third edition in one volume in 1894 with important alterations. Two early Islamic historians exhausted entirely the available material on the life of the Prophet. Archaeological studies added some material on pre-Islamic culture. Muir, however, exhausted whatever material was available up to his time. The other biographies, written after him, had no further material to be added. But different biographies look at the matter differently.

The other important biography written by a Westerner is *Mohammed and the Rise of Islam*, written by D.S. Margoliouth. Margoliouth, a great linguist and scholar, and for a long time a professor of Arabic at the University of Oxford, was also a minister of the Church of England. His biography was published as a part of a long series in 1905. "The stand point from which, his book was written," Margoliouth writes: "is suggested by the title of the series. I regard Mohammad as a great man, who solved a political problem of appalling difficulty,—the construction of a state and an empire out of the Arab tribes. I have endeavoured, in recounting the mode in which he accomplished this, to do justice to his intellectual ability and to observe towards him the respectful attitude which his greatness deserves; but otherwise this book does not aim at being either an apology or an indictment. Indeed neither sort of work is now required."[1]

Margoliouth wants to maintain respectful attitude towards the Prophet; he does not want his book to be apologetic or biased. And, indeed, his book is free from Christian bias, about which he indirectly mentions, while remarking about the biographies of Amir Ali and Muir. He writes: "The charming treatise of Syed Ameer Ali[2] is probably the best achievement in the way of an apology for Muhammad that is ever likely to be composed in an European language, whereas indictments are very numerous—some dignified and moderate, as is the work of Sir William Muir; others fanatical and virulent. These works are ordinarily designed to show the superiority or inferiority of Mohammad's religion to some other system; an endeavour from which this book will be found to be absolutely free."[3] Margoliouth, in a way, sums up the situation; a large number of publications were either unduly critical and biased, or hagiographic and apologetic. Margoliouth, on his part, was free from Christian bias, but not from Euro-Christian colonial bias; Bedouin manners and institutions, like other non-European manners and institutions, were savage ones for him.

When European scholars started working on the biography of the Prophet, the only text available for them was the biography of Muhammad by Abu'l Fida of 732 AH (1322 AD). As it was a book written by a late authority, many scholars were not satisfied. But gradually, earlier works came to light; the Arabist and Persian knowing European scholars, of course, used original Arabic and Persian texts. The scholars, who discovered and used original texts, "were G. Weil, Caussin de Perceval, F. Wustenfeld, A. Sprenger, and William Muir;" and as Margoliouth writes: "the Lives of Mohammed by the last two of these writers are likely to be regarded as classical so long as there are students of Oriental history in Europe; notwithstanding the fact that Muir's Life is written with confessedly Christian bias, and that Sprenger's is defaced by some slipshod scholarship and untrustworthy archaeology."[4]

Muir, on his part, wanted to base his biography of the Prophet on facts derived from the Original sources. He, while discussing the inaccuracies of Washington Irving's biography, *Life of Muhammad*, stressed the need for a "life of the Prophet of Arabia which is based on sound, orthodox Muslim sources."[5] Muir wrote a number of articles in Calcutta Review in mid-1840s, which gives an idea as what he expected his 'Life of Muhammad' to be or to achieve. Ram Swarup has summed up his ideas: "He wanted to oppose two kinds of biographies; 'one was by the Missionary writers who were careless about their facts, slipshod in their scholarship, hostile in their intent, unsympathetic in treatment, and uninhibited in expressing their opinions. For example, A. Sprenger, his contemporary, a Missionary and an Islamist of great repute, regarded Muhammad as having a "weak and cunning mind." Muir disagreed and argued that such a man "could never have accomplished the mighty mission which Mahomet wrought." Others called Islam "a spurious faith" and its founder "a false Messiah." Muir probably shared these opinions, but he discouraged their too open expression. He thought that if the Missionaries used such epithets, how could they get the hearing of the Muslims? He probably also thought that stating facts should do, for they should speak for themselves."[6]

Another kind of Biographies of the Prophet, which Muir wanted his Life to oppose were written by native Muslim writers, current among devout Muslims. As Ram Swarup sums up, "These were highly fanciful and extravagant and were based on fabricated traditions of which the early biographers of the Prophet were quite innocent. For illustration, Muir discusses a biography of the Prophet, *Maulud Sharif* or "The Ennobled Nativity" written by Ghulam Imam Shahid, during the 1840s. It was very popular among the Muslims and it had already seen a dozen editions. In this biography, the author, an ornate writer, informed us how Allah wishing to manifest himself formed the "light of Muhammad a thousand years before creation;" how when the light was at last transferred to the womb of Ameena, Muhammad's mother, "200 damsels of Coreish died of envy;" how angels rejoiced at his birth; how as he came out of the womb he was already circumcised; and how he repeated the kalima."[7]

We do not find what Ghulam Imam Shahid has written in early traditions of Islam, or while going through the pages of *Sirat Rasul Allah* of Ibn Ishaq. Muir wanted his biography to be faithful to the early tradition. He thought that such a biography would be respected by the Muslims; it would therefore serve the Missionary cause better. Muir argued: "If we can from their own best sources, prove to them that they are deceived and superstitious in many important points ... we shall have gone a great way to excite honest enquiry and induce the sincere investigator to follow our lead."[8] He wanted to present this biography to "thinking Mohammedans, who are turning their attention to the historical evidence of their faith; and are comparing them with Christianity." Thus, Muir fondly hoped that thinking Muslims may come to accept Christianity to their own faith. But his hope, for rationality on the part of 'thinking Muslims, was dashed. Sir

Sayyad Ahmed also wrote a biography of Prophet Muhammad in reply to Muir's biography. He argued, whether the Biblical miracles of Moses and Jesus should not be considered from the same rational viewpoint? Whether the Christians beliefs should not be rationally analysed?[9] The Christians, however, remained dogmatic; they had learnt to believe that while the miracles of Jesus were historical and well attested, those found in rival faiths were irrational. The stories of the immaculate Conception, the Virgin Mother and only Begotten Son will satisfy the historical sense of the believing Christians, and pass the test of rationality for them, but not for the others. Naturally, the one-sided rationality failed to bring the result.

A recent biographical publication, titled *The First Muslim*,[10] has come out recently. Lesley Hazleton, basing on the original sources, traces the life journey of a posthumous doubly orphaned person moving from powerlessness to power, from anonymity to renown, from insignificance to lasting significance. She deals her subject from diverse angles of history, politics, religion and psychology. The book is a valuable addition in the field of Islamic study.

References

1. Margoliouth, D.S., Mohammed and the Rise of Islam, Reprint, New Delhi, 1985; Preface, pp. vi-vii; hereafter Margoliouth.
2. *The Spirit of Islam*, London, 1896, Calcutta, 1902.
3. Margoliouth, p. vii.
4. Ibid, op. cit, pp. iii-iv.
5. Muir, *The Life of Mahomet*, New Delhi, 2002; Introduction of the Reprint by Ram Swarup, p. 1.
6. Ibid, pp. 1-2.
7. Ibid, p. 2.
8. Ibid.
9. Ibid.
10. Lesley Hazleton, *The First Muslim*, Atlantic Books, London, 2013.

Pre-Prophetic Phase

Birth and Childhood of Prophet Muhammad

Muhammad, the posthumous child of the Meccan parents, Abdallah (*Servant of God*; Hebrew, *Abdiel*) and Amina (also written Aminah; meaning, *safe* or *secure*), was born in the autumn of the year 570. The event occurred about fifty-five days after the attack of Abraha. Accordingly, his date of birth computed by Caussin de Perceval falls on August 20. His father died before his birth. His mother sent the good news after his birth to his grandfather, Abd al-Mutalib. The old man, who was sitting in the holy precinct of Ka'ba, was very happy to hear the news; he met Amina, who informed the past happening to him. The old man took the child in his arms, went to Ka'ba. Standing beside the Holy house, he gave thanks to Allah. The child was given the name Muhammad. It was a rare name among the Arabs. Derived from the root *Hamada,* it signified 'The Praised.' "Another form" of the name, according to Muir, "is Ahmed, which having been erroneously employed as a translation of 'The Paraclete' in some Arabic version of the New Testament, became a favourite term with Muslims, especially in addressing Jews and Christians; for it was (they said) the title under which the Prophet had been in their books predicted."[1] Here, it needs mention that 'Mahmud' is also a variety of the name 'Muhammad.'

Muir has detailed the marriage and death of Prophet Muhammad's father. It was some months previous to the incident of the attack of Abraha on Mecca, that the Prophet's grandfather, Abd al-Muttalib, then of more than 70 years of age, and a person who enjoyed rank and consideration as the foremost chief of Mecca, took his youngest son, Abdallah, then 24 years of age, to Medina, "to the house of Uheib (Wahb), a distant kinsman descended from Zuhra, brother of the famous Kosai; and there affianced him to Amina, the niece of Uheib, under whose guardianship she lived. At the same time, 'Abd al-Muttalib, notwithstanding his advanced age, bethought him of a matrimonial alliance on his own account, and married Halah, the cousin of Amina and daughter of Uheib; of this late marriage, the famous Hamza was the firstfruits."[2]

The marriage took place at Medina and Abdallah died away from home during a trading expedition, when Muhammad was yet to be born. Muir writes: "As was customary in a marriage at the home of the bride, 'Abdallah remained there with her for three days. Not long after, he left his wife with child, and set out on a mercantile expedition to Gaza in the south Syria. On his way back he sickened at Medina, and was left behind by the caravan with his father's maternal relatives. 'Abd al-Muttalib, on learning of 'Abdallah's sickness, dispatched his son Al-Harith to take care of him. Reaching Medina, Al-Harith found that his brother had died about a month after the departure of the caravan. He returned with these tidings, and his father and brethren mourned for 'Abdallah. He was but five-and-twenty years of age, and Amina had not yet been delivered. He left behind him five camels fed on wild shrubs, a flock of goats, and Um Aiman, a slave girl (called also *Baraka*), who tended the infant born by his widow. This little property, and the house in which he dwelt, were all the inheritance Muhammad received from his father; but, little as it was, the simple habit of the Arabs required no more; and instead of being evidence of poverty, the possession of a female slave was rather an indication of prosperity and comfort."[3]

According to a custom, better class of women at Mecca did not suckle their children. Either the nurses were procured for them, or they were given out to nurse among the neighbouring Bedawi tribes. The practice continued among the Sherifs of Mecca. Eight days old child used to be sent to them, and except for a visit at the sixth month, the child did not return to the parents till he attained the age of eight or ten. The infant Muhammad also was made over to Thuweiba, the slave of his uncle, Abu Lahab, for suckling, shortly after his birth. Thuweiba had also lately suckled to his uncle Hamza. After several days of nursing by Thuweiba, a party of the Beni Sa'd of Hawazin tribe arrived at Mecca with ten women, offering themselves as nurses. All of them got children except Halima, who had to be persuaded to take Muhammad. The difficulty with him was that he was fatherless, and it was the father from whom they expected to receive rewards for nursing the baby. Any way, the baby was taken; Halima brought him back to his mother after two years; the mother was delighted to see his healthy and robust appearance; he looked like a child of double the age. Amina asked Halima to take him back again to the desert. She said: 'Take him with thee again to the desert; for I fear the unhealthy air of Mecca.' So, she took him back with her to return again after two years. This time, it was due to some occurrence of strange event, which greatly alarmed her. "It was probably a fit of epilepsy;" as

Muir writes: "but Muslim legend has invested it with so many marvelous features as makes it difficult to discover the real facts. It is certain that the apprehensions of Halima and her husband were aroused; for Arab superstition wont to regard the subject of such ailments as under the influence of an evil spirit. They resolved to rid themselves of the charge, and Halima carried the child back to its mother. With some difficulty, Amina obtained from her an account of what had happened, calmed her fears, and entreated her to resume the care of her boy. Halima loved her foster child, and was not unwillingly persuaded to take him back once more to her encampment. There she kept him for about a year longer, and with such care that she would not suffer him to move out of her sight. But uneasiness was again excited by fresh symptoms of a suspicious kind; and she set out finally to restore the boy to his mother when he was about five years of age."[4]

Staying with Bedouins benefited Muhammad in many ways in his later life. The Bedouins attached 'vast importance to the study of eloquence, of fluent and correct delivery; Muhammad may have had some early practice in this accomplishment, in which he afterwards excelled.' He was proud of his tongue, and said: 'Verily, I am the most perfect Arab amongst you; my descent is from the Koraish, and my tongue is the tongue of the Beni Sa'd.' He developed love for horses during that period, which helped him afterwards. Again, staying with them gave him robust health.[5]

While coming to his mother, Muhammad was lost in Mecca. Halima was worried. She reported the matter to his grand-father. Ibn Ishaq writes: "It is alleged by some, but God knows the truth, that when his foster mother brought him to Mecca he escaped ftom her in the crowd while she was taking him to his people. She sought after him and could not find him, so she went to 'Abdu'l Muttalib and said: 'I brought Muhammad tonight and when I was in upper part of Mecca he escaped me and I don't know where he is.' So 'Abdu'l Muttalib went to the Ka'ba praying to Allah to restore him. They assert that Waraqa[6] and another man of Quraysh found him and brought him to 'Abdu'l Muttalib saying: 'We have found the son of yours in the upper part of Mecca." Abdu'l Muttalib took him and put him on his shoulder as he went round the Ka'ba confiding him to Allah's protection and praying for him; then he sent him to his mother Amina."[7]

Muhammad's five years stay with Beni Sa'd in a steppe across the forbiddingly jagged mountain chain called Hijaz (meaning 'barrier') only fifty miles away from Mecca, yet enormously distant, had tremendous impact in his making. It was a distinct world with distinct way of living. He lived there and learnt things the way they learnt. Lesley Hazleton writes: "The high desert steppe was an early education in the power of nature and the art of living with it; how to gauge the right time to move from winter to summer grazing and back again, how to find water where there seemed to be none; how to adjust the long black camel hair tents to give shade in summer and create warmth on winter nights, Every child did whatever work he or she was capable of. As soon as he could walk, Muhammad was sent out to herd the flocks under the protective wing of one of his foster sisters, Shayma. As older children do with youngsters in large families, she carried him on her adolescent hip when his legs gave out, and kept a watchful eye on him. He in turn watched her, learning how to handle the goats and camels and becoming to all intents and purposes a Beduin boy except that he was always called "the Qurayshi," the one from the Quraysh tribe."[8]

Handling domestic animals and getting the feel of the beasts and forces of nature was not new for him at the age of five. "By the age of five," as Hazleton writes, Muhammad "could handle the animals by himself. He'd wait by a well while the camels drank seemingly endlessly, their humps fattening as the red blood cells in them hydrated; fight sleep as he stood night watch, guarding the flocks against hyenas howling at the scent of prey; listen for the rustle of desert foxes in the brush or restless anxiety of his charges as a mountain lion prowled silently nearby, its tracks clear in the dust next morning. He didn't need to be told that the desert was a lesson in humility, stripping away all pretense and ambition. He knew in his body how large and alive the world was, and how small a human being within it."[9]

Prophet Muhammad had soft feeling for his foster mother and the foster sister. He always retained a grateful impression of the kindness experienced during his stay among Beni Sa'd and reciprocated in his later life. Muir wrote:

"Muhammad ever retained a grateful impression of the kindness he had experience as a child among the Beni Sa'd. Halima visited him at Mecca after his marriage with Khadija. It was (the tradition runs) a year of drought, in which much cattle perished; and Muhammad spoke to Khadija and she gave to Halima a camel used to carry a litter, and forty sheep; so she returned to her people.' Upon another occasion he spread out his mantle for her to sit upon—a token of especial respect—and placed his hand upon her bossom in an affectionate and familiar way. Many years after, when on the expedition against At-Taif, he attacked the Beni Hawazin and took a multitude of them captive; they found ready access to his heart by reminding him of the days when he was nursed among them. About the same time a woman called Seima (Shayma) was brought in with some other prisoners to the camp. When they threatened her with their sword, she declared that she was Prophet's foster sister." On being satisfied, Muhammad gave her the option of remaining in honour and comfort with him, but she preferred to stay with her people.[10]

Prophet Muhammad spent the sixth year of his life in Mecca under the care of his mother. Then her mother took him to Medina to show him to the maternal relatives of his father. Muhammad, his mother and her slave girl Um Aiman, rode upon two camels, arrived at Medina, and alighted at the house where his father had died and was buried. As Muir writes: "The visit was of sufficient duration to imprint the scene and the society, notwithstanding his tender age, upon the memory of Mohammad. He used in later days to call to recollect things that happened on this occasion. Seven and forty years afterwards, when he entered Medina as a refugee, he recognised the place and said: 'In this house I sported with Uneisa, a little girl of Medina; and with my cousin I used to put to flight the birds that alighted upon the roof.' As he gazed upon the mansion, he added: 'Here it was my mother lodged with me; in this place is the tomb of my father; and it was there, in that very pond, that I learnt to swim.'[11] When Prophet Muhammad was six years old his mother died in Abwa, midway between Mecca and Medina, when she was returning with him from Medina, after sojourning there for a month. After her death, the slave girl brought Muhammad to Mecca, and handed him over to Abdu'l Muttalib. The loss of his mother at such an early age might have been responsible, as is natural, for the pensive and meditative character of Muhammad. While visiting his mother's tomb, during his pilgrimage from Medina to Al-Hodeibiya, Muhammad raised his voice and wept, and his followers around him did the same. When his followers enquired concerning his weeping, he said: This is the grave of my mother; the Lord hath permitted me to visit it. And I sought leave to pray for her salvation, but it was not granted. So I called my mother to remembrance, and tender memory of her overcame me, and I wept.[12] Muhammad remembered his mother and the state of his being an orphan even while recounting mercy of God towards him. The Qur'an says: "Did He not find thee an orphan, and furnish thee with a refuge?[13]

Muhammad's grandfather died when he was eight years of age; it was eight years after the 'year of elephant.' Ibn Ishaq mentions about an episode showing Prophet's grandfather's affection for him. The apostle was left to the care of his grandfather after the death of his mother when he was six years old. His sons made a cot for him in the shade of Ka'ba, and they used to sit around the cot. But, none of them sat upon it out of respect for him. 'The apostle, still a little boy, used to come and sit on it and his uncles would drive him away. When 'Abdu'l Muttalib saw this he said: 'Let my son alone, for by Allah he has a great future.' Then he would make him sit beside him on his bed and would stroke his back with his hand. It used to please him to see what he did.[14]

When his grandfather died, Muhammad was left to the care of Abu Talib, who, probably, employed him in looking after the sheep and camels which he kept at Uranah, near Mt. Arafat, just as his son Ja'far was employed in looking after sheep at Badr.[15] He accompanied Abu Talib as a member of the trading expedition, and after acquiring experience, managed the caravan of Khadija. It needs mention that Abu Talib was the brother of Muhammad's father from the same mother. As discussed elsewhere in the book, he gave lifelong protection to Muhammad.

References

1. Muir, Sir William, *The Life of Mahomet* (Hereafter, Muir), pp. 4-5.
2. Muir, p. 4; refers At-Tabari.
3. Muir, p. 4.
4. Muir, pp. 5-7; p. 5, Note 1.
5. Margoliouth, *Mohammed and the Rise of Islam*, (Hereafter, Margoliouth), pp.52-53; Muir, p. 7.
6. Full name of Waraqa is 'Waraqa b. Naufal b. Asad'; Waraqa, son of Naufal, son of Asad.
7. Ibn Ishaq, *Sirat Rasul Allah,* hereafter, Ibn Ishaq; English translation by A. Guillaume; pp. 72-73.
8. Lesley Hazleton, *The First Muslim*, p. 28.
9. Ibid, pp. 28-29.
10. Muir, pp. 7-8; Margoliouth, pp. 50-51.
11. Muir quoting Ibn Sa'd; p. 8.
12. Muir, pp. 8-9.
13. Qur'an, 93:6.
14. Ibn Ishaq, p. 73.
15. Margoliouth, p. 51.

Life of Prophet Muhammad: Pre-Prophetic Phase

The life of Prophet Muhammad, till he had the first revelation at the age of forty, or rather, till he started having regular revelations after a couple of years after the first one, is in no way much different from the life of an ordinary Meccan. But, he was a man of keen observation, sharp mind and highly experienced, which made a difference. His higher exposure and tenacious nature were the added factors. He strategically planned all his moves, leading to ultimate success.

Personal Appearance

'The personal appearance of the Prophet in middle life,' as Margoliouth writes: 'was recorded by many persons. According to the ordinary tradition, he was "of middle height, bluish coloured, with heir that was neither straight nor curly; with a large head, large eyes, heavy eyelashes, a reddish tint in his eyes, thick bearded, broad shouldered, with thick hands and feet;"[1] another description adds "with a large mouth, with eyes horizontally long, and with little flesh on the heels;[2] according to one account his hands were abnormally soft, which the palmists tell us signifies" a natural tendency towards the miraculous."'[3]

Lesley Hazleton, basing on earlier sources, writes: "The earliest sources describe him with infuriating vagueness for those of us who need images. "He was neither tall nor short," they say. "Neither dark nor fair." "Neither thin nor stout." But here and there, specific details slip through, and when they do, they are surprising. Surely a man spending night after night in solitary meditation would be a gaunt, ascetic figure, yet far from being pale and wan, he had round, rosy cheeks and a ruddy complexion. He was stockily built, almost barrel-chested, which may partly account for his distinctive gait, always "leaning forward slightly as though he were hurrying toward something." And he must have had a stiff neck, because people would remember that when he turned to look at you, he turned his whole body instead of just his head. The only sense in which he was conventionally handsome was his profile: the swooping hawk nose long considered a sign of nobility in the Middle East.'[4] He was a person of affectionate nature[5] and with common sense.[6]

Style of Dress

As Margoliouth writes: 'His style of dress seems to have varied at different times: his favourite costume being a striped dress of Yemen make[7] though some times he wore a Syrian *jubbah* with narrow sleeves, (refers Musnad) or a cloak (*mirt*) of tristed black hair[8], or a red gown (*hullah*).[9] On the day of the taking of Meccah he wore a black turban.'[10]

Lesley Hazleton also, while referring to his meditation, writes about his dress: "There was a hint, perhaps in his clothing. By now he could certainly have afforded the elaborate embroidered silk of the wealthy, but his clothing was low-key. His sandals were worn, the leather thongs sun-bleached paler than his skin. His homespun robe would be almost threadbare if it hadn't been so carefully patched, and it was hardly enough to shield him against the night-time cold of the high desert.[11]

The dress code, prohibiting certain clothes, was prescribed by Muhammad when his prophetic career started. It will be dealt with, while discussing about the Muslim identity formation.

Prophet's Tastes and Habits

Basing on the traditions, Margoliouth has also had written about Muhammad's tastes and habits. He writes: 'What is recorded of his tastes and habits exhibits ordinarily a high degree of refinement and delicacy. He abhorred anything that produced an evil odour; garlic and onion were described by him as evil vegetables,[12] and his loathing of anything that tented the breath was used as lever by members of his harem. When sovereign he found fault with those whose hair was untidy, or whose clothes were dirty,[13] being himself particular about as to his appearance. He disliked yellow teeth,[14] and almost made the use of toothpick a religious ordinance.'[15]

Ambitious Person: Divine Solace

According to Qur'an, Muhammad was a young man of promise, and, indeed, should expect that the astounding talents which he afterwards displayed would give evidence of themselves in youth. The divine consolation: "Have we not expanded thy breast and exalted thy name?"[16] gave him solace and comfort, when there were hurdles in meeting his ambitions and few things were going well with his project.[17]

Childhood with Beni Sa'd, its Benefits

As is already discussed, Muhammad's five years stay among the Beni Sa'd was advantageous for him in many ways. The eloquence and purity of language and the use of standard dialect, which he acquired during his childhood, became enormously helpful for him in public life. He understood the importance of horse, especially in warfare and raids, as none before him in Arabia. Robust constitution and free and independent characters were the added advantages.[18]

During his stay with the Beduins in his childhood, Muhammad learned to handle camels properly. Lesley Hazleton writes: "His years with the Beduins had served him well. He had a way with camels, among the most ornery of animals unless one knows how to cajole them: the particular clicks of the tongue, the exact tug on the lead rope, the hand on the flank with just the right amount of pressure to make them stand or kneel. Those who were bad with camels yelled at them and jerked the ropes, making the animals all the more stubborn and hard to control. Dealing with them was a skill, and the best handler was one whom nobody noticed because he never had to stamp and prod, and never yelled. The sound he made to urge the camels on were so soft and sibilant, they were more like breath than noise."[19] She further writes: "At first Muhammad worked just with the milk camels. Only when he'd proven himself with them was he allowed to work with the castrated males that made Mecca's trade possible. These single-humped dromedaries had been introduced from Ethiopia in the third century, and turned out to be perfectly suited to the climate and terrain of Arabia. Not only they vary their body temperature according to conditions, but they could store water in their red blood cells (legends of parched travelers slitting open the hump to drink from it may spark the imagination, but the hump actually stores fat, not water). This meant that they could go for days without drinking, spanning the distances between wells or spring. They were, that is, uniquely well adapted to the desert. But humans weren't which is why so many caravan traders, like Muhammad's father, never returned."[20]

Under the Guardianship of Abu Talib

Abu Talib, the uncle of Muhammad, became his guardian after the death of his grandfather. He lived the life of a camel boy under his guardianship. Lesley Hazleton writes about his life under the guardianship of Abu-Talib: "Muhammad appears to have been more an appendage to the extended Abu-Talib household than an essential part of it. And he would have to earn his keep. So while wishful accounts would have it that the uncle took special care of his nephew from the beginning, the record is clear that Muhammad was put to work as a lowly camel boy, and that within two years he was working in that capacity on the Meccan trade caravans."[21] The fact that Abu Talib suffered due to poverty, and had to give two of his sons as adopted sons of Muhammad and Abbas, gives credence to the fact mentioned above.

Lessons at Okaz

The sacrilegious war during 580 to 590 AD was fought in the vale of Mecca and the surrounding country, when Muhammad was young. It was a sacrilegious war, because it was fought within the sacred territory during the sacred month, which was traditionally prohibited. In Okaz, a place within three days' journey east of Mecca, a fair was held annualy in Dhu'l-Ka'da, the sacred month preceding the annual pilgrimage. It was a place with shady palm and cool fountain, which 'offered a grateful resting place to the merchant and traveller after their toilsome journey.' In the fair, chivalrous and poetical contests were held. The root cause of the war was the rivalrous spirit between Kuraysh of Mecca and Hawazin tribe dwelling between Mecca and At-Taif. On several occasions, tense situations were created, the sword was unsheathed, blood flowed, and the leaders calmed the people to prevent the escalation of conflict; on one occasion, an arrogant poet, vaunting the superiority of his tribe, was struck by an indignant Hawazinite; on other occasion, a maid of Hawazine descent was rudely treated by some Koreishite youth; on yet another occasion, an importunate creditor was insolently repulsed. The precautions, however, could not prevent the war; the hostilities precipitated by a murder, ultimately, resulted into four years war in which Omeiyad and Hashimite, both participated, and even Muhammad took part in the same.[22]

The probable influence of Okaz on Muhammad was that he learnt the lessons of poetry and rhetoric by hearing the Arabic poets. The second impact was that he got acquaintance with the Christians and Jews, and their doctrines, and probably with Catholic system also. Muir writes about what Muhammad might have learnt at Okaz: his contact with them, thus: "The struggle for pre-eminence, indeed, and the contests of eloquence, at the annual fair, must have possessed for the youthful Muhammad a more engrossing interest than the combat of arms. At these spectacles, while his patriotism was no doubt aroused and desire after personal distinction simulated by the whole atmosphere of the rivalry, he had rare opportunities of cultivating his genius, and learning from the greatest masters and most perfect models of the art of poetry and power of rhetoric. But another and a nobler lesson might also be learnt in the concourse of Okaz. The Christianity, as well as the chivalry, of Arabia had their representatives there; and, if we may believe tradition, Muhammad while a boy heard Koss, bishop of Nejran, preach a purer creed than that of Mecca, in accents which agitated and aroused his soul. And many at that fair, besides the venerable Koss, though influenced it may be by a less catholic spirit, yet professed to believe in the same revelation from above, and preach the same tidings. There too were Jews, serious and earnest men, surpassing the Christians in number, and equally with them appealing to an inspired Book. The scene thus annually witnessed by Muhammad as he advanced into mature years, had, we can not doubt, a deep influence upon him."[23]

Occupation as a Shepherd

Muir also writes about Muhammad's occupation as a shepherd: "The youth of Muhammad passed away without any other incidents of interest. At one period he was employed, like other lads, in tending the sheep and goats of Mecca upon the neighbouring hills and valleys.[24] He used when at Medina to refer to this employment and to say that it comported with his prophetic office, even as it did with that of Moses and David. On one occasion, as some people passed him carrying a load of *Arak* berries, the Prophet said to his companions: 'Pick me out the blackest of them, for they are sweet; — even such was I wont to gather when I fed the flock of Mecca at Aiyad. Verily there hath been no prophet raised up, who performed not the work of a Shepherd.' The hire received for this duty would contribute towards the support of his needy uncle, Abu Talib, and the occupation itself was congenial with his thoughtful and meditative character."[25]

According to Muir, his shepherd life had probable effect on his later life, especially on his contemplative and meditative character, and 'a deep and earnest faith in the Deity as an ever-present, all-directing Agent;—a faith which in after days the Prophet was wont to enforce from the memories, no doubt, of these early days, eloquent and heart-stirring appeals to the sublime operations of Nature and the beneficent adaptations of an ever-present diety.'[26]

Accompanies Abu-Talib in his Trading Expedition

Abu-Talib undertook a trading expedition to Syria in 582 AD and wanted Muhammad to leave behind him, as he had already attained the age of twelve by then and was able to take care of himself. However, when all preparation for the departure of the caravan was made, Abu Talib was about to mount, Muhammad, overcome by the prospect of long separation, clung to his uncle;

the latter was moved, and carried him together. The expedition, extending to Bosra, perhaps further, took several months. Muhammad had the opportunity to see places of Jewish and Christian people; some visited places, such as Petra, Jerash, 'Amman, were of historical or religious or commercial importance; some had remains of former mercantile grandeur. The wild legendary story of the valley of Al-Hijr, 'its lonely deserted habitations hewn out of the rocks, and the related tale of divine vengeance descending on the cities of the plains over which now rolled the waves of the dead sea," exciting apprehension and awe, must have been deeply imprinted on his reflective young mind. All these had linkages with strange history, tragical Jewish tradition and local legend. During that journey, the young man came in contact with Jewish and Christian settlements, and their churches and synagogues. All these must not have gone without impact on his young mind. Of course, such journey was renewed at least twice. Moreover, Jewish and Christian preachers, as stated above, always visited the fare of Ukaz, and biblical stories were not unknown to the Meccans.[27] Muir has refered Ibn Hisham, At-Tabari and Ibn Sa'd for the information. Meccans also had Christian converts, such as Waraqa, among them. The Jews of Medina had trade contact with the Kuraysh of Mecca.

The mercantile expedition, in which Muhammad took part as a manager, was repeated after thirteen years on the insistence of Abu Talib, when he attained the age of twenty-five. One day Abu Talib called him and addressed thus: "I am as thou knowest, a man of small substance; and truly the times deal hardly with me. Now there is a caravan of thine own tribe about to start for Syria, and Khadija, daughter of Khuweilid, needeth men of our tribe to send forth with her merchandise. If thou wert to offer thyself, she would readily accept thy services." Muhammad replied: "Be it so as thou hast said." Then Abu Talib went to Khadija, and inquired whether she wishes to hire her nephew, but he added: "We hear that thou hast engaged such as one for two camels, and we should not be content that my nephew's hire were less than four." She discreetly answered: "Hadst thou asked this thing for one of a distant or alien tribe, I would have granted it; how much rather now that thou askest it for a near relative and friend!" Thus the matter was settled, and Muhammad prepared for the journey. Abu Talib commended Muhammad to the men of the company, at the time the caravan was just to set out. Meisara, the servant of Khadija, was in charge of her property, and Muhammad accompanied him. The caravan took the same route to Syria, as it took thirteen years earlier. The caravan reached Bosra, on road to Damascus, about sixty miles to the east of Jordon. Muhammad handled the barter with natural sagacity and shrewdness, which carried him prosperously through the undertaking, and, thereby returning with a balance more than usual in his favour. Skillful management of the work of a business manager was not an easy job; but Muhammad handled the job properly.

The caravan trade benefited the society economically; it benefited the individuals due to their exposure to outside world, they became experienced and knowledgeable. Muhammad could also know about the world around due to his participation in the expeditions; he could know a lot, as discussed about the Jews and Christians, and their religion, before his prophetic career. But, participation in such expeditions was also risky. Hazleton writes: "It's a measure of how much they risked that of the four ancestors who had given their names to the main clans of the Quraysh, only one had died at home in Mecca; the other three, including Muhammad's forebear Hashim, had ended their lives far away in Gaza, in Iraq, and in the Yemen."[28]

Rebuilding of Kaaba

An important role played by Muhammad in his early life was in resolving the conflict during the rebuilding of Kaaba. As discussed elsewhere, the Kaaba was destroyed during a flood, and different clans quarreled as to who would replace the Black Stone in the rebuilt Kaaba. The problem was that everyone wanted to have the honour of replacing the stone, and none wanted to cede it. "Within minutes," Lesley Hazleton writes: "the process that had been a model of co-operation between the various clans of the Quraysh broke down into such violent disagreement that it seemed actual violence was imminent. One clan even produced a bowl filled with animal blood, then thrust their hands into it and held their bloody palms high for all to see, swearing that they were willing to shed their own blood for the right of one of their own to lift the stone into its newly built niche. Fists were bunched and hands reaching for daggers when one of the elders, distressed at the prospect of bloodshed in this of all places, found a way to diffuse the situation. They were all too exhausted with the effort of intense labour to make such a weighty decision, he said. Instead, they should leave the decision to God by agreeing that the first man to enter the precinct from that point on, no matter to which clan he belonged to, should decide whose hands would lift the stone. As it happened—or, depending on your point of view, as it was predestined—that man was Muhammad."[29] In reality, he went their for circumambulation of the Kaaba, but the people there, as soon as they saw him, declared: "This is the amin, the trustworthy one, and we will be satisfied with his decision."

Muhammad asked them to bring a cloak. They brought it, spread it on the ground and placed the Black Stone at its centre, as instructed by Muhammad. Then he asked elders of each of the clans to take hold of the edge of the cloak and lift it together at the right level. When they did it, Muhammad took it and placed it at the proper place himself.[30]

References:

1. Margoliouth, *Mohammad and the Rise of Islam*, p. 63; he refers Musnad and Bukhari; hereafter Margoliouth.
2. Sahih Muslim, pp. ii, 217.
3. Margoliouth, pp. 63-64.
4. Lesley Hazleton, The First Muslim. p. 3; hereafter Hazleton.
5. Margoliouth, p. 71.
6. Margoliouth, p. 79.
7. Refers *Hibrah*, *Muslim,* pp. ii., 154.
8. Ibid.
9. Bukhari (K.) pp. ii., 392.
10. Musnad, pp. iii., 393.
11. Lesley Hazleton, *The First Muslim*, p. 4, hereafter Hazleton.
12. Musnad, pp. iv., 19.
13. Musnad, pp. iii,. 356.
14. Ibid, pp. iii., 442.
15. Margoliouth, p. 64.
16. Qur'an, xi: 65.
17. Margoliouth, pp. 66-67.
18. Muir, *William, The Life of Mahomet*, p.7, hereafter Muir.
19. Hazleton, pp. 48-49.
20. Ibid, p. 49.
21. Ibid, p. 48.
22. Muir, pp. 14-15.
23. Ibid, p. 16.
24. Ibid, p. 18; based on Ibn Sa'd's account.
25. Ibid, pp. 18-19.
26. Ibid, p. 19.
27. Ibid, pp. 11, 16.
28. Hazleton, p. 49.
29. Ibid, p. 74.
30. Ibid, pp. 74-75.

The Prophet Muhammad and His Family

Prophet Muhammad belonged to Beni Hashim clan of the Quraysh community of Mecca, where he was born on Monday, 12th Rabi *Al Awwal*, the 22 April 571 AD His father's name was Abdullah,[1] who died outside Mecca before Muhammad was born. His mother, Aminah[2] was from Yathrib (Medina), who died when Muhammad was only six years old. He spent his childhood with his Bedouin foster mother, whose name was Haleema.[3] His mother took him to Medina after his return from the care of his foster mother. While returning to Mecca, she died halfway between Medina and Mecca, at a place called Abwa, where she was buried.

Being doubly orphaned, he spent his childhood under the loving care of his grandfather, Abdul Muttalib. But, his grandfather also died after two years, when he was just eight years old. After that, he not only spent his childhood, but even up to late forties of his life, under the protection of his uncle, Abu Talib.

Muhammad Marries Khadija

According to a tradition, Khuwaylid, the father of Khadija, and according to another, 'Amr, her brother, married Khadija to Muhammad, who gave her twenty she-camels as dowry. She was the first, among the thirteen women, whom Muhammad married; and she was the mother of all the children of the Prophet, except Ibrahim. Earlier, she was married to 'Utayyiq b. 'Abid, and then to Abu Hala. Her children from Utayyiq were 'Abdullah and Jariya, and the children from Abu Hala were Hind b. Abu Hala and Zaynab.[4]

Khadija was a Koreshite (Qurayshite) lady, distinguished by fortune as well as birth. Her father, Khuweilid, was the grandson of Asad, and Asad was the grandson of Kosai. He commanded in the Sacrilegious War a considerable section of Koreish (Quraysh), and so did his nephew 'Othman.[5] As William Muir informs: "Her substance, whether inherited or acquired through her former marriages, was very considerable; and by means of hired agents, she had increased it largely in mercantile speculation. To the blessing of affluence, she added the more endowments of discretion, virtue, and an affectionate heart; and, though now mellowed by a more than middle age, she retained a fair and attractive countenance. The chief men of Koreish were not insensible to these charms, and many sought her in marriage; but choosing rather to live on in dignified and independent widowhood, she had rejected all their offers. The tender emotions, however, excited by the visit of Mohammad overpowered her resolution."[6] She deputed a sister (according to another account, a servant) to sound his views to Muhammad. On being asked the reason of his remaining unmarried at so mature an age, he replied: 'I have nothing in my hands wherewithal I might marry. 'But if haply that difficulty were removed, and thou wert invited to espouse a beautiful and wealthy lady of noble birth, who would place thee in affluence, wouldest thou not desire to have her?' Muhammad startled at the novel thought, asked about the identity of the person, and knowing her to be Khadija, he immediately consented to marry her. After receiving Muhammad's consent, she dispatched a messenger to him or his uncle appointing a time for their meeting. But, as she dreaded the refusal of her father, she provided a feast for him. He was well fed, had well drunk and was merry; perfume of saffron or ambergris was cast over him; he was dressed in marriage raiment. The old man, while under the effects of wine, united his daughter Khadija to Muhammad in presence of Hamza, the uncle of Muhammad. But, soon after coming to his senses, and knowing about the marriage, the old man "fell into violent passion, and declared that he would never consent to give away to that poor youth a daughter courted by the great men of Kureish. The friends of Muhammad replied indignantly that the alliance had not originated in their wish, but was the act of no other than his own daughter. Weapons were drawn, and blood might have been shed, when the old man became pacified, and at last was reconciled."[7]

Khadija: In the List of the Companions of the Prophet

In the list of the 'Merits of the Companions of the Prophet,' the names of only four of his wives are mentioned, which are, Khadija, Ayesha, Salama, and Zainab. Khadija, Muhammad's first employer, was fifteen years senior to him in age. She was the first to encourage him in his apostolic mission. According to the Prophet, she was the best of the women of her time, just as Mary, the daughter of Imran, was the best of the women of her time.[8] Muhammad did not marry any other women in her life-time. As Lesley Hazleton rightly observes: "For twenty-four years, she had been Muhammad's pole star—his refuge, his rock, his confidante, his solace. From the beginning, she had seen what was in him more accurately and more presciently than anyone else. She had defied social norms to marry him, lifting him out of insecurity into respectability. Together they had raised four daughters and two sons, one formally adopted and the other in effect adopted, both of whom had become as close as birth sons. It had been in her arms that he had sought shelter from the terror of that night on Mount Hira, and her voice that had reassured him. Together they had faced hardship and boycott, scorn and derision. They had persevered."[9]

Aisha says: "Never did I feel jealous of any woman as I was jealous of Khadija. She had died three years before he (Muhammad) married me. I often heard him praise her, and his Lord … had commanded him to give her the glad tidings of a palace of Jewels in Paradise, and whenever he slaughtered a sheep he presented its meat to her female companions"[10] Once, in fit of jealousy, Ayesha told Muhammad: "Why do you remember one of those old women of the Quraish with gums red and who is so long dead—while Allah has given you a better one in her stead?"[11] Anyway, her superiority was, undoubtedly, a fact.[12]

Muhammad's Other Wives

Prophet Muhammad married many other women. Mirkhond provides information about his eleven wives and four concubines. At-Tabari mentions the names of twenty-three, besides five more to whom proposals were made, but there was no success.[13] According to Ibn Ishaq's accounts, Muhammad married thirteen women. His first wife was **Khadija** d. Khuwaylid (d. = daughter of; Arabic, *bint*). The nine wives, as reported to Hisham by more than one traditionists, were **'A'isha** d. Abu Bakr; **Hafsa** d. 'Umar bin Khattab; **Umm Habiba** d. Abu Sufyan; **Umm Salama** d. Abu Ummaya b. al-Mughira (b. =bin = son of); **Sauda** d. Zama'a b. Qaya; **Zaynab** d. Jahsh b. Ri'ab; **Maymuna** d. al-Harith b. Hazn; **Juwayriya** d. al-Harith b. Abu-Dirar; and **Safiya** d. Huyay b. Akhtab. These nine wives survived after his death; **Khadija**, the first, and **Zaynab/ Zeinab** d. Khuzayma b. al-Harith b. 'Abdullah b. 'Amr b. 'Abdu Manaf b. 'Amir b. Sa'sa'a, the fourth wife, died before him; Zaynab, widow of his cousin Obeida, killed at Badr, was famous for her charity and known as the 'mother of the poor.' Of course, Reihana, the Jewess, also died a year before him, but it is not certain whether she was a wife or a concubine. He married the fifth wife, Um Selama, within a month of the fourth one. The two others, with whom he did not consummate his marriage, were **Asma**' d. al-Numan, a Kindite woman, and **'Amra** d. Yajid, a Kilap woman, who was an unbeliever. He married Asma and found her to be suffering from leprosy, and therefore returned her to her people with suitable gift. Amra, when she came to the apostle said: "I seek

God's protection against you." Muhammad replied that one who did that was inviolable, and then sent her back to her people.[14]

Marriages After Khadija's Death

Muhammad, in his late life marriages, had three wives within three years of Khadija's death, the first being with **Sawda (Sauda)**. The marriages with **Aisha** (Ayesha, 'A'isha), Abu Bakr's daughter, and **Hafsa**, Umar's daughter, followed.[15] According to Muir, Sauda 'had been for three or four years his only wife.'[16] The marriage with Sauda, a Kureshite quiet, mature-aged lady, the widow of Sakran, was solemnized within 2 or 3 months from the death of Khadija. Both – Sauda and Sakran – became early converts to Islam, and migrated to Abyssinia; Sakran died after return to Mecca. Muir, in a note, observes about her: "On the conquest of Kheibar, eight years after, Sauda had her portion assigned her from its revenues with the Prophet's other wives. In the following year it is said somewhat obscurely that either on account of her age, or some doubt of her fidelity, Muhammad wished to put her away, but was afterwards reconciled. She is also said to have given up her turn to 'A'isha. She survived Muhammad ten years. She had by Sakran a son who was killed in the wars under Omar."[17]

'A'isha was the only virgin bride of Muhammad; his other wives were married before they came to him. The three years affianced 'A'isha was only of ten years of age at the time of her marriage with the Prophet. She was married at her father's residence in the suburb of Sunh, and then brought back to the bridal home with her 'sister' Sauda.[18]

Hafsa (Hafsah), daughter of Umar and the widow of Khoneis, an early convert, who died six-seven months earlier, was the third wife of Muhhammad, whom he married during 624 AD. By his marriages with Ayesha (Aisha, 'A'isha) and Hafsa, Muhammad bound himself closer in friendship to their fathers, Abu Bakr (Abu Bekr) and Umar (Omer), who became first two caliphs of Islam after the death of Muhammad. Now, both of them were connected equally with the Prophet, and they had access to his ears through their daughters. Of course, there was much rivalry between Ayesha and Hafsa; but youth, vivacity, and beauty maintained the supremacy of Ayesha.[19] Hafsa was a woman of violent nature, who had to be put down often. The death of her husband gave Prophet Muhammad to the chance of allaying with his faithful follower, Umer, who offered his daughter to Abu Bakr and Othman, but these persons preferred to leave her to Muhammad.[20]

Muhammad married, as Ibn Hishama writes: "**Umm Habiba,** whose name was Ramla d. Abu Sufyan. Khalid b. Sa'id b. al-As, married her to him when they were both in Abyssinia and the Negus gave her on behalf of the apostle four hundred dinars. It was he who arranged the marriage for the apostle. She had been married to 'Ubaydullah b. Jahsh al-Asadi."[21] As is well-known, some early converts to Islam migrated to the Christian kingdom of Abyssinia; the king was sympathetic to them and the Prophet was in correspondence with him, and in one of the dispatches, "the Prophet begged that his remaining followers might now be sent to Medina; and the request was added that before their departure, the Prince would betroth to him Um Habiba, daughter of Abu Sufyan, whose early charms, though she was now five-and thirty years of age, still held a place in his imagination. Her former husband, Obeidallah, one of the 'Four Inquirers,' after emigrating a Muslim in Abyssinia, had there embraced Christianity, and died in its profession."[22] Um Habiba survived the Prophet some thirty years, and died during the Caliphate of her brother Mu'awiya.[23]

Juweiriya, the seventh wife of Muhammad, was one of the captives of the Beni'l Mustalik brought to Medina along with the booty. She was of about twenty years of age, married to a chief. Being a beautiful comely damsel of birth and rank, the citizen, to whose lot she fell, kept the high ransom price of nine ounces of gold. As it was not possible for her tribe to pay such high sum, she, being despaired, approached Muhammad sitting in Ayesha's apartment, and pleaded for some remission.[24] Muir writes about what happened after that: "A qualm passed over Ayesha, as she saw the Prophet listening to the fair and winning suppliant, and soon perceived that the conquerer has become the captive of his prisoner. 'Wilt thou hearken,' he said, 'to something that may be better than what thou askest of me?' Marvelling at his gentle accents, she asked what that might be. 'Even that I should pay thy ransom, and take thee for myself!' The maiden was nothing loth. And so the ransom was paid. Muhammad, taking her at once to wife, built a seventh house for her reception. As soon as the marriage was noised abroad, the people said that, the Beni Mustalik having now become their relatives, they would let rest of the prisoners go free as Juweiriya's dower; 'and so,' Aisha used in after days to say, 'no woman was ever a greater blessing to her people than this Juweiriya.'[25]

Seventeen year old beautiful **Safiya,** the daughter of a leading chief, and bride of Kinan, the chief of Kheibar, became the eighth wife of Muhammad, and his second Jewish one, after the defeat of Kheibar, and torture and death of Kinan.[26]

During AH 6, Mukankis, the Roman Governor of Egypt, in response to Prophet's letter, sent his polite reply, expressing his unbelief, with valuable presents including two slave Coptic Christian beauties – **Marya** and Sirin. He wrote: "I am aware that a prophet is yet to arise; but I am of opinion that he will appear in Syria. Thy messenger hath been received with honour, I send for thine acceptance two sisters, such as are prized among the Copts, a present of raiment, and a mule for thee to ride upon." Muhammad retained Mary for him and presented the other one to Hassan, the poet. The white mule, a rarity and highly prized in Arabia, was retained for his use. Here, it needs mention that both Coptic maids were comely, but it was not lawful, according to his own strict precept for the Prophet, to place two sisters in his harem; therefore he kept Mary, having fairer complexion, delicate features adorned by a profusion of black curling hair. She was placed separately with Um Sulem, the wife of his servant Abu Rafi, entrusted with the new charge, in a garden house prepared for her in Upper Medina, where in the heat of the summer and the date harvest, she used to receive the visit of the Prophet. The garden, according to Beladhuri, was one of the seven properties escheated from the Beni an-Nadir, and given to Mukheirik the Jew, and on his death left by him to Muhammad. As it is shown to the present day, it lies on the South-East side of the city in the quarter called Ambariya on the junction of the roads emerging to Yanbo and Mecca. There used to be a mosque, called Masjid Mashrabat Um Ibrahim, the mosque of the summer house of the mother of Ibrahim' on the spot.[27] Ibrahim, as we know was the son of Muhammad and Mary, who died during infancy.

Prophet Muhammad took **Meimuna** (Maimuna), aged 26 years, to wife while in Mecca during his 'lesser pilgrimage.' The widowed Meimuna was the sister-in-law of his uncle Abbas. As three days period allowed by the Meccans for his stay in Mecca lapsed, Muhammad was asked to leave the city; he gave immediate marching orders to all the pilgrims placing his bride in charge of his servant Abu Rafi.' The marriage was, therefore, consummated at a place called Sarif, some eight to ten Arabian miles away from Mecca. Meimuna survived Muhammad fifty years. She died at the ripe age of eighty years. She was buried, as desired by her, on the spot of her marriage.[28]

With his marriage with Meimuna, the number of Prophet Muhammad's *Harim* was completed. Muir writes: "The harim of Muhammad has now reached its limit; for this was the last marriage contracted by him. There were in it at this time ten wives, besides two servile concubines, but Zeinab, daughter of Khozeima, died before him; so that the number was then reduced to nine, or, including concubines, eleven. Some other women are mentioned by tradition, whose intended marriage was at the last stage broken off. The details in most instances are obscure. Of one case, at any rate, there can be no doubt."[29] Meimuna survived the Prophet fifty years; she was, by her desire, buried on the spot on which she had celebrated her marriage with him.[30]

The *Sahih Muslim* has a long *Hadis,*[31] relating to the scandal involving Ayesha, the favourite wife of the Prophet. But a revelation proved her innocence. During the fifth year of the Hijra (December 626 AD), Ayesha and Muhammad's other wife Umm Salama accompanied him during the surprise attack on the tribe, Banu 'l-Mustaliq, in which a large number of prisoners, including Juweiriya, were captured. As Ayesha reported, and Ibn Ishaq details, "When the apostle intended to go on an expedition he cast lots between his wives which of them should accompany him. He did this on the occasion of the raid on B. al-Mustaliq and the lot fell on me, so the apostle took me out. The wives on those occasions used to eat light rations; meat did not fill them up so that they were heavy. When the camel was saddled for me I used to sit in my howdah; then the men who saddled it for me would come and pick me up and take hold of the lower part of the howdah and lift it up and put it on the camel's back and fasten it with a rope. Then they would take hold of the camel's head and walk with it."[32]

"When the apostle finished his journey on this occasion he started back and halted when he was near Medina and passed a part of the night there. Then he gave permission to start and the men moved off. I went out for a certain purpose having a string of Zafar beads on my neck. When I had finished it, it slipped from my neck without my knowledge, and when I returned to the camel I went feeling my neck for it but could not find it. Meanwhile, the main body had already moved off. I went back to the place where I had been and looked for the necklace until I found it. The men who were saddling the camel for me came up to the place I have just left and having finished the saddling they took hold of the howdah thinking that I was in it as I normally was, picked it up and bound it on the camel, not doubting that I was in it. Then they took the camel by head and went off with it. I returned to the place and there was not a soul there. The men had gone. So I wrapped myself to my smock and then lay down where I was, knowing that if I missed they would come back for me, and by Allah I had but just lain down when Safwan b. al-Muattal al-Sulami passed me; he had fallen behind the main body for some purpose and had not spent the night with the troops. He saw my form and came and stood over me. He used to see me before the veil was prescribed for us, so when he saw me he exclaimed in astonishment "The apostle's wife" while I was rapped in garments. He asked me what has kept me behind but I did not speak to him. Then he brought up his camel and told me to ride it while he kept behind. So I rode it and he took the camel's head going forward quickly in search of the army, and by Allah we did not overtake them and I was not missed until the morning. The men had halted and when they were rested up came the man leading me and the liars spread their reports and the army was much disturbed. But by Allah I knew nothing about it."[33]

The gossip started soon after the return of Ayesha and Safwan together, which very soon developed into a scandal. There were both – the ansars and the emigrants – among the gossip-mongers, which included Abdullah ibn Ubayy, a member of the Khazrajite clan of 'Auf and a leading citizen of Medina, poet Hassan, Hamna, the daughter of Jahsh and sister of the Prophet's wife Zainab, and Mistah, a relative and dependant of Abu Bakr. Prophet Muhammad was much disturbed. Perhaps, he had his own suspicions and turned cold towards Ayesha, who sought permission to go to her father's home; the permission was given. He consulted his close relatives, specially Ali and Usama b. Zaid. Usama said: "Allah's Messenger, they are your wives and we know nothing about them but goodness." Ali advised him to divorce her. He said: Allah has not put any unnecessary burden on you in regard to your wives. There are a number of women besides her. "He also suggested that Ayesha's maid, Burayra be questioned. Ali struck her and warned her to speak the truth. Burayra could not throw any light on the incident; she said that she had never found any wrong in Ayesha except that "she goes to sleep while kneading the flour and the sheep lamb (Tabari – 'pet lamb') eats that."[34]

As Ayesha became very ill after her return to Medina, she did not know about these developments, but she could feel the lack of warmth and apostle's accustomed kindness to her. Ayesha said: "When he came to see me when my mother was nursing me, all he said was, "How is she?" so that I was pained and asked him to let me be taken to my mother so that she could nurse me. "Do what you like," he said, and so I was taken to my mother, knowing nothing of what had happened until I recovered from my illness some twenty days later. Now we were an Arab people; we did not have those privies which foreigners have in their houses; we loath and detest them. Our practices was to go out into the open spaces of Medina. The women used to go out every night, and one night I went out with Umm Mistah d. Abu Ruhm b. al-Muttalib b. Abu Manaf. Her mother was Sakhr b. Amir b. Ka'b b. Sa'd b. Taym, aunt of Abu Bakr. As she was walking with me she stumbled over her gown and exclaimed, "May Mistah stumble," Mistah being the nickname of 'Auf. I said, "That is a bad thing to say about one of the emigrants who fought at Badr." She replied, "Haven't you heard the news, O daughter of Abu Bakr?" and when I said that I had not heard she went on to tell me of what the liars had said, and when I showed my astonishment she told me that all this really had happened. By Allah, I was unable to do what I had to do and went back. I could not stop crying until I thought that the weeping would burst my lever. I said to my mother, Allah forgive you! Men have spoken ill of me (T. and you have known of it) and have not told me about a thing about it." She replied. "My little daughter, don't let the matter weigh on you. Seldom is there a beautiful woman married to a man who loves her but her rival wives gossip about her and men do the same."[35]

After a month passed, Muhammad went to the pulpit, and pointing towards the scandal-mongers, reprimanded his Muslim followers, and asked: "Who would exonerate me from imputations of that person who has troubled me in regard to my family? By Allah, I find nothing in my wife but goodness and the person whom the people have mentioned in this connection is, according to my knowledge, a thoroughly pious person, and he never get into my house but along with me." His appeal touched a loyal chord in the hearts of Sa'd bin Mu'az and Usaid bin Huzair, who stood up and promised to punish any delinquent, if Muhammad so desired. Sa'd said, "Allah's Messenger, I defend your honour against him. If he belongs to the tribe of Aus we would strike his neck and if he belongs to the tribe of our brother Khazraj and you order us we would comply with your order. Then Sa'd bin 'Ubada, the chief of the Khazraj tribe, an "otherwise a pious man," but "having somewhat tribal partnership in him," stood up and said to Sa'd bin Mu'adh: "By the everlasting existence of Allah, you are not stating the fact, you will not be able to kill him and you will not have power to do so." Then Usaid bin Hudair, the first cousin of Sa'd bin Mu'adh, stood up and said, "By the everlasting existence of Allah, you are not stating the fact. We would kill him. You are a hypocrite and so you argue in defence of the hypocrites." Thus, both the tribes, Aus and Khazraj, were flared up, and were about to fall upon one another. Muhammad, ultimately, had to pacify them. After that, he decided to put an end to the matter, and went to Abu Bakr's house. He asked Ayesha to confess if she had done anything wrong and seek forgiveness of Allah." Ayesha maintained her innocence, and to her great astonishment and relief, a Quranic revelation (*Wahy matlu*) descended vindicating her innocence and honour.[36] After the revelation, 'Ayesha observed, as mentioned in the *Hadis*, "I was innocent but I did not expect that Allah would descend *wahy matlu* in my case as I did not think myself so much important. … I only hoped that Allah would in vision give an indication of my innocence to Allah's messenger." After 'Ayesha was exonerated by Allah and the Prophet Muhammad, coming out of the prophetic trance or fit, announced the news: '"Ayesha, there is a glad tiding for you. Verily Allah has vindicated your honour," everyone was happy, and her mother wanted 'Ayesha to get up and thank the Prophet, which she refused, and said: "I shall not thank him and laud him but Allah who has descended revelation vindicating my honour."[37]

When the Quran came down, "the apostle had not moved from where he was sitting … he was wrapped in his garment … Then the apostle recovered and sat up and there fell from him as were drops of water on a winter day, and he began to wipe the sweat from his brow;" He announced the good tiding and went out to the men and addressed them and recited the Quran, which descended. After that "he gave orders about Mistah b. Uthath and Hassan b. Thabit and Hamna d. Jahsh who were the most explicit in their slander and they were flogged with prescribed number of stripes" which was eighty. This was, because Allah, in the revelation, not only vindicated 'Aisha's innocence but ordered punishment for the persons spreading unproved calumnies against chaste women; Allah, at the same time did not refrain from administering an admonition to all the wives of the Prophet. The Quran said: "And those who launch charges against chaste women, and produce not four witnesses to support their allegation, flog them with eighty stripes and reject their evidence ever after, for such men are wicked transgressors."[38] It also took to task those Muslims who have given ear to the scandal. It said: "And why did not the believers, men and women, when ye first heard of the affair, put the best construction on it in their own minds and say, 'This charge is an obvious lie?' And why did they not bring four witnesses to prove it? When they had not brought the witnesses, such men, in the sight of Allah, stand forth themselves as liars."[39] Administering admonition to the wives of the Prophet, Allah said: "O Women of the Prophet! If any one of you should be guilty of unseemly conduct, your punishment will be doubled and that is easy for Allah." It further said: "And stay quietly in your houses, and make not a dazzling display, like that of the former times of ignorance.[40] Abu Bakr wanted to withdraw his support to his relative Mistah. He, however, revised his stand in the light of the revelation, which said: "Let not those among you who are endowed with grace and amplitude of means resolve by oath against helping their kinsmen, those in want and those who have left their homes in God's cause."[41]

The poet Hassan, in one of his poems, lampooned Safwan, who brought Aisha to Medina. The latter, in retaliation, gave Hassan a sword wound. Safwan sang:

Here's the edge of my sword for you
When you lampoon a man like me you don't get a poem in return.[42]

The relative's of Hassan, however, captured Safwan and kept him as a prisoner, in spite of Muhammad's intervention, till Hassan's wound was healed.

Safwan hotly contested the allegation, and died soon after, though young. Hadis quotes his statement and that of Aisha. He said, "Hallowed be Allah, by one, in Whose hand is my life, I have never unveiled any woman." As Aisha said, "then he died as a martyr in Allah's cause."[43] Ibn Ishaq quotes another *Hadis*, according to which "Safwan was impotent."[44]

As stated above, Ayesha used to accompany Muhammad in the expeditions. There is no mention of her accompanying him in the next expedition to Tabuk, or to other ones. Umm Salama's name comes in her place. Muhammad kept Ali behind to look after his family during the Tabuk expedition.

Marriage with Zaynab **(Zeinab, Zainab bint Jahsh)** was the other occasion when a divine command justified the marriage. Muir, basing on At-Tabari's account, has given an account of the marriage.[45] It happened when Muhammad was sixty. Lesley Hezleton has also given the account basing on Ibn Ishaq's account.[46] "One day Muhammad had gone to visit his adopted son Zayd, but found only Zayd's wife Zaynab at home. Expecting Zayd and not Muhammad, she was in "a state of disarray," as Ibn Ishaq tactfully puts it. Flustered by the sight, Muhammad rushed away murmuring, "Praise be to God who affects men's hearts!" When Zayd heard about this, he took it as a sign of Muhammad's desire, and in a fit of filial devotion—or possibly, by some accounts, because it hadn't been the best of marriages in the first place—he divorced Zaynab so that Muhammad could marry her instead." As it was against the existing Arabic tradition, it was taboo to marry one's adopted son's wife; the Quranic revelation justified it on the basis that Zayd was not Muhammad's biological son. According to the Quranic revelation: "God hath not given two hearts within him ...Nor hath He made your adopted sons your (real) sons. This your speech proceedeth from your mouth; but God speaketh the Truth; and He directeth in the right way. Let your adopted sons go by their own father's names. This is more just with God."[47]

It allows the marriage with the wife of one's adopted sons, and revealation even names Zayd: "And when thou saidst to him on whom God hath bestowed favours, and upon whom thou too hast bestowed favours; '*Keep thy wife to thyself and fear God*;' and thou didst conceal in thy breast that which God was minded to make known, and thou fearedst man—whereas God is more worthy to be feared. And when Zeid had fulfilled her divorce, We joined thee with her in marriage, that there might hereafter be no offence to Believers to marry the wives of their adopted sons, when they have fulfilled their divorce; and the command of God is to be fulfilled... Muhammad is not the father of any man amongst you. Rather he is the Apostle of God, and the Seal of the Prophets; and God knoweth all things."[48]

Muhammad asked Zayd after he divorced Zaynab, whether he had ever seen anything to dislike in her, to which his reply was, 'only good.' The revelation, naturally brought the sense of superiority in Zeinab, who is reported as saying that 'God had given her in marriage to His Prophet, whereas his other wives were given to him by their relatives.'[49] On the other hand, tart-tongued Aisha remarked: "Truly, God makes haste to do your bidding."[50]

Muhammad, after mass killing of Jews of Beni Koreiza, took the captive **Reihana** for his concubine. Reihana, whose husband and all the male relatives were just massacred, declined to be his wife, and chose to remain his slave or concubine, and a Jew.[51] Another Jewess, Zaynab **(Zeinab)**, sister of the warrior Marhab, also denied Prophet's wifehood to her after her capture at Kheibar; she remained a concubine and Jew, and poisoned him in due course. Prophet, however, survived that time, but continued to suffer from its effect.[52]

Children of Muhammad

Muhammad and Khadija had four daughters and one son, Qasim (Al-Qasim, Al-Kasim). But Qasim died before his second birthday.[53] However, according to another tradition, as stated by Muir, he had two sons and Qasim died at the age of two. Muir writes about the children of Muhammad: "Within next ten or twelve years, Khadija bore to Muhammad two sons and four daughters. The firstborn was named Al-Kasim; and after him, according to Arabian custom, Muhammad received the title of Abu'l-Kasim, 'Father of Al-Kasim.' This son died at the age of two years. Meanwhile, his eldest daughter Zeinab was born; and after her, at interval of one or two years, three other daughters, Rokeiya, Fatima and Um Kulthum. Last of all was born his second son, who died in infancy. Seima, maid of Safiya Muhammad's aunt, officiated as midwife on these occasions. Khadija sacrificed at the birth of each boy two kids, and one at the birth of every girl. Her children she nursed herself. Many years after, Muhammad used to look back to this period of his life with fond remembrance. Indeed so much did he dwell upon the mutual love of Khadija and himself, that the envious 'A'isha declared herself more jealous of this rival whom she had never seen, than all the other wives who contested with her the affection of the Prophet.[54]

Daughters' Marriage

Khadija prevailed upon Muhammad to join Abu'l As, her sister's son, whom she loved, and who was respected for his uprightness and mercantile success, in marriage with their eldest daughter Zeinab, who had reached the age of womanhood, by then. The next two daughters of Muhammad were given in marriage to 'Otba and 'Oteiba, the sons of Abu Lahab, Muhammad's uncle. Um Kulthum was married to Uthman, as a substitute, when Zeinab died. Fatima, who was a child then, was married later on to Ali, the son of Muhammad's other uncle Abu Talib.[55] They had two sons – Hasan and Hussain— who became forefathers of Saiyids, meaning 'masters.' Muhammad's daughter Rokeiya bore Othman a son, two or three years before the Flight; but he died during his childhood, as his eyes were pecked out at Medina by a fowl.

Adoption of Ali and Zeid

Muhammad adopted his cousin Ali, when he was not above the age of five or six. Muir, basing on At-Tabari's account, has detailed how, during a season of severe scarcity in Mecca, Muhammad and Abbas, his uncle, adopted two sons of Abu Talib–Ali and Ja'far respective–leaving two other, Akil and Talib, with him.[54] Zeid, (also written Zayd, Zaid) son of Haritha, a Christian slave, whose both the parents were Christian, was presented to him by Khadija. His father offered a large payment for his ransom to Muhammad, who left the option on Zeid to go or stay. Zeid preferred to stay with him, after that Muhammad adopted him as a son; Haritha returned happily to his home; Zeid, a freed man after that, was called 'Zeid ibn Muhammad' (Zeid, the son of Muhammad). By Muhammad's desire, Zeid married his old attendant, Um Aiman, who was of nearly double his age. Their son, Osama was the leader in the expedition to Syria, when Muhammad was fatally ill.[56]

Prophet's Relatives

Muhammad's prominent relatives were Abu Bakr and Umer, his fathers-in-laws and Othman and Ali, his sons-in-law. All of them became caliphs, one after the other, after the death of the Prophet.

Prophet's Attitude Towards his Near and Dear Ones

Prophet's attitude towards his near and dear ones was very soft and cordial. He broke down seeing his daughter, Zaynab's ransom for the release of his son-in-law Abul As.[57] Muhammad could not sleep with anxiety to hear that some one wanted to kill his uncle, Abbas, and till he was freed.[58] According to Sahih Muslim, the Prophet said to an enquirer that the fathers of both of them were in hell, but for Abu Talib, he said that "I found him in the lowest part of the Fire and I brought him to the shallow part."[59] Thus, he was more kind to his uncle, Abu Talib.

Domestic Life

Prophet Muhammad lived a simple domestic life. He lived in his wive's apartments in turns; the apartments were built of unburnt brick and thatched with palm-branches. Each apartment, twelve or fourteen feet square in dimension, had the roof so low to be reached by hand. The doorways, except in the case of Ayesha's, which was wooden, was protected by a screen of goat and camel hair. The furnishing of the apartments was also simple.[60] As he has many wives, the inter-familial discord was natural, as happened in case of Hafsa-Marya discord.[61] Polygamy, naturally, was to impact family life.[62] The revelations imposed veil and other restrictions on Prophet's wives and the wives of the believers.[63] Believers were advised not to enter their apartments unless especially called for.[64] The Prophet's wives were known as 'the Mothers of the Faithful,' as per a revelation which said: "The prophet is nearer unto the Believers than their own souls, and his Wives are their Mothers."[65]

Notes and References

1. The Arabic personal names are usually accompanied by the name of the father; this makes the identity of the person more clear. Thus, the name of Abdullah is usually written as 'Abdullah Ibn Abdul Muttalib' (Abdullah son of Abdul Muttalib; Ibn = bin = b. = son).
2. Aminah Bint Wahhab Ibn Abd Manaf Ibn Zahrah (Ameenah, daughter of Wahhab, son of Abd Manaf, son of Zahrah). For fuller identity, the names of not only the father, but even that of the higher generations is also taken.
3. Haleema Bint Abu Dhuaib (Haleema, daughter of Abu Dhurab); also, Haleema Al-Sadiyah.
4. Ibn Hisham's Note no. 918; in Ibn Ishaq's *Sirat Rasul Allah;* English translation *The Life of Muhammad* by A. Guillaume; Oxford University Press, Karachi, 1996; p. 792; hereafter IBN Ishaq.
5. William Muir, The Life of Mahomet from Original Sources, New Delhi, Reprint, 2002; p. 23; hereafter, Muir.
6. Ibid, pp. 23-24.
7. Ibid, pp. 24-25.
8. *Sahih Muslim*, *Hadis* no. 5965.
9. Lesley Hazleton, *The First Muslim*, London, 2013; pp. 133-34; hereafter Hazleton.
10. *Sahih Muslim*, *Hadis* 5971; Muir, p. 106 note.
11. SM: 5976.

12. Hazleton, pp. 64-65.
13. Ram Swarup, *Understanding Islam through Hadis*, p. 173; note; hereafter Ram Swarup.
14. Ibn Hisham's Note no. 918; in Ibn Ishaq's *Sirat Rasul Allah;* English translation *The Life of Muhammad* by A. Guillaume; Oxford University Press, Karachi (1996), pp. 792-94.
15. Hazleton, p. 213.
16. Muir: p. 172.
17. Ibid: p. 113; 113 Note 1.
18. Ibid, p. 177.
19. Ibid, p. 250.
20. Margoliouth, p. 307.
21. Ibn Ishaq, p. 793.
22. Muir, pp. 372, 372 note.
23. Ibid, p. 372.
24. Ibid, p. 298.
25. Ibn Ishaq, p. 493. Muir, pp. 298-99.
26. Muir: pp. 376-78.
27. Ibid, pp. 425-26; note 2.
28. Ibid, p. 389.
29. Ibid, p. 390.
30. Muir, p. 389.
31. *Sahih Muslim, Hadis* 6673.
32. Ibn Ishaq, p. 494.
33. Ibn Ishaq; pp. 494-95.
34. Ibn Ishaq, p. 495; *Sahih Muslim, Hadis* 6673.
35. *Sahih Muslim, Hadis* 6673; Ibn Ishaq, pp. 495-97.
36. Ibn Ishaq. p. 497.
37. Quran 24:4.
38. Quran 24:12-13; also 24:16.
39. Quran 33:30.
40. Quran 24:22.
41. Ibn Ishaq, p. 498.
42. *Sahih Muslim, ahadis* 6674-6675.
43. Ibn Ishaq, p. 499.
44. Muir, pp. 291-92.
45. Hezleton, pp. 223-24.
46. Qur'an 33:4f.

47. Qur'an 33:37f, 40.
48. Muir, p. 291 note.
49. Hazleton, p. 224.
50. Muir, p. 319.
51. Ibid, p. 379.
52. Ibid, p. 25.
53. Ibid, pp. 33-34; pp. 250-51.
54. Ibid, p. 250.
55. Ibid, pp. 34-35.
56. Muir, pp. 344-6; 345 note 1 Ibn Ishaq – 313-15.
57. Ibn Ishaq, p. 301.
58. *Sahih Muslim*, *Hadis* 409.
59. Muir, pp. 201-2.
60. Margo, pp. 416-18.
61. Muir, pp. 514-15.
62. Qur'an 33:59ff; 24:31.s
63. Qur'an, 33:53.
64. Qur'an, 33:5.

Revelation, Call, and Preaching in Mecca

The Revelations

It was the night of glory for Islam, when the Qur'an started coming down. The Qur'an says, "We sent it down on the night of glory."[1] And again, it happened when Muhammad was forty, and forty is considered to be an auspicious number throughout Middle-East.[2] During the first three or four years after the assumption of the prophetic office by Muhammad, the Muslim converts amounted to nearly forty souls.[3] During the night of the first revelation, Muhammad was in the cave on Mount Hira, where he used to go and stay in seclusion for days together. Ibn Ishaq writes about the first revelation.[4]

"When it was the night on which Allah honoured him with his mission and showed mercy on His servants thereby, Gabriel brought the command of Allah. 'He came to me,' said the apostle of Allah, 'while I was asleep, with a coverlet of brocade whereon was some writing, and said, "Read!" I said, "What shall I read?" He pressed me with it so tightly that I thought it was death; then he let me go and said, "Read!" I said, "What shall I read?" He pressed me with it the third time so that I thought it was death and said "Read!" I said, "What then shall I read?"—and this I said only to deliver myself from him, lest he should do the same to me again. He said:

"Read in the name of thy Lord who created,
Who created man of blood coagulated,
Read! Thy Lord is the most beneficent,
Who taught by the pen,
Taught that which they knew not unto men."[5]

Ibn Ishaq further writes: "So I read it, and he departed from me. And I awoke from my sleep, and it was as though these words were written on my heart."

The very first chapter of the *Sahih Al-Bukhari* is the 'Book of Revelation.' *Sahih Muslim* does not have the 'Book of Revelation.' A Hadis of *Sahih Al-Bukhari,*[6] based on the account credited to Ayesha, said almost the same. It, however, mentions only following three ayats, of the Qur'an, whereas Ibn Ishaq mentions five: "Read! In the name of your Lord, who created: He created man from a clinging form. Read! Your Lord is the Most Generous."[7]

Narrations, however, slightly differ, which is natural. Hazleton writes: "What actually happened on Mount Hira? We have what appear to be Muhammad's own words, but they come relayed through others, at several removes, with each narrator struggling to translate the ineffable into terms they could understand." He illustrates by quoting an account: "One account is credited to Aisha, the youngest and the most outspoken of the wives he would marry after Khadija's death: "He said: 'When the angel came to me, I had been standing, but I fell to knees and crawled away, my shoulders trembling … I thought of hurling myself down from a mountain crag, but he appeared to me as I was thinking this and said, 'Muhammad, I am Gabriel and you are the messenger of Allah.' Then he said, 'Recite!' I said, 'What shall I recite?' He took me and pressed me tightly three times until I was nearly stifled and thought that I should die, and then he said, 'Recite in the name of thy Lord who created, created man from a clot of blood, that thy Lords the most munificent, who teaches by the word, teaches man what he knew not.'"[8]

Awe-Inspiring Experience

The experience was not the least blissful; it was rather a awe-inspiring experience. Ibn Ishaq writes: "Now none of the Allah's creatures was more hateful to me than an (ecstatic) poet or a man possessed: I could not even look at them. I thought, Woe is me poet or possessed—Never shall Quraysh say this of me! I will go to the top of the mountain and throw myself down that I may kill myself and gain rest. So I went forth to do so."[9] And when Muhammad was midway on the mountain, he heard a voice from heaven saying, "O Muhammad! Thou art the apostle of Allah and I am Gabriel." He raised his head towards heaven to see, and saw Gabriel in the form of a man with feet astride the horizon, who said the same again. He continued to gaze at him, standing at the same place, and while turning his face he saw him as before. After he returned home, he came to Khadija, sat by her thigh, and drew close to her. She enquired, "O Abu'l-Qasim,[10] where hast thou been? By Allah, I sent my messenger in search of thee, and they reached the high ground above Mecca and returned to me." Muhammad replied, "Woe is me poet or possessed." She said, "I take refuse in Allah from that O Abu'l-Qasim, Allah would not treat you thus since he knows your great truthfulness, your fine character, and your kindness. This can not be my dear. Perhaps you did see something." "Yes, I did," he replied, and narrated what had happened.. She said, "Rejoice, O son of my uncle,[11] and be of good heart. Verily, by Him in whose hand is Khadija's soul, I hope that thou wilt be the prophet of this people." After that, she went to Waraqa, her cousin, and a Christian convert, who, after hearing her, cried, 'Holy! Holy! Verily by Him in whose hand is Waraqa's soul, if thou hast spoken to me the truth, O Khadija, there hath come to him the greatest Namus (meaning Gabriel) who came to Moses aforetime, and lo, he is the prophet of this people. Bid him be of good heart.'[12]

According to a Hadis of *Sahih Bukhari*, when the Allah's Messenger returned with the Inspiration and with his heart beating severely to Khadija, he said, "Cover me! Cover me! They covered him till his fear was over and after that he told Khadija everything that hast happened, and said, "I fear that something may happen to me." Khadija replied, "Never! By Allah, Allah will never disgrace you, You keep good relations with your kith and kin, help the poor and the destitute, serve your guests generously and assist the deserving calamity-afflicted ones."[13]

Waraqa Confirms Muhammad's Prophethood, Warns Him of Future Problems

When the Prophet Muhammad calmed down, Khadija accompanied him to her cousin, Waraqa, who was old and blind, and knew Hebrew and Christian Gospels, and said, "O my cousin! Listen to the story of your nephew." Allah's Messenger described whatever he had seen. Waraqa said, "This is the same one (who keeps the secrets i.e. angel Jibrael; Gabriel), whom Allah had sent to Musa (Moses). I wish I were young and could live upto the time when your people would turn you out." Allah's Messenger asked, "Will they drive me out?" He replied in the affirmative and said, "Anyone (man) who came with something similar to what you have brought, was treated with hostility; and if I should remain alive till the day (when you will be turned out) then I would support you strongly." Waraqa, however, died after a few days, and the Divine Inspiration was also paused for a while.[14] Ibn Ishaq also wrote the same: 'Waraqa brought Muhammad's head near him and kissed it. Waraqa's statement about the prophethood gladdened him, it 'added to his confidence and lighted his anxiery.[15]

Khadija Confirms Gabriel as an Angel

Ibn Ishaq, based on the authority of Khadija, conveyed by Isma'il, son of Haki writes that she said to the apostle of Allah, "O son of my uncle, are you able to tell me about your visitant, when he comes to you?' He replied that he could, and she asked him to tell her when he came. So when Gabriel came to him, as he was wont, the apostle said to Khadija, 'This is Gabriel who has just come to me.' 'Get up O son of my uncle.' She said, 'and sit by my left thigh.' The apostle did so, and she said, 'Can you see him?' 'Yes,' he said. She said, 'Then turn round and sit on my right thigh.' He did so and she said, 'Can you see him?' When he said that he could, she asked him to move and sit in her lap. When he had done this, she again asked if he could see him, and when he said yes, she disclosed her form and cast aside her veil, while apostle was sitting in her lap. Then she said, 'Can you see him? And he replied, 'No.' She said, O son of my uncle, rejoice and be of good heart, by Allah he is an angel and not a Satan.[16]

The Way Divine Inspiration was Revealed

Sahih Bukhari has the ahadis mentioning the way the Divine Inspirations were revealed. As narrated by Ayesha in a Hadis, Al-Harith, son of Hisham asked Allah's Messenger, "O Allah's Messenger! How is the Divine Inspiration revealed to you?" Allah's Messenger replied, "Sometimes it is (revealed) like ringing of a bell. This form of Inspiration is the hardest of all and then this state passes off after I have grasped what is inspired. Sometimes the angel comes in the form of a man and talks to me and I grasp whatever he says." Ayesha further said, "Verily, I saw the Prophet being inspired (divinely) and (noticed) the sweat dropping from his forehead on a very cold day as the Inspiration was over."[17]

In another Hadis, narrated by Ibn Abbas, "Allah's messenger used to bear the revelation with great stress and hardness, and used to move his lips (quickly with Inspiration)." Ibn Abbas moved his lips saying, "I am moving my lips (in front of you) as Allah's Messenger used to move his."[18] The Quranic revelations forbade him to do so afterwards. It said: "(Prophet), do not rush your tongue in an attempt to hasten (your memorization of) the Revelation: It is for us to make sure of its safe collection and recitation. When We have recited it, repeat the recitation and it is up to Us to make it clear."[19]

As Ibn Ishaq writes, "The apostle began to receive revelations in the month of Ramadan.[20] The Battle of Badr was also fought on 17th of Ramadan, after which the revelation came fully to the apostle. Ibn Ishaq writes: "Then revelation came fully to the apostle while he was believing in Him and in the truth of His message. He received it willingly, and took upon himself what it entailed whether of man's goodwill or anger. Prophecy is a troublesome burden—only strong, resolute, messengers can bear it by Allah's help and grace, because of the opposition which they meet from men in conveying Allah's message. The apostle carried out Allah's orders in spite of the opposition and ill treatment which he met with."[21]

Khadija: The First Believer

Khadija, the wife of the Prophet, was the first believer, which helped his work immensely. Ibn Ishaq writes: "Khadija believed in him and accepted as true what he brought from Allah, and helped him in his work. She was the first to believe in Allah and His apostle. He never met with contradiction and charges of falsehood, which saddened him, but Allah comforted him by her when he went home. She strengthened him, lightened his burden, proclaimed his truth, and belittled man's opposition."[22]

Revelations Temporarily Stop Coming

As Ibn Ishaq writes: "revelation stopped for a time so that the apostle of Allah was distressed and grieved."[23] Margoliouth writes that "the revelations ceased for a time after they had begun…Khadija is credited with having consoled the Prophet during the temporary suspense of the divine visitations; which perhaps we may interpret as meaning that the strong-minded woman who kept him faithful during the years in which his master-passion must have been strongest compelled him to adhere to the line which he had taken. But indeed he was compelled to continue by Abu Bakr, who immediately started proselytizing."[24]

Opinions differ about the suspension of revelations. Muir writes: "The period succeeding the revelation of the 96th Sura, during which inspiration was suspended, and Mohammad in despondency contemplated suicide, is generally represented of longer duration than in the above statement. The interval (which is called the *fetra*) is variously held to have lasted from six months to three years. At its close, the 74th and 93rd Suras, containing assurance of mercy and command to preach, were delivered. The accounts, however, are thoroughly confused, and sometimes contradictory; and we can only gather with certainty that there was a time (corresponding with the deductions already drawn from the Kor'an itself) during which the mind of Mohammad hung in suspense, and doubted the reality of heavenly mission."[25]

Despair and Hope

The stoppage of revelations caused deep despair, and the Prophet meditated even suicide. Muir writes: Now the first Sura revealed to Muhammad was the 96th, verses 1-5, *Recite in the name of the Lord*, etc.; and that descended on him in the cave of Hira. After this he waited some time without seeing Gabriel.

And he became greatly downcast, so that he went out now to one mountain, and then to another, seeking to cast himself headlong thence. While thus intent on self-destruction, he was suddenly arrested by a voice from heaven. He looked up, and behold it was Gabriel upon a throne between the heaven and the earth, who said:'*O Mohammad! Thou art the Prophet of the Lord, in truth, and I am Gabriel.*' Then Mohammad turned to go to his own house; and the Lord confronted him, and strengthened his heart. And thereafter revelations began to follow one upon another with frequency."[26]

A Hadis from Sahih Bukhari speaks differently about the revelation after the period of pause. According to that Hadis the Prophet says: "While I was walking, all of a sudden I heard a voice from the sky. I looked up and saw the same angel, who had visited me at the cave of Hira, sitting on a chair between the sky and the earth. I got scared of him and came back home and said, 'Wrap me (in blankets)' And then Allah revealed following verses (of the Qur'an) "You wrapped in your cloak, arise and give warning! Proclaim the greatness of your Lord; cleanse yourself; keep away from ar-Rujz (the idols).[27] After this revelations started coming strongly and frequently in succession one after the other."[28]

The frequency of the visit of the Gabriel to teach Qur'an to the Prophet increased during the Ramadan, and he came every night to do so.[29]

The early Meccan Sura, "Morning Brightness," was addressed to the Prophet to reassure him, when he did not receive revelation for some time. It said, "By the morning brightness and by the night when it grows still, your Lord has not forsaken you (Prophet), nor does He hate you, and the future will be better for you than the past; your Lord is sure to give you (so much) that you will be well pleased. Did He not find you an orphan and shelter you, find you lost and guide you, find you in need and satisfy your need? So do not be harsh with the orphan and do not chide the one who asks for help; talk about the blessings of your Lord."[30]

The timings of the revelations, during early, days were not known. The forms and contents also differed. Lesley Hazleton writes, "In these first few years, Muhammad never knew when a revelation was about to come. One may follow hard on the heels of another, or there might be weeks or even months between them. But unpredictability of timing was itself part of the process. If revelation had come on a regular basis, the words piling up like those of a writer determined to fulfill a daily quota, one might suspect too much neatness for credibility, as though a direct line had been established between human and divine, one that could be dialed into on demand. Instead, the verses themselves taught him how to receive them. "Be not hasty in your recitation before the revelation of it is finished." He'd be told. Let it come in full, that is, before trying to repeat it. "Be patient," he was told again and again. It was a a kind of ongoing lesson in how to surrender to the process. He was not to fight it nor attempt to hurry it, but allow it to take shape."[31]

About the style and content, Hazleton writes, "These early revelations were like exquisite poems, some so short and dense as to be almost haiku-like. Later, they'd become long and densely involved with the issues of the moment, and these longer revelations would form the suras, or chapters, that would be placed toward the beginning of the Qur'an when it was written down and compiled shortly after Muhammad's death, arranged not chronologically but more or less by length, from longest to shortest."[32]

Go Ahead to Go Public

At first, Hazleton writes: "only Khadija heard Muhammad recite these early verses, as though they needed to be incubated in a safe place before they could be recited to the wider world. It would be another full year until the sign came to go public with them. According to Ibn Ishaq, the go ahead came from the angel Gabriel, who appeared to Muhammad with precise instructions." As discussed elsewhere, the Prophet did accordingly.[33]

Initial Reaction of the Pagan People

The intial reaction of the pagans of Mecca was not of opposition, as discussed in the book.[34] However, the antagonism gradually developed between them forcing the Prophet to migrate to Medina.

References

1. Qur'an 97:1.
2. Hazleton, Lesley, *The First Muslim*, p. 76; hereafter Hazleton.
3. Muir, p. 60.
4. Ibn Ishaq, *Sirat Rasul Allah;*English translation by A Guillaume, p. 106; hereafter Ibn Ishaq.
5. Quran 96:1-5.
6. *Sahih Al-Bukhari, Hadis* no. 1:3.
7. Qur'an 96:1-3.
8. Hazleton, pp. 77-78.
9. Ibid, p. 78.
10. The *kunya* or 'name of honour of Prophet Muhammad;' meaning, 'father of Qasim.'

11. 'Son of my uncle' is the Arabian way of addressing the husband.
12. Ibn Ishaq, pp. 106-107.
13. *Sahih Bukhari*, op. cit.
14. Ibid.
15. Ibn Ishaq, p. 107.
16. Ibid.
17. *Sahih Bukhari*, Hadis no. 1:2.
18. Ibid, *Hadis* no. 1:4.
19. Qur'an 75:16-19.
20. Ibn Ishaq, p. 155.
21. Ibid.
22. Ibid.
23. Ibid.
24. Margoliouth, *Mohammed and the Rise of Islam*, p. 95; hereafter Margoliouth.
25. Muir, *The Life of Mahomet*, p. 51; hereafter Muir.
26. Ibid, p. 50.
27. Qur'an 74: 1-5; the translator of the Qur'an translates ar-Rujz as 'the filth.'
28. *Sahih Bukhari, Hadis* 1:3 (B).
29. Ibid, *Hadis* no. 1:5.
30. Qur'an, Sura 93.
31. Hazleton, pp. 94-95.
32. Ibid, p. 94.
33. Hazleton, p. 95.
34. Ibn Ishaq, p.118.

Islam: The Meccan Period

Islam, during the Meccan period passed through three phases after revelation. Firstly, it worked in a very limited circle; the reading of the Qur'an and the prayers were done secretly. In essence, it remained a secret society.[1] The second phase started when Allah ordered the Prophet to go public and preach openly. The people did not oppose the Islam during that phase.[2] The third phase began when the Prophet and his followers started talking against the Arabic deities, which, ultimately, led to conflict situation between the Muslims and the pagans.

Secrecy Maintained During the Initial Phase

As Margoliouth writes: Islam was a secret society before Allah ordered the Prophet to go public. "The *salat* (prayer) was during this early period performed in strict privacy, and doubtless meetings of believers were fixed with great caution. Whatever part the converted had previously taken in the Meccan worship they doubtless continued to take. Whether the sanctity of Ka'bah was maintained at this time by the Prophet, we do not know: most probably it was rejected. And if the question of a direction to be taken in prayer was considered at this time, we can scarcely doubt that the Temple of Jerusalem was the point to which he turned. The connection of the Abraham myth with the Ka'bah appears to have been the result of later speculation, and to have been fully developed only when a political need for it arose."[3]

The Prophet expressly discouraged publicity. Margoliouth further writes: "Publicity was expressly discouraged by him. A Syrian ('Amr, son of 'Abasah) who claimed at a later time to have been the fourth Moslem, asserted that having himself abandoned the worship of idols, he had come to Mohammed, who, he heard, was in possession of the truth; he found Mohammed bent on maintaining the secrecy of his mission: he offered to join Mohammed openly, but was forbidden to do so, (since he would serve the cause better by returning to his country) and—we may presume—playing the part of Abu Bakr. Some early revelations are said to have been delivered in a cave, a natural forms of hiding place; and in the anecdotes that have already been told Mohammed is found in seclusion; when Abu Dharr, afterwards a famous ascetic, came from a distance to learn about the Prophet's views (according to one account), the latter was hiding in the mountains."[4]

Allah Commands to Publish His Religion

Islam remained a secret religion for three years. After that Allah commanded the Prophet to publish it. Ibn Ishaq writes: "People began to accept Islam, both men and women, in large numbers, until the fame of it was spread throughout Mecca, and it began to be talked about. Then Allah commanded His apostle to declare the truth of what he had received and to make known His commands to men and to call them to Him. Three years elapsed from the time that the apostle concealed his state until Allah commanded him to publish his religion, according to information which has reached me.[5] The Qur'an said: "So proclaim openly what you have been commanded (to say) and ignore the idolaters"[6] Qur'an further said: "Warn your nearest kinsfolk and lower your wing tenderly over the believers who follow you."[7] And again, Allah proclaimed, "But We sent down the angels only to bring justice and then these people will not be reprieved. We sent down the Qur'an Ourself, and We Ourself will guard it."[8]

Ibn Ishaq further writes basing on the statements emanating from Ali, "When these words 'Warn thy family, thy nearest relations' came down to the apostle he called me and said: "Allah has ordered me to warn my family, my nearest relations and the task is beyond my strength. I know that when I made the message known to them I should meet with great unpleasantness so I kept silence until Gabriel came to me and told me that if I did not do as I was ordered my Lord would punish me. So get some food ready with a leg of mutton and fill a cup with milk and then get together the sons of 'Abdu'l Muttalib so that I can address them and tell them what I have been ordered to say. I did what he ordered and summoned them. There were at that time forty men more or less including his uncles Abu Talib, Hamza, al-'Abbas and Abu Lahab. When they were assembled, he told me to bring in the food which I had prepared for them, and when I produced it the apostle took a bit of the meat and split it in his teeth and threw it into the dish. Then he said, 'Take it in the name of Allah.' The men ate till they could eat no more and all I could see (in the dish) was the place where their hands had been. And as sure as I live if there had been only one man he could have eaten what I put before the lot of them. Then he said, 'Give the people to drink,' so I brought them the cup and they drank until they were all satisfied, and as sure as I live if there had been only one man he could have drunk that amount. When the apostle wanted to address them Abu Lahab got in first and said, 'Your host has bewitched you'; so they dispersed before the apostle could address them."[9]

Here, it needs mention that traditions differ about the happenings in this case. According to some tradition, as mentioned elsewhere in the book, Abu Lahab interrupted only after hearing part of what the apostle said, and the meeting came to an end. And again, whenever, an element of magic comes in, Ibn Ishaq usually inserts the comment, such as 'only Allah knows the reality,' which is missing in the above mentioned account, in which the eatables and drink, consumable by a single individual, satisfied some two score persons. Anyway, the process, as Ibn Ishaq wrote, was repeated next day, and after the food was served and consumed by all, except Abu Lahab, who did not attend, the apostle addressed the kinsmen. Ali said: "On the morrow he (the apostle) said to me: "This man spoke before I could, and the people dispersed before I could address them, so do exactly as you did yesterday." Everything went as before and then the apostle said: 'O sons of 'Abdu'l-Muttalib, I know of no Arab who has come to his people with a nobler message than mine. I have brought you best of this world and the next. Allah has ordered me to call you to Him. So which of you will co-operate with me in this matter, my brother, my executor, my successor being among you?' The men remained silent and I, though the youngest, most rheumy-eyed, fattest in body and thinnest in legs, said: 'O Prophet of Allah, I will be your helper in this matter.' He laid his hand on the back of my neck and said, "This is my brother, my executor, and my successor among you. Hearken to him and obey him.' The men got up laughing and saying to Abu Talib, 'He has ordered you to listen and obey your son!'"[10]

Warning Quraysh of Allah's Punishment

According to a tradition, when the verse came down to the apostle, he stood in the vale of Mecca, and warned different tribes of Quraysh, naming them one after another, of Allah's punishment. He said, 'I call you to Allah and I warn you of his punishment.'[11]

The First Bloodshed in Islam

The companions of the apostle used to go to the glens so that their people could not see them praying. One day, while Sa'd, son of Abu Waqqas, and a number of the apostle's companions were praying in one of the glens of Mecca, a band of polytheists came upon them; they rudely interrupted them, and blamed them for what they were doing. Ultimately, they came to blows, and Sa'd smote a polytheist with the jawbone of a camel and wounded him.[12]

Kuraysh did not Oppose the Prophet on Open Display of Islam.

It was not the open display of Islam, which caused the withdrawal of the people from Prophet Muhammad, and enmity between the two. The cause of the conflict and enmity was that the Prophet started speaking disparagingly against their gods. Ibn Ishaq writes: 'When the apostle openly displayed Islam as Allah ordered him his people did not withdraw or turn against him, so far as I have heard, until he spoke disparagingly of their gods.'[13]

The Enmity and Conflicts

As mentioned above, the polytheists of Mecca turned against the apostle only when he started speaking disparagingly against their gods. Ibn Ishaq further writes: 'When he did that they took great offence and resolved unanimously to treat him as an enemy, except those whom Allah had protected by Islam from such evil, but they were a despised minority.'[14]

Polytheists Attempt to Compromise

The polytheists of Mecca tried, at least twice to have the compromise. The first time, when they met Abu Talib, uncle and the protector of Prophet Muhammad, then they ventilated their grievances to him, and said: 'O Abu Talib, your Nephew has cursed our gods, insulted our religion, mocked our way of life (the term 'ahlam' is used, which means 'civilization and virtues of the pre-Islamic Arabia..) and accused our forefathers of error; either you must stop him or you must let us get at him, for you yourself are in the same position as we are in opposition to him and we will rid you of him.' 'Abu Talib gave them a conciliatory reply and a soft answer and they went away.' The Quraysh leaders, who met Abu Talib, were Utba and Shyba, sons of Rabi'a, Abu Sufiyan, son of Harb, Abu'l Bakhtar whose name was al-'As, son of Hisham, al-Aswad, son of al-Muttalib, Abu Jahl (whose name was 'Amr, his title being Abu'l Hakam), son of Hisham, al-Walid, son of Mughira, and two sons of al-Hajjaj, namely, Nubayh and Munabbih, and al-As, son of al-Wa'il. The attempt, however, did not bring any change. The situation further deteriorated. 'The apostle continued on his way, publishing Allah's religion and calling men thereto. In consequence his relations with Quraysh deteriorated and men withdrew from him in enmity. They were always talking about him and inciting one another against him. After that, they attempted at the compromise the second time, went to Abu Talib, and said, 'You have a high and lofty position among us, and we have asked you to put a stop to your nephew's activities but you have not done so, By Allah, we can not endure that our fathers should be reviled, our customs mocked and our gods insulted. Until you rid us of him we will fight the pair of you until one side perishes,' or words to that effect.' Thus saying, they went off. Abu Talib was deeply distressed at the breach with his people and their enmity but he could not desert the apostle and give him up to them.[15]

Traditional Protection Mechanism

Abu Talib continued to protect Prophet Muhammad during his lifetime. After his death, Abu Lahab, his next uncle gave him protection for a brief period only. After that, the Prophet attempted to get protection at At-Taif, but failed. On assurance of protection from a Meccan, he, however, returned to Mecca, but ultimately, he had to migrate to Medina. It needs mention here that the Prophet, who was fighting against the traditional culture of Mecca, and in reality of Arabia, availed fully their protection mechanism for his own safety.

Social Boycott and Migration to Abyssinia

Prophet Muhammad was protected during the lifetime of Abu Talib, his uncle and clan leader. The clan, however suffered due to social boycott. The unprotected Muslim converts, from weaker social background, however, migrated to Abyssinia.[16] The Christian king of that country declined the request of the Meccans to send back the migrants to Mecca.. The migrants came back after some time,[17] and then re-migrated to that country.[18]

References

1. Margoliouth, pp. 83-117.
2. Ibn Ishaq, p. 118.
3. Margoliouth, pp. 103-104.
4. Ibid, pp. 107-108.
5. Ibn Ishaq, p.117.
6. Qur'an 15:94.
7. Qur'an 26: 214-15.
8. Qur'an 14:8-9.
9. Ibn Ishaq, pp. 117-18.
10. Ibid, p. 118.
11. Ibid.
12. Ibid.
13. Ibid.
14. Ibid, p. 118.
15. Ibid, pp. 118-19.
16. Muir, p. 69.
17. Ibid, pp. 80, 82, 86.
18. Ibid, pp. 86, 87, 91.

Early Converts to Islam

As discussed elsewhere, Prophet Muhammad was not free from doubt about his prophethood after the first revelation. He could, however, emerge only towards the forty-fourth year of his age 'from doubt and obscurity, clearly and unequivocally asserting that he was ordained a prophet with a commission to the people of Arabia; reciting his warnings and exhortations as messages that emanated direct from Allah; and himself implicitly believing (to all outward appearance) his call and mission to be divine.' The first ones, convinced in his prophethood, and in turn convincing him about the same, were his wife, Khadija, and her aged cousin, Waraqa, 'who died before Muhammad had entered upon his public ministry.' Among the first converts of Islam were Khadija, Zeid, the adopted son and intimate friend of Muhammad, Ali, his cousin and Abu Bakr. Ali grew up from a child in the faith of Islam. According to Ibn Ishaq, Ali was the first male Muslim, followed by Abu Bakr and his converts.[1] By the time he was convinced of his prophethood, Muhammad was 'already surrounded by a little band of followers, all animated by ardent devotion to his person, and the belief that his guide and inspirer was Allah himself.'[2]

Abu Bakr accepted the faith after Khadija. Abu Bakr lived in the same quarter of the city where Khadija lived, and when Muhammad shifted to her residence, both of them became intimate friends. 'Every convert brought to Muhammad exhibited some repugnance, except Abu Bakr. This was afterwards acknowledged by the prophet. But he did not state what it was that the newcomers disliked. Nor have we any record of the procedure at these solemn scenes: at most we hear that the Prophet taught the proselytes to pray.'[3]

Abu Bakr started proselytization soon after, though in profound strict secrecy, as desired by the Prophet. According to Margoliouth, it needs mention, the Islam initially was a secret society.[4] During initial years, two persons played important roles in Muhammad's life. His wife, Khadija, and Abu Bakr. The first strengthened his faith in his prophethood, and the second, Abu Bakr, initiated proselytization. Margoliouth writes: "Khadija is credited with having consoled the Prophet during the temporary suspense of the divine visitations; which we may perhaps interpret as meaning that the strong-minded woman who kept him faithful during the years in which his master-passion must have been strongest compelled him to adhere to the line which he has taken. But indeed he was compelled to continue by Abu Bakr, who immediately started proselytizing. Doubtless at the Prophet's desire the Mission was conducted with profound secrecy. Abu Bakr communicated nothing save to persons in whom he had confidence; and on whom he was able to obtain some leverage. But neither he nor the Prophet were impatient, and they were satisfied if the first year of Abu Bakr's propaganda produced three converts. There is strong reason for thinking that he was helped from the first by an Abyssinian slave, Bilal, of whose antecedents we should gladly know more; for Omar declared that Bilal was a third part of Islam; and, lest we should mistake the meaning of the phrase, a later follower used to call himself the quarter of Islam, because, when he visited Muhammad at Ukaz, he found him followed as yet by one freeman, Abu Bakr, and one slave Bilal."[5] Bilal, after a time, it needs mention, was purchased and manumitted by Abu Bakr.[6]

Abu Bakr gained five converts in the very beginning. Muir writes about them: "To have such a man a staunch adherent of his claims was for Muhammad a most important step. Abu Bakr's influence was freely surrendered to the cause of Islam, and five of the earliest converts are attributed to his exertions and example. Three were but striplings. *Sa'd*, the son of Abu Wakkas, converted in his sixteenth or seventeenth year, was the nephew of Amina, mother of the Prophet. *Az-Zubair*, probably still younger, was at once the nephew of Khadija, and the son of Muhammad's aunt Safiya. About the same age was Talha, a relative of Abu Bakr and a renowned warrior after age. The fourth was Othman, son of Affan (successor of Umar in the Caliphate), who, though of the Omeiyad stock, was also, on his mother's side, grandson of Abd al-Muttalib. Muhammad's daughter Rokeiya, being now, or shortly after, free from her connection with Otba (son of the hostile Abu Lahab), the Prophet gave her in marriage to Othman, whose wife she continued until her death ten or twelve years afterwards. Othman was at this period between thirty and forty years of age. The fifth was *Abd ar-Rahman*, ten years younger than the Prophet, a man of wealth and character. Abd ar-Rahman, Othman, and Talha were, like Abu Bakr, merchants."[7]

Mikdad was one of the earliest converts, who had fled from his own tribe for a murder, and been received by the Kindah. He shed blood even there, and fled to Mecca, where he was adopted by a man called Al-Aswad, who belonged to the tribe of Muhammad's mother. Margoliouth writes about his conversion: "Abd al-Ka'bah advised him (in conversation) to marry, yet refused him his daughter, with scorn; but he found consolation from Muhammad, who gave him the daughter of Zubair, already dead, on the same conditions (we suspect) as those to which Othman had been compelled to assent. …With Mikdad there was won another convert, Utbah, son of Ghazwan, also a client, and probably poor."[8]

The four persons accompanied Abd ar-Rahman, namely, *Obeida*, son of Muhammad's uncle Al-Harith; *Abu Selama, Abu Obeida*, subsequently a warrior of note; and *Othman*, son of Mazun, when he visited the house of the Prophet; they embraced Islam at the same time. 'The latter had already abandoned wine before his conversion, and was with difficulty persuaded by Muhammad to renounce the asperities of an ascetic life. His family apears to have been well inclined to Islam,' for the names of his two brothers, a son, and other relatives, is found in the list of believers.[9]

Many slaves were manumitted by Abu Bakr, and converted to Islam, Most of them knew something about Christianity and Judaism, and were well-inclined towards Islam and Prophet Muhammad. *Amir ibn Fuheira, Abdallah ibn Masud*, and *Khabbab*, a blacksmith, were among the early converts. Apart from the twenty converts, whose name came to light, there were thirteen more during initial few years of Islam; and as Muir mentions, the number of converts reached to nearly forty souls in the first three or four years. This included wives and daughters of some of the converts.[10]

As mentioned earlier, Abu Bakr manumitted many slaves and got them converted. Uthman loved the daughter of Muhammad, and Abu Bakr, by facilitating their marriage, succeeded in making him Muslim. The persons dissatisfied with pagan beliefs approached the Prophet and got converted. Abu Bakr managed to bring many such persons to the Islamic fold.

After three years of secret preaching and private solicitation, Muhammad started openly preaching the Quraysh at large.[11] This happened after he received the command to 'arise and preach.'[12] Ibn Ishaq writes about the developments: "People began to accept Islam, both men and women, in large numbers until the fame of it was spread throughout Mecca, and it began to be talked about. Then Allah commanded his apostle to declare the truth of what he had received and to make known His commands to men and to call them to Him. Three years elapsed from the time that the apostle concealed his state until Allah commanded him to publish his religion, according to information which has reached me. Then Allah said, 'Proclaim what you have been ordered and turn aside from the polytheists.'[13] And again, 'Warn thy family, thy nearest relations, and lower thy wing to the followers who follow thee.'[14] And 'Say, I am the one who warns plainly..'[15]

Muir writes about the change in the relationship of Prophet Muhammad with the Quraysh: "An important change now occurred in the relations of Muhammad with the citizens of Mecca. Hitherto they had treated his teaching as that of a harmless enthusiast. But now their hostility was aroused and believers were subjected to indignity and molestation. The main ground of the opposition was the deep-seated attachment of Quraysh to the Ka'ba. The same spirit was aroused in them as caused the multitude of old to shout 'Great is Diana of the Ephesians.' Their shrine, the glory of Mecca and the centre of pilgrimage from all Arabia, was in danger to be set at nought. The new doctrine must be crushed, and its followers forced to abandon it. By degrees the persecution grew hot. Those who were citizens for the most part escaped serious injury, being protected as a point of honour by their families; but slaves, who had no such support, were exposed to much suffering."[16]

Ibn Ishaq has detailed the after developments, leading to intense opposition of Muhammad by the Quraysh, as he insulted their gods; the first blood was shed in Islam by Sa;d, a Muslim;[17] Muhammas's protection by Abu Talib, conversion of Hamza, attempts of Utba towards compromise, converts emigrating to Abyssinia, Meccans failure to bring the emigrants back, proclamation of the boycott against the Prophet's clan, and annulling of the boycott.[18] These aspects have been discussed in the book elsewhere. Muir has pointed out that even the opposition by the unbelievers benefited Muhammad: "Persecution, though it may sometimes have deterred the timid from joining his ranks, was eventually of unquestionable service to Muhammad. It furnished in after years a plausible excuse for casting aside the garb of toleration; for opposing force to force against those who 'obstructed the ways of the Lord;' and last of all for the compulsory conversions of the unbelievers. Even before the Hijra it drove the adherents of the Prophet in self-defence into a closer union, and made them stand forth with a more resolute aim and bolder front. The severity and injustice of Quraysh, overshooting the mark, aroused at once personal and family sympathies; unbelievers sought to avert or mitigate the sufferings of the followers of the Prophet; and in so doing they were themselves sometimes gained over to his side."[19]

The general opposition to Muhammad was, however, highly delayed. Muir writes: "It was not, however, till three or four years of his ministry had elapsed, that any general opposition to Muhammad was organized. Even after he had begun publicly to summon his fellow-citizens to the faith, and his followers had multiplied, the people did not gainsay his doctrine. They would only point at him slightingly as he passed, and say: *There goeth the Fellow from among the children of Abd al-Muttalib, to speak unto the people about the Heavens.* But (adds tradition) when the Prophet began to abuse their idols, and to assert the perdition of their ancestors who died in unbelief, then they became unpleased and began to treat him with contumely. Hostility, once excited, soon showed itself in acts of violence. Sa'd, it is related, having retired for prayer with a group of believers to a valley near Mecca, some of his neighbours passed unexpectedly by. A sharp contention arose between them, followed by blows. Sa'd struck one of his opponents with a camel goad; and this was the first blood shed in Islam."[20]

After the killing of an unbeliever by Sa'd, Muhammad shifted his residence to the house of a convert, Al-Arkam, situated at a short distance from his own house, upon the gentle rise of the Safa. This, he did, to enable him to prosecute his mission peaceably and without interruption. Many persons, who visited him there, including Umar, got converted to Islam, making the house famous as *the House of Islam*. Omar was converted there at the close of the sixth year of the mission; he was the last brought to that house, as his influence enabled Muhammad then to dispense with secrecy.[21]

It my be interesting to know about a few more converts before closing the chapter. Mus'ab, son of Umair, was one of the earlier convert; he was sent to Medina, with the Muslim converts, 'to lead prayer and teach such portions of Qur'an as had already become part of the ritual.' He was an earnest man, and Prophet's first choice of a lieutenant. He had been a fop in his early life, 'who rejoiced in fine raiment and dainty perfumes.' He had concealed his conversion till the secret was betrayed to his parents by one who saw him pray. Then he openly espoused the cause, losing his all. He fled to Abyssinia, and returned with the others. Poverty and privation has changed his dainty complexion so that the Prophet wept to see it; rags scarcely sufficient to cover him were the substitute for his smart apparel. Presently a martyr's death awaited him. If other Muslim's reaped some of the reward in this world the first \Refugee reaped none.[22] The valuable Muslim converts won by him were Muhammad, son of Maslamah, and other two—Usaid, son of Haraith, and Sa'd, son of Mu'adh, the two chieftains of the Aus—whose conversion decided the fortunes of Islam at Yathrib.[23] Sa'd became so enthusiastic about Islam that he "not only brought Mus'ab and As'ad into his lodge, but vowed to converse with none of his clan, the Banu Abd al-Ashhal, till they were converted; and this energetic measure led to the conversion of the whole clan."[24]

The conversion produced a complex scenario in Mecca. The experience of the young ones, adopting the new faith silently, differed. The reactions of the mothers of Mus'ab, son of Omeir (*Mos'ab ibn Omeir*) and that of Toleiba, son of Arwa, a daughter of Abd al-Muttalib vividly shows the contrast. When Mus'ab, about whom we have written above, returned from Abyssinia to Mecca, and met his mother, he looked so altered and wretched that his mother had not the heart to abuse him. Afterwards, when he came back from Medina, and his mother came to know about the same, then she sent to him saying: 'Ah, disobedient son! Wilt thou enter a city in which thy mother dwelleth, and not first visit her?' 'Nay, verily,' he replied, 'I shall never visit the house of anyone before the Prophet of Allah.' He, therefore, went to his mother only after greeting Muhammad. His mother accosted him, and said: Well! I suppose thou art still a renegade? The son answered: 'I follow the Prophet of the Lord, and true faith of Islam.' 'Art thou then well satisfied with the miserable way thou hast fared in the land of the Abyssinia, and now again at Medina?' Perceiving a design to seize him, he exclaimed: 'What! Wilt thou force a man from his religion? If ye seek to confine me, I will assuredly slay the first person that layeth hands upon me.' His mother said: 'Then depart from my presence,' and she began to weep. Mus'ab was moved; he said: 'Oh my mother! I give thee affectionate counsel. Testify that there is no God but Allah, and that Muhammad is his servant and messenger.' His mother replied: 'By the sparkling stars! I shall never make myself a fool by entering into thy religion. Begone! I wash my hands of thee and thy concerns, and cleave steadfastly unto mine own faith.'[25] The mother of Toleiba, when informed by his son that he had silently got converted, to Islam, approved his action. At the same time, she expressed her willingness to become Muslim.[26]

References

1. Ibn Ishaq, *Sirat Rasul Allah*, pp. 114-117; hereafter, Ibn Ishaq.
2. Muir, Sir William, *The Life of Mahomet*, pp. 55-57; hereafter Muir.
3. Margoliouth, D.S., *Mohammed and the Rise of Islam*, p. 101; hereafter Margoliouth.
4. Ibid, pp. 83-117.
5. Ibid, pp. 95-96.
6. Ibid, p. 96.
7. Muir, p. 58.
8. Margoliouth, p. 100.

9. Muir, pp. 58-59.
10. Ibid, pp. 59-60.
11. Ibid, p. 61; Ibn Ishaq, pp. 117.
12. Qur'an 74:1ff; the biographers of Muhammad, however, cite another passage of the Qur'an as the first command, which is cited below: "And preach to (or warn) thy nearer kinsfolk And lower thy wing to the believers that follow thee. And if they rebel against thee,' … (Qur'an 26:214ff. Muir, anyway, does not agree that the above mentioned passage was the first one, commanding to preach. (See Muir, p. 61 note 1).
13. Quran 15:94.
14. Qur'an 26:214, i.e. 'deal gently with.'
15. Qur'an 15:8, 9.
16. Muir, p. 62.
17. Ibn Ishaq, p. 118.
18. Ibid, pp. 130-74.
19. Muir, p. 62.
20. Ibid, pp. 62-63.
21. Ibid, pp. 63-64; p. 63 note 2.
22. Margoliouth, pp. 198-200.
23. Ibid, p. 199.
24. Ibid, p. 200.
25. Muir, pp. 64-65.
26. Ibid, p. 65.

Medinan Phase

Medinan Society Before the Prophet's Migration

The Settling of Medina

Amalekites, according to Arab legend, were the earliest tribes to settle in northern Arabia. They belonged probably to the Abrahamic races of the non-Israelitish descent. Waves of Jewish settlers moved southwards in northern Arabia after their dispersal due to sack of Jerusalem by Nebuchadnezzar, the attack of Pompey 64 years before the Christian era, the attack of Titus 70 years after it, the bloody retribution inflicted by Hadrian on Judea during 136 AD, and such other factors. The Jews formed the majority population of Medina (the ancient *Yathrib*) before the northward movement of numerous Arabian tribes migrating from the Yemen during early fourth century, and their settlement on the Syrian border, which included the settlement of Aus and Khazraj in Medina. Thus, the society in Medina, when Prophet Muhammad migrated there, consisted of two Arabian tribes—Aus and Khazraj—and three Jewish settlements in its neighbourhood. The three Jewish tribes residing in these settlements were An-Nadir, Koreiza, and Kainuka. Thus, the Jews were the earlier settlers there.[1]

Jewish Ethnicity

The Jews, apart from their migration from Cannan, might have migrated northwards from the south also after the break-up of the Jewish state in South Arabia. Thus, the possibility of the Jewish origin, as well as Judaised Arabs among them may not be ruled out. Margoliouth writes:

"It rather appears as if these tribes had kept aloof from the affairs of their pagan neighbours till shortly after the commencement of Islam. Yet the fact of these tribes having names with specifically Arabic consonants requires some explanation. Israelites in most countries take names by which they are assimilated to their neighbours; but the fact of their doing so implies that they feel themselves to be aliens, and would, at least to a certain extent conceal this circumstance. Had these Israelites, coming from their home in Canaan, colonized a new country, they would surely have retained both their language and their national names. Now, it seems clear that these Jews of Medina were no more retentive of the former than of the latter. They spoke Arabic—an idiom of their own, it would appear, but not more different from the language of their neighbours than is Yiddish from German."[2]

Margoliouth further writes:

"Hence we cannot credit the Arabic tale, and yet the obvious hypothesis that these tribes were not of Jewish origin, but Judaised Arabs, can only be accepted to a moderate extent. The characteristic which they are found displaying are too national for us to suppose they had imbibed their Judaism from strangers. Perhaps, then, these tribes had migrated to Yathrib after the break-up of the Jewish state in South Arabia."[3]

Aus and Khazraj Supplanting the Jews

As the Aus and Khazraj gained a footing in Medina, and soon encroached upon the Jews, the enmity sprang up between them. These two Arab communities, aided by their Syrian brethren, treacherously massacred the leading Jews assembled at a banquet, and thereby became the masters of Medina; they took possession of the richest land of Medina.[4] Though, some of the Jews professed to have settled at Medina even during the time of Moses, and 'Jewish settlers were certainly to be found in most of the oases that lie between Syria and Yemen,' they formed a minority population of Medina at the time of the migration of the Prophet.[5] Again, as the population of Arabs increased, 'they incurred the envy and suspicion of the wealthy Jewish residents, who, imitating the treatment of their ancestors by Pharaoh, proceeded to oppress the settlers: one Jewish chieftain (with the curious name Bedchamber) even exacting the *jus primae noctis*.' This, naturally, led to retaliation, and further developments, which ultimately resulted into the subdued social position of the Jews. Margoliouth writes: "By an expedient which rarely failed in anecdotes of this style, the brother of one of the brides, disguised in bridal attire, assassinated the tyrant; and presently by two acts of gross perfidy the supremacy had been won for the incomers. A Ghassanide king, at the instance of a Khazrajite, Malik, son of 'Ajlan, had invited the chiefs of the Jews to a banquet and beheaded them, leaving Malik to achieve the work of subduing the Jews. Malik accomplishes this by a second banquet, which the remaining chiefs were credulous and infatuated to attend. After this double massacre, the Jews were no longer able to make head against the newcomers, but sank into a condition of vassalage. When a Jew was attacked, instead of calling his brethren to help him, he besought the help of an Arab patron."[6] Of course, As Margoliouth writes, "Beni Kainuka, who owned the market of Yathrib, were dependents of Khazraj, …"[7]

Margoliouth further writes: "It cannot now be discovered whether the above story contains any germ of truth, or whether it is wholly the product of fancy. It is certainly true that to many of the Yathrib tribes Jews were attached: but the victims of the treachery cannot well have been the tribes Nadir or Kuraizah, who play a part in the scenes to which we are coming; for at the commencement of Islam, these were not in a condition of vassalage.[8]

Better equipped with instruments for agriculture, with the understanding of many industries to which the Arabs were strangers, and having reputation for learning, the Jews, in many respects, were well-placed in Medina, and in Arabian society. Although adept in black art, and preferring the weapons of the black art to those of open warfare, they had some renown as warriors also. The Jews had considerable wealth, which they acquired by aid of their peaceful industry, and to some extent by money-lending. Banu Nadir of Medina, had palaces, which an Arabian poet of early Islam couples with those of the Persian and Byzantine monarchs. As he thinks, the deterioration of the race had led to the fall of all alike.[9]

Intra-Societal Conflict in Medina

Once established in Medina, there started conflict and violence between Aus and Khazraj also. The Jews were also divided between the two Arab clans. Muir writes:

"Thus established, it was not long before the Aus and the Khazraj fell out among themselves; and in the beginning of the 6th century we find them in a state of chronic enmity, if not actual warfare with each other. Four or five years previous to the period of our history, hostilities had reached a crisis between them. Each was reinforced by allies from other Arab tribes; the Jews were divided, the Beni Koreiza and An-Nadir siding with the Aus, Kainuka with the Khazraj. In the year 616 AD there was fought the great battle of Bo'ath (Boʿath; also Bu'ath). At first the Aus were worsted and fled; but their chief, in indignation, pierced himself and fell; and at the sight, stung by shame, they returned to the charge and fought so bravely that they dispersed the Khazraj with great slaughter. They burned the date groves of their enemy, and were scarce restrained from razing their fortified houses to the ground."[10] In the battle, both the chiefs, leading the Aus and the Khazraj, were killed.[11]

Muir further writes: "The Khazraj were humbled but not reconciled. No open engagement after this took place, but numerous assassinations from time to time were indicative of hardly suppressed ill-blood. Wearied with the protracted discord, both parties were about to take 'Abdallah ibn Obei, a distinguished citizen of the Khazraj, as their chief. This man had resented the treacherous murder by his own tribe of certain Jewish hostages; he had taken no part in the field of Bo'ath; and he was respected by both factions. But his bright prospects were destined to be eclipsed by the rising fortunes of the stranger driven from Mecca."[12]

Jewish Involvement in the Conflict

The Jews remained uninvolved in the intra-tribal conflict in Medina till the battle of Bo'ath; they had been cultivating their fields in peace, and even in case of the loss of life, they preferred a battle of curses and imprecations to the use of sword or spear. But the situation changed and the Jewish tribes of 'Kuraizah and Nadir had to participate in the battle of Bo'ath against the Khazraj; the third Jewish tribe, however, fought with the Khazraj. Margoliouth writes, how the Khazraj made the two Jewish tribes their enemy:

"The defeated Aus, catching like drowning men at a straw, negotiated with these tribes for assistance in their war, and the Khazraj, hearing of this, sent to warn the Jews against interference, and demanded forty lads as hostages. These were provided: but the real purpose of the Khazraj was to force the Jews into a quarrel with a view of obtaining their lands, and the game which they played was afterwards imitated by Muhammad with most signal success. The Khazaraj demanded the lands of the Jews under threat of killing their hostages; and the Jews suffered the hostages to be killed. So the Jews were driven to help the Aus, and to take part in the war of which they had kept clear. They opened their doors to the fugitive Nabit. Fighting under foreign commanders, and by the side of brave men, the Jews have often proved themselves as good soldiers as other men; and in the battle which resulted after long preparation, the Khazraj were defeated by the Aus with their Jewish allies. In following up the victory and exacting full vengeance the Jews were not restrained by the usages which the Arabs respected."[13]

Khazraj Meet Prophet Muhammad, Accept Islam

The strife-torn society of Medina was ideally placed to accept Islam. Ibn Ishaq writes about the meeting between Prophet Muhammad and the Khazraj: "When Allah wished to display His religion openly and to glorify His prophet and to fulfil His promise to him, the time came when he met a number of the Helpers at one of the fairs; and while he was offering himself to the Arab tribes as was his wont he met at al-'Aqaba a number of the Khazraj whom Allah intended to benefit. ... when the apostle met them he learned by inquiry that they were of the Khazraj and allies of the Jews. He invited them to sit with him and expounded to them Islam and recited the Quran to them. Now Allah had prepared the way for Islam in that they lived side by side with the Jews who were people of the scriptures and knowledge, while they themselves were polytheists and idolaters. They had often raided them in their district and whenever bad feeling arose the Jews used to say to them, 'A prophet will be sent soon. His day is at hand. We shall follow him and kill you by his aid as 'Ad and Iram perished.' So when they heard the apostle's message they said one to another: 'This is the very prophet of whom the Jews warned us. Don't let them get to him before us!' Thereupon they accepted his teaching and became Muslims, saying, 'We have left our people, for no tribe is so divided by hatred and rancour as they. Perhaps Allah will unite them through you. So let us go to them and invite them to this religion of yours; and if Allah unites them in it, then no man will be mightier than you.' Thus saying they returned to Medina."[14]

Thus, it is clear that Medina was well prepared for Islam before the *Hijr*, and its unexpected success at Medina was also not without perceptible cause. Muir also writes: "There was, first, the vague expectation, derived from the Jews, of a coming prophet. When the Jews, dividing their allegiance between the Aus and Khazraj clans, used to fight on either side, they would say: *A prophet is about to arise; his time draweth nigh. Him shall we follow; and then we shall slay you with the slaughter of the ungodly nations of the old.* So when Muhammad addressed the pilgrims of Medina at Mina, they spoke one with another: *Know surely that this is the prophet with whom the Jews are ever threatening us; wherefore let us make haste and be the first to join him.* Such is the Muslim tradition, and there is truth, no doubt, though exaggerated and distorted, in it."[15]

Muir further writes: "In their close and constant intercourse with the Arabs of Medina, the expectation of a Messiah must in some form or other have been communicated by the Jews to their heathen neighbours. Nor could the people live in daily contact with a race professing the pure theism and stern morality of the Old Testament without realizing its practical protest against the errors of heathenism, and its contrast with the worship of the one true God. Moreover, Medina was only half the distance of Mecca from the Christian tribes of Syria; the poet Hassan ibn Thabit, and men of his stamp in Medina, used to frequent the Christian court of the Ghassanide king; and thus Christianity as well as Judaism had probably wrought a more powerful effect upon the social condition of Medina than upon any other part of the Peninsula."[16]

As Muir further writes, internal strife neutralized the fear of foreign influence and Medina was prepared to accept Muhammad before his arrival.[17]

Belief in 'Victory of Bu'ath Due to Allah's Intervention'

As the Jews joined victorious Aus in the battle of Bu'ath, they regarded the victory due to the intervention of Allah, their God. Margoliouth writes: "The history which has come down to us is meager and one sided; we hear little of the triumph of the Aus or of the pride of the Jewish tribes in their victory over their oppressors. When men have had to endure failure and humiliation, a little success turns their heads. That the victory of Bu'ath was regarded by the Jews as a direct intervention by their God can scarcely be doubted; and since the gods of the Aus had failed to secure them victory, it prepared their enemies to recognize the transcendent power of the Israelitish God, whose emissary and agent Muhammad claimed—as we have seen, with some Jewish support—to be. Perhaps Mohammed confirmed them in this view of the situation. What more natural than that Allah should help his worshippers? The Khazrajites returned home with much food for reflection."[18]

Medinan Soil Prepared for Islam

The victory, according to Margoliouth, was due to the aid of Allah; he writes: "Thus we can interpret the saying of the keen-witted Ayesha. In the civil war at Yathrib the side that had long been defeated had won a signal victory by the aid of Allah, the God of the Jews. The Jews however care little to make proselytes, and took no advantage of the event for religious propaganda. But some of the defeated side learned of a man who could obtain for them the favour of Allah, and so were disposed to give a favourable hearing to Mohammad's preaching; and to the victors the name of Allah was associated with success, and they were not willing that the favour of his assistance should be transferred to those whom they had defeated. The expedient which had originally been intended for the continuance of the civil war resulted in uniting the parties."[19] Margoliouth, blaming the Jews for not deriving benefit from the changed situation further writes: "The Jews of Yathrib, impolite and un-foreseeing in the extreme, are likely to have attested the correctness of the first principles of Islam which reached them—the Unity of God, necessitating the destruction of idols, and the resurrection of the dead; the fact that prayer was to be directed towards their Temple clinched the matter. Moreover a century before they had made a convert of an Arab chieftain who had established a Jewish throne in South Arabia. Further, there are classical precedents of a prophet being called in to treat a state which was suffering from *statis* (internal dissention); some new cult was the expedient whereby the disease was curable. Such precedents were not indeed known to the Yathribites, but history is homogeneous."[20] Hence, as Margoliouth writes: "the soil of Medina, suffering due to internal dissention, was thoroughly prepared for Islam. In a healthy community like that of Meccah it gained no hold; but in one that was ailing from long years of civil strife it could spread apace."[21]

The Converts Return with the Promise to Meet Next Year

The Medinans, who met the Prophet, return back with the promise to meet him again after a year. The long wait was a period of expectation and anxiety for the Prophet. Muir writes:

"To return to Mecca, the year AD 620 was to Muhammad one of expectation and anxiety. Would the handful of Medina converts remain steady to the cause? Would they succeed in winning adherents from amongst their fellow citizens? If they should prove unfaithful, or fail to success, what then? He might be forced to flee to Syria or Abyssinia; and seek refuge at some Christian court, or with the Ethiopian Negus, or amongst the tribes of the northern deserts. Such are the doubts that must have exercised his soul during this long year of waiting."[22]

The First Pledge of 'Akaba

The Prophet's apprehensions, however, were dispelled. Twelve converts, ten Khazraj and two Aus, came and met him after the wait of a year in April AD 621, when the days of pilgrimage at last came round at the appointed place, in a narrow sheltered glen near Mina, to acknowledge him their prophet. After meeting him, they plighted their faith in the Prophet thus: '*We will not worship any god, but Allah; we will not steal, neither will we commit adultery, nor kill our children; we will not slander in anywise; nor will we disobey the Prophet in anything that is right.*' This was called the 'First Pledge of the 'Akaba' (also al-'Aqaba). named, after the name of the little eminence or defile wheither Prophet with the twelve retired. It was afterwards called the Pledge of Women, "because, as not embracing any stipulation to defend the Prophet, it was the only oath required of the female sex. When the twelve had taken this engagement, Muhammad replied: '*If ye fulfil the pledge, Paradise shall be your reward. He that shall fail in any part thereof, to Allah belongeth his concern either to punish or to forgive.*' A Mosque marks the spot of the pledge."[23] The twelve Medinan converts returned to Medina as the missionaries of Islam, with the promise to come back in greater number during the next year's pilgrimage, and meet Prophet Muhammad for the Second Pledge of 'Akaba (Aqaba).

Second Pledge of 'Akaba

A year passed after the first pledge of Akaba; the season of pilgrimage came. A delegation of converts came in the company of the polytheist pilgrims from Medina, who came for *hajj* and wanted to meet the apostle. Mos'ab, the missionary sent by the apostle to Medina, also came and informed about the amazing success of Islam in Medina. Ibn Ishaq writes: "Then Mos'ab came to Mecca and the Muslim Ansar came to the fair there with the pilgrims of their people who were polytheists. They met the apostle at al-'Aqaba in the middle of the day of *Tashriq*, (The three days, following the day of sacrifice, are known as days of Tashriq) when Allah intended to honour them and to help His apostle and to strengthen Islam and to humiliate heathenism and its devotees."[24] The converts from Medina were enthusiastic to crowd him, but there was need of caution and secrecy. Muir writes: "Messages and reports of the amazing success of Islam had no doubt reached Mohammed; but he could hardly have been prepared for the enthusiastic numbers ready to crowd to his standard, and swear allegiance to him as prophet and master. But the occasion was critical, and it was necessary to proceed with caution. Koreish, if aware of the hostile confederacy—hostile because pledged to support a faction in their community—would have good ground for umbrage; the sword might prematurely be unsheathed, and the cause of Islam endangered. The movement, therefore, was conducted with the utmost secrecy. Even the great body of Medina pilgrims, in whose company the converts travelled, were unaware of their object."[25]

Proper care was taken in the selection of time and place of the meeting of the Medinan converts with Prophet Muhammad. Muir writes: "To elude the security of the citizens the meeting between Mohammad and his new adherents was to be by night; and that the strangers, in case suspicion is aroused, might be as soon as possible beyond reach of their enemies, the time was deferred to the close of the pilgrimage when, the ceremonies and sacrifices being finished, the multitude would on the following morning disperse to their homes. The spot was to be the same secluded glen of Al-'Akaba, outside Mina, where the men of Medina had met Muhammad before. They were to move thither cautiously, after all had retired to rest;—'walking not the sleeper, nor tarrying for the absent.'"[26] The internal meeting had been kept profoundly hidden even from his own followers at Mecca, so that to secure the greater secrecy; and only Al-'Abbas, his uncle, 'the wealthiest sons of 'Abd al-Muttalib, who was said to be 'weak in character' and who 'ordinarily sailed with the wind and tide,' and not a convert, accompanied him.[27]

Ibn Ishaq writes about what an adherent narrates about the happening. It said: 'We slept that night among our people in the caravan until when a third of the night had passed we went stealing softly like sandgrouse to our appointment with the apostle as far as the gully by al-'Aqaba. There were seventy-three men with two of our women… We gathered together in the gully waiting for the apostle till he came with his uncle al-'Abbas who was at that time a polytheist; albeit he wanted to be present at his nephew's business and see that he had a firm guarantee. When he sat down he was the first to speak and said: "O people of al-Khazraj (the Arabs used the term to cover both Khazraj and Aus). You know what position Muhammad holds among us. We have protected him from our own people who think as we do about him. He lives in honour and safety among his people, but he will turn to you and join you. If you think that you can be faithful to what you have promised him and protect him from his opponents, then assume the burden you have undertaken. But if you think that you will betray and abandon him after he has gone out with you, then leave him now. For he is safe where he is." We replied, "We have heard what you say. You speak, O apostle, and chose for yourself and for your Lord you wish."[28]

Then, the apostle spoke and recited the Qur'an and invited men to Allah and commended Islam and then said: "I invite your allegiance on the basis that you protect me as you would your women and children." Al-Bara took his hand and said, "By Him Who sent you with the truth we will protect you as we protect our women. We give our allegiance and we are men of war possessing arms which have been passed on from father to son." Another adherent, Abu'l Haytham interrupted him and said: "O apostle, we have ties with other men (he meant the Jews) and if we sever them perhaps when we have done that and Allah will have given you victory, you will return to your people and leave us?" The apostle smiled and said: "Nay, blood is blood and blood not to be paid for is blood not to be paid for. I am of you and you are of me. I will war against them that war against you and be at peace with those at peace with you."[29]

When the adherents of Medina were asked to pledge, there arose, at once, a confused tumultuous noise, which 'was the eager voice of the 'Seventy' testifying their readiness to take the pledge, and protesting that they would receive and defend the Prophet even at the cost of life and property.' After that Al-'Abbas, 'holding his nephew's hand, called aloud: 'Hush! There may be spies abroad. Let your men of years stand forth, and speak on your behalf. Of a truth, we are fearful for your safety if our people should discover us. Then when you have plighted your faith depart silently to your camp.' After that, their chief men stood forth. The Al-Bara said: 'Stretch out your hand, O Mohammad!' After he stretched out, Al-Bara struck his thereon, as the manner was in taking oath of fealty. The Seventy came forward one by one, after that, and did the same.[30] Then the apostle said, "Bring out to me twelve leaders, that they may take charge of their people's affairs." They produced nine from al-Khazraj and three from al-Aus." The apostle named the 'Twelve' as their chief men, and said: '*Moses chose from amongst his people twelve leaders. Thus shall ye be the leaders and sureties for the rest, even as the apostles of Jesus were; and I am the surety for my people.*' They agreed to what he said.[31] Here, it needs mention that the tradition differs as to who was the first to strike his hand in fealty.[32]

When the process of striking the hand in fealty was over, "the voice of one crying aloud, a straggler perchance, searching for his company, was heard at hand. Excited fancy conjured up a Koreishite if not an infernal spy."[33] Ibn Ishaq calls it the voice of Satan.[34] When the apostle commanded them to disperse and go back to their caravan, one of them said, 'By Allah, if you wish it we will fall on the people of Mina tomorrow with our swords.' The apostle replied: 'We have not been commanded to do that; but go back to your caravan.' So they went back to their caravan and slept.[35]

As was natural, such 'large gathering could not be held close by Mina without rumours reaching the Koreish enough to rouse suspicion; they considered it to be a hostile movement, came to their camp, and enquired. The pagan, as they did not know about the development denied it. 'Their chief, 'Abdallah, son of Obei, assured the visitors that none of his people would have ventured on such a step without consulting him.' Koreish, being satisfied left their camp. But the incident could not remain secret; even 'Mohammad cared to keep secret now;' they pursued the Medina caravan in the hope that they might lay hands on some of the delinquents, but ultimately found only two. As one of the two persons escaped, they maltreated the remaining ones.[36]

After the Second Pledge of 'Akaba, five things happened: (i) The conflict intensifies in Mecca; (ii) Mohammad gave command to emigrate to Medina; (iii) The apostle receive order to fight; (iv) The Muslims, after coming to Medina, started openly professing Islam; (v) the idol of Manat of a chief of Medina was repeatedly thrown in dirty places, and ultimately tied to a dead dog and thrown in a pit.[37]

References

1. Muir, Sir William, *The Life of Mahomet*, pp. 114-15. (Hereafter, Muir).
2. Margoliouth, D.S., *Mohammed and the Rise of Islam*; p. 188. (Hereafter,

Margoliouth).

3. Ibid.
4. Muir, p. 115.
5. Margoliouth, p. 186.
6. Ibid, pp. 186-87.
7. Ibid, p. 187.
8. Ibid, pp. 187-88.
9. Ibid, pp. 187-89.
10. Muir, p. 115.
11. Ibn Ishaq, *Sirat Rasul Allah*, English translation, *The Life of Muhammad*, A. Guillaume; p. 261; (Hereafter, Ibn Ishaq).
12. Muir, pp. 115-16.
13. Margoliouth, pp. 193-94.
14. Ibn Ishaq, pp. 197-98.
15. Muir, p. 116.
16. Ibid.
17. Ibid, pp. 116-17.
18. Margoliouth, pp. 196-97.
19. Ibid, p. 197.
20. Ibid, pp. 197-98.
21. Ibid, p. 198.
22. Muir, p. 118.
23. Ibid.
24. Ibn Ishaq, pp. 201-202.
25. Muir, p. 128.
26. Ibid, pp. 128-29.
27. Ibid, p. 129.
28. Ibn Ishaq, p. 203.
29. Ibn Ishaq, pp. 203-204.
30. Muir, p. 130.
31. Muir, p. 130; Ibn Ishaq, p. 204.
32. Ibn Ishaq, p. 205.
33. Muir, p. 130.
34. Ibn Ishaq, p. 205.
35. Ibid.
36. Ibid, pp. 205-207; Muir, pp. 131-32.
37. Ibid, pp. 207-213; Muir, pp. 131-33.

Migration and After

Khadija and Abu Talib: The Pillars of Strength

Khadija, prophet's wife, and Abu Talib, his uncle, were pillars of strength for the apostle. Khadija 'had been a faithful support to him in Islam, and he used to tell her of his troubles. Abu Talib, 'a strength and stay in his personal life,' was 'a defence and protection against his tribe.' The Prophet bothered least about his ill-wishers during their lifetime.

Death of Khadija and Abu Talib

Both, Khadija and Abu Talib died one after another in the same year; and with Abu Talib's death, three years before his migration to Medina, the 'Quraish began to treat him in an offensive way which they would not have dared in his uncle's lifetime.' After the death of Abu Talib, when a 'young lout actually threw dust on his head, he said: 'Quraish never treated me thus while Abu Talib was alive.' After this happened, 'the apostle went into his house with the dust still on his head and one of his daughters got up to wash it away, weeping as she did so.' 'Don't weep, my little girl,' the apostle said: 'for Allah will protect your father.'[1]

When Abu Talib was seriously ill, some Quraish notables—Utba, Shayba, Abu Jahl, Umayya, Abu Sufyan and some sundry other notables—went to him and said: 'You know your rank with us and now that you are at the point of death we are deeply concerned on your account. You know the trouble that exists between us and your nephew, so call him and let us make an agreement that he will leave us alone and we will leave him alone; let him have his religion and we will have ours.' When the Prophet came, Abu Talib said: 'Nephew, these notables have come to you that they may give you something and to take something from you.' 'Yes,' he answered, 'you may give me one word by which you can rule the Arabs and subject the Persians to you.' 'Yeah,' said Abu Jahl, 'and ten words.' He said: "You must say, 'There is no God but Allah and you must repudiate what you worship beside him.' 'They clapped their hands,' and then said: 'Do you want to make all the gods into one Allah, Muhammad? That would be an extraordinary thing.' After that, they said one to another, 'This fellow is not going to give you anything you want, so go and continue with the religion of your fathers until Allah judge between us.' After that they departed.[2]

After the departure of Kuraish leaders, Abu Talib said: 'Nephew, I don't think that you asked them anything extraordinary.' On hearing his statement, Prophet Muhammad hoped that he would accept Islam, and said, 'You say it, uncle, and then I shall be able to intercede for you on Resurrection Day.' Abu Talib replied: 'Were it not that I fear that you and your father's sons would be abused after my death and that Quraish would think that I had only said it in fear of death, I would say it. I would only say it to give you pleasure.'[3]

When Abu Talib felt that his life was coming to an end, 'he summoned his brethren, the sons of 'Abd al-Muttalib, around his bed; commended his nephew to their protection; and, relieved of the trust, died in peace, and was buried near Khadija's grave. Mohammad wept as he followed the bier, and not without reason.'[4] Muir writes: 'For forty years, Abu Talib had been his faithful friend,—the prop of his childhood, the guardian of his youth, and in later life a very tower of defence. His unbelief only made his influence the stronger. So long as he survived, Mohammed needed not to fear violence and attack. But there was no strong hand now to protect him from his foes.'[5]

Abu Lahab's Guardianship

The next leader of the Hashim clan, Abu Lahab ('Father of flames'; half-brother of Abu Talib), was a vehement opponent of Muhammad. Things 'might have continued to work out, since it seemed at first that their mutual grief over abu-Talib's death might bind the two men together,' and Abu-Lahab assured his nephew of the protection he needed. But he could not continue to give him protection for long, as he was incensed at the Islamic idea of the ancestors of the Hashim clan going to hell.[6] Muir writes: "Grieved and dispirited by these bereavements following so closely one upon the other, and dreading the new unchecked insolence of Koreish, Mohammad seldom went abroad. The dying behest of Abu Talib had now an unexpected effect; for Abu Lahab, heretofore the avowed enemy of Mohammad, was softened by his despondency and distress, and spontaneously became his guardian. *'Do,' he said, 'as thou hast been in the habit of doing while Abu Talib was yet alive. By Al-Lat! No one shall hurt thee while I live.'* But the pledge was not long observed, for Abu Lahab was soon gained back again by Koreish, and became his enemy more determined than before. At first, indeed, he was rather praised by Koreish for his attempt to 'bind up family differences.' But, bid by Abu Jahl to ask where 'Abd al-Muttalib was, and on the Prophet confessing that he was in the place of the lost, Abu Lahab left him in indignation, saying, 'I will not cease to be thine enemy for ever;' and so he did remain. The embittered relations between Abu Lahab and his nephew, notwithstanding that two of his sons married daughters of Mohammad, may be gathered from a memorable passage in the Qur'an. The Prophet, we are told, called his relatives together to hear his message. When he had delivered it, 'Blast the fellow!' cried Abu Lahab; 'is that all that he hath called us for together?"[7] The revelation, chiding the blasphemer, and cursing his wife, who had strewn thorns in his path, came down, It said:

> Blasted be the hands of Abu Lahab! And let himself be blasted!
> His riches shall not profit him, nor that which he hath gained.
> He shall be cast into the broiling *flame*;
> His wife also laden with fuel,
> A halter of palm-coir round her neck.[8]

Withdrawal of clan protection meant that any physical harm on Muhammad would no longer be taken by the Hashims as cause for blood-revenge. That means "his blood was licit."[9]

The situation was becoming more critical. New persons were almost not joining Islam, especially the important ones, such as Umar and Hamza, who joined him 3-4 years earlier. Under such situation, and due to growing hostility of the Quraish, the apostle resolved to make travel of At-Ta'if, the nearest city, some 60-70 miles to the east, to seek help from Thaqif, through the three principal men of the city, and brothers, and their defence against his tribe.

Oppressive Behaviour of the Neighbours

Some of the neighbours, who used to ill-treat the apostle, were Abu Lahab, al-Hakam, Uqba, Adiy and Ibnu'l Asda. One of them, al-Hakam, became Muslim afterwards. As Ibn Ishaq reports, 'one of them used to throw a sheep's uterus at him while he was praying; and one of them used to throw it into his cooking pot when it had been placed ready for him. Thus, the apostle was forced to retire to a wall when he prayed. … when they threw this objectionable thing at him the apostle took it out on stick, and standing at the door of his house, he would say, "O Banu Abdu Manaf, what sort of protection is this?" Then he would throw it into the street.[10]

Journey to At-Taif and Ignominious Expulsion

The Prophet undertook the journey to At-Ta'if during January, 620, ten years after the revelations started coming down, and just after the death of Abu Talib. His only companion was Zeid. At-Taif people had numerous links by frequent intermarriages with the people of Mecca; many rich Meccans had fruit gardens there. They had the chief idol of al-Lat there. The inhabitants of that city were, however jealous of the Quraysh. Muhammad thought it to be possible, by appealing to their tribal pride as well as conscience, to enlist them on the side of Islam against the people of Mecca. He was, however, advised to seek protection elsewhere. Then he met other influential men of the city during his ten days' stay there. Ultimately, failing to receive positive response from them, 'he solicited only one favour; that they would not divulge the object of his visit, for he feared on his return the taunts and aggravated hostility of Quraysh. But this, even if it had been possible, the men of At-Taif were little likely to concede.'[11] Not only that he was ignominiously expelled from At-Taif. Muir writes: 'For first few days, perhaps, the common people regarded with awe the prophet who had turned Mecca upside down, and whose preaching probably most of them had heard at some of the neighbouring fairs or at the yearly pilgrimage. But the neglect manifested by their chiefs, and the disproportion to outward eye between the magnitude of the prophet's claim and his present solitary helpless condition, turned fear into contempt. Stirred up to hasten the departure of the unwelcome visitor, the people hooted him through the streets, pelted him with stones, and at last obliged him to flee the city pursued by a relentless rabble. Blood flowed from both his legs; and Zeid, endeavouring to shield him, was wounded in the head. The mob did not desist unless they had chased him two or three miles across the sandy plain to the foot of the surrounding hills. There, wearied and mortified, he took refuge in one of the numerous orchards, and rested under a vine.'[12] Who knew that Muhammad, slightly after a decade, would become the master of At-Ta'if, where he suffered such a humiliation? In this case, Muir rightly observes: "In this the day of his humiliation, little did even his unwavering faith anticipate that in little more than ten years he should stand upon the same spot at the head of a conquering army; and that the great idol of At-Taif, despite the entreaties of its votaries, would be demolished at his command.'[13]

After ouster from At-Ta'if, Muhammad rested at a garden in the outskirts of At-Ta'if, which belonged to two Quraysh, Otba and Sheiba. They watched his flight, and being moved with compassion, sent a tray of grapes for his refreshment. After a little, after being composed and reassured, he prayed movingly to Allah, with the touching petition in which his burdened soul gave vent to its distress:

"O Lord! I make my complaint unto thee of my helplessness and frailty, and my insignificance before mankind. But thou art the Lord of the poor and the feeble, and thou art my Lord. Into whose hands wilt thou abandon me? Into the hands of strangers that beset me round about? Or of the enemy thou hast given at home the mastery over me? If thy wrath be not upon me, I have no concern; but rather thy favour is the more wide unto me. I seek refuge in the light of thy countenance. It is thine to chase away the darkness, and to give peace both for this world and the next; let not thy wrath light upon me, nor thine indignation. It is thine to show anger until thou art pleased; and there is none other power nor any resource but in thee."[14]

Stay at Nakhla and Return to Mecca

Fearing the reception at home which, after the failure of his mission at At-Ta'if, might await him, he halted halfway in the vale of Nakhla for few days.. And here, "as he arose at night to prayer, or perhaps in a dream or trance, his excited imagination pictured crowds of Genii pressing forward to hear his exhortations, and ardent to embrace Islam."[15] The Quranic revelation provide romantic scene of the same.[16]

From Nakhla, he went on towards Mecca, but rather than entering the city, he turned aside by a northward path to his ancient haunts on Mount Hira, as he feared to enter the city without a protector, as by now the object of his visit to At-Taif must have been known to the Meccans. From Mount Hira, he sent twice to solicit the guardianship of certain influential chiefs, but failed. Ultimately, he thought of Al Mut'im, one of the persons who had helped to procure the removal of the ban against the Hashims; and then sent word beseeching that he would bring him into the city under his protection. The chief assented; he then summoned his sons, bade them buckle on their armour and take their stand by Ka'ba. Muhammad, on being assured of his guarantee, re-entered Mecca along with Zeid. After they reached Ka'ba, Al-Mut'im stood upright on his camel and called aloud: 'O ye Quraysh! Verily I have given pledge of protection unto Mohammad; wherefore, let not any one amongst you molest him.' After that Mohammad went forward, kissed the cornerstone, and returned to his house guarded by Al-Mut'in and his party.[17]

Prophet Offers Himself to the Tribes

After return of the Prophet from At-Taif to Mecca, 'his people opposed him more bitterly than ever, apart from the few lower class people who believed in him.' He offered himself to the tribes of the Arabs at the fairs, and it was one such occasion that he met the people of Yathrib, which ultimately led to his migration there.[18]

One day, when Abu Abu Jahl saw the Prophet in the Ka'ba, he said, 'This is your prophet, O B. 'Abdu Manaf.' 'Utba, son of Rabi' a replied: 'And why should you take it amiss if we have a prophet or a king?' The Prophet was told of this, or he may have heard it, and he came to them and said, 'O'Utba, you were not angry on Allah's behalf or his apostle's behalf, but on your own account. As for you, O Abu Jahl, a great blow of fate will come upon you so that you will laugh little and weep much; and as for you, O leaders of Quraysh, a great blow of fate will come upon you so that you will experience what you must abhor and that perforce!'[19]

Muslim Converts of Yathrib Pledge to Protect the Prophet

After return from At-Ta'if, Muhammad married Sauda and was betrothed to Ayesha. He used to visit the camps of various Arabian tribes coming for pilgrimage or attending the fairs, and preach Qur'an to them. In one of such meetings, the pilgrims from Yathrib evinced interest in accepting Islam. In the subsequent two annual visits the number of Muslim visitors increased; and they met the Prophet at Al-Aqaba. In the second meeting at Al-Aqaba they pledged protection to him, and invited him to come to Yathrib. Thus, the second pledge of Aqaba, ultimately, led to his migration along with that of his followers to Yathrib.

Muslims Migrate to Medina

The exodus of the Meccans started just after the second Aqaba. Some persons, such as Abdallah, son of Abs al-As'ad, even escaped after the first Aqaba, and he was named the first refugee. The Meccans attempted to stop the migration; they pursued some and brought them back by force or deceit; some, even precluded from access to the new refuge; they fell away and returned to paganism. Omar, Hisham, son of Al'Asi, and 'Ayyash made the arrangement to escape together; Omar and 'Ayyash could get away, but Hisham was detained. 'Ayyash was afterwards lured back. Nu'aim, son of Sallam, was a famous philanthropist; the Meccans feared to lose the advantage of his presence, and therefore, according to one tradition, persuaded him to stay, with the right of holding any religion he chose. 'But the same half-heartedness, which led to the collapse of the Meccan resistance,' Margoliouth observes: 'made most of their measures abortive.' The greater number of the persons, among those who wished to migrate, succeeded in doing so.[20]

Hazleton notes: "At the word from Muhammad, they began to leave for Medina ahead of him, in small groups so as to attract the least attention. But in a city as crowded as Mecca, it was impossible to leave unobserved. Fathers and mothers, brothers and sisters, uncles and aunts and cousins quickly realized what their relatives were planning, and moved to forestall them sometimes by force."[21]

Atomization of the Family

The experience of Umm Salama, who later on married Prophet Muhammad, described by Ibn Ishaq, is worth quoting. It is a case of atomization of family due to the recent developments, and it was not a lone case of its kind. Ibn Ishaq writes: "When Abu Salama had decided to set out for Medina he saddled the camel for me and mounted me on it together with my son Salama who was in my arms. Then he set out leading the camel. When the men of B. al-Mughira b. 'Abdullah b. 'Umar b. Makhzum saw him, they got up and said: 'So far as you are concerned you can do what you like; but what about your wife? Do you suppose that we shall let you take her away?' So they snatched the camel's rope from his hand and took me from him. Abu Salama's family, the B. Abdu'l Asad, were angry at this and said: 'We shall not leave our son with her seeing you have torn her from our tribeman.' So they dragged at my little boy Salama between them and they dislocated his arm, and the B. al-Asad took him away, while B. al-Mughira kept me with them, and my husband Abu Salama went to Medina. Thus I was separated from my husband and my son. I used to go out every morning and sit in the valley weeping continuously until a year or so had passed when one of my cousins of B. al-Mughira passed and saw my plight and took pity on me."[22]

Human Sentiments and Values at Work

But that was not the end of the story. The cousin of Umm Salama went and "He said to his tribesmen, 'Why don't you let this poor women go? You have separated husband, wife and child.' So they said to me, 'You can join your husband if you like;' and then the B. 'Abdu'l Asad restored my son to me. So I saddled my camel and took my son and carried him in my arms. Then I set forth making for my husband in Medina. Not a soul was with me. I thought I could get food from anyone I met on the road until I reached my husband. When I was in Tan'im[23] I met 'Uthman b. Talha b. Abu Talha, brother of B. Abdu'l-Dar, who asked me where I was going and if I was all alone. I told him that except for Allah and my little boy I was alone. He said that I ought not to be left helpless like that and he took hold of my camel's halter and went along with me. Never have I met an Arab more noble than he. When we halted he would make the camel kneel for me and then withdraw; when we reached a stopping place he would lead my camel away, unload it, and tie it to a tree. Then he would go from me and lie down under a tree. When evening came he would bring the camel and saddle it, then go behind me and tell me to ride; and when I was firmly established in the saddle he would come and take the halter and lead it until he brought me to a halt. This he did all the way to Medina."[24]

Ultimately, when Uthman saw a village, where Abu Salama was actually present, he said: 'Your husband is in this village, so enter it with the blessing of Allah.' Then he went off on his way back to Mecca. Umm Salama used to say, 'By Allah, I do not know a family in Islam which suffered what the family of Abu Salama did. Nor have I ever seen a noble man than Uthman, son of Talha.'[25] Her comment certainly needs no elaboration!

The Deserted Houses

As many Muslim converts migrated to Medina, their houses remained locked and deserted. One such house was that of Banu Jahs. When Utba, al-'Abbas and Abu Jahl were passing by it to the upper part of Mecca, Utba looked at it with its doors blowing to and fro, empty of inhabitants; he sighed heavily and said:

> Every house however long its property lasts
> Will one day be overtaken by misfortune and trouble.

He further said: 'The house of B. Jahs has become tenantless.' Then Abu Jahl replied, 'Nobody will weep over that.' He further said pointing towards Abbas: 'This is the work of this man's nephew. He has divided our community, disrupted our affairs, and driven a wedge between us.'[26]

But all the houses were not left locked and undisturbed. There were cases when the deserters' houses were sold by even their relatives, as was the case when Akil[27], the son of Abu Talib, and brother of Ali sold the house of the Prophet and Ali, when they migrated. Margoliouth writes: "Akil, an unconverted son of Abu Talib, seized and sold the dwellings of Mohammad and the other Moslem members of his family; and a similar raid was made on the houses and goods of the other Refugees. For a time the city was to enjoy complete rest."[28]

Prophet Delays Migration

The sagacious Prophet Muhammad delayed migrating to Medina, and waited till the end, though Abu Bakr continued to urge him to do so; the latter cried for joy when at last the former resolved to do so. The Prophet, before leaving Mecca, wanted the faith of the people of Yathrib to be tested before committing himself to them. Margoliouth writes about what he thought: "If they were to receive him, they must first receive his followers. If they welcomed in the name of Allah and his Prophet all those hungry mouths, the Prophet might leave his stronghold and enter into his palace. But even if the people of Yathrib should prove fickle, these Refugees would form a bodyguard of desperate men, of whose loyalty he could be absolutely sure. "When we return," said a Hypocrite at a later time, "the stronger of us shall eject the weaker." The stronger were those who had sacrificed every hope and every conviction to one."[29]

There was yet another reason for delaying migration, and that was his timidity in undertaking the journey, Margoliouth further writes: "The hesitation of Muhammad to migrate to Yathrib may have been in part due to unwillingness to encounter those physical horrors, which though less trying to an Arab than to an European, are not likely to have been underrated; and indeed he hated traveling, and in the Koran couples exile with death. The Prophet was, like many men, timid at the start, courageous when he had the experience."[30]

Though the Prophet had journeyed in Arabia in his early days, but the same was certainly arduous and difficult. Margoliouth quotes what Keane wrote about such journey. "Every yard in that dead barren waste with its constant flitting mirage phantoms, made you feel more dismal and insignificant than an hundred miles into the bright, sparkling, briny ocean: even the Red Sea itself, with a temperature of one hundred degree in the shade, is nothing to the desert for downright misery and helplessness."[31] He also quotes the opinions of Burckhardt, comparing part of the way to Nubian desert, and Burton speaking of the same as "a desert peopled only with sand: a place of death for what little there to die in it: Nature scalped, flayed, discovering all her skeleton to the gazer's eye."[32] But that is certainly an image exaggerating the difficulty, as thousands of people continued to traverse these routes annually for trade and pilgrimage.

The Enemies Plan Prophet's Assassination

Migration of Makkan Muslims and the increasing number of his followers kept the inhabitants of the city worried. They discussed the plan of putting the Prophet to jail or throwing him out of the country. But these plans were not accepted. Ultimately, they agreed on the plan of assassinating him, which forced him to decide to migrate.[33] In the meantime, Mut'im, his protector, was dead. Ibn Ishaq writes that Gabriel warned him about the assassination plan. He wrote: "Then Gabriel came to the apostle and said: 'Do not sleep tonight on the bed on which you usually sleep.' Before much of the night had passed they assembled at his door waiting him to go to sleep so that they might fall upon him. When the apostle saw what they were doing he told Ali to lie on his bed and to wrap himself in his Hadrani mantle; for no harm will befall him. He himself used to sleep in this mantle."[34]

When the Prophet decided to migrate, he visited Abu Bakr at unusual time to inform him about the same. He used to visit Abu Bakr's house every day either in the early morning or in night, but that day, when Allah permitted him to migrate, he visited him at noon. Abu Bakr was overjoyed and wept when he heard that he was also permitted to accompany the Prophet.[35] The Qur'an said about the scheming of the disbelievers: "Remember (Prophet) when the disbelievers plotted to take you captive, kill, or expel you. They schemed and so did Allah. He is the best of schemers."[36] The Qur'an further said: "By the grace of your Lord (Prophet) you are neither oracle nor madman. If they say, 'He is only a poet: we shall await his fate,' say 'Wait if you wish; I too am waiting'—"[37] They were permitted to migrate after that.

The information about what Quraysh planned and wanted to do, was brought to them by Abdallah, son of Abu Bakr. He, possessing some talent for espionage, managed to be present at their deliberations. The enemies 'met in their Senate-house, and bethought them of one plan after another; and the final issue was that Muhammad should be assassinated, every tribe in Mecca sending a representative to take part in the murder. Muhammad's tribe too weak to demand blood-vengeance from all the other tribes would have to accept blood-money, which would be easily paid, perhaps even readily received."[38] As the Prophet was quickly apprised of the development, the measures were taken to outwit them. When the assassins reached his house to execute their plan, they found Ali sleeping on his bed. He had already escaped from a window in the back of Abu Bakr's house. Abu Bakr accompanied him with his possession of five thousand dirhems.

The remarks of Margoliouth on these developments provides an insight on the way the Quraysh acted under such situation. He wrote: "Arabia would have remained pagan had there been a man in Mecca who could strike a blow; who would act, and be ready to accept the responsibility for acting. But many as were Muhammad's ill-wishers, there was not one of them who had this sort of courage; and, as has been seen, there was no magistracy by which he could be tried." And again, his remark about leaving Ali free. He writes: "The son-in-law, Ali, was sleeping in Muhammad's blanket, and would have served for a hostage.

But the Kurashites were too chivalrous to take so mean an advantage of their foe. They satisfied themselves with offering a reward of one hundred camels for the heads of the Prophet and Abu Bakr, and employing professional trackers to follow their trail."[39]

The Prophet Migrating to Medina

Before leaving Mecca, Prophet Muhammad and Abu Bakr planned about the escape route and the strategy properly. As Yathrib was located towards the north of Mecca, they thought wisely that the search party shall ordinarily move towards the direction of that town. Therefore, they moved towards the south to a cave in the mountain called Thaur in the region called Mafjar. "Few of the Meccans were cunning enough to search for him in the direction which was opposite to that in which Yathrib lay, or if they searched, they failed to find the hiding place, though one Kurz, son of 'Alkamah, professed afterwards to have followed the Prophet's trail as far as the cave.[40] Again, only a few trusted persons, which included 'Amir, son of Fuhayrah, freedman of Abu Bakr, and an early convert, and another one, the guide, who knew the way from Mecca to Yathrib, were admitted to the secret. Amir, whose conversion had won him his liberty, had served in Abu Bakr's household, and had presently shared his employer's camel in the flight. Visiting the cave at evening, he undertook the difficult task of providing the fugitives with food. The guide, a pagan called Abdallah, son of Arkat, kept the camels procured for the journey, and brought them to the cave at the appointed time.[41] During their stay in the cave, Abdalla used to bring intelligence, and Asma used to bring food during the night. They stayed for three days in the cave. When the Quraish could not locate them then they offered a hundred she-camels to anyone who would bring the apostle back. A person tried to use the divined arrows and pursue them, but failed.[42]

In the cave, as the Qur'an says, the Prophet comforted Abu Bakr, and assured him of the Allah's help. The Qur'an says: "Even if you do not help the Prophet, Allah helped him when the disbelievers drove him out: when two of them were in the cave, he (Muhammad) said to his companion, 'Do not worry, Allah is with us,' and Allah sent His calm down to him, aided him with forces invisible to you, and brought down the disbelievers' plan. Allah's plan is higher: Allah is almighty and wise."[43]

On the third day of the search, "when the bounty hunters had widened their rearch and reached Mount Thaur, thousands of spiders appeared from nowhere and spun a thick maze of webs across the cave entrance. Seeing the dense network of filaments, the searchers concluded that no body had entered that cave in years, and passed on by leaving us with the image of Muhammad and Abu-Bakr hidden by grossamer threads, nature itself conspiring to protect them.[44]

Ibn Ishaq quotes the statement of Asma, the daughter of Abu Bakr, about what Abu Jahl did when he came to their house to enquire about Abu Bakr's whereabouts. She said: 'When the apostle and Abu Bakr had gone, a number of Quraysh including Abu Jahl came and stood at the door. When I went out to them they asked where my father was and when I said that I did not know Abu Jahl, who was a rough dissolute man, slapped my face so violently that my earring flew off, Then they took themselves off and we remained for three days without news ...'"[45]

When the search was relaxed, they moved out, first taking the direction of south, then west and lastly to the north towards Medina. The path chosen for journey to Medina was difficult and unfrequented one. Margoliouth writes that "Those who have accomplished this journey once only do not make light of its difficulties and terrors. Part of it lies over bare rocks, through narrow ravines; part over a great glaring plain." He further writes: "The road followed by the guide appears to have been not quite identical with any of the four mentioned by the Burton. The first two days' journey brought them near Usfan, thirty-six miles from Mecca; this is at the extreme edge of the hills, and apparently retained its name as late as Burckhardt's time. Of the rest of the names that figure in the narrative of the Prophet's flight few would seem to be known to European travelers. The guide intentionally followed bye-paths, only occasionally crossing the ordinary route."[46] The camel of the Prophet broke down after reaching 'Arj in the land of Aslam (meaning 'safest; taken to be good omen by the Prophet), a branch of Khuza'ah tribe, who remembered that they had been ousted from the privileges by the Quraysh. A person of the family, with whom a daughter of Abu Bakr was being nursed, supplied him the camel, and also a guide acquainted with a short cut to Medina over the difficult Rakubah. Incidently, it needs mention that in Rakubah, the Prophet succeeded in pressing a couple of robbers into his service; and he reconciliated Aslam tribe as the first step towards the recovery of Mecca.[47]

They reached Kuba, near Medina, on Monday, the 8th of Rabi'I of the year 1 AH, corresponding to September 20 of the year 622 AD, and decided to stay there till Ali joins them. Moreover, he wanted to ascertain the truth about the welcome he was to receive. Anyway, Ali arrived on Thursday, and he departed for nearby Medina on Friday, September 24, 622 AD. He performed the service in the way. Friday, as a Muslim sacred day, was, however, declared later on at the suggestion of a Medenese after the relations with the Jews deteriorated. During his passing through Medina, each tribe desired the honour of his presence and stay with him. He, however, allowed his camel to move on, and alighted where it stopped. Thus, he allowed his camel to choose the site; and it was that place where the future mosque and his residence was made. The Prophet, anyway, accepted temporary hospitality till his own house was built. According to a tradition, five hundred of the helpers came out to meet him, and an Abyssinian war dance was got up by way of welcome.[48]

The Prophet, during his early days in Medina, lived cautiously. Margoliouth writes: "We know that he was at first unable to sleep at night owing to his alarm, and could only close his eyes when he found that some of his faithful adherents from Mecca were mounting guard. The terror of the attempted assassination and of the days and nights in the cave were still on him. And he was aware also that one of his new adherents, Naufal', son of Al-Mu'alla, had been murdered before his arrival in consequence of the blood-feud.[49]

Suffering at Medina

The Muslim emigrants from Mecca suffered in Medina due to
(i) extreme poverty, about which we have discussed in the book, and (ii) fever, as Medina was the most fever-infested place at that time. Ibn Ishaq quotes Ayesha's statement, conveyed by Hisham and others, about the fever-infested companions of the Prophet: "When his apostle came to Medina it was the most fever-infested land on earth, and his companions suffered severely from it, though God kept it from His apostle. 'Amir b. Fuhayra and Bilal, freedman of Abu Bakr, were with him in one house when the fever attacked them, and I came in to visit them, for veil had not then been ordered for us. Only God knows how much they suffered from the fever. I came to my father and asked him how he fared and he said:

"Any man may be greeted by his family in the morning
While death was nearer than the thong of his sandal."

I thought that my father did not know what he was saying. Then I went to 'Amir and asked how he was and he said:

"I have experienced death before actually tasting it:
The coward's death comes upon him as he sits.
Every man resists it with all his might
Like the ox who protects his body with his horns.

On being asked Bilal also gave similar answer. The apostle, on her query, remarked that "they were delirious and out of their minds with a high temperature." He, then said: "O God, make Medina as dear to us as Mecca and even dearer!

And bless to us its food, and carry its fever to Mahya'a."[50] Incidentally, it needs mention that Mahya'a was once a large village with a pulpit on the road from Medina to Mecca about four stages distant from the latter. It was the rendezvous of the Egyptians and Syrians if they wished to avoid Medina."[51] The fever made the emigrants so weak that they could not stand during the prayer, on which Muhammad said: "Know that prayer of the sitter is only half as valuable as the prayer of the stander,' after which 'they painfully struggled to their feet despite their weakness and sickness, seeking a blessing.'[52]

Changing Social Scenario After *Hijr*

The social scenario of Yathrib considerably changed after the migration of Prophet Muhammad. The relationship between the Aus and Khazraj got normalized, especially among the Muslim converts. It, however, needed stabilization. Here, an incident, described by Ibn Ishaq, needs mention. Shas, son of Qays, 'an old man hardened in unbelief and most bitter against the Muslims' and exceedingly 'envious of them' passed by a number of the apostle's companions from Aus and Khazraj in a meeting while they were talking together. When he saw their amity and unity and their happy relations in Islam after their enmity in pagaṇ times he was filled with rage and said: "The chiefs of B. Qayla in this country having united there will be no firm place for us with them." So he gave orders to a Jewish youth who was with them to go to them and sit with them and mention the battle of Bu'ath and the preceding events, and recite to them some of the poetry composed by each side.[53] As the youth did so, 'the people began to talk and to quarrel and to boast until two men of the two clans leapt up. … They began to hold forth against each other until one of them said: 'If you wish we will do the same again.' Thereupon both sides became enraged and said: 'We will. Your meeting place is outside—that being the volcanic tract—To arms! To arms!' So out they went and when the news reached the apostle, he went out with such of the emigrants as were with him and said to them: 'O Muslims, remember Allah. Remember Allah. Will you act as pagans while I am with you after Allah has guided you to Islam and honoured you thereby and made a clean break with paganism; delivered you thereby from unbelief; made you friends thereby?' Then the people realized that the dissension was due to Satan and the guile of their enemy. They wept and people of Aus and Khazraj embraced one another. Then they went off with the apostle, attentive and obedient, Allah having quenched the guile of the enemy of Allah Shas, son of Qays.[54]

Forbidding Friendship with the Jews

Some Muslims remained friends of the Jews due to tie of mutual protection and alliance subsisting between them. Even Prophet Muhammad had treaty with the Jews of Medina. But such friendship was forbidden very soon.[55] Ibn Ishaq cites the Qur'anic revelation forbidding such friendship; it reads: "O you who believe, do not chose those outside your community as intimate friends. They will spare no pains to corrupt you longing for your ruin. From their mouths hatred has already shown itself and what their breasts conceal is greater. We have made the signs plain to you if you will understand. Behold you love them but they love not you and you believe in the book—all of it."[56]

The deteriorating relationship between the Prophet and the Jews ultimately resulted into the ouster of the latter from Medina and their destruction. The economic condition of the migrants improved. They did not remain dependent on the Ansars for their livelihood. The frequent raids and wars ultimately brought entire Arabia under the Muslim rule. In the aftermath of the same a vast Islamic Empire was established within a century. The Arab economy registered enormous growth, which was mainly based on spoils of war, and not on productive activities, and trade and commerce. All these developments have been discussed elsewhere in detail in the book.

References

1. Ibn Ishaq, *Sirat Rasul Allah*, p. 191. (Hereafter, Ibn Ishaq).
2. Ibid, pp. 191-92.
3. Ibid, p. 192.
4. Muir, *The Life of Mahomet*; p. 106 hereafter Muir.
5. Ibid.
6. Lesley Hazleton, *The First Muslim*, pp. 136-37. (Hereafter, Hazleton).
7. Muir, pp. 106-107.
8. Qur'an, Sura 111.
9. Hazleton, p.137.
10. Ibn Ishaq, p. 191.
11. Muir, p. 109.
12. Ibid.
13. Ibid, pp. 109-110.
14. Ibid, p. 110; quotes At-Tabari.
15. Ibid, pp. 110-11.
16. Qur'an 46:28ff; 72:1ff.
17. Muir, p. 112.
18. Ibn Ishaq, p. 194.

19. Ibid.
20. Margoliouth, *Mohammed and the Rise of Islam*, p. 205; hereafter Margoliouth.
21. Hazleton, p. 157.
22. Ibn Ishaq, pp. 213-14.
23. Tan'im is a place two parasangs, i.e. six miles away from Mecca.
24. Ibn Ishaq, p. 214.
25. Ibid.
26. Ibid, pp. 214-15.
27. Also written 'Akil, 'Aqil.
28. Margoliouth, p. 212.
29. Ibid, p. 206.
30. Ibid, p. 210.
31. Ibid.
32. Ibid.
33. Ibn Ishaq, pp. 221-22.
34. Ibid, p. 222.
35. Ibid.
36. Qur'an, 8:30.
37. Qur'an 52:29-31.
38. Margoliouth, p. 207.
39. Ibid, pp. 207-208.
40. Ibid, p. 208.
41. Ibid, pp. 208-209.
42. Ibn Ishaq, pp. 223-36.
43. Qur'an 9:40.
44. Hazleton, p. 163; refers Ibn Ishaq's observation.
45. Ibn Ishaq, pp. 224-25.
46. Margoliouth, pp. 209-11.
47. Ibid, p. 211.
48. Ibid, pp. 213-14.
49. Ibid, p. 214.
50. Ibn Ishaq, pp. 279-80.
51. Ibid, p. 280, note 2.
52. Ibid, p. 280.
53. Ibid, p. 261.
54. Ibid, p. 262.
55. Ibid.
56. Qur'an 3.114.

Poverty to Riches

Muslims Migrants in Utter Poverty

The Muslim migrants (*Muhajirun*, Refugees, muhajirs; *Muhajir*, singular) from Mecca to Yathrib (old name of Medina) suffered due to extreme poverty. Even the Prophet, after few months at Medina, found himself at the end of his resources. The extreme poverty forced him to be parsimonious to the extent that when, seven months after his arrival at Medina, he married Ayesha, there was no wedding feast. Abu Bakr, his father-in-law, provided the bridegroom with the indispensable gift to the bride. There were no helpers (*Ansars* in Arabic, Muslim converts of Medina; this word is also used in Qur'an for twelve apostles of Jesus) to receive fresh arrivals of refugees from Mecca, as happened in the case of Mikdad, son of Amr. Many of the refugees found themselves without shelter, sufficient clothing for decency and food; their only shelter was the mosque. Thus, not only the refugees from Mecca, but even, the Prophet himself, and his family members, suffered due to extreme poverty.[1]

Straitened Means of Prophet Muhammad

Muir, based on many traditions, has also described the straitened means of Prophet Muhammad at Medina. He writes: "Fatima once brought Muhammad a piece of bread; it was the first that has passed his lips for three days. 'A'isha tells us that for months together Muhammad did not get a full meal. 'Months used to pass,' she says again, 'and no fire would be lighted in Muhammad's house either for baking bread or cooking meal. *How, then, did ye live?* By the "two black things (dates and water), and by what the citizens used to send unto us; the Lord requite them! Such of them as had milch cattle would send us a little milk. The Prophet never enjoyed the luxury of two kinds of food the same day; if he had flesh there was nothing else; and so if he had dates; so likewise if he had bread. We possessed no sieves, but used to bruise the grain and blow off the husk. One night Abu Bekr sent Muhammad the leg of a kid. 'A'isha held it while the Prophet cut off a piece for himself in the dark: and in his turn the Prophet held it while 'A'isha cut off a piece for herself. *"What,"* exclaimed the listener, *"and ye ate without a lamp!"* "Yea," replied 'A'isha; "had we possessed oil for a lamp, think ye not that we should have lighted it for our food?""[2]

Muir further writes about the scarcity situation based on Abu Hureira's explanation. He writes: "Abu Hureira explains the scarcity thus: 'It arose,' he says, 'from the great number of Muhammad's visitors and guests; for he never sat down to food but there were some followers with him. Even the conquest of Kheibar did not put an end to the scarcity; because Medina has an intractable soil, which is ordinarily cultivated for dates only, the staple food of its inhabitants. There did not exist in the country means of support sufficient for the greatly increased population. Its fruits are the commonest products of the soil, which want little water; and such water as was needed the people used to carry on their backs, for in these days they had few camels. One year, moreover, a disease (pre-mature shedding) smote the palms, and the harvest failed. It is true that a dish used to be sent for the Prophet's table from the house of Sa'd ibn 'Obada, every day until his death, and also in the same manner by other Citizens; and the Refugees used to aid likewise; but the claims upon the Prophet increased greatly, from the number of his wives and dependents.'"[3]

Muir, basing on several other stories, further observes: "I have repeatedly noticed these stories, and have attributed them to the frugal habits of Muhammad compared with the sudden growth of wealth and splendour in the Caliphate. The products of the surrounding country were, no doubt, at first inadequate to the wants of the great numbers who flocked with Muhammad to Medina. But it is evident that although Muhammad, in the early years of the *Hijr*, may have been reduced to common fare; he could hardly have ever suffered *want*, especially with so many devoted followers about him. It is the vivid contrast between the 'luxury prevalent in the days when tradition was growing up, and the simple life of Muhammad, which mainly gave rise to these ideas. Thus 'Abd ar-Rahman, when in after years he used to fare sumptuously on fine bread and every variety of meats, would weep while looking at his richly furnished table, thinking of the Prophet's straitened fare. Another upbraids his comrade who could not live without bread made of the finest flour: 'What!' said he; 'the Prophet of the Lord, to the last hour of his life, never had two full meals on the same day, of bread and of oil; and behold, thou and thy fellows vainly luxuriate on the delicacies of this life, as if ye were children!'"[4]

Extreme Poverty of the Migrants

Several *ahadis* throw light on the poor condition of the emigrants. They were so poor that they even lacked cloth to cover adequately their nakedness. Earlier, the women were allowed to go to the mosque for prayer; but, they were told not to precede men in lifting their heads from prostration.[5] This was, as the note explaining the process indicates, to give the poor men time to adjust their clothes before the women raised their heads. The translator of the Hadis, *Sahih Muslim*, explains that the *Hadis* relates to a period when the Companions of the prophet were very poor and could not afford proper clothing.[6] In yet other Hadis, Utba tells, "I was seventh amongst seven who had been with Allah's messenger and we had nothing to eat but the leaves of the tree. … We found a sheet which we tore in two and divided between myself and Sa'd b. Malik. I made the lower garment with half of it and so did Sa'd. … and today there is none amongst us who has not become the governor of a city."[7]

During the massacre of the Jews of Banu Quraiza, a Jew, named Huyayy, was brought out for execution with his hands bound to his neck with a rope. He was wearing a flowered robe, in which he had made holes about the size of the finger-tips in every part so that it should not be taken from him as spoil.[8] Although he had come in a shirt so torn and tattered that it was not worth taking as a spoil, but he had still the fear of the same. And, therefore, before dying, he said to his executioner 'Ali: I beseech thee not to take off my robe from my body"[9] This illustrates, apart from other facts, as to how poor were the executioners that they even took torn and tattered cloths covering the dead bodies, as booty, and thereby forcing a Jew to be executed to go in tatters so that his dress shall not be removed.

Casual and private generosity was failing; the Prophet lacked source of revenue. But he fully shared the misery of his followers; he refused to employ the alms for his private needs. As Ayesha, wife of the Prophet, stated, months used to pass without fire being lighted in their house;[10] dates and water was their food; Fatima, his daughter, was stunted; she used to complain about her misery after her marriage. Often, the Prophet starved; but occasionally, charitable persons invited him, seeing his face pinched with hunger. Sometimes, presents of food were sent to him, which he shared with the "people of the Shade," the homeless Muslims, compelled to seek refuge in the Mosque.[11]

Under such situation, the Prophet had to teach them that what was enough for two was enough for three or even for four; one date per day, eked out with some of the herbs on which camels browse, counted as a man's ration. To get rid of the difficulty, an arrangement had been, originally, made that the Refugees should assist the Helpers in their field work, but the former knew nothing about the palmiculture, and thus could perform only the most menial services; some of them literally hewed wood and drew water; some others were employed in watering palms, carrying skins on their backs.

Hard Labour at Medina

The first year at Medina was a very difficult one for the Refugees; they had to put hard labour for sustenance. As Lesley Hazleton writes: "They were city people, their muscles new to the demands of physical labour. They knew little about construction or agriculture, and had to learn the hard way."[12] Moreover, "many of them struggled with sickness, their resistance worn down by sheer physical exhaustion. It is one thing to bravely break old ties and commit oneself to a new way of being, but quite another to actually live that new life on a day-to-day basis, dealing with it in literally down-to-earth terms."[13] Here, it needs mention that the Refugees, although they worked harder, but even that did not bring enough for sustenance. Ali, at least on one occasion, earned sixteen dates by filling buckets with water, and emptying them over mould for brick-making at a rate of a date a bucket. Evidently, it was hardly enough for the meal, he shared with the Prophet.[14] One day, when Ali worked as a labour with brick-workers and came to Muhammad with his body full of dust, Muhammad jokingly called him 'Abu-Torab' i.e., 'father of dust.' For Muir, it was an instance of the pleasantry in which the prophet indulged sometimes; but, in reality, it was a case illustrating that the Refugees were forced to do any available petty job due to utter poverty. Muir writes:

"An instance of the pleasantry in which the Prophet sometimes indulged is here recorded. 'Ali had fallen asleep on the dusty ground under the shade of a palm-grove. Muhammad espied him lying thus, all soiled with the dust, and, pushing him with the foot, called out, 'Ho! Abu Torab! (*Father of dust*) is it thou? Abu Torab, sit up!' Ali, half-ashamed, sat up; and the sobriquet ever after clung to him."[15]

Refugees Performing Petty Jobs for Sustenance

The Refugees, under trying situation of extreme poverty did whatever work was available for them. Some of them adopted retail trade for livelihood; Abu Bakr sold clothes in the Market; Othman, son of 'Affan, became a fruiter buying dates of the Banu Kainuka (Qaynuqa), a Jewish community of Medina, and selling them at a higher price; Abd al-Rahman, son of 'Auf, set up as a milkman; Omar spent much time bargaining in the market. Others got the name of "the hucksters," Muhammad altered the name to "the Merchants." Ali and Omar also tried to carry on foreign trade. But these measures did not bring an end to their sufferings; the grinding poverty continued to haunt them; they remained, some how, starved, naked and frozen. Moreover, the date-growing industry had been severely hit that year, producing artificial scarcity at a time, when plenty was specially required. This was caused due to Prophet's order forbidding artificial fertilization, and prohibiting loans on the security of the prospective produce. At one stage, Abu-Bakr, driven by poverty, went to a Jew, asking for loan, saying, 'lend Allah money'.

New Fraternity: The Brotherhood Ties Between *Ansars* and *Muhajirs*

Prophet Muhammad, in order to raise the spirit of his home-sick and suffering followers from Mecca, the *muhajirs*, and to draw them into nearer relations with the *ansars*, established the new fraternity between them. 'Become brethren every two and two of you', he said, and set the example by taking 'Ali, or according to other tradition, 'Othman, for his brother. According to the same, each of the refugees selected one of the Citizens as his brother; about forty to fifty refugees were thus united to as many Citizens of Medina. This bond, as Muir writes, 'was of the closest description, and involved not only a special devotion to each other's interests in the persons thus associated, but in case of death the 'brother' inherited the property of the deceased. Abd ar-Rahman of Mecca, on his first arrival at Medina, was lodged by Sa'd ibn ar-Rabi (Sa'd, son of ar-Rabi), a convert of Medina, to whom Muhammad had united him in brotherhood. As they sat at meal, Sa'd addressed Abd ar-Rahman: 'My brother! I have abundance of wealth; I will divide with thee a portion. And behold my two wives! Choose which of them thou likest best, and I will divorce her that thou mayest take her to thyself to wife.' And 'Abd ar-Rahman replied: 'The Lord bless thee, my brother, in thy family and in thy property!' So he married one of the wives of Sa'd. When Muhammad met him with the nuptial attire of saffron, he asked: 'How is this?' 'I have married me a wife from amongst the people of Medina,' replied Abd ar-Rahman. 'For what dower?' 'For a small gold piece the size of a small date stone,' was the reply. 'And why not a goat?' said Muhammad. This incident shows at once the familiar and friendly footing on which, at least, some of the strangers were received by the Citizens; it also shows of their manners of life, as well as poor economic status of the Refugees. 'This peculiar custom lasted only for about a year and a half, when Muhammad, finding it after the victory of Badr to be no longer necessary for the encouragement of his followers, and probably attended with some inconvenience and unpopularity as overriding the ties of nature, abolished the bond and suffered inheritance to take its usual course.'[16]

Alms to the Poor

The Prophet also wanted rich people to share their wealth. The institution of *Zakat* (poor-tax) was developed. Keeping the same in mind, the Prophet warned Abd ar-Rahman against his penuriousness: 'Oh son of 'Auf! Verily thou art amongst the rich, and thou shalt not enter paradise but with great difficulty. Lend therefore to thy lord, so that He may loosen thy steps.' And he departed by Muhammad's advice to give away all his property. But the Prophet sent for him again, and told him by Gabriel's desire that it would suffice if he used hospitality and gave alms.[17] Of course, giving alms to the poor, later on payment of poor-tax (*zakat*), became only possible when Muslims became rich after adopting the profession of sword.

Need of New Sources of Revenue

Due to poverty, there was need of new sources of revenue,[18] and it was the 'profession by sword,' which Muhammad decided to choose. Raiding expeditions were organized; many failed; but, as Margoliouth notes, 'even the failures impressed on the Refugees the necessity of earning their livelihood by sword.'[19]

Livelihood by Sword

The main source of livelihood of the Companions of Muhammad, after the Prophet established himself in Medina, became loot from raids on non-Muslim tribes. The booty, at times used to be enormous. As for example, the booty in a single raid, the raid on Hawazin, included 24,000 camels, 40,000 sheep and goats, and 4,000 ounces of silver, apart from 6,000 prisoners, who were either to be ransomed or sold as slaves.[20]

As discussed, it needs mention that the spoils of war were made lawful in Islam.[21]

Prophet's Share in Booty

The Prophet's share was a fifth of all the spoils taken from the enemy. Apart from that, he also had the first choice in everything, including slaves, or women or property. The spoils obtained without a battle went entirely to him, and none received a share in the same. This happened in case of the properties of the Banu Nazir (Banu Nazir), an exiled Jewish tribe of Medina, confiscated by Muhammad. The Prophet distributed some of them among his Quraysh followers, but kept a large part for himself; the *ansars* were not given any part of the same. Muhammad turned one plot of land from the confiscated properties into "summer garden of Mary," his Coptic slave-wife. Muhammad also had seven other gardens in Medina. This property, according to one source, was bestowed on him by a Jew named Mukhayriq; according to others, however, it was a portion of the confiscated estates of Banu Nazir. The Prophet had also the properties at Kheibar, as part of the spoils that accrued to him when the Jewish community of that place was defeated.[22]

The above mentioned facts clearly indicate that Muhammad and his family suffered due to poverty and resource-crunch at Medina, only for a brief period. After rapid flow of booty started, he had more than enough to support his family, as well to use the remaining resources for the purchase of men, horses and the weapons for furthering the cause of *Jihad*. Umar said: "The properties abandoned by Banu Nazir were the ones which Allah bestowed upon His Apostle for which no expedition was taken either with cavalry or camel. These properties were particularly meant for the Holy Prophet. He would meet the annual expenditure of his family from the income thereof, and would spend what remained for purchasing horses and weapons as preparation for *Jihad*."[23]

Emigrants Becoming Rich enough

Regular flow of war spoils made the emigrants rich enough not only to live comfortably, but even to pay back the *ansars* for their help and gifts.[24] After Muhammad migrated to Medina, "a person placed at his disposal some date-palms, which the Prophet returned after he came back to Medina from Kheibar.[25]

Many Muslims Became Enormously Wealthy

The situation drastically changed after the 'Profession by Sword' was adopted as a novel way of livelihood and revenue generation. As a result, Muslims, both migrants and the helpers, became rich; and some of them became very wealthy. Here, the case of Abd ar-Rahman may be cited, who was very poor when he migrated to Medina, but subsequently became enormously wealthy. As an index of the journey from extreme poverty to newly acquired riches, his case may be cited, who, at his death, 'left gold in such quantities that it was cut with hatchets till the people's hands bled.' He had 1,000 camels, 3,000 sheep and 100 horses. He had issues by sixteen wives, besides children by concubines. Each of his four widows inherited 100,000 dinars.[26] Zubair, Muhammad's cousin and son-in-law of Abu Bakr, embraced Islam at an early age of 15 or 16; he became owner of a thousand slaves, and was the richest man of Arabia at that time. This was partly due to his political connections.[27]

Muslims: The Beneficiaries of the Expanding Islamic Empire

The solid foundations of the Islamic Empire, led by Prophet Muhammad, and its unprecedented growth, brought enormous wealth to Mecca and Medina, of which every Muslim became beneficiary. As "the nascent Muslim state grew into an empire and the tribute poured into the coffers of Medina," the share in the tithes received by every Meccan and Medinan Muslim started growing. It "was only 9 dirhems for the first year and 20 dirhems for the next year" during two years of the Abu bakr's caliphate. "But within two decades everything changed, thanks to the enormous revenue received from the outlying colonial regions in the neighbourhood of the Arabian Peninsula. The *diwan*, or Civil List, established by 'Umar specified that each of Muhammad's widows was to receive 12,000 dirhams a year, each of the more than three hundred veterans of the Battle of Badr, 5,000 dirhams a year, everyone who had converted to Islam before that date, 4,000 dirhams a year, and their children, 2,000 dirhams a year. Every Muslim had a place in this classification. Officers of the Arab occupation armies in the different cantonment areas of the empire received yearly from 6,000 to 9,000 dirhams, and every boy born in these military quarters received from his birth 100 dirhams annually."[28] Thus, every Muslim became a partner, and a beneficiary, in the endeavour of Islamic Empire formation.

References

1. Margoliouth, D.S., *Mohammed and the Rise of Islam*, Reprint, New Delhi (1985); hereafter, Margoliouth; pp. 234-36.
2. Muir, Sir William, *The Life of Mahomet*, Reprint, New Delhi (2002); hereafter, Muir; p. 528.
3. Ibid, pp. 528-29.
4. Ibid, p. 529.
5. *Sahih Muslim*, Kitab Bhawan, New Delhi, 2004; *Hadis* no. 883.
6. *Sahih Muslim*, note 665; Ram Swarup, *Understanding Islam through Hadis*, New Delhi, 2001; hereafter, Ram Swarup; p. 28.
7. *Sahih Muslim, Hadis* no. 7075.
8. Ibn Ishaq, *Sirat Rasul Allah*, English translation by A. Guillaume; Oxford University Press, Karachi, 1996; p. 464; hereafter Ibn Ishaq.
9. Mirkhond, *Rauzat-us-Safa*, vol. II, Part II, p. 476; cited by Ram Swarup, p. 113.
10. *Sahih Muslim, Hadis* no. 7089.
11. Margoliouth, pp. 235-36.

12. Leslie Hazleton, *The First Muslim*, Penguin Group, U.S.A., 2013; hereafter, Hazleton; p. 165.
13. Ibid, pp. 165-66.
14. Ibid.
15. Muir, p. 208; At-Tabari referred.
16. Muir, p. 174; Hazleton, p. 166.
17. Muir, p. 175 note 1.
18. Margoliouth, pp. 234-37, Muir, p. lvi.
19. Margoliouth, p. 239.
20. Muir, p. 417.
21. Qur'an 8:69.
22. Ram Swarup, p. 107.
23. *Sahih Muslim, Hadis* no. 4347.
24. Ibid, *Hadis* no. 4375.
25. Ibid, *Hadis* no. 4376.
26. Muir, p. 175 note 1; p. 347 note 2.
27. Ram Swarup, pp. 177-78; *Sahih Muslim, Hadis* no. 5938.
28. Ram Swarup, p. 27 note; fuller account of the Civil List is given in the *Tarikh Tabari*, Vol. II, pp. 476-477.

Prophet and the Poets

Arabia had the old tradition of poetry writing, and their love of poetry is well-known.[1] Often, there used to be poetical contests, especially where the people of different places gathered. The rivalrous spirit generated during such poetical contests, as happened in the fair of Okaz, when an arrogant poet, vaunting the superiority of his tribe, was struck by an indignant Hawazinite, leading to 'Sacrilegious War' between Kuraysh and Hawazin tribe,[2] often led to conflicts. Nevertheless, Arabia had ample use of the poets.

The tradition of poetry and satire-writing started since remote past. There were many poets, as discussed below during the days of Muhammad. The poets, like Asma, Abu Afak and Ka'b ibn al-Ashraf, composed satires to criticize him The Prophet dealt with them ruthlessly. On the other hand, even he himself employed poets, such as Ka'b ibn Malik, Hasan ibn Sabit and Ka'b ibn Zuhair, who celebrated his prophethood and victories; they denounced his enemies, and wrote satires against them. Muhammad generously rewarded them by giving them money, houses and even slave girls.

Part of War Machinery

The Poets in Arabia were part of the war machinery. Margoliouth writes: "In nomad Arabia; they (poets) were part of the war equipment of the tribe: they defended their own, and damaged hostile tribes, by the employment of a force which was supposed indeed to work mysteriously, but which, in fact, consisted in composing dexterous phrases of a sort that would attract notice, and would consequently be diffused and remembered widely."[3] At least in one case, Ibn Ishaq has written about an appeal being made to a poet to help in war efforts, which the poet declined, as he did not like to work against Prophet Muhammad, who once pardoned him.[4]

A poetic contest, which Prophet Muhammad allowed, took place between the chief orator, Ut arid, and the chief poet, Al-Akra of Banu Tamim tribe on one side, and the poet Hassan, son of Thabit, and orator Thabit, son of Kais, on the side of the Prophet. Hassan was the poet, it needs mention, 'whom Muhammad had taken pains to conciliate after he had been justly punished.' Banu Tamim, though converted to Islam, declined to pay the Alms, and the Prophet, sent a group to quell the insubordination. The group captured considerable number of their men, women and children, and brought them to Medina. As Beni Tamin were already Muslims and allies, Muhammad 'had no hesitation in letting the old fashioned debate commence.' As Margoliouth writes: "The rival poets and orators boasted of the achievements of their respective tribes in fluent phrase and rolling verse. The conclusion however was a foregone one: the Tamim would not have resorted to a verbal contest had they had any intention of fighting; nor would the Prophet have permitted it, except as an act of courtesy."[5]

Muhammad Did Not Like the Poets

There were many poets, including the women poets, who wrote satires against Prophet Muhammad. The poets, as Margoliouth writes, had given the Prophet "considerable trouble."[6] This was perhaps the reason that he did not like the poets, and got many of them assassinated. As a *Hadis* mentions, he once saw a poet reciting a poem at a place called 'Arj. "Catch the Satan," he commanded, and said: "Filling the belly of a person with pus is better than stuffing his brain with poetry."[7]

Muhammad Taunted as Poet

One of the reasons of Muhammad not liking the poets was that he was himself taunted as a poet,[8] and some times as a soothsayer, which he declined, as it detracted him from the dignity of apostleship, the only status he cared to claim.[9] Anyway, the fact remains that he disliked to be called a poet.[10] The Qur'an said about the same: "This is the speech of an honoured Apostle; it is not a speech of a poet nor of a soothsayer."[11]

Muhammad's Utilitarian View of the Poets

The Arabian poets used to write satires about the prevailing situations. They did so about Prophet Muhammad also, who took a utilitarian view of them.[12] As far as the poets, and their relationship with Prophet Muhammad is concerned, they may be of the following three categories:

i. More inconvenient ones, such as Asma, the daughter of Marwan, the centenarian poet Abu Afak, and Kab ibn Ashraf, whom the Prophet had got eliminated, even by the method of assassination.

ii. The poets, such as Ka'b ibn Malik, Hassan ibn Sabit,[13] and Ka'b ibn Zuhair, learnt to behave. The more pliable among them were even employed and honoured by the Prophet.
iii. The poets, like Ibn Zib'ra and Hubayra, fled in all directions after Prophet Muhammad captured Mecca, and killed the poets, who had satirized him.[14]

Dealing with the poets

The poets were very effective voice during seventh century Arabia. Muhammad, however, made the poetic venture very costly as well as rewarding, depending on whether it opposed or favoured him. The words of the Arabian poets were no doubt sharp-edged, but in the changed situation, 'they could also bring sharp edge of a sword in return,' Lesley Hazleton writes: "Being a poet could be equally dangerous. However marginal poets may seem in the twentieth century West, they were the rock stars of seventh century Arabia, and not only because of their famed odes and elegies. The other great form of Arabic poetry was satire: verses laced with vivid and often bawdy puns and double entendres, the more biting the better. But if words could be as sharp-edged as a sword, they could also bring the sharp edge of a sword in return. And this is what exactly happened in Arabia."[15]

Asma Meets Her End

One of the pithiest Arabian wordsmiths was Asma bint Merwan (Asma, daughter of Merwan); she belonged to Aus tribe, a disaffected tribe. Her family, as yet, was pagan, and she did not hide her dislike for Islam. As a poetess, she composed some couplets after the battle of Badr, mentioning 'the folly of receiving and trusting a Stranger, who has risen against his own people, and slain the chief of them in battle.' The following is one of the verses written by her:

Will you be cuckolds
Allowing this stranger to take over your nest?
You put your hopes in him like men greedy for warm barley soup.
Is there no man who will set up and cut off this cuckoo?"[16]

Blaming Islam and its followers, she wrote:

I despise B. Malik and al-Nabit
And 'Auf and B. al-Khazraj.
You obey a stranger, who is none of yours,
Not one of Murad or Madhij.[17]

Do you expect good from him after the killing of your chiefs
Like a hungry man waiting for a cook's broth?
Is there no man of pride who would attack him by surprise
And cut off the hopes of those who expect aught from him?[18]

Hassan b. Thabit, the court-poet of Prophet Muhammad, answered her:

Banu Wa'il and B. Waqif and Khatma
Are inferior to B. al-Khazraj.
When she called for folly woe to her in her weeping,
For death is coming.
She stirred up a man of glorious origin,
Noble in his going out and his coming in,
Before midnight he dyed her in her blood
And incurred no guilt thereby.[19]

Her verses travelled from mouth to mouth, and ultimately reached the Muslims and the Prophet, making them highly offended. Prophet Muhammad, after the Badr, was highly powerful. "Who will rid me of Merwan's daughter?" Muhammad said.[20] Omeir, a blind kinsman, and according to another source, a former husband of Asma, was the one for whom Muhammad's wish was the command; he did the job the same night. He belonged to the same kindred group B. Khatma.[21] It was the first case of assassination in Medina, which took place within a week of the battle of Badr.[22] But, according to Ibn Ishaq, she was killed after Abu Afak, and thus second among the Arabian poets to be killed.[23]

Muir has detailed the incident: "It was a few days after the return of Prophet Muhammad from Badr that this man, in the dead of night, crept into the apartment where Asma with her little ones lay asleep. Feeling stealthily, he removed her suckling babe, and plunged his sword into her breast with such force that it transfixed her to the couch. Next morning, in the Mosque at prayer, Prophet Muhammad, who was aware of the bloody design, said to Omeir: 'Hast thou slain the daughter of Merwan?' 'Yes,' he answered; 'but tell me now, is there cause of apprehension?' 'None,' said Prophet Muhammad; 'a couple of goats will hardly knock their heads together for it.' Then turning to the people assembled in the Mosque, he said: 'If ye desire to see a man that hath assisted the Lord and his Prophet, look ye here!' 'What!' cried Omar, 'the blind Omeir!' 'Nay,' replied the Prophet, 'call him not blind; call him rather '*Omeir the Seeing.*'[24]

In the aftermath of the assassination, three things were observed:

i. The assassin had no apprehension of retaliation; rather he became further bold to threaten the aggrieved party. Muir writes: "As the assassin returned to his home in Upper Medina, he passed the sons of Asma burying their mother; they accused him of the murder, which without compunction he avowed, and added that if they dared to repeat things such as she had uttered he would slay the whole clan of them."

ii. As per the old traditional Arabian social norm one was to expect immediate retaliation from the aggrieved party, and the chain of murders; but the situation in Medina had drastically changed, and such thing was no more possible. There was terror al-around, which became denser after further assassinations.

iii. The bloody threat, as Muir writes, had the desired effect. "Those of the family who had secretly espoused the cause of Prophet Muhammad now openly professed their faith, and the whole tribe soon succumbed before the fierce-determination and growing influence of the Prophet's followers."[25]

The incident has tremendous impact in Medinan society. Muir cites the opinion of Sprenger: "In short, as Sprenger remarks, the only alternative to a hopeless blood-feud was the adoption of Islam."[26]

Tribes of the Assassinated Persons Adopt Islam

Ibn Ishaq has written about the impact of the assassination, thus: "The day after Bint Marwan was killed the men of B. Khatma became Muslims because they saw the power of Islam. Margoliouth also writes that "Tribes of the murdered persons adopted Islam in consequence."[27] Of course, this statement is only true for the pagans, and not for the Jews, who were forced to migrate or were destroyed.

Assassination of Abu Afak

Abu Afak was murdered after a few weeks after that of Asma, for the similar offense, 'by expressed authority of Muhammad.' A Jewish proselyte of more than hundred years of age, he belonged to the Beni 'Amra, but in spite of the change in faith, he still lived with his tribe in Upper Medina.[28] As Ibn Ishaq writes, "He showed his disaffection when the apostle killed al-Harith b. Suwayd b. Samit (b. = *bin* = son of; the Harith, son of Suwayd, son of Samit). He said:

Long have I lived but never have I seen
An assembly or collection of people
More faithful to their undertaking
And their allies when called upon
Than the sons of Qayla when they assembled,[29] Men who overthrew

mountains and never submitted. A rider who came to them split them in two (saying) 'Permitted', 'Forbidden'[30] of all sorts of things. Had you believed in glory or kingship You should have followed Tubba.[31]

Prophet Muhammad, on hearing all these, said, 'Who will deal with this rascal for me?' whereupon Salim b. Umayr went forth and killed him.[32] The murderer was a Muslim convert of the same tribe, 'falling unawares upon the aged man, as he slept in the courtyard outside his house, dispatched him with his sword. The death shriek drew his neighbours to the spot; but though they vowed vengeance against the murderer, he escaped unrecognized."[33]

Impact of the Murder

The impact was the same, as of earlier assassinations. Muir writes about the impact of this murder thus: "These lawless and sanguinary acts alarmed all that party at Medina which still regarded the strangers and the new faith with suspicion and dislike. And above all, terror crept over the hearts of the Jews. There was good reason for it."[34]

Ka'b ibn Ashraf Assassinated

Ka'b, son of Ashraf, a member of the Jewish Nadir tribe, temporarily went to Mecca with fifty other young men after the war of Badr, calling on the Quraysh to take revenge. He wrote:

"For such battles, tears and rain flow in torrents,
The flower of the Quraysh perished around the wells of Badr,
Where so many of noble fame were cut down."[35]

Hassan ibn Thabit, the poet of Prophet Muhammad wrote back:

"Weep on like pup following a little bitch.
God has given satisfaction to our leader
And shamed and cast down those who fought him."[36]

A Muslim woman also wrote in response to Ka'b:

"This slave shows great concern
Weeping over the slain untiringly.
May the eye that weeps over the slain at Badr weep on"[37]

In response to the poem of the Muslim lady, Ka'b wrote:

"Drive off that fool of yours that you may be safe
From the talk that has no sense!
Do you taunt me because I shed tears
For people who loved me sincerely?
As long as I live I shall weep and remember
The merits of people whose glory is in Mecca's houses."[38]

Ka'b, foolishly or bravely came back from Mecca to Medina. Muhammad asked: 'Who will rid me of Ibnu'l-Ashraf?' Muhammad, son of Maslama, said, 'I will deal with him for you, O apostle of God, I will kill him.' Muhammad said, 'Do so if you can.' After that Muhammad b. Maslama returned and waited for three days without food and drink, apart from what was absolutely necessary. When Muhammad was informed about the same, he summoned him, and said, 'All that is incumbent upon you is that you should try.' 'O apostle of God, we shall have to tell lies.' said he. Muhammad answered, 'Say what you like, for you are free in the matter.' Ibn Ishaq has detailed what happened after that.[39] Muir has summarized the incident, which needs to be given in full:

"By the advice of Sa'd, the conspirator chose four other men from the same clan as accomplishes, and, taking them to Muhammad, obtained his sanction to their plan of throwing the victim off his guard by fair words and pretence of unfriendliness to the Prophet's rule. Abu Na'ila, foster brother of Ka'b, being deputed to pave the way, complained to him of the calamities and poverty which the advent of Muhammad had brought upon them, and begged that he would advance corn and dates for the sustenance of himself and a party like-minded with him. Ka'b taken in the snare, demanded security; Abu Na'ila agreed that they should pledge their arms, and appointed a late hour of meeting at the house of Ka'b, when the bargain would be completed. Towards evening, the conspirators assembled at the house of Muhammad. It was a bright moonlight night, and the Prophet accompanied them to the outskirts of the town. As they emerged from the low shrubs of the Muslim burying ground, he bade them god-speed: 'Go!' said he; 'the blessing of Allah be with you, and assistance from on High!' The house of Ka'b was near one of the Jewish suburbs, two or three miles from the city. When they reached it he had retired to rest. Abu Na'ila called aloud for him to come down, and Ka'b started from his couch. His bride (for he had been lately married, and the biographers omit nothing that adds to the heartlessness of the affair) caught him by the skirt, and warned him not to go. 'It is but my brother Abu Na'ila,' he said; and, as he pulled the garment from her, gaily added the verse; 'Shall a warrior be challenged and not respond?' Descending, he was not alarmed to find the party armed, as the weapons were to be left with him in pledge. They wandered along, conversing on the misfortune of Medina, till they reached a waterfall, and upon its banks they proposed to pass some part of the moonlight night. Meanwhile, his foster brother, having thrown his arm around Ka'b, was familiarly drawing his hand through his long locks, and praising their sweet scent, which Ka'b said was that of his bride. Suddenly the traitor seized his hair, and dragging him to the ground, shouted! *'Slay him! Slay the enemy of Allah!'* Drawing their Swords, they fell upon the victim. The wretched man clung so close to his foster brother that he was with difficulty put to death. As he received the fatal wound he uttered a fearful scream, which resounded far and near amongst the strongholds of the Jews, and lights were seen at the windows of the affrighted inhabitants. The assassins, fearful of pursuit, retired in haste, carrying in their arms one of their member who had received two sword-cuts aimed at Ka'b. As they regained the burying ground, they shouted the well-known *takbir*, 'Great is the Lord'; which Muhammad hearing knew that their work had been successfully accomplished. At the gate of the mosque he met them, saying: 'Welcome; for your countenances beam of victory.' 'And thine also, O Prophet,' they exclaimed, as they cast the ghastly head of their victim at their feet. Then Muhammad praised Allah for what had been done and comforted the wounded man."[40] Incidentally, it may be interesting to provide some information about the palace of Ka'b, given in a note in Ibn Ishaq's book. The note says: "A photograph of Ka'b's castle is given in the *Islamic Review*, Sept. 1953, p. 12. There Dr. M. Hamidullah writes: "Towards the south (of Medina) in the eastern lava plain near Wadi Mudhanib, there is a small hillock. On this the walls of the palace of Ka'b Ibn al-Ashraf still stand, about a yard or a yard and a quarter in height, built of stone. Inside the palace there is a well....In front of the palace, on the base of the hillock, there are rims of a big cistern of water, built of lime and divided into several sections, each connected with the other by means of clay pipes.[41]

Poet Ka'b b. Malik wrote about the assassination:

"Of them Kab was left prostrate there
(After his fall al-Nadir were brought low),
Sword in hand we cut him down
By Muhammad's order when he sent secretly by night
Ka'b's brother to go to Ka'b.
He beguiled him and brought him down with guile
Mahmud was trustworthy, bold."[42]

Killing with Guile

In the above quoted poem, Ka'b, son of Malik, writes that the killer 'beguiled him and brought him down with guile.' Benzamin, a Muslim convert from Ka'b's tribe, when asked by Merwan, the Governor of Medina, one day, 'in what manner Ka'b met his death,' said: 'by guile and perfidy.' Incidentally, Mohammad, son of the assassin, Maslama, a very aged man by that time, was also sitting there. Mohammad exclaimed: 'What, O Merwan! could the Prophet of the Lord, thinkest thou, be guilty of perfidy? By the Lord! we did not kill him but command of the Prophet. I swear that no roof, save that of the Mosque shall cover thee and me.' Then turning to Benzamin, he swore that if he had had a sword in his hand, he would have cut off his head. Unfortunate Benzamin could leave his house after that only after ascertaining that Mohammad was out of the way. Unfortunately, Benzamin was caught one day at a funeral; Mohammad seized a bundle of date branches from a woman passing by, and broke every one of them over the face and back of Benzamin. Murmurers against the incidents were thus silenced during early days of Islam.[43] Here, it needs mention that Islam accepts that "War is deceit"[44] and the issue of 'killing with guile' need to be understood in the same framework.

Jews Terrorized

Ibn Ishaq writes about the observation of the assassins on the impact of Ka'b's murder on the Jews: "Our attack on God's enemy cast terror among the Jews, and there was no Jew in Medina who did not fear for his life."[45]

Competitiveness for Killing

When Aus tribe of Medina killed Ka'b b. Ashraf (Ibnu'l Ashraf), the other tribe, Khazraj killed Sallam, son of Huqayq (Sallam b. Huqayq; Ibnu'l Huqayq), another man hostile to Muhammad, with the permission of the latter. This happened as both tribes were in competition to keep them equally useful in the eye of the Prophet.[46] Hassan B. Thabit, the court poet of Muhammad wrote on killing of Ka'b and Sallam, son of Abu'l-Huqayq:

> "What a fine hand you met, O Ibnu'l-Huqayq,
> And you too, Ibnu'l Ashraf,
> Traveling by night with their light swords
> Bold as lion in their jungle lair
> Until they came to you in your quarter
> And made you taste death with their deadly swords,
> Seeking victory for the religion of their prophet
> Counting their lives and wealth as nothing."[47]

Poets Writing Against the Enemies of Islam

Some poets acted as the court poets of Prophet Muhammad. There were poets, such as Hassan ibn Thabit and Ka'b ibn Malik, whose writings, besides illustrating specific facts, exhibiting the spirit of the first Muslims towards their unconverted brethren, were full of biting satire against the enemies of Islam. Hassan's poems throw ample light on 'Battle of the Ditch' and on the 'taking of Mecca;' the poems of Ka'b ibn Malik, on the other hand, throw light on the oath of fealty by the Medina converts at the 'Second pledge of Al-'Akaba and other such incidents.'[48] These poets were also chastised as the occasion demanded. They were, however pliable, and even rewarded by the Prophet.

Ka'b ibn Zuhayr Submits to the Prophet

Ka'b, the son of Zuhayr, was a poet who satirized Prophet Muhammad; his brother Bujayr was a Muslim. The poems given below express the views of the two brothers on religion. Ka'b had said:

"Give Bujayr a message from me;
Do you accept what I said, confound you?
Tell us plainly if you don't accept what I say
For what reason other than that has he led you
To a religion I cannot find his fathers ever held
And you can not find that your father followed?
If you don't accept what I say I shall not grieve
Nor say if you stumble God help you!
Al-Ma'mun[49] has given you a full cup to drink
And added a second draught of the same.[50]

His brother Bujayr said to Ka'b:

"Who will tell Ka'b that that for which you wrongly blame me
Is the better course?
To God alone not al-Uzza and al-Lat
You will escape and be safe while escape is possible,
On a day when none will escape
Except a Muslim pure of heart,
Zuhayr's religion is a thing of naught
And religion of Abu Sulma is forbidden to me.[51]

Bujayr was, however, extremely worried for the safety of his brother Ka'b. He wrote to his brother Ka'b that the apostle had killed some of the men in Mecca who had satirized and insulted him and that the Quraish poets who were left, had fled in all the directions. He advised him: "If you have any use for your life then come quickly to the apostle, for he does not kill anyone who comes to him in repentance. If you do not do that, then get to some safe place."[52]

Ibn Ishaq writes about further development in this case: "When Ka'b received the missive he was deeply distressed and anxious for his life. His enemies in the neighbourhood spread alarming reports about him saying that he was as good as slain. Finding no way out, he wrote his ode in which he praised the apostle and mentioned his fear and slanderous reports of his enemies. Then he set out for Medina and stayed with a man of Juhayna whom he knew, according to my information. He took him to the apostle when he was praying morning prayers, and he prayed with him. The man pointed out the apostle to him and told him to go and ask for his life. He got up and went and sat up by the apostle and placed his hand in his, the apostle not knowing who he was. He said, 'O apostle, Ka'b b. Zuhayr has come to ask security from you as a repentant Muslim. Would you accept him as such if he came to you? When the apostle said that he would, he confessed that he was Ka'b b. Zuhayr." After that, one of the ansars leapt upon him and asked for allowing him to behead the enemy of Allah. But "the apostle told him to let him alone, because he had come repentant breaking away from his past."[53]

To signalize his gratitude, as Muir writes, "Ka'b composed the famous 'Poem of the Mantle,' in which he lauded the generosity and glory of his benefactor." While reciting the poem, he came to the following verse:

> Verily, the Prophet is a light to illuminate the world,
> A naked sword from out of the armory of Allah.

Hearing which, Muhammad, unable to restrain his admiration and delight, threw his mantle from off his shoulders upon Ka'b. This immediately made the poem famous in the Islamic history.[54]

Prophet Permitted Reciting Poetry of Pagan Era

The apostle, according to a tradition, gave permission to recite the poetry of pagan era, except two odes, including ode of Umayya about Badr. Later on, even that was allowed; 'when. Islam was generally accepted and hatred and enmity ceased,' there was no harm in reciting them.'[55] The Ode of Umayya is given below:

> O eye, weep with overflowing tears for Abu'l Harith
> And hold not thy tears for Zama'a
> Weep for 'Aqil b. Aswad, the bold line,
> On the day of battle and dust of war,
> Those Banu Aswad were brothers like Gemini,
> No treachery and no deceit was in them,
> They are the noblest family of Ka'b,
> The very summit of excellence.
> They produced sons as many as the hairs of the head
> And established them in impregnable positions,
> When misfortune visited their kinsmen
> Their hearts eched for them,
> They gave their food when rain failed,
> When all was dry and no cloud could be seen.[56]

This ode expresses sympathy for the enemies of Prophet slain at Badr; at the same time it brings out the positive aspects of Arabian Pagan society, such as distribution of food to the needy during draught and famine.

Notes and References

1. Muir, *The Life of Mahomet*, p. lxxiv n; hereafter, Muir.
2. Ibid, pp. 13-14.
3. Margoliouth, *Mohammed and the Rise of Islam*, pp. 411-12; hereafter Margoliouth.
4. Ibn Ishaq, *The Life of Muhammed*, English translation by Guillaume, p. 370; hereafter, Ibn Ishaq.
5. Margoliouth, pp. 414-15.
6. Ibid, p. 411.
7. *Sahih Muslim, Hadis* 5611; hereafter, Muslim.
8. Muir, pp. 48, 78, 127.
9. Ram Swarup, *Understanding Islam through Hadis*, p. 150; hereafter, Ram Swarup.
10. Muir, p. 175n.
11. Qur'an 69:40-42.
12. Ram Swarup, p. 150.
13. 'Sabit'also written as 'Thabit.'
14. Ram Swarup, pp. 150-51; Ibn Ishaq, pp. 597-98.
15. Lesley Hazleton, *The First Muslim*, p. 194; hereafter Hazleton.
16. Ibid, p. 194.
17. Murad and Madhij were the tribes of Yamani origin.
18. Ibn Ishaq, pp. 675-76.
19. Ibid, p. 676.
20. Ibid.
21. Banu, in short B., is used to denote the ancestorship.
22. Hazleton, pp. 194-95, Margoliouth, p. 278; Muir, p. 239.
23. Ibn Ishaq, p. 675.
24. Muir, pp. 239-40.
25. Ibid, p. 240.
26. Ibid, p. 240.
27. Margoliouth, p. 278.
28. Muir, p. 240, Margo, p. 277.
29. Qayla was the putative ancestor of Aus and Khazraj tribes of Medina.

30. A gibe on the language of Qur'an.
31. Ibn Ishaq, p. 675; Tubba was a king and a man of great reputation, who once attacked Medina. The poet asks: 'if Muhammad, then why not Tubba?'; Note 4 on p. 675.
32. Ibid.
33. Muir, p. 240.
34. Ibid.
35. Ibn Ishaq, pp. 365-66; LH, 195.
36. Ibid, p. 366.
37. Ibid.
38. Ibid.
39. Ibid, pp. 367-69.
40. Muir, pp. 247-48.
41. Ibn Ishaq, p. 368, Note 2.
42. Ibid, pp. 368-69.
43. Muir, pp. 248-49 note 1; this is based on the writings of Ibn Hisham, At-Tabari and Al-Wakidi.
44. *Sahih Muslim, Hadis 4311.*
45. Ibn Ishaq, p. 368.
46. Ibid, p. 482.
47. Ibid, p. 369.
48. Muir, p. lxxv.
49. Ibn Ishaq, p. 598; Ka'b used the title al-Mamun, as Ibn Ishaq informs, "simply for the reason that Quraysh used to name the apostle thus."
50. Ibid, pp. 597-98.
51. Ibid, p. 598.
52. Ibid. p. 597.
53. Ibid, p. 598.
54. Muir, p. 437.
55. Ibn Ishaq, p. 355 note 1.
56. Ibid, p. 355.

Muhammad and the Hypocrites

When Prophet Muhammad migrated to Medina, enmity between Aus and Khazraj communities was suppressed. The number of converts increased; idolatry and skepticism was suppressed; the 'body of unconverted inhabitants were at the first neutral, or at least outwardly passive. There was no active opposition, nor, as at Mecca, any open denial of Muhammad's supernatural claims; neither was his temporal authority over his adherents questioned. The constitution of the society enabled him to exercise absolute and unquestioned control over his own people, without for the present arrogating jurisdiction over others.' Jews were an important sections of the Medinan society, and Muhammad wanted 'to gain the Jews over to his cause.' Therefore, it was natural for him 'to enter into a close and binding union with the Jews, and this he did in a formal manner shortly after reaching Medina.'[1]

In Medina, 'Judaism and Islam came rapidly into antagonism.'[2] Ibn Ishaq has written about the rabbis who accepted Islam hypocritically; there were hypocrites, who were talking against the Prophet, sitting in the mosque, and talking in low voice against him, who were expelled from the mosque, as ordered by the Prophet. As written by Ibn Ishaq, "The first hundred verses of the *sura* of the Cow came down in reference to these Jewish rabbis and the hypocrites of Aus and Khazraj, according to what I have been told, and Allah knows best."[3]

Though Islam spread rapidly in Medina, the real belief in Medina was not equally growing. Muir writes: "Real belief in Muhammad was not, however, always of such rapid growth. Doubts and jealousies possessed the hearts of many; and in private, and at convenient distance, found free expression. They have foolishly espoused an Exile's cause which would make them run the gauntlet of all Arabia; and for what return? Only to lose their liberties, and bring themselves under bondage to a foreign usurper! The class which cherished these sentiments are named Hypocrites in Qur'an. But *hypocrisy* and *disaffection* are, in its vocabulary, nearly synonymous; and as the views of this party developed into political rather than into religious antagonism, it will be more correct to call them the *DISAFFECTED*." [4]

Based on Ibn Ishaq's writings, Ibn Hisham described the situation: 'When Jewish doctors were filled with hatred and envy of Muhammad, because Allah has chosen a prophet from amongst the Arabs, there joined them certain men of the Aus and Khazraj, who were in reality little removed from heathenism and unbelief, only that Islam had by its prevalence overpowered them. So they took the faith outwardly as a shield unto them from death; but in secret they were traitors, and their hearts were with the Jews in their rejection of the Prophet.'[5] Here, it needs mention that Prophet Muhammad took steps to eliminate Jews from Arabia. The poets, who criticized him were also either eliminated or silenced. These have been detailed separately in this book. The Aus and Khazraj hypocrites were gradually made ineffective.

Hypocrites, or *Munafiqin*, as they were called, were the Muslims, who, according to Islamic literature, did not believe in the Islamic faith. Qur'an has referred to the hypocrites twenty- five times, and it has a *Sura*, called *Al-Munafiqin*.[6] Qur'an warns Muhammad about the hypocrites, and warns the hypocrites also to fear from the wrath of Allah. The Qur'an says: "The (hypocrites) wait to see what happens to you and, if Allah brings you success, they say, 'Were we not on your side?' but if the disbelievers have some success, they say to them, 'Did we not have the upper-hand over you, and (yet) protect you from the believers?' … The hypocrites try to deceive Allah, but it is He who causes them to be deceived. …"[7]

According to Qur'an, hypocrites, and rejecters of faith, shall dwell in the hell. It says: "Allah has promised the hypocrites, men and women, and rejecters of Faith, the Fire of Hell; therein shall they dwell. … For them is the curse of Allah and an enduring punishment."[8] The last two *ahadis* of the *Kitab Sifat al-Munafiqin wa Ahkamihim* of *Sahih Muslim* describe those who have neither the support of a faith nor that of the philosophy, and who are subject to the doubts and temptations of ordinary men. Ibn Umar narrates what the Prophet said: "The similitude of a hypocrite is that of a sheep which roams aimlessly between two flocks. She goes to one at one time and to the other at another time."[9]

The name "hypocrite", as Ram Swarup writes, does not derive from any moral category but was applied to people who no longer believed in the prophethood of Muhammad in their hearts but were afraid to admit it openly in public. They were doubtless, skeptics, men of incomplete faith, men who began to entertain questions about the apostleship of Muhammad.[10]

Ibn Ishaq has written about two persons, who were highly respected ones in Medina, before the arrival of Muhammad. Abdullah, son of Ubayy, belonged to Khazraj community. As Ibn Ishaq attested, 'none of his own people contested his authority and Aus and Khazraj never rallied to one person before or after him until Islam came, as they did to him. With him was Abu Amir, who had been an ascetic in pagan days and had worn a coarse hair garment and was called a monk. He belonged to the Aus and that community obeyed him. Abu Amir never accepted Islam. He went to Mecca with his ten followers to get away from Islam and the apostle. After the capture of Mecca, he went to Taif; and, after Taif was captured by apostle, then to Syria, where he died. Apostle said about him: 'Don't call him monk, but the evil-doer.[11] Ibn Ubayy became Muslim after some time.

Prophet Muhammad, while going to see Sa'd during his illness, saw Ibn Ubayy sitting among some of his men; he alighted from the ass, went and met him out of politeness. After sitting a little while, the apostle recited Qur'an, invited him to Allah, admonished and warned him, and preached the good news to him. When the apostle stopped speaking, Ibn Ubbay said, "There would be nothing finer than what you say if it were true. But sit in your own house and if anyone comes, talk to him about it; but don't importune those who do not come to you, and don't come into a man's gathering with talk which he does not like." Prophet Muhammad left him and went to meet Sa'd. When he met Sa'd, his face was showing the emotions raised by Ibn Ubayy. On asking the reason of his angry face, he told Sa'd what Ibn Ubayy told him. Sa'd said: 'Don't be hard on him; for Allah sent you to us when we were making a diadem to crown him, and by Allah he thinks that you have robbed him of a kingdom.'[12]

Abdullah, son of Rawaha, who was sitting with Ibn Ubayy, on hearing what Ibn Ubayy told Muhammad, said to the apostle: "Nay, do come to us with it and come into our gatherings and quarters and houses. For by Allah it is what we love and what Allah has honoured us with, and guided us to." Abdulla b. Ubayy, seeing that his people were opposed to him, said:

> When your friend is your opponent you will always be humiliated
> And your adversaries will overthrow you.
> Can the falcon mount without his wings?
> If his feathers are clipped he falls to the ground.[13]

Ibn Ishaq has cited some cases of the persons, who did not hide their unbelief. Yazid, son of Hatib, "was grievously wounded at the battle of Uhud and was brought to his people's settlement at the point of death. His kinsmen gathered around and the men and women began to say to him, 'Good news of the garden (of paradise), O son of Hatib.' Now Hatib was an old man who had lived long in the heathen period and his hypocrisy appeared then, for he said, 'What good news do you give me? Of a garden of rue?'[14] By Allah, you have robbed this man of his life by your deception (and brought great sorrow for me.' Tab.)[15]

Ibn Ishaq has also written about another person, a stranger of unknown origin called Quzman, who also fought the battle of Uhud, and killed seven or eight polytheists single-handed. He was a stout warrior. Being disabled by wound, he was carried to the quarter of B. Zafar. The Muslims began to say to him, "You have done gallantry, Quzman, be of good cheer!" "Why should I," he said, "I only fought for the honour of my people; but for that I should not have fought." And when pain of his wounds became unbearable he took an arrow from his quiver, (T. cut the veins of his wrist, and bled to death) and killed himself."[16]

Ahadis, narrated by Jabir, gives an account of another such hypocrite. One day, the Prophet declared: "He who climbed this hill, the hill of Murar, his sins would be obliterated." Many availed of the opportunity, and took advantage of this divine amnesty, and "there was a ceaseless flow of persons." All, except owner of a red camel, were pardoned. People went to him and advised him that he should also go and obtain pardon. The man replied: "By Allah, so far I am concerned the finding of something lost is dearer to me than seeking of forgiveness for me by your companion (the Holy Prophet), and he remained busy in finding out his lost thing."[17] The Hadis does not give us his name; According to another tradition, he was Harr, son of Qays, who refused to take the "pledge of the Tree;" he was called a "hypocrite" by the believers. Ram Swarup has likened him to a Zen philosopher; he wrote: "Was he a Zen philosopher who lived one day at a time? Sufficient unto the day is the work of the day. Hereafter will take care of itself."[18]

Abdullah, son of Ubayy, is considered to be the arch-Hypocrite by the Muslims. He was, however, the only Medinan, whom the two warring factions of Aus and Khazraj liked, and wanted to make their king.. "In the crime of murdering the hostages' during the war between Aus and Khazraj, as Margoliouth writes, Abdullah would not participate; he endeavoured to dissuade the others, and sent back the hostages that were deposited with him. From the battle too, he kept aloof—out of conscientious scruples. Hence when the tide of fortune had turned the Khazraj he was able to secure the deliverance of his own fortress."[19] Margoliouth further writes about him, "This arch-Hypocrite" was a man who commanded respect by his talents and virtues—both of them of a sort which is of little use to a statesman, especially in times of trouble and confusion. He disliked bloodshed; he abhorred treachery. His mental powers placed him above all the theological disputants; He cared little for these things. When he tried to interfere in politics he failed through want of practice, of readiness, and of dexterity."[20]

The Sura 'The Hypocrite' declares hypocrites as liars; the hypocrites, the Qur'an says: "use their oaths as a cover and so bar others from Allah's way: what they have been doing is truly evil—because they professed faith and then rejected it, so their hearts have been sealed and they do not understand." Further, Qur'an warns Muhammad, "When you see them (Prophet), their outward appearance pleases you; when they speak, you listen to what they say. But they are like propped-up timber—they think every cry they hear is against them—and they are the enemy. Beware of them. May Allah thwart them! How devious they are..[21] *Sahih Bukhari* includes these in the six aspects of hypocrisy in belief.[22]

But, "was Ibn Ubayy really an enemy? Or even a hypocrite? Lesley Hazleton raises the question, and answers. She writes: "The line between rhetoric and demagoguery is some times a very thin one. To translate *munafiqun* as "hypocrites" is to overload the word, which is better if more clumsily rendered as "those who had reservations or held back." Literally, it means "those who crept into their holes," the way desert voles turn tail in fright and dig deep into the earth. In fact, ibn Ubayy neither lied nor rejected *Islam*. Instead he reserved the right to question Muhammad's political decisions. Far from hiding his true opinion as the word "hypocrite" implies, he spoke out openly in favour of what in modern terms would be called separation of church and state."[23]

She further writes: "The new coinage was a challenge to all those who had accepted *Islam* but did not necessarily accord every statement of Muhammad's the power of divine authority. They distinguished, that is, between the messenger and the politician, and it was this distinction that the Quranic voice seemed to blur. The messenger was fast becoming the prophet, no longer simply "one of you," but to be thought of as divinely directed in every aspect of his life."[24]

Some months after the massacre of Banu Qurayza, Banu Mustaliq, an Arabian tribe inhabiting a region about eight days' march from Medina, were attacked and plundered. While returning with huge booty, a quarrel broke out between an ansar named Sinan and a refugee named Jihja, who was a servant of Umar. Jihja struck Sinan. Both called out men of their own communities; tempers were frayed on both sides, and the quarrel soon spread to others. Ibn Ubayy was angry; he said, 'Have they really done this? They dispute our priority, they outnumber us in our own country, and nothing so fits us and the vagabonds of Quraysh as the ancient saying "Feed a dog and it would devour you." By Allah when we return to Medina the stronger will drive out the weaker.' Then he went to his people who were there and said "This is what you have done to yourself. You have let them occupy your country, and you have divided your property among them. Had you but kept your property from them they would have gone elsewhere.' Zayd, son of Arqam, then a young boy, went to the Prophet and reported the matter to him. Umar, who was with the apostle, said, Tell Abbad, son of Bishr, to go and kill him.' The apostle replied, 'But what if men should say Muhammad kills his own companions? No, but give orders to set off. Although that was not the time when he used to do so, but the men duly moved off."[25]

It is interesting to note what different persons said and did after the incident. After getting the marching order, the apostle 'walked with the men all that day till nightfall, and through the night until the morning and during the following day until the sun distressed them. Then he halted them, and as soon as they touched the ground they fell asleep." According to Ibn Ishaq, 'He did this to distract their minds from what Abdullah b. Ubayy had said the day before.' When Abdullah bin Ubayy heard that Zayd had reported what he said to the apostle, he went to him, swore and said that he had not said so. The opinion of the *ansar* people was favorable to him. Ibn Ishaq writes, 'He (Ibn Ubayy) was a great man among his own people and the Ansar who were present with the apostle said: 'It may well be that the boy was mistaken in what he said, and did not remember the man's words,' sympathizing with Ibn Ubayy and protecting him.[26]

After the apostle began the journey, Usayd, son of Hudayr, met and saluted him, and asked, 'You are traveling at a disagreeable time, a thing you have never done before.' Prophet Muhammad said, 'Have you not heard of what your friend said? He asserted that if he returns to Medina the stronger will drive out the weaker'. Usayd answered, 'But you will drive him out if you want to; he is the weak and you are the strong.' He added, 'Treat him kindly, for Allah brought you to us when his people were stringing beads to make him a crown, and he thinks that you have deprived him of a kingdom.'[27] The Prophet 'accepted the denial' of Ibn Ubayy that time, 'but it rankled in his mind,[28] and later, at a more opportune moment, Allah confirmed it openly in a Quranic verse.[29] In the *sura* which came down, Allah mentioned the disaffected with Ibn Ubayy and those like-minded with him. Then the apostle took hold of Zayd's rear, and said, 'This is he who devoted his ear to Allah." The son of Ibn Ubayy heard it; he came to the apostle and offered to kill his father and bring his head to him. The reason given by him for doing so, and Prophet Muhammad's tolerating Ibn Ubayy earlier, is insightful and worth knowing.

Abdullah, Abdullah b Ubay's son (It is strange that Ibn Ishaq has given the same name to the father and the son.) said to the Prophet: 'I heard that you want to kill Abdullah b. Ubayy for what you have heard about him. If you must do it then order me to do it and I will bring you his head, for al-Khazraj know that they have no man more dutiful to his father than I, and I am afraid that if you order some one else to kill him my soul will not permit me to see his slayer walking among men and I shall kill him, thus killing a believer for an unbeliever, and so I should go to hell.' Prophet Muhammad replied, 'Nay, but let us deal kindly with him and make much of his companionship while he is with us.'[30]

After this incident, 'it happened that if any misfortune befell it was his own people who reproached and upbraided him roughly. Prophet Muhammad came to know of the same and told Umar, 'Now what do you think, Umar? Had I killed him on the day you wanted me to kill him the leading men would have trembled with rage. If I ordered them to kill him today they would kill him.'[31] Umar, who wanted Ibn Ubayy to be killed, confessed the wisdom of the Prophet.[32] The situation gradually changed, it was not possible for Ibn Ubayy to help the Jew allies stay in Medina possible, and to keep the promise, as revealed in the Quran.[33] Nevertheless, the credit goes to Ibn Ubay that he saved the lives of Banu Nadir, and made it possible for them to leave Medina triumphantly.

While ordering Banu Nadir to quit, the Prophet used the term 'my city,' rather than Yathrib or Medina. The political reality of the day was not hidden from anyone; and as Lesley Hazleton writes: "Branding Ibn Ubayy a hypocrite was a political move more than the religious one.[34]

References

1. Muir, Sir William, *The Life of Mahomet*, pp. 180-83; hereafter, Muir.
2. Ibid, p.185.
3. Ibn Ishaq, *Sirat Rasul Allah*, pp. 246-47; hereafter Ibn Ishaq.
4. Muir, p. 182.
5. Ibid, p. 182 note 1; quotes Ibn Hisham, p. 361.
6. Sura 63 of the Qur'an is titled *Al-Munafiqin*.
7. Qur'an 4:141-42.
8. Qur'an 9:68.

9. *Sahih Muslim*, *Hadis* no. 6698.
10. Ram Swarup, *Understanding Islam through Hadis*, p. 233; hereafter Ram Swarup.; Ibn Ishaq, pp. 277-78.
11. Ibn Ishaq, p. 278.
12. Ibid, pp. 278-79.
13. Ibid.
14. The dead were buried with rue at their feet those days in Arabia.
15.. Ibn Ishaq, p. 383.
16. Ibid, pp. 383-84.
17. *Sahih Muslim*, *Hadis* no. 6691.
18. Ram Swarup, p. 242.
19. Margoliouth, *Mohammed and the Rise of Islam*, p. 194; hereafter Margoliouth.
20. Ibid, pp. 201-202.
21. Qur'an, 63:1-4.
22. *Summarised Sahih Al-Bukhari*, p. 1078.9.
23. Lesley Hazleton, *The First Muslim*, pp. 206-207; hereafter, Hazleton.
24. Ibid, p. 207.
25. Ibn Ishaq, pp. 490-91; Muir, pp. 296-97.
26. Ibid, p. 491.
27. Ibid.
28. Ram Swarup, p. 240.
29. Qur'an 63:7,8.
30. Ibn Ishaq, pp. 491-92.
31. Ibid, p. 492; Muir, pp. 297; 297 note 1.
32. Ibn Ishaq, p. 492,
33. Qur'an 59: 11-13.
34. Hazleton, p. 208.

Society, Politics, and Economy

Islamic Identity

Introduction

Islamic Identity formation has taken place at three levels, which are (a) distinct theological conceptualization about (i) God-head, (ii) Prophethood and (iii) Life after death; (b) changes in kinship patterns and the formation of Islamic Ummah, and (c) changes in the externals – the distinct physical look, and social and behavioural pattern. This paper deals with the third aspect of Islamic identity. Other aspects of this matter are discussed elsewhere in the book.

Differences in Physical Look and Behavioural Pattern

When Prophet Muhammad and his Companions migrated to Medina, he directed them to bow towards Jerusalem in their prayers; Jewish festivals and holidays were adopted by them. But this did not continue for long. The Jews refused to become Muslims; Muhammad became powerful enough; there was change of the *Qiblah*, i.e., the Muslims were directed to bow towards Kaaba, rather than towards Jerusalem; enmity between the two communities led to the expulsion of the Jews from Medina and then their destruction. The numerous changes followed, which led to a Muslim identity distinct from that of the Jews, Christians and the Pagans

The distinct Muslim identity, as discussed above was a well-planned phenomenon. It was based on its ideology and its fundamentals; the clear picture of the same emerges after careful study of the Qur'an and the *Hadis*. The Islamic identity formation was a gradual process. On several occasions, when the Prophet came to know about a certain custom or practice – religious or secular – followed by the believers to be identical with that of the infidels, Jews or the Christians, he brought an immediate change in the same. Thus, the Muslim ones became distinct. An attempt was made from the very beginning to see that Muslims not only have different look, but also differ otherwise – in their belief system, way of prayer, social and cultural customs and values from the Pagans, Jews and the Christians.

Residual Pagan Elements

Although Prophet Muhammad brought numerous changes towards distinct Islamic identity formation, it neither happened, nor was it possible to obliterate all the pre-existing Pagan and Semitic beliefs and practices; therefore, much of the Pagan elements survived in the Islamic society, which is discussed elsewhere in the book.

Steps Taken for Distinct Islamic Identity Formation

As stated above, Prophet Muhammad took steps to bring gradual change for the distinct Islamic identity formation by ordering the Muslims to follow his edicts. By which, he ensured that Muslims look differently, differ in dress, behave differently, i.e., they have different mode of behaviour, culture, prayer, etc. from that of the Pagans, Jews and the Christians. Numerous *ahadis* came out with the edict to "Do the opposite of what the Pagans do," or, "Jews and Christians do such things, so do the opposite of what they do," or "Do not do like the Jews." Thus, the criteria on which he based his edicts was to find what the others did, and how they did, and then to prescribe the opposite of those.

Distinct External Appearance

Thc pagans of Arabia, in the days of Muhammad, used to keep their moustaches and cut their beards. The Prophet ordered Muslims to take out the moustaches and grow the beards According to the *Hadis*, the Prophet said: "Do the opposite of what the Pagans do, cut the moustaches short and leave the beard". We find this *Hadis* in both *Sahih Al-Bukhari*[1] and *Sahih Muslim*[2] Another *Hadis* says: "Jews and Christians do not dye their hair so you do the opposite of what they do"[3]

When Abu Quhafa, hundred year old father of Abu Bakr, with his head and beard white like hyssop, met Muhammad, the Prophet said: "Change it with something but avoid black."[4] Abu Huraira reported Prophet as saying: "The Jews and the Christians do not dye (their hair), so oppose them."[5]

A man met Muhammad who used to wear cloth dyed in saffron. Muhammad disapproved it, on which the man wanted to wash it, but Muhammad told him to burn that cloth.[6] The reason: "It is not permissible for a Muslim to wear clothes of yellow colour,"[7] as "these are the clothes usually worn by the non-believers."[8] Here, it needs mention that the Prophet forbade the use of saffron according to *Sahih Bukhari*.[9] According to another *Hadis*, not only clothes, but even hair, should not be dyed in saffron. Silk is also forbidden, which is usually of yellow colour. The *Hadis* says: "Do not wear silk, for one who wears it in this world will not wear it in the Hereafter.[10] The Prophet forbade the Muslims from lining their clothes with silk and from putting silk over their shoulders, as doing such was the way of Ajamis (the non-Arabs, particularly the people living to the East of Iraq.)[11]

Although Islam brought numerous other changes discussed below, the changes discussed above were responsible for appearance difference of a Muslim, his very distinct look, by which it is possible to distinguish a Muslim from a non-Muslim. This is precisely the reason that Islamic religious scholars over-emphasize such items and bring out *fatwas* in favour of the same.[12]

Shifting the Time of Prayer

The Arabian Pagans used to do prostrations to the rising and setting sun, as Hindus do during *Surya-Namaskar*; Hindus also worship the rising and setting sun while performing *Sandhya*. The Prophet shifted the time of morning and evening *namaz*, keeping the infidel practice in mind. He directed the Muslims: "Do the morning *namaz* before the sun rises because it rises between the two horns of Satan when the infidels do prostrations to it… Wait for the evening *namaz* till the sun has set because it sets between the two horns of Satan when the infidels do prostrations to it…"[13]

Dress for Namaz

About the dress during *namaz*, the Prophet said: "He among you who has two pieces of cloth should wear them both for doing *namaz*. If he has only one cloth, he should use it as a *tabband* and not let it hang as the Jews do."[14] Regarding the use of shoes and socks during the *namaz*, he said: "Do the opposite of what the Jews do. They do not do *namaz* with shoes and socks on."[15]

Azan, the Call for Prayer

In the beginning, when the Muslims came to Medina, they used to guess about the time, and then come for the prayer; they were not called for the prayer. Various suggestions were made to call the people for prayer at a fixed time, such as, raising a flag, or use of horn, as the Jews do, or the use of the bell like the Christians. The Prophet rejected the use of horn, "because it meant acting like the Jews and Prophet did not like similarity with the People of the Book in matters of Faith." The Prophet rejected the use of the bell also; he said: "This is what the Christians do." Ultimately, he decided to use the human voice for the same, and then ordered Bilal to call out the *azan*.[16]

Friday, as the Day of Special Prayer for the Muslims

Friday is a special day for the Muslims. It precedes Saturday, the special day for the Jews, and Sunday, the special day for the Christians. As Prophet Muhammad said: "The best day on which the sun has risen is Friday; on it Adam was created, on it he was made to enter Paradise, on it he was expelled from it. And the last day will take place on no other day than Friday."[17]

The Prophet further said: "It was Friday from which Allah diverted those who were before us. For the Jews (the day set aside for prayer) was *Sabt* (Saturday), and for the Christians it was Sunday. And Allah turned towards us and guided us to Friday (as the day of prayer) for us. In fact He (Allah) made Friday, Saturday and Sunday (as day of prayer). In this order would they (Jews and Christians) come after us on the Day of Resurrection. We are the last of (the *Ummahs*) among the people in this world and the first among the created to be judged on the Day of Resurrection."[18]

The Days of Fasting

Prophet Muhammad, like other Quraysh, used to fast on the day of *Ashura* (the tenth day of Muharram). Even after his migration to Medina, he used to do so and asked the believers also to do so. But he shifted it to Ramzan soon after, and it was no longer obligatory for Muslims to fast on Ashura.[19] As mentioned in *Sunam Abu Dawudi*, the Companions of the Prophet informed him that Jews and Christians also honoured Ashura on tenth day of Muharram. Prophet Muhammad then observed that if he remained alive at the end of that year, then he would observe the fast on the ninth day of Muharram. But he passed away before the year ended, and the change could not take place.

Morning Meal and Breaking of the Fast

The Muslims delay the morning meal (*Sahri*) before sunrise as far as possible, and break the fast (*Iftar*) as early as possible after sunset. The *ahadis* say: "Take meal a little before dawn, for there is a blessing in taking meal at that time"[20] and "the people will continue to prosper as long as they hasten the breaking of the fast."[21] Here, it needs mention that Jews and Christians ate early and broke their fasts late; they waited for the stars to appear. The Prophet said: "The difference between our fasting and that of the People of the Book is eating shortly before dawn." As per the translator's note, it "distinguishes the *Ummah* of Islam from other *Ummahs*," and "hammers" into its consciousness the sense of "its separate entity which is the first step towards prosperity of any nation." In addition, the note mentions: "taking meal late in the dawn and breaking fast early at the sunset indicate the fact that one feels the pangs of hunger. ...This feeling inculcates in one a spirit of humility rather than of stoic pride."[22] Thus, "both the morning meal and the breaking of the fast were devised so as to set the Muslims apart from the Jews and Christians, and the Prophet was at pains to make sure that the followers saw them as such."[23] Pointing to the morning meal (*sahri*), the Prophet remarked: "This is the difference between our way of fasting and that of the People of the Book – the eating of *sahri*."[24] Regarding the ending of the fast (*Iftar*), he advised: "The *Din* will prevail so long as people hurry in ending the fast, because the Jews and the Christians delay the *Iftar*."[25]

Changes in Pre-Islamic Hajj Rituals

Basically the rituals related to Hajj pilgrimage, including minor pilgrimage, *umra*, remain the same as during the pagan period. The Muslims, like the Pagans, circumambulate the holy temple, use single unsewn cloth, shave the hair, take bath before the worship. But pagan did not run between Safa and Marwa, the two hills adjacent to the Kaba, considered it to be sin, which the Qur'an prescribes.[26] These two hills, according to Islamic tradition, a pilgrim and visitor should walk up and down in commemoration of what Hagar did in search of water for her baby, Ishmael, the ancestor of the Muslims. According to a *Hadis*[27], Prophet Muhammad ran between Safa and Marwa, only after the Quranic revelation.

The Pagans, while performing the *Hajj*, used to leave Mazdalfah/Madhdalfah after the sun rose; when the Prophet learnt from Umar, son of Khattab, that 'they used to start after sunshine had brightened the hills of Sabir,' then the Prophet did the opposite. Umar left the place before sunrise.[28] According to another *Hadis*, the Prophet said that the infidels are not to be imitated. He said: "Do not slaughter with teeth or fingernails and I will tell you why: It is because teeth are bones (i.e. can not cut properly) and fingernails are the tools used by the Ethiopians (whom we should not imitate for they are infidels."[29]

General Conduct: Some Aspects

Once Prophet Muhammad came bending on a stick, and the persons present there stood up in his honour. The Prophet said, "Do not stand up as the Ajamis do for honouring particular person."[30]

Sulaiman, a Companion of the Prophet informed him that he read in the *Taurat* (Jewish Scripture, Old Testament) that it was propitious to wash before breakfast. On hearing the same, the Prophet observed that it was propitious to eat before washing and to wash after eating. The *Hadis* further said: "One day the Prophet came out of the lavatory, people asked him if water was to be brought for him to wash; he said that he had been ordered to wash only before standing for *namaz*."[31]

In yet another *Hadis*, it is said that Sulaiman informed the Prophet that he had read in the Taurat about doing wuzu after meals and sought his ruling. The Prophet then said to do wuzu both before and after meals.[32]

Prophet and the Dead

A Jew died, and Prophet Muhammad saw his people weeping. He forbade believers from weeping audibly over their dead; he said that the dead suffer torment in the grave if his people weep over his death.[33] On another such occasion, he instructed believer women to weep taking the name of Hamza, his uncle killed in the war.

Prophet Muhammad, while accompanying the bier used to remain standing till the bier was lowered into the grave. One day, a learned Jew, who was passing by, came near the Prophet and said, "O Muhammad, we also do the same." The Prophet immediately sat down and told his Companions: "Do the opposite of what they do."[34] *Mishkat-ul-Masabih* discusses some more *ahadis*, which need mention. According to one, the Prophet commanded his Companions to stand up on seeing a bier, but later he sat and commanded them also to sit.[35] In another *Hadis*, Prophet commands his Companions, "When the bier of a Jew or a Christian or a Muslim passed by, you should stand for it. You are not standing in its honour, but you stand for the angels who are with it."[36] In yet another time the Prophet gave similar answer when he stood up seeing a bier, and was pointed out that it was the bier of a Jew; he said: "I stood up (in reverence of) the angels."[37]

But there are other *ahadis*, which give different explanations for his standing. In one *Hadis*, Muhammad stood up seeing a bier passing, and when pointed out that it belonged to a Jew, remarked: "Was it not a human being?"[38] In another *Hadis*, Hasan, son of Ali, remarked, "He disliked that the bier of a Jew should be higher than his head, therefore he stood up."[39] Here, it needs mention that such traditions did not develop uniform impact on the followers of Muhammad. When Hasan, son of Ali, stood up seeing a bier passing, and Ibn Abbas, sitting by his side, did not do so, the former asked him: "Has not the Messenger of Allah stood (in reverence of) the bier of a Jew?" The reply was: "Yes, but later he sat down."[40]

Non-Segregation of the Women Under Menses

The Jews used to segregate menstruating women; they neither ate or drank with her, nor allowed her to stay in the same house. When the Companions of the Prophet asked about the practice, the Quranic verse descended, which said: "They ask you (Prophet) about Menstruation. Say, 'Menstruation is a painful condition, so keep away from women during it. Do not approach them until they are cleansed; when they are cleansed, you may approach them as God has directed you.'"[41] Prophet Muhammad directed them, as usual, the course opposite to what the non-believers were doing, and thereby allowed the Companions to let the women in menses eat and drink with them and allowed them to live in the same house. Except for the sex, they were allowed to do everything with them.[42]

Food and the Way of Eating

On being asked about the food eaten by the Christians, Prophet Muhammad said: Let no such thing come to your mind as is like that of the Christians.[43] He ordered the believers: "Do not slice meat with knife, because that is what the Ajamis do; instead bite it with your teeth – that is very pleasant."[44]

Substituting the Days of Sports and Merriment

When Muhammad came to Medina, he found that the people used to sport for two days, on which he said that "Allah has substituted the two days of sports by better two days of *Id-ul-Adha* and *Id-ul-Fitr*."[45]

Forbidding Celibacy, Ascetic Life and Self-Denial

In Arabia, like in India and elsewhere, there were people, who wanted to live the life of celibacy and self-denial. Muhammad did not like such things, and therefore forbade it.[46]

Name Change

The Prophet used to change the names of the converts wherever the same had any linkages with the traditional gods and goddesses or had some how any derogatory meaning.[47]

Notes and References

1. *Sahih Bukhari*, The Book of dress, Chapter 11; *Summerized Sahih Al-Bukhari*, p. 949; *Original Bukhari*, 7:781; this Hadis was narrated by Umar, as said by Allah's messenger.
2. *Sahih Muslim*, Vol. I, p. 389.
3. *Sahih Al-Bukhari*, Ibid, Ch. 12; OB 7:786); narrator – Abu Huraira.
4. *Sahih Muslim*, *Hadis* 5244.
5. Ibid, *Hadis* 5245.
6. Ibid, *Hadis* 5175.
7. Ibid, *Hadis* 5173-5178.
8. Ibid, *Hadis* 5173.
9. *Sahih Bukhari*, Ch. 6; OB 7:737; narrator – Anas.
10. *Sahih Muslim, Hadis* 5150.
11. *Mishkat Sharif*, Volume II, Rabbani Book Depot, Delhi, n.d., *Hadis* 4158/ 46, p. 150.
12. Shourie, Arun, *The World of Fatwas*, pp. 124-41.
13. *Sahih Muslim Sharif*, Volume II, p. 299.
14. *Sunam Abu Dawud Sharif*, Volume I, Hadis 633, p. 264.
15. Ibid, *Hadis* 647, p. 269.
16. *Sunam Abu Dawud Sharif*, Volume I, *Hadis* 495, pp. 212-13; the remark of the translator is worth noting: "This *Hadis* has been interpreted by some people as a prohibition of keeping any similarities with the Jews and Christians." Also see *Jama Tirmizi*, Volume I, pp. 113-14; *Sahih al-Bukhari Sharif*, Maulana Akhtar Shahjahanpuri (tr.), Delhi, 1984, Volume I, *Hadis* 573-74, p. 290).
17. *Sahih Muslim, Hadis* 1857.
18. Ibid, *Hadis* 1862.
19. *Jama Tirmizi*, Volume I, p. 291.
20. *Sahih Muslim, Hadis* 2412.
21. *Sahih Muslim, Hadis* 2417.
22. Ibid, Note 1491.
23. Shourie, op. cit.,pp. 615-16.
24. *Sunam Nasai Sharif*, Volume II, *Hadis* 2170, p. 51.
25. *Sunam Abu Dawud Sharif*, Volume II, *Hadis* 581, p. 237.
26. Qur'an 2:158.
27. *Sunam Nasai Sharif*, Volume II, *Hadis* 2972, p. 296; *Sahih Muslim Sharif*, Volume III, pp. 314-15.

28. *Sahih al-Bukhari Sharif,* Volume I, *Hadis* 1571, p. 620; *Jama Tirmizi*, Volume I, p. 335; *Sunam Ibn Maja*, Volume II, *Hadis* 239, p. 233.
29. *Summarised Bukhari – Hadis* 1133; Original *Sahih al-Bukhari*, *Hadis* 3:668, narrator – Rafi bin Khadij.
30. *Mishkat Sharif,* Volume II, *Hadis* 4493, 4496.
31. *Jama Tirmizi*, Allama Badi al-Zaman (tr.) Aitqad Publishing House, Delhi, Volume I, pp. 667-68.
32. *Mishkat Sharif,* Volume II, *Hadis* 4023, 4046; p. 125.
33. *Zama Tirmizi*, Volume I, p. 371.
34. Ibid, p. 376; *Mishkat-ul-Masabih*, Volume III, p. 189, *Hadis* 1681; this is based on Tirmizdhi/Tirmizi, Abu Dawud, and Ibn Majah.
35. Ibid, *Hadis* 1682.
36. Ibid, *Hadis* 1685.
37. Ibid, *Hadis* 1686.
38. Ibid, *Hadis* 1680.
39. Ibid, *Hadis* 1684.
40. Ibid, *Hadis* 1683; based on Nasa'i.
41. Qur'an 2:222.
42. *Mishkat Sharif,* Volume II, *Hadis* 4493, 4496; p. 219.
43. Mushkat Sharif, Volume II, *Hadis* 3908/24.
44. Ibid, *Hadis* 4029/52, p. 126.
45. *Mishkat-ul-Masabih, Hadis* 1439; based the *Hadis* of *Sunam abu-Dawud.*
46. Muir, *The Life of Mahomet*, pp. 59, 180; Margoliouth, D.S., *Mohammed and the Rise of Islam*, p. 43, p. 151; *Sahih al-Bukhari, Hadis* 1432; pp. 677-98.
47. Ibn Ishaq, p. 302; Margoliouth, p. 110.

Women in Islam

Prophet Muhammad linked the behavioural status of women in general with that of Biblical Eve and said: "Had it not been for Eve, women would have never acted unfaithfully towards the husbands."[1] This concern regarding the original sin was, undoubted, responsible for many changes in the prevailing customs about women, which brought changes in the status of the Muslim women. Many prevailing customs were, however, retained, which the following write-up brings out. The women did not practice veil and some other restrictions during pre-Islamic days. They even used to go to the war zones to encourage their fighting men. The veil and other restrictions were introduced afterwards.

Removal of Certain Marriage Restrictions

Certain marriage restrictions of the pagan days were removed during the Islamic period. As for example, the marriage with the wife of the adopted son was a taboo during the pagan days, but the practice was abandoned for the Prophet, and then for other Muslims. The Quranic revelation made it clear that Muhammad was the seal of the Prophets and not the father of any one of the men:

"Muhammad is not the father of any one of you men; he is Allah's Messenger and the seal of the prophets; Allah knows everything."[2]

The Quranic revelation, however, freed other Muslims also from marrying the wives of their adopted sons, and the old pagan practice was thus abandoned. The Qur'an further says: "…you were afraid of the people, but it is more fitting that you fear Allah. When Zayd no longer wanted her, We gave her to you in marriage so that there might be no fault in believers marrying the wives of their adopted sons after they no more wanted them. Allah's command must be carried out: the Prophet is not at fault for what Allah has ordained for him."[3]

About the permitted marital relations, the Qur'an says: "Prophet, We have made lawful for you the wives whose bride gift you have paid, and any slave Allah has assigned you through war, and the daughters of your uncles and aunts on your father's and mother's side, who migrated with you. Also any believing woman who has offered herself to the Prophet (waiving any bride gift) and whom the Prophet wishes to wed—this is only for you (Prophet) and not the rest of the believers; We know exactly what We have made obligatory for them concerning their wives and slave girls—so you should not be blamed; ..."[4] Thus, Allah provided for the exclusive marital relationship for the Prophet.

Marriage is not permitted when one has put on the ritual garb of pilgrimage. As the Hadis says: "A *Muhrim* should neither marry nor make the proposal of marriage."[5] But the Prophet himself "married Maimuna while he was a *Muhrim*."[6]

Changes Exclusively for the Prophet

As mentioned above, Allah provides for the exclusive marital relationship for the Prophet. Otherwise also, the followers of Islam have no freedom to claim everything on the matters decided by Allah and his Messenger, concerning them. The Qur'an says:

"When Allah and His Messenger have decided on a matter that concerns them, it is not fitting for any believing man or woman to claim freedom of choice in that matter."[7]

Celibacy and Self-Denial is Not Allowed

The Prophet did not allow a person to lead celibate life.[8] He discouraged the person living the life of self-denial, such as 'not eating meat,' 'not marrying.'[9] The prophet disapproved of not marrying and of getting castrated. As narrated by Sa'd, son of Abi Waqqas, "he did not allow Uthman, son of Mazun, to keep away from marrying, and if he had allowed him, we would have gotten ourselves castrated."[10]

Marriage Essential

"Those among you who can support a wife should marry, for it restrains eyes from casting evil glances and preserves one from immorality," said the Prophet. According to *Hadis*, "Allah's Messenger saw a woman and so he came to his wife, Zainab, as she was tanning leather and had sexual intercourse with her. He then went to his Companions and told them: "The woman advances and returns in the shape of a devil, so when one of you see a woman, he should come to his wife, for that will repel what he feels in his heart."[11] Thus, woman was safety valve, and a married man, if aroused by some women, is advised to go to his wife.

Introduction of Veil and Other Restrictions

The *Veil* and other restrictions were imposed on the wives of the Prophet and then on the others. Muir writes: "The seclusion of the *Veil* or curtain was at this time enjoined upon the wives of Mohammad. Himself well stricken in years, surrounded by six wives, some of them sprightly, young, and beautiful, and with a continual concourse of courtiers, visitors, and suitors, such a restriction was not un-needed. Indeed, he has himself proved in the case of Zeinab the danger that might arise from the too free admission of friends or strangers; and his followers could hardly expect to be free of temptation than the Prophet himself. No one unless bidden was to enter his wives' apartments; they were not to be spoken to but from behind a curtain; and to slake the last embers of jealousy (or uneasiness as it is euphemistically called), an interdict is declared against their ever marrying again, even after his death. Henceforward they were known as *'the Mothers of the Faithful.'*"[12] The Qur'an says:

"Believers, do not enter the Prophet's apartments for a meal unless you are given permission to do so; do not linger until (a meal) is ready. When you are invited, go in; then, when you have taken your meal, leave. Do not stay on and talk, for that would offend the Prophet, though he would shrink from asking you to leave. Allah does not shrink from the truth. When you ask from his wives for something, do so from behind a screen: this is purer both for your hearts and for theirs. It is not right for you to offend Allah's Messenger, just as you should never marry his wives after him: that would be grievous in Allah's eye. Allah has full knowledge of all things, whether you reveal them or not."[13]

The Muslim men and women were told to restrain their eyes and to preserve their modesty. The Qur'an says: "(Prophet), tell believing men to lower their eyes and guard their private parts: that is purer for them. … And tell believing women that they should lower their eyes, guard their private parts, and not display their charms beyond what (it is acceptable) to reveal; they should draw their coverings over their necklaces and not reveal their charms except to their husbands, their fathers, their husbands' fathers, their sons, their husband's sons, their brothers, their brothers' sons, their sisters' sons, their womenfolk, their slaves, such men as attend them who have no desire, or children who are not yet aware of women's nakedness; they should not stamp their feet so as to draw attention to any hidden charms."[14]

Qur'an also directs on restrictions of less stringent nature upon dress and demeanour, placed at that time. It says: "Prophet, tell your wives, your daughters, and women believers to make their outer garments hang low over them so as to be recognized and not insulted."[15]

Rules Regulating Strangers' Visit to Neighbours' Homes

Prescription of rules, as precautionary measures to regulate the visits of strangers to the houses of the neighbours, was aimed at ensuring the privacy of the believers, and preventing intrusion without warning. The Qur'an writes: "Believers, your slaves and any who have not yet reached puberty should ask your permission to come in at three times of day: before the dawn prayer; when you lay your garments and in the mid-day heat; and after the evening prayer. These are your three times of privacy; at other times, there is no blame on you or them if you move around each other freely."[16] ı ne children, after reaching puberty, like the elders, should also take permission for entering the house.[17] According to *Sahih Bukhari*, a man should not stay with a woman in seclusion unless he is a *Dhu-Mahram* (a person who is legally not allowed to marry that woman, e.g. her father or brother, etc). And it is unlawful to enter upon a woman whose husband is absent.[18]

There are yet some other restrictions worth noting. A woman should not look at or touch the body of another woman to describe her to her husband. And according to another *Hadis*, "If a man is away or absent from his family for a long time, then on returning home, he should not enter his house at night (lest he should find something which might arouse his suspicion as regards his family, or lest he should discover their defects.)[19] According to another *Hadis*, the prophet said, "If you enter (your town) at night (after coming from a journey), do not enter upon your family till the woman whose husband was absent (from the house) shaves her pubic hair and the women with unkempt hair, combs her hair."[20]

The Woman's Testimony

Woman's testimony (*shahadah*), according to Qur'an has half the weight of a man's.[21] The evidence of two men or one man and two women is required in a dispute regarding property or debt.[22]

Half Blood-Price for Women's Murder

The blood price (*diyah*), in case of the murder of woman, is only half in comparison to that of a man.[23]

Women and *Salat*

Women were allowed to go to mosque for prayer, but with certain restrictions. As Hadis says, the women "should not apply perfume."[24] The men were, however, not denied from doing so. The women were also not allowed to raise their heads before the men during prayer.[25] The translator of the *Hadis* relates it to the poverty of the Muslims during the early days, and explains it that the men, having scanty cloths needed time to adjust them before the women lifted their heads.[26]

The Prophet commanded the believers to "take out unmarried women and purdah-observing ladies for 'Id prayers, and he commanded the menstruating women to remain away from the place of worship of the Muslims."[27] The translator's note regarding women's accompanying men in prayer, says, "The fact is that the Holy Prophet deemed it preferable for women to say their prayers within the four walls of their houses or in the nearest mosque."[28]

Woman Observing *Saum* (Fasting)

According to *Hadis*, the Prophet said: "A women should not observe *Saum* (fast) (optional ones) except with his husband's permission if he is at home (staying with her). And a woman should not allow anyone to enter her husband's house except with his consent. And whatever she spends of his wealth in charitable gifts in Allah's Cause without being ordered by him, he will get half of the reward."[29]

Husband's Rights

"Your wives are (like) your fields, so go into your fields whichever way you like,"[30] Qur'an says Likewise, the *Hadis* says, "Your wives are your tilth; go then unto your tilth as you may desire.[31] Thus, a husband has complete sexual right over his wife. There are other *ahadis* also expressing such things.[32] Yet another *Hadis* says, "When a woman spends the night away from the bed of her husband, the angels curse her till morning."[33] Thus, it is the duty of a wife to be responsive to all of her husband's overtures. A *Hadis* also advises one to treat one's family in a polite and kind manner,[34] Thus one's rights need behavioral adjustment also.

Sahih Bukhari writes about the *Ghira* (honour, prestige or self-respect) of a husband, and quotes the statement of a husband (Sa'd, son of Ubada), who said: "If I saw a man with my wife, I would strike him with the sharp edge of the sword." Then the Prophet said to his Companions, "Are you astonished by Sa'd's (*Ghira*) sense of honour?" By Allah, I have greater sense of *Ghira* than he has, and Allah has still more greater sense of *Ghira* than I have.[35]

Women's Rights

A woman is entitled to a dowry (*mahr*) or "hire" (*ujurat*), which she can claim after divorce.[36] She is entitled to lawful maintenance (*nafaqah*), failing which she can seek a divorce.

She has the right to be consulted in the choice of her husband. The *Hadis* says, "A women who has been previously married (*Sayyib*) has more right to her person than her guardian. And a virgin should also be consulted, and her silence implies her consent."[37] Though, a Muslim woman is entitled to make her marriage contract, in reality, her nearest kinsman, the father (called 'compelling *wallis*, gurdians) do the same; a minor girl, given in marriage by the guardian other than father or grandfather, according to some schools, may even seek dissolution of marriage after attaining majority.[38]

The Qur'an also mentions about women's earning and their heirs,[39] the Hadis, cited below, mentions about the wealth of a women. Khadija, the first wife of the Prophet herself was a wealthy woman. There are certain traditions in Islam regarding polygamous families.

Deportment Towards One's Wives

As per *as-Sunna*, if someone marries a virgin and he has already a matron wife (with him) then he should stay with the virgin for seven days; and if someone marries a matron (and he has already a virgin wife with him) then he should stay with her for three days.[40] When a person has many wives, and he intends to go on a journey, then he should draw lots among his wives to select one to accompany him.[41] *Sahih Muslim* also says that one should spend seven days with newly wed virgin wife and three days if she is a widow, if there are many wives in the family.[42]

When the Prophet married Umm Salama, he spent three nights with her. After that, he intended to leave her, then she caught hold of his garment. The Prophet, then told her, "If you wish I can stay with you for a week, but then I shall have to stay for a week with all my wives.[43]

Prophet Muhammad followed the rule of rotation for his stay with his wives, as according to him, the husbands should divide his days equally among all his wives. It was, however, provided that a wife could forego her turn to the other,[44] as Sauda did when she became old and Allah's Messenger "allotted two days to Aisha."[45] Of course, it also happened that the Prophet would ask a wife to forgo her day; On such happenings, one wife told him, "If I had the option in this I would not have allowed anyone to have precedence over me."[46]

The rule of rotation was, however, eventually withdrawn altogether by a special dispensation of Allah. The revelation says: "Thou may differ the turn of any of them that thou pleasest, and thou may receive any thou pleasest: and there is no blame in thee if thou invite one whose turn thou hast set aside."[47] This was going to benefit Ayesha, who taunted the Prophet, pointing Allah to be very accommodating. She said to him: "It seems to me that your Lord hastens to satisfy your desire."[48]

In case of polygamy, the *Hadis* advises a particular wife not to show her pride to other co-wives.[49] Seeking refuge with Allah is the greatest surety of protection for a Muslim lady. As the tradition says: "Once, the daughter of Al-Jaun was brought before Prophet Muhammad as bride. She said: "I seek refuge with Allah from you." The Prophet said: "You have sought refuge with The Most Great; return to your family."[50] In this *Hadis* and in others[51] one finds it permissible to cast a glance at the woman whom a person intends to marry.

Woman's Marriage Eligibility

Only the Muslim women are eligible for marriage to a Muslim.[52] The unbelieving women may only be the concubines. However, the *Hadis* also writes about four eligibility criteria of a woman for marriage. The Prophet said: "A women is married for four (things), i.e., her wealth, her family status, her beauty and her religion. So you should take possession of (Marry) the religious women (otherwise) you will be a loser."[53]

Period of Mourning (*Idda*)

There is a fixed period (*idda*) of mourning for four months and ten days for the wife, and three days for others.[54] A widow must abstain from all adornments during the *idda* period.[55] A woman is also debarred from re-marriage during the *idda* period; it, however, ends sooner if the woman gives birth to a child.[56]

Inferior Position of Women and Female Slaves

Muslim women and female slaves, according to Muir, occupy inferior position in Islam. Muir writes: "But in respect of the marital state (which in the east embraces practically the whole sex during the greater part of their lives), condition of woman is that of a dependant, destined for the service of her lord, liable to be cast off without the assignment of any reason and without the notice of a single hour. While the husband possesses the power of divorce, absolute, immediate, unquestioned, no privilege of a corresponding nature has been reserved for the wife. She hangs on, however unwilling, neglected or superseded, the slave of her Lord,—if such be his will. When divorced, she can, indeed, claim her dower,—her *hire*, as in too plain language it is called; this, however, is but a poor security against capricious taste, and in the case of female slaves, even that is wanting. The power of divorce is not the only power that may be arbitrarily exercised by the tyrannical husband: Authority to confine and to beat his wives is vested in his direction"[57] The wives are, however, to be beaten, as the Qur'an says, when they show deviant behaviour:

"Husbands should take good care of their wives; with (the bounties) Allah has given to some more than others and with what they spend out of their own money. Righteous wives are devout and guard what Allah would have them guard in their husband's absence. If you fear high-handedness from your wives, remind them (of the teachings of Allah), then ignore them when you go to bed, then hit them. If they obey you, you have no right to act against them"[58] The Islamic tradition (*Hadis*) advises treating them in polite way.[59]

The Qur'an, of course, advises arbitration in the case of discord between the couple. It says: "If you (believers) fear that a couple may break up, appoint one arbiter from his family and one from hers. Then, if the couple want to put things right, Allah will bring about a reconciliation between them."[60]

Prohibited Marital Relations

Islam prohibits certain marital relationships. Quran writes about the prohibited marital relations, thus: "Do not marry women that your fathers married—with the exception of what is past—this is indeed a shameful thing to do, loathsome and leading to evil. You are forbidden to take as wives your mothers, daughters, sisters, paternal and maternal aunts, the daughters of brothers and daughters of sisters, your milk mothers and milk sisters, your wives' mothers and stepdaughters in your care—those born of women with whom you have consummated the marriage, if you have not consummated the marriage, then you will not be blamed—wives of your begotten sons, two sisters simultaneously—with the exception of what is past…"[61] The list further includes 'women already married, other than your slaves."[62]

The Qur'an forbids marriage with an unbeliever.[63] This prohibition was, however, relaxed later on, and a male Muslim was allowed to marry a Jew or a Christian.[64] But, there was no such relaxation for a female believer under any circumstances.

Further restrictions on marriage included marriage with one's wife's father's sister, her mother's sister,[65] daughter of one's foster brother, and the sister of one's wife, if the wife is alive and not divorced.[66]

The exchange marriage (*Shighar*), the marriage, which says: 'Marry me your daughter or sister, and in exchange I will give you in marriage my daughter or sister,' is prohibited in Islam.[67]

The remarriage with one's divorced wife is prohibited unless she subsequently marries someone else; the new husband had sex with her and then divorced her.[68] A *Hadis* brings such a case to notice, according to which a married divorcee wanted to return to her old husband. While seeking the permission of the Prophet, she told him that all the new husband possessed was "like the fringe of the garment" (i.e., he was sexually weak). The Prophet "laughed" but withheld the permission. He told her, "You can not do that unless you tasted his (the new husband's) sweetness and he has tasted your sweetness.[69] This, however, happens in case of the divorce on third time. Muir writes:

"In the conditions of Divorce, there is one which (such as I might desire) can not be passed over in silence. A husband may twice divorce his wife, and each time receive her back again. But when it has been thrice repeated, the divorce is, with a hateful exception, irreversible. However unjust or injurious the action, how much soever the result of passion or caprice, however it may affect the interests not only of an innocent wife, but also of her innocent children, however desirous the husband may be of undoing the wrong,—the decision can not be recalled; the divorced wife can return to her husband but on one condition, and that is that she shall first be married to another, and after cohabitation be again divorced."[70]

Marriage relations between the parties of unequal rank or status (*kafa'ah*) are disallowed.[71] Prophet Muhammad found a person ineligible for marriage, as he was poor and incapable to pay any dowry. On being refused the hand of a captive girl, when the man was returning back, the Prophet enquired whether he knew any verse of the Qur'an and could recite them. The man said yes. Then the prophet decided and said: "Go, I have given her to you in marriage for the part of the Qur'an which you know."[72]

A person is advised not to outbid one's brother. "A believer is a brother of a believer, so it is not lawful for a believer to outbid his brother, and he should not propose an agreement when his brother has thus proposed until he gives it up."[73]

Marriages with Virgin Preferred

The Prophet preferred marriage with a virgin. According to a *Hadis* narrated by Ayesha, she asked the Prophet, "O Allah's Messenger! Suppose you landed in a valley where there is a tree of which something has been eaten and then you found trees of which nothing has been eaten, of which tree would you let your camel graze?" He said, "(I will let my camel graze) of the one of which nothing has been eaten before." (Narrator added: 'Aisha meant that Allah's Messenger had not married a virgin beside herself.)[74]

A Young Lady's Marriage to an Elderly Man

Ayesha narrates an interesting discussion about her marriage with Prophet Muhammad in a Hadis titled the above mentioned one. As she narrated: "The Prophet asked Abu Bakr for (Ayesha's) hand in marriage. Abu Bakr said: "But I am your brother." The Prophet said: "You are my brother in Allah's Religion and His Book, but she (Ayesha) is lawful for me to marry.[75]

Restriction on Number of Wives

Number of wives for a Muslim is restricted to four;[76] but there is no restriction on the number of concubines. The marriage laws, as the divorce laws, derive from the practice and pronouncements of Prophet Muhammad. But there are cases showing the difference. As for example, Muslims are allowed four wives at a time, whereas Prophet Muhammad had nine.

Captive Women

Islam does not allow marriage with the married women, unless they are divorced. Adultery and fornication are also punishable. But the married pagan women, captured in *Jihad*, are exceptions. The Qur'an says: "Also (prohibited) are women already married, except those whom your right hands possess.[77] This verse descended when Allah's Messenger, at the Battle of Hunain, sent an army to Autas, who defeated the enemy and captured their women. The companions of the Prophet "seemed to refrain from having intercourse with captive women because of their husbands being polytheists. Then Allah, Most High, sent down" the verse regarding that.[78]

Captive women had to suffer sexual abuse, but as the captors wanted ransom, they practiced *coitus interruptus* (*Al-'Azl*) to avoid conception. Of course, otherwise also, their fate was to be sold as slaves, or to be kept by the captors as concubines. The companions of the Prophet sought his advice in this case, and, according to him, *Al-'azl* was permitted, but it is useless if the object is to prevent conception, for that is in the Allah. Abu Sirma reported: "We went out with Allah's Messenger on the expedition … and took some excellent Arab women; and we desired them … but we also desired ransom from them. So we decided to have sexual intercourse with them but by observing '*azl*." On consultation, the Prophet advised: "It does not matter if you do not do it, for every soul that is to be born up to the day of Resurrection will be born."[79]

Temporary Marriage (*Mut'a*, *Nikah-al-Mut'a*) with Captive Women

According to a *Hadis*, 'Abdullah, son of Mas'ud reported: "We were on an expedition with Allah's Messenger and we had no women with us. We said: Should we not have ourselves castrated? The Holy Prophet forbade us to do so. He then granted us permission that we should contract temporary marriage for a stipulated period giving her a garment (for a dowry)." At this 'Abdullah became happy and remembered the Quranic verse: "The believers do not make unlawful the good things which Allah has made lawful for you, and do not transgress. Allah does not like transgressors."[80]

In another *Hadis*, Jabir reports: "We contracted temporary marriage giving handful of dates and flour as dower."[81] Such temporary marriages continued during the period of Abu Bakr and Umar also. In another *Hadis*, Jabir said: "Yes, we had been benefiting ourselves by this temporary marriage during the time of Abu Bakr and 'Umar also."[82] This kind of marriage, as yet another *Hadis* says, was allowed by Prophet Muhammad in the year of *Autas*, after the Battle of Hunain during A.H. 8, and then forbidden.[83] Sunnis regard this kind of marriage unlawful now a days, but Shias still practice it in Persia.[84]

Vow of Abstinence (*Zihar*)

There were two kinds of vows of separation from the wife during the period of Prophet Muhammad, namely *zihar* and *Ila*. *Zihar* was the customary vow of abstinence by a husband from his wife for the brief period, in which her husband vowed that his wife would be unto him as the back (*zahr*) of his mother and then stayed away from her for the specified period. Its purpose could be penitential or devotional; on the other hand, the vow might be taken in a fit of anger. The formula was also used as a form of divorce. The Qur'an condemned divorce by this formula;[85] he allowed a husband who had taken a vow to go back to his wife. The Muslims also, according to some traditions, used to take this vow during fasting. There was provision for the expiation for the broken vow by making *kaffarah* (literally, "that which covers a sin"), which, in this case, was either a fast for two months, or feeding of sixty poor men or women.[86]

In *Ila* ("to swore"), the husband swore an oath to abstain from sexual intercourse with his wife. During the pagan days, the Arabs regarded it as a form of divorce, which, in reality, did not fully dissolve the marriage. Sometimes, this oath was taken to penalize the wife and extort ransom from her. The Qur'an, however, forbade it.[87] The man, taking such a vow, was to go back to his wife without any blame to himself; but if he did not do so, "the marriage was ipso facto legally dissolved at the end of four months." There was provision for expiation for the broken vow in this case also. As a *Hadis* says: "When a man declares his wife unlawful for himself that is an oath which must be atoned, ... There is in the Messenger of Allah a model pattern for you."[88]

Prophet Muhammad's Separation (*Ila*) from his Wives

As discussed, Prophet Muhammad himself underwent a separation of 29 days under *Ila*, Umar calmed down his anger, and when he was relaxed, a verse, freeing him from his oath respecting Mary, threatening his wives with divorce, and incorporating 'Umar's assurance that all the angels and believers supported him, descended. Allah said: "Prophet, why do you prohibit what Allah has made lawful to you in your desire to please your wives? Yet Allah is forgiving and merciful; He has ordained a way for you (believers) to release you from (such) oath—Allah is your helper. He is All Knowing, the One who decides. The Prophet told something in confidence to one of his wives. When she disclosed it to (another wife) and Allah made known to him, he confirmed part of it, and said nothing about the rest. When he confronted her with what she had done, she asked: 'Who told you about this?' and he replied: 'The All Knowing, the All Aware told me.' If both of you (wives) repent to Allah—for your hearts have deviated—(all will be well); if you collaborate against him, (be warned that) Allah will aid him, as will Gabriel, and all righteous believers, and angels too will back him. His Lord may well replace you with better wives if the Prophet decides to divorce you: wives who are devoted to Allah, true believers, devout, who turn to Him repentance and worship Him, given to fasting, whether previously married or virgins. … Allah has given examples of disbelievers: the wives of Noah and Lot who married two of our righteous servants but betrayed them."[89]

The matter was settled; the two—Ayesha and Hafsa—became his wives again. The Prophet "had taken an oath of remaining away from them (his wives) and now only twenty-nine days had passed, (but) he visited them." Aisha mischievously reminded him that it was not yet one month but only twenty-nine days; the reply was: "At times, the month consists of twenty-nine days."[90]

As the matter blew over, Umar stood at the door of the mosque and called out at the top of his voice: "The Messenger of Allah has not divorced his wives. A revelation, chiding the followers against the rumour-mongering, followed, which said: "Whenever news of any matter comes to them, whether concerning peace or war, they spread it about; if they referred it to the Messenger and those in authority among them, those seeking its meaning would have found it out from them. If it were not for Allah's bounty and mercy towards you, you would almost all have followed Satan."[91]

Prophet's Threat to Divorce His Wives

It was discussed that Prophet Muhammad suffered due to lack of money during the early days in Medina. This led to family discord, and the Prophet was sad.

Abu Bakr and Umar, while visiting him on one such occasion, found him "sitting sad and silent with his wives around him." He told them, "They (his wives and their daughters) are around me as you see, asking for extra money." Hearing that, Abu Bakr "got up, went to Ayesha and slapped her on the neck; and 'Umar stood up and slapped Hafsa." The Prophet, on the occasion, gave them the option of divorce if they "cared more for this world and its adornments than for Allah and His Apostle and the abode of Hereafter."[92] His wives, of course chose to stay with him.

Invoked Curse (*Li'an*): A Way of Separation

Literally, the word *li'an* means "oath," but it is technically a different kind of oath. This form of oath brings about separation between husband and the wife with the help of four oaths and one curse.

It relates the problem of a person witnessing his wife's adultery. The person can neither kill the man, nor accuse the wife unless he has four witnesses, which is difficult to procure, as such acts are not done in public. And if he accuses without four witnesses, he receives eighty stripes for making a false accusation against the chastity of a woman. An Ansar raises the problem to the Prophet; he asked, him, "If a man were to find with his wife a man and if he were to talk about it, you would lash him; and if he killed, you would kill him, and if he were to keep quiet, he would consume anger." The Prophet said, "Allah solve (this problem) and he began to supplicate (before Him).[93] Then the verses pertaining to *li'an* were revealed: "Those who accuse their wives and have no witnesses except themselves."[94]

In *li'an*, a husband's solitary evidence can be accepted if he bears witness four times with an oath by Allah that he is solemnly telling the truth and then invokes the curse of Allah upon himself if he is lying. The wife, similarly denies the allegation four times followed by the invocation of the wrath of Allah on herself if his accuser husband is telling the truth. As the oath of both can't be true, they stand separated.[95]

Triple Talaq

Separation between husband and wife, i.e., undoing the marriage, or divorce is called *talaq*, which means "undoing the knot." The word *talaq* had to be pronounced three times before it becomes operative.[96] Opinions, however, differs as to whether it has to be pronounced on three separate occasions, after three successive menses, or whether three times at one sitting is enough. As the translator of the *Sahih Muslim* notes, "traditions are not lacking in which three pronouncements at one sitting were held as irrevocable divorce even during the time of the Prophet."[97]

Divorce at the Women's *Iddah*

Divorce is not permitted to a women during her menstrual period.[98] Abdullah, son of 'Umar, divorced his wife during her menstrual period. When 'Umar informed it to the Prophet, he ordered that Abdullah should take her back, and when she is pure he may divorce her.[99] According to *Sahih Bukhari*, Allah's Messenger told 'Umar, "Order him (your son) to take her back and keep her till she is clean from her menses and then to wait till she gets her next period and becomes clean again, whereupon, if he wishes to keep her, he can do so, and if he wishes to divorce her he can divorce her before having sexual intercourse with her; and that is the prescribed period which Allah has fixed for the women meant to be divorced.[100]

The Qur'an said about the same: "When you divorce women, divorce them at their *Iddah* (prescribed periods) and count (accurately) their *Iddah*.[101]

Maintenance Allowance not Allowed for a Divorcee

When a lady, named Fatima, daughter of Quais, was divorced "when he was away from home," she angrily reported the matter to the Prophet, who told her: "There is no lodging and maintenance allowance for a women who has been given irrevocable divorce." The Prophet, however, mercifully helped her to find another husband for her. Prophet Muhammad advised her against her two suitors—Abu Jahm and Mu'awiya—as the former did "not put down his staff from his shoulder" (i.e., he used to beat his wife), and the latter was poor.[102]

Later on, 'Umar ruled that the husbands should provide a maintenance allowance to their divorced wives during the period of *'idda.* He did so on the ground that the true purpose of the Prophet's words had been misunderstood by Fatima, a mere woman. He said: "We can not abandon the book of Allah and Sunnah of our apostle for the words of a women."[103]

Easy Separation Adversely Affected the Sanctity of the Women

The triple *talaq*, and maintenance allowance for such a brief period, putting no burden on the husband, made the separation very easy, and adversely affected the sanctity of the women. Wives could be easily disposed off by gifting or divorce, as was done by Sa'd, son of Rabi, to 'Abdar Rahman, the former's adopted brother in faith. As both of them sat at supper, Sa'd said: "Behold my two wives and choose one you like the best."[104]

Islam allowed four wives at a time, but the wives were constantly replaced. As a result, Abu Bakr, 'Umar and Abdar-Rahman had children from sixteen wives each, apart from the children from their concubines. Hasan, the son of Ali and grandson of Prophet Muhammad, married "seventy—some say ninety—times. People used to call him the 'Divorcer.'[105]

Women of At-Taif Crying on the Destruction of Al-Lat

When At-Taif was captured by Prophet Muhammad, he wanted the idol of Al-Lat to be destroyed. The people of that place refused to do it by their own hands. Then Abu-Sufyan and Al-Mughira, friends of the local people were sent to do the job. The destruction of great image was done amid the cries and wailing of the women. The women of Thaqif came out with their heads uncovered bewailing her and saying:

O weep for our protector
Poltroons would neglect her
Whose swords need a corrector[106]

Muir remarked about the attitude of the people of that place towards the destruction of the idol: "At-Taif was the last stronghold that held out against the authority of Mohammad. It is remarkable also as the only place where the fate of an idol excited the sympathy of the local people."[107]

Islam and the Female Infanticide

Apart from the reference of the female infanticide in Qur'an, referring to "when the baby girl buried alive is asked,"[108] the Islamic source materials, practically, provide no information on female infanticide. Ibn Ishaq does not detail it. Muir in his *The Life of Mahomet* has referred about it, at three places only in three sentences, and that too not exclusively on the topic.[109] Strangely, the topic, so much in circulation, is conspicuously absent from the discourse. There is no instance of a single case of female infanticide, where the Prophet either witnessed it, or intervened in it during his pre-Prophetic or Prophetic career. A female Muslim convert is said to have denied the existence of the very practice. The possibility of its existence among some tribe of Arabia, however, may not be ruled out. Margoliouth, while describing how he prevented certain practices of cruelty towards the animals, such as, 'not hitting the horses on the cheek, not branding or hitting the asses on the face, not even cursing the cocks and camels, writes about the innovation of Islam, which is quoted below:

"To the same genuine humanity we may ascribe the one innovation of Islam which ordinarily receives praise even from its enemies: the abolition of the practice of burying girls alive. The tradition records the thrill of horror with which the Prophet heard the recital of a man who had covered with earth a girl whom her mother owing to the father's absence, has ventured to save and bring up. Our sources do not tell us within what limits this practice prevailed: some of the archaeologists confined it to particular tribes, whereas from the Koran we should imagine that the fate of each daughter born hung in the balance. On the other hand one of the women who adopted Islam at the taking of Meccah indignantly repudiated the charge of infanticide."[110]

References

1. *Sahih Muslim, Hadis* 3471.
2. Qur'an 33:40.
3. Qur'an 33:37-38.
4. Qur'an 33:50.
5. *Sahih Muslim, Hadis* 3281.
6. Ibid, *Hadis* 3284.
7. Qur'an 33:36.
8. *Sahih Muslim*, *Hadis* 3239.
9. Ibid, *Hadis* 3236.
10. *Sahih Bukhari*, *Hadis* 7:11.
11. *Sahih Muslim*, *Hadis* 3240.
12. Muir, Sir William, *The Life of Mahomet*, p. 292. (Hereafter Muir).
13. Qur'an 33:53-54.
14. Qur'an 24:30-31.
15. Qur'an 33: 59.
16. Qur'an 24:58.
17. Qur'an 24:59.
18. *Sahih Bukhari*, *Hadis* 7:159.
19. Ibid, *Hadis* 7:171.
20. Ibid, *Hadis* 7:173.
21. Qur'an 2:282.
22. Ram Swarup, *Understanding Islam through Hadis*, p. 96. (Hereafter Ram Swarup).
23. Ibid, p. 87.
24. *Sahih Muslim, Hadis* 893.
25. *Ibid, Hadis* 883.
26. Ibid, translator's note 665.

27. *Ibid, Hadis* 1932.
28. Ibid, note 668.
29. SM note 668.
30. Qur'an 2:223.
31. *Sahih Muslim*, *Hadis* 3363.
32. Ibid, *Hadis* 3365.
33. Ibid, *Hadis* 3366.
34. Ibid, *Hadis* 717.
35. *Sahih Bukhari*, *Hadis* 7:150.
36. Qur'an 4:24, 33:50.
37. *Sahih Muslim*, *Hadis* 3307, *Sahih Bukhari*, *Hadis* 7:67-68.
38. Ram Swarup, p. 61; *Sahih Bukhari*, *Hadis* 7:61.
39. Qur'an 4:31-33.
40. *Sahih Bukhari*, *Hadis* 7:140.
41. Ibid, *Hadis* 7:138.
42. *Sahih Muslim*, *ahadis* 3443-3449.
43. Ibid, *ahadis* 3443-3445.
44. Ibid, *ahadis* 3451-3452.
45. Ibid, *Hadis* 3451.
46. Ibid, *Hadis* 3499.
47. Qur'an 33:51.
48. *Sahih Muslim*, *ahadis* 3453-54.
49. *Sahih Bukhari*, *Hadis* 7:146.
50. Ibid, *Hadis* 7:18.
51. *Sahih Muslim*, *Hadis* 4981; note 2424.
52. *Sahih Bukhari*, *Hadis* 7:25.
53. Ibid, *Hadis* 7:27.
54. *Sahih Muslim*, *Hadis* 3539.
55. Ibid, *Hadis* 3539-3552.
56. Ibid, *ahadis* 3536-3538.
57. Muir, op. cit., pp. 335-36.
58. Qur'an 4:34.
59. *Sahih Bukhari*, *Hadis* 7:117.
60. Qur'an 4:35.
61. Qur'an 4:22-23.
62. Qur'an 4:24.
63. Qur'an 2:220-221.
64. Qur'an 5:5.

65. *Sahih Muslim*, *ahadis* 3268-3277.
66. Ibid, *ahadis* 3412-3413; *Sahih Bukhari*, *ahadis* 7:36-39.
67. *Sahih Muslim*, *ahadis* 3296-3301.
68. Ibid, *ahadis* 3354-3356.
69. Ibid, *Hadis* 3354.
70. Muir, op. cit., p. 337.
71. Ram Swarup, op. cit., p. 59.
72. *Sahih Muslim*, *Hadis* 3316; *Sahih Bukhari*, *Hadis* 7:58.
73. *Sahih Muslim*, *Hadis* 3294; *Sahih Bukhari*, *Hadis* 7:73.
74. *Sahih Bukhari* , *Hadis* 7:14.
75. Ibid, *Hadis* 7:18.
76. Qur'an 4:3.
77. Qur'an 4:24.
78. *Sahih Muslim*, *Ahadis* 3432-34.
79. Ibid, *Hadis* 3371.
80. Ibid, *Hadis* 3243; Qur'an 5:87.
81. Ibid, *Hadis* 3249.
82. Ibid, *Hadis* 3248.
83. Ibid, *Hadis* 3251; *Sahih Bukhari*, *Hadis* 7:52.
84. Ram Swarup, op. cit., p. 58.
85. Qur'an 58:1-3.
86. Qur'an 58:4-5.
87. Qur'an 2:226.
88. *Sahih Muslim*, *ahadis* 3494-3495.
89. Qur'an 66:1-5, 10.
90. *Sahih Muslim*, *ahadis* 3507-3511.
91. Qur'an 4:83.
92. Qur'an 33:28-29.
93. *Sahih Muslim*, *Hadis* 3464.
94. Qur'an 24:6.
95. *Sahih Muslim*, *Hadis* 3553-3577.
96. Ibid, *ahadis* 3491-3493.
97. Ibid, Translator's note 1933.
98. Ibid, *ahadis* 3473-3490.
99. Ibid, *Hadis* 3485.
100. *Sahih Bukhari*, *Hadis* 7:178.
101. Qur'an 65:1.
102. *Sahih Muslim*, *Hadis* 3512.

103. Ibid, *Hadis* 3524.
104. Ram Swarup, op. cit, p. 69.
105. Ibid.
106. Ibn Ishaq, *Sirat Rasul Allah*, p.616.
107. Muir, op. cit., p. 451.
108. Qur'an 81:8.
109. Muir, pp. 36, 466, 521.
110. Margoliouth, *Mohammed and the Rise of Islam*, pp. 459-460.

Arab and Quraysh Supremacy Among the Muslims

Arab supremacy among Muslim Umma, and Quraysh (also Quraish, Kuraish) supremacy among the Arabs is an established fact. Evidently, the Arab supremacy among the Muslims is accepted because, the holy places of Islam, Mecca and Medina, are located in al-Hijaz in Arabia, the sacred book of Islam, Qur'an, is in Arabic, and the Prophet Muhammad was an Arab. The Prophet said: "Love the Arabs for three reasons: (i) I am an Arab, (ii) the Holy Qur'an is in Arabic, and (iii) the language of the paradise shall also be Arabic.[1] It is obligatory for every Muslim to go to Mecca for pilgrimage at least once in his life-time. Kaaba (Ka'ba), located in Mecca, is the *qibla* of Islam, which every Muslim faces during prayer. On death, a Muslim is buried facing Mecca. It is taboo for a Muslim to defecate facing Kaaba.

Numerous *ahadis*, point towards the supremacy of the Quraysh, and affirm the fact that the people (Muslims) are subservient to the Quraysh and Caliphate is their right.[2] About them, Prophet Muhammad said: "The Caliphate will remain among the Quraysh even if only two persons are left (on the earth)."[3] In another *Hadis*, he said: "People are subservient to the Quraysh: the Muslims among them being subservient to Muslims among them, and the disbelievers among them being subservient to disbelievers among them."[4] According to yet other *ahadis*, the Prophet Muhammad said that "Islam will continue to be triumphant until there have been twelve Caliphs" and "all of them will be from Quraysh."[5]

Almost for six hundred years the caliphate remained with an Arab and the Quraysh till Halaku, the grandson of Genghis Khan, murdered the last caliph (also Khalifa, Khalifa) at Baghdad; this remained so, in spite of the shift of the centre of the Islamic power from Medina to Damascus to Baghdad with shifting dynasties. A shadowy Quraysh caliphate, shorn of temporal power, although Quraysh, emerged in Egypt. After that, the caliphate passed on to Turkish Sultan Usman (Usman, Uthman; 1299-1326). The titles, which Usman added to his many others, included 'Protector of the Two Lands (al-Hiijaz and Syria; the holy lands of Islam),' 'Successor of the Apostle of God,' and the 'Ruler of the Faithful.' The dynasty of Usman continued till the end of 1920, when the Turk leader, Kamal Pasha declared the abolition of the caliphate.

Although the Usman dynasty caliphate survived for about six centuries, "the sentiment that the Khalifa should be a Quraish or at least an Arab was so strong that the Sultan of Turkey was never given universal recognition by Muslim theologians."[6] The question, however, "whether Caliphate is the privilege of the Quraysh is one of those debatable issues over which there has been a good deal of difference of opinion amongst the scholars. The one view which is held by a section of the scholars is that a Caliph should necessarily be a Quraysh. The overwhelming majority of scholars, however, do not subscribe to this view and assert that a Quraysh is to be preferred as a Caliph provided he eminently possesses all other requisite qualifications, which are rightly expected of a Caliph in Islam. The Quraysh have no right to be Caliphs merely because of their being connected with their tribe of Quraysh."[7]

The note is followed by the following two *ahadis* to affirm that the Holy Prophet has himself stated the same:

"The Caliphate will remain with the Quraysh and those who would contend with them would be overthrown on their faces, so long as they would establish the *Din* (Islam)[8]

The other *Hadis*, given in support of the note, is the following:

"The Caliphs would be amongst the Quraysh so long as they would rule with justice, fulfill their promises, and treat (their people) mercifully." [9]

Yet, according to another *Hadis*, the caliphate is not the permanent prerogative of the Quraysh. It says:

"Hear and obey, even though your Amir be an Abyssinian slave with a head like that of raisins (or with crinky hair)"[10]

No sooner than Prophet Muhammad died, the struggle for power raged between the ansars and the muhajirs on one hand, and on the other Ali and Abbas, cousin and son-in-law, and the uncle of Muhammad took charge of the burial work and allowed none to participate in the same. The *ansars* gathered in the hall of Banu Sa'ida to choose Sa'd, son of Obada, one of the Medinite, as their chief. When Abu Bakr and Umar got the information about the same, they rushed to the spot with their supporters. Abu Bakr told the Medinans to accept Quraysh as caliph as Arabs may not accept Ansars on that post. He said: "O Ansar, whatever you say about you, you in fact deserve that, and there is no doubt that you are deeply attached to Allah's Apostle and most of his wives belong to your tribe, but the Arabs would not accept the Caliphate (of anyone else) but that of the people of Quraysh"[11]

Abu Bakr told the Ansars that the Quraysh were the "best of the Arabs in blood and country," and that the "Arabs will recognize the authority only in this clan of Quraysh." He told them: "We are the *Ameers*; and you are our *Wazeers*." The Ansars protested; situation became tense. Then it was proposed that each party should choose its own separate *Ameer*. The emigrants did not agree to that proposal. Ultimately, Abu Bakr was chosen as Ameer only after Umar and some others threatened to kill Sa'd. Abu Bakr declared himself the caliph of Islam next day.[12] Likewise, Ali was also threatened by Umar to accept Abu Bakr as caliph.[13]

References

1. *Mishkat*, Vol. 3, *Hadith* no. 5751.
2. *Sahih Muslim, Hadis* no. 4473-4483.
3. Ibid, *Hadis* no. 4176.
4. Ibid, *Hadis* no. 4473, 4474.
5. Ibid, *ahadis* 4480, 4481, 4482.
6. Ram Swarup, *Understanding Islam through Hadis*, p. 120.
7. *Sahih Muslim*, English translator's note no. 2287.
8. Ibid; refers: Bukhari, *"Bab al-Umara" min al-Quraish."*
9. Ibid; refers: Abu Dawud, Tayalisi, *Munsad Ahmad.*
10. Ibid; quotes *Fath-ul-Bari*, Vol. XVI, pp. 239-40.
11. *Ibn Jarir Tabari*, Vol. II, p. 457.
12. Ibn Ishaq, *Sirat Rasul Allah*, pp. 683-687.
13. Ibn Ishaq, op. cit., p. 687; *Tarikh Tabari*, Vol. I, pp. 527-529.

Terror: An Instrument of Islamic War

Prophet Muhammad Helped by Terror

Prophet Muhammad once admitted that he was helped by terror and plunder. He said: "I have been helped by terror (in the hearts of enemies) and while I was asleep I was brought the keys of the treasures of the earth which were placed in my hand." Abu Hurraira, the narrator of the Hadis, added, Messenger of Allah has left for his heavenly abode and you are now busy in getting them."[1] "Keys denote riches, honour and power and victory, and all these things were conferred upon the Holy Prophet. He was given both the worldly and the spiritual wealth," adds the translator of the Hadis, in his note.[2] The very first plunder, which the Prophet got without war, was the houses and the belongings of the Jewish tribe, Banu An Nadir; and the terror played great role in achieving the same. Ibn Ishaq writes: "God cast terror into their hearts."[3]

The 'Quranic Sura of Exile'[4] writes, how due to terror they destroyed their own houses and departed.

Allah Casts Terror

Terror is an instrument of Jehad, and Allah himself helped Muhammad and the believers by terrorizing their enemies. A Quranic verse says how Allah helped Muhammad by casting terror into the hearts of Banu Quraiza, a Jewish tribe:

"Allah did take them down from their strongholds, and cast terror into their hearts; (so that) some ye slew, and some ye made prisoners. And He made you heirs of their land, their houses, and their goods."[5]

Qur'an says again:
"I shall cast terror
Into the hearts of the infidels
Strike off their heads
Maim them in every limb."[6]

Ibn Ishaq writes about the coming down of the *Sura Unfal*[7], which came down after the battle of Badr.); it talks about 'striking terror' in the hearts of the non-believers.[8] Allah, in that Sura says, how He showed enemy's strength less to encourage the believers, and believers strength more to terrorize the Quraysh.[9]

It was not only Allah, who terrorized unbelievers, but even Gabriel, the arch-angel, also did the same. When Dihya, son of Khalifa al-Kalbi, riding on a white mule with a saddle covered with a piece of brocade, passed through the settlement of Qurayza Jews, before their massacre, Ibn Ishaq writes, what the apostle said: "That was Gabriel who has been sent to B. Quraiza to shake their castles and strike terror to their hearts."[10] The Quraiza were terrorized by Allah when the apostle besieged them for twenty-five days. Ibn Ishaq writes: "The apostle besieged them for twenty-five nights until they were sore pressed and Allah cast terror into their hearts."[11]

As discussed in separate chapter, when Prophet Muhammad got his critic poets of Medina killed, the Jews got terrorized. Even the killers admitted the fact of getting terrorized. Ibn Ishaq writes: "Our attack on Allah's enemies cast terror among the Jews, and there was no Jew in Medina who did not fear for his life."[12]

After the killings of the poets, the apostle ordered Muslims to kill any Jew coming in his way. He said, 'Kill any Jew that falls into your power.' Ibn Ishaq narrates an interesting development after that, which also indicates how terror facilitated conversion to Islam. After apostle's declaration, Ibn Ishaq writes: "Muhayyisa, son of Mas'ud, leapt upon Ibn Sunayna, a Jewish merchant with whom they had social and business relations, and killed him. Huwayyisa was not a Muslim at that time though he was the elder brother. When Muhayyisa killed him, Huwayyisa, his elder brother, began to beat him, saying: 'You enemy of Allah, did you kill him when much of the fat on your belly comes from his wealth?' Muhayyisa answered: 'Had the one who ordered me to kill him ordered me to kill you I would have cut your head off.' He said that this was the beginning of Huwayyisa's (also Huweisa) acceptance of Islam. The other replied, 'By Allah, if Muhammad had ordered you to kill me would you have killed me?' He said, 'Yes, by Allah, had he ordered me to cut off your head I would have done so.' He exclaimed: 'By Allah, a religion which can bring you to this is marvelous!' and he became a Muslim.[13]

Ibn Ishaq gives the following lines, composed by Muhayyisa, in his book:

"My mother's son blames me because if I were ordered to kill him
I would smite his nape with a sharp sword,
A blade as white as salt from polishing,

My downward stroke never misses its mark.
It would not please me to kill you voluntarily
Though we owned all Arabia from north to south."[14]

On Suneina's (also written Sunayna's) killing, Muir observes: "On the morning after the murder of Ka'b, Muhammad, exasperated at the opposition (or, as tradition puts it, the treachery) of the Jews, accorded a general permission to his followers to slay them wherever met. Accordingly, Muhayyisa,[15] having encountered Ibn Suneina, a Jewish merchant, slew him, though a confederate of his tribe. The occurrence is alluded to by the biographers rather for the purpose of explaining the sudden conversion of assassin's brother Huweisa, than to record the murder of a petty Jewish trader. Huweisa upbraided his brother for killing the confederate Jew, and appropriating his wealth; heard his replies, as stated above, "'Strange indeed!' Huweissa responded; 'hath the new religion reached to this? Verily, it is a wonderful faith.' And Huweisa was converted from that very hour."[16] Muir further writes, "The Progress of Islam begins to stand out in unenviable contrast with that of Christianity. Converts were gained to the faith of Jesus by witnessing the constancy with which its confessors suffered death; they were gained to Islam by the spectacle of the readiness with which its adherents inflicted death. In the one case conversion imperiled the believer's life; in the other, it was the only means of saving it."[17]

Prophet Muhammad did not tolerate opposition. He eliminated his opponents from his way or made them ineffective. At the same time he exhibited extreme ruthlessness, generating terror, which ultimately led to submission of entire Arabia before him. Hazleton writes: 'By expelling the Nadir, Muhammad had not only made it clearer than ever that he would tolerate no challenge to his authority;' and he forced his will on ibn Ubayy.[18]

Massacre of Qaynuqa was the ultimate step of extreme ruthlessness exhibited by him, which has been discussed elsewhere.

Yet another such extreme case was the death meted out to a old lady. Um Kirfa, A strong force, led by Zeid, was sent to punish a marauding tribe, Bani Fezara, who waylaid and plundered a mercantile expedition to Syria, with ventures from many of the citizens. Approaching stealthily, they surprised and captured the marauders' stronghold, Um Kirfa, aunt of Oyeina, and 'a lady who had gained celebrity as mistress of this nest of robbers,' and her daughter. Muir writes about her barbaric death: "Nether the sex, nor great age of Um Kirfa, saved her from a death of extreme barbarity. Her legs were tied each to a separate camel. The camels were driven asunder, and thus she was torn in pieces. Two young brothers were also put to death. Zeid, on his return, hastened to Muhammad, who hurried forth to meet him with dress ungirded; and, learning the success of the expedition, embraced and kissed him."[19]

Here, it needs mention that the inhuman torture and death of the aged lady did not bring any adverse reaction. Muir further writes: "We do not read of disapprobation at the inhuman treatment of the aged female. The daughter was given to Ayesha as her waiting-maid; but the brigand spirit survived in her, and a few years after we find her slain in a similar encounter with Khalid."[20]

The instances of brother killing a brother,[21] a son proposing to kill his own father,[22] Umar proposing the use of sword as the answer of each and every opposition or the voice of dissent, such as to propose to kill ibn Ubayy[23] were certainly not normal situations. Quran, Hadis and Prophet's biographies have many other sayings or acts where utility of terror was shown. Muir writes how terror caused conversion of the murdered person's brother to Islam[24]

References

1. *Sahih Muslim, Hadis* no. 1068.
2. Ibid, note 731.
3. Ibn Ishaq, *Sirat Rasul Allah*, p. 437; hereafter Ibn Ishaq.
4. Qur'an, Sura 59.
5. Qur'an, 33:26-27.
6. Qur'an, 8:12.
7. Qur'an, Sura 8.
8. Ibn Ishaq, p. 326.
9. Qur'an, 8:44.
10. Ibn Ishaq, p. 461.
11. Ibid.
12. Ibid, p. 368.
13. Ibid, p. 369; ibid, p. 752, Ibn Hisham's note 580.
14. Ibid, p. 369.
15. The names are differently written by different writers. Ibn Ishaq's book writes Muhayysa, Huwayysa, Sunayna; Muir writes Muheisa, Huweisa, Suneina, like that. I have retained the spellings of different writers in the quotes of their respective books.
16. Muir, *The Life of Mahomet*, p. 249; hereafter Muir.
17. Ibid.
18. Hazleton, p. 212.

19. Muir, pp. 347-48.
20. Ibid, p. 348.
21. Ibn Ishaq, pp. 752-53.
22. Ram Swarup, *Understanding Islam through Hadis*. p. 190.
23. Hazleton, p. 212.
24. Muir, p. 249.

Dhimmis and Dhimmitude

Dhimmis or Zimmis

Dhimmis (also called Zimmis) are the members of tolerated religions, who had to pay tributes (*Jizya/Jizyah*). As defined by the *Dictionary of Islam*, Zimmi is "a member of the Ahlu'z-Zimma, a non-Muslim subject of a Muslim government, belonging to the Jewish, Christian, or Sabean creed, who for the payment of a poll- or capitation tax, enjoys security of his person and property in a Muslim country."[1] With the expansion of Islamic empire, the Hindus and Buddhists also, from time to time, acquired the status of Dhimmis (Zimmis, 'responsibility' of the Muslim state), and had to pay *Jizya*.

The Qur'an, provided for the payment of the *Jizya* by the People of the Book, It said: "Fight those who believe not on Allah, nor the Last Day, nor hold that forbidden which has been forbidden by Allah and His Apostle, nor acknowledge the Religion of Truth, (even if they) are of the People of the Book, until they pay the *Jizya* with willing submission, and feel themselves subdued."[2]

Dhimmi Status and Dhimmitude

When it was not possible either to convert to Islam or to throw out a non-Muslim from a Muslim state, then that non-Muslim used to acquire the status of a Dhimmi or Zimmi, who had to pay *Jizya* and stay there with certain disabilities imposed on him. Needless to say that Dhimmitude, on the other hand is the attitude acquired by the non-Muslims in a Muslim state. It is a state of mind induced in the victims of Islamic terror, especially among the non-Muslims of a Muslim state. It is just like the 'Stockholm Syndrome,' which afflicts hostages by turning them into defenders of their kidnappers.

The Egypt-born scholar Bat Ye'or (Her pen name; meaning 'Daughter of the Nile') has done pioneering work in the study of Dhimmitude. Sufferers of Islamic terror, especially the non-Muslim subjects under harsh Islamic rule, develop a peculiar mindset, under which they start defending their oppressors. This syndrome is called Dhimmitude, from which a section of the Hindus also suffer. After all in Stockholm Syndrome, the hostages turn into defenders of their kidnappers. This happens to be due to the impact of terror.

The Beginning

When Prophet Muhammad attacked Jew settlements of Khaibar, Fadak and Wadi al-Kora, hundred miles to the north of Medina between Medina and Damascus in Syria, the land gained as *fai*, which were partly distributed among his loyal followers of Al-Hodeibiya and partly as crown possession, were left in the occupation of the Jewish cultivators, on the condition that they were to give half of the produce to the Muslims. This was necessitated as there were not enough Muslims to settle there and Prophet needed men for his raiding teams. At the same time, the continuing cultivation in that fertile valley was to solve the acute food problem, which used to force the Muslims to eat the flesh of ass. Thus, the Jews of Khaybar (Khaibar) and neighbouring settlements became the first Dhimmis.[3] These Jews were, anyway, expelled from their homes during the caliphate of Umar.

After Khaybar, there were numerous cases of making treaty with Muhammad, becoming Muslims or dhimmis, and payment of poll-tax. During Prophet Muhammad's raid on Tabuk, the Christian governors of Ayla, and the people of Jarba and Adhrub met him, made treaty and paid poll-tax. He wrote to Yuhanna, son of Ru'ba, the governor of Ayla: 'In the name of Allah the Compassionate and Merciful. This is a guarantee from Allah and Muhammad the Prophet, the apostle of Allah, to Yuhanna, b. Ru'ba and people of Ayla, for their ships and their caravans by land and sea. They and all that are with them, men, of Syria, and Yemen, and seamen, all have the protection of Allah and the protection of Muhammad the prophet. Should any one of them break the treaty by introducing some new factor then his wealth shall not save him; it is the fair prize of him who takes it. It is not permitted that they shall be restrained from going down to their wells or using their roads by lands or sea.'[4] The delegations meeting the Prophet, making treaties, followed by payment of poll-tax continued throughout his lifetime. Christianity was allowed to exist on sufferance.[5] Some Christian communities agreed to demolish their church[6]; many paid poll-tax.[7]

Muhammad bin Qasim introduced *Jizya* in Sindh.[8] Thus, it was levied from the very beginning of the Muslim rule in India. It was an instrument for humiliating non-Muslims; the payment procedure used was also humiliating one.[9] It was levied throughout the Sultanate period; abolished by Akbar, and re-imposed by Aurangzeb.[10] The poorest Hindus were hit the hardest due to it.[11]

Jizya became a means of spreading Islam in India;[12] Feroz Tughlaq was delighted by flood of conversions by imposition of jizya;[13] Aurangzeb also rejoiced on conversion due to the same.[14] Thus *Jizya*, in a way, helped forcible conversion to Islam.[15]

Disabilities Imposed on Dhimmis were the following:

1. They will not build new temples.
2. They will not rebuild or repair any old dilapidated temple fallen into disrepair.
3. Muslim travellers will not be prevented from staying in the temples.
4. Muslim travellers will be provided hospitality by Dhimmis/Zimmis in their own houses for three days.
5. Dhimmis/Zimmis will neither act as spies nor give spies shelter in their houses.
6. If any relation of a Dhimmi is inclined towards Islam, he should not be prevented from doing so.
7. Dhimmis will respect Muslims.
8. Dhimmis will courteously receive a Muslim wishing to attend their meetings.
9. Dhimmis will not dress like Muslims.
10. They will not take Muslim names.
11. They will not ride horses with saddle and bridle.
12. They will not posses swords, bows and arrows.
13. They will not wear signet rings.
14. They will not openly sell or drink intoxicating liquor.
15. They will not abandon their traditional dress, which is a sign of their ignorance, in order that they may be distinguished from Muslims.
16. They will not openly practice their traditional customs amongst Muslims.
17. They will not build their houses in the neighbourhood of Muslims.
18. They will not carry or burry their dead near Muslim graveyards.
19. They will not mourn their dead loudly.
20. They will not buy Muslim slaves.[16]

References

1. *Dictionary of Islam*, p. 710.
2. Qur'an 9:29.
3. Muir, *The Life of Mahomet*, pp. 380-82.
4. Ibn Ishaq, *Sirat Rasul Allah*, p. 607.
5. Muir, pp. 460-61.
6. Ibid, p. 461.

7. Ibid, pp. 452-467.
8. K.S. Lal, *The Legacy of Muslim Rule in India*, p. 70.
9. Ibid, pp. 119, 320.
10. K.S. Lal, *Theory and Practice of Muslim State in India*, p. 115.
11. Ibid, p. 122.
12. Ibid, pp. 120-21.
13. Ibid, pp. 120, 292.
14. Ibid, p. 121.
15. Ibid, p. 292.
16. Quoted in *A History of Sufism in India*, pp. 295-96, from *Zakhiratu'l Muluk*, pp. 117-18; Refered by Sita Ram Goel, in his *India's Secularism: New Name for National Subversion*, pp. 106-107.

Origin and Growth of Islamic Arab Empire

Only two months after his return from the farewell Pilgrimage, during the beginning of the AH XI, when Prophet Muhammad was of sixty-three years of age, that he gave orders for the expedition to the Syrian frontier. It was the forerunner of the Arab Empire formation, which he initiated, and his Companions pursuing it realized his vision and dream in no time. Syria, Iran and Egypt became parts of the emerging Arab empire within a decade. Subjugation of parts of Asia, Africa and South-West Europe followed.

Unprecedented success of the Islamic Imperialism, in terms of its spread, is unparallel in human history. Perhaps, no other empire, except that of Chenghese Khan, spread as rapidly as the Islamic Empire. It was so, both in terms of the time frame and the geographical spread. Within eighty years of the death of the Prophet, it spread from Iberian Peninsula, consisting of Spain and Portugal, in the Western Europe, to Sindh, in the Western fringe of India, in the East; and from Yemen and Egypt in the South to the parts of Central Asia in the North.

The credit for such unprecedented success of the empire-building goes to the Prophet of Islam himself; and partly, to earlier caliphs, specially Umar, the second caliph. But the credit for the origin and maturing of the ideology, goes to Prophet Muhammad, Arab Imperialism owes almost everything—its vision, its ideology, modus operandi, resource mobilization, strategies, creation of war-machinery, and all—to the Prophet. Not only his Companions, i.e., the first four caliphs, but other Islamic kings and generals continued to follow him even up to today. The history, the period, and geography of the region also played important role in the success of the endeavour.

Difficulties After the Death of the Prophet

There were initial difficulties for the Muslims after the death of the Prophet. "The Prophet had hardly departed this life," writes Muir, "when Arabia was convulsed by the violent endeavour of its tribes to shake off the trammels of Islam and regain their previous freedom. The hordes of the desert rose up in rebellion, and during the first year of his caliphate, Abu Bakr had to struggle for the very existence of the faith. Step by step, the wild Bedawin were subdued and forced to tender their submission."[1]

Abu Bakr has to fulfil two tasks immediately after the death of Prophet Muhammad. The first was to suppress the rebellion in different parts of Arabia; the second was 'to fulfil the dying wish of Muhammad' to dispatch the Syrian Army. Many, including Umar opposed the move, urging 'that the Muslim force should not be sent just yet upon this distant expedition.' Umer joined the cry: 'scatter not the believers, rather keep our army here: we may have need of it yet to defend the city.' 'Never!' replied Abu Bakr; 'the command of the Prophet shall be carried out, even if I be left here in the city all alone, prey to the wolves and beasts of the desert.' Now, they wanted a more experienced soldier to be the command chief. The caliph arose in wrath and cried, 'Out upon thee!' He seized Umar by the beard, and said: 'Hath the Prophet of the Lord named Osama to the leadership, and dost thou counsel me to take it from him.' This silenced all; Osama's expedition was successful.[2]

They fulfilled the Prophet's last command by ravaging the land; 'with the well-known cry of Ya Mansur amit ("Strike ye conquerors!"), "they slew all who ventured to oppose them in the field, and carried off captive the remainder. They burned the villages, the fields of standing corn, and the groves of palm-trees; and there went up behind them, as it were, a whirlwind of fire and smoke."[3] This was the beginning of the Arab Empire building. Osama, by his actions, fulfilled the last wish of Muhammad by avenging the defeat of Muta, and the murder of his father during the previous expedition. Earlier, he could not proceed for the expedition due to the sudden death of the Prophet.

Stages of Islamic Arab Imperialism

There were two stages of the Islamic Arab Empire formation:

i. Bringing entire Arabia under single unified Islamic State: The state entity, thus formed, may be termed as the Islamic Empire of Arabia.
ii. Bringing foreign lands under Islamic Caliphate: With incorporation of the foreign lands—Syria, Iraq, Iran, Central Asia, Egypt and other parts of the North Africa, and Iberian Peninsula—under Islamic Caliphate, the State entity formed was the Arab Empire. The core content of the State was no doubt Islam, but it imposed Arabian language, culture and way of life also on the defeated people.

Pre-Islamic Arabian Society and the Change Brought by Islam

Pre-Islamic Arabian society consisted of the (i) sedentary people in the permanent settlements like, Mecca, Medina, At-Taif, Khaybar, Tabuk, Najran and Sanna; and (ii) nomadic Beduin tribes. Prophet Muhammad and his followers endeavoured and brought the following changes in Arabia:

i. Paganism was replaced by Islam;
ii. Jews and Christians were either forced to migrate, eliminated, or made second class citizens (*dhimmis*);
iii. Arabia was brought under unified control. In another language, we may say that the process of the formation of Islamic Empire of Arabia was complete; its strengthening, of course, was done mostly by the first two caliphs.
iv. The process of taking Islam outside the boundaries of Arabia, and bringing other countries within Islamic Arab Empire was initiated by the Prophet himself.

Ideology

There components of the ideology behind Arab Islamic Imperialism were:

i. Ideology of Jehad: The ideology is based on belief of one God (Allah) and two humanities—the believers and non-believers—as enemies of each other, and the fight by the believers against the unbelievers till the end.
ii Arab nationalism and sense of superiority inculcated by Prophet Muhammad especially among his companions, and Arabs in general.
iii. Vision of the Arab Islamic Empire: The Prophet conceived the idea that Arabs shall conquer Persians, Romans, Turks, and others.

Vision of Islamic Empire

Prophet Muhammad had a sense of Arab superiority, and the dream of Arab imperialism, which his followers realized soon after his death. He had the sense of Arab and Quraysh superiority and tried to inculcate the same in others. Once, he saw a Persian bow in the hand of a person, and commanded him to throw that away, and use the other (Arab) bow and spear, telling him that "Allah shall help you to conquer other countries with the Arab bows and spears."[4]

About the future Arab conquest of the other countries, the Prophet said: "Before long, you (the Arabs) will conquer many countries and cities. Qazvin, shall be one of such places. The person, who takes part in that battle for forty nights or forty days, will be given a gold pillar in paradise encrusted with jades and rubies. He will enjoy residing in a palace, having seventy thousand gates, and each gate shall be attended by a *hurie* as his wife."[5] The longer period of forty days, mentioned above, clearly indicates that he was conscious of the longer period required for battles in distant lands. He was also conscious of the inevitability of the sea-battle, and said, accordingly, "The one who receives martyrdom in a sea-battle is equal to two martyrs of a land-battle ..."[6]

Perusal of different *ahadis* makes it clear that Prophet Muhammad had the prior perception of the war with the Turks of the Central Asia, and with Khurasan and other areas. Thus, he somehow planed about the future Arabic Islamic Empire, and his dream was fulfilled after his death in a big way. About Turks, he said: "One of the portents of the hour is that you will fight with people wearing shoes made of hair; and that you will fight with broad-faced people whose faces will look like shields coated with leather."[7] He further said about the Turks: "The hour will not be established until you fight with the Turks: people with small eyes, red faces, and flat noses. Their faces will look like shields coated with leather. The hour will not be established till you fight with people whose shoes are made of hair."[8]

About Khosrau (Iran) and Caesar (Rome; Constantinople), Prophet Muhammad said: "Khosrau will be ruined, and there will be no Khosrau after him, and Caesar will surely be ruined and there will be no Caesar after him and you (the Muslims) will spend their treasury in Allah's cause." He said: "War is deceit."[9]

There was gradual change in the purpose of jehad. It evolved from self-protection to Muslim dominance in Arabia, and ultimately to Islamic imperialism.[10] For achieving that purpose he promoted archery and horse riding.[11]

Keeping in view the importance of horse-rearing, the Prophet said: "He who reared a horse for the sole intention of using it in a Jehad, then he will be rewarded on virtue for each grain he gave the horse as a feed."[12] Keeping the importance and utility of horse in war in mind, he decided to give three shares of war-booty to a warrior with horse, and only one share to the warrior without the horse.[13]

Modus Operandi

Different modus operandi were adopted depending on the situation:

i. Muhammad followed the policy of atomization and destruction of the pagans. The pagans were attacked, their menfolk were massacred, and women and children were enslaved and sold.

ii. If the communities or families captured during the raid, consented to accept Islam, then, as happened in the case of Beni Hawazin, their cases were sympathetically considered. Hawazin, as it happened, were given the option to retain either their confiscated property or the family members. Naturally, they preferred to retain the latter.

iii. Two Jewish tribes of Medina were ousted and their lands, houses and properties were confiscated.

iv. If their presence was found beneficial, as in the case of the Jews of Khaybar, the unbelievers were allowed to stay, either temporarily or permanently, as Dhimmis.

v. In many countries, Islamic rulers were forced to tolerate the unbelievers.

Arab Participation Ensured

After overcoming the initial difficulties after the death of the Prophet, the Arabian tribes were made partners in the game of war and plunder, and the same accelerated the processes of Arab empire-building; it ensured Arab participation in the empire building efforts. Muhammad knew the historical reality of Persian-Greek conflict, and his sympathy in the conflict lied with the Caesar of the Abrahmic faith, rather than with the fire-worshipping Persians.[14] A Quranic verse pointed towards the same.[15] In reality, It was the understanding of the inner weaknesses of the Greeks and Persians, due to which Prophet Muhammad believed that the Arabs shall one day defeat the Greeks, Persians and others. Fortunately for the Arabs, Abu Bakr shared the optimism of the Prophet towards the Arab empire formation.

Bridging the Intra-Arab Divide by Partnership in Gains of War

The Intra-Arab divide was reversed by the masterstroke of the policy, which made the Arab tribes partners in war and plunder. The Bedawin tribes, by a masterstroke of policy, Muir writes: "were induced again to take up their arms, and aroused by the prospect of boundless spoil, to wield them on the side of Islam. Like bloodhounds eager for the chase, they were let forth upon mankind—the whole world their prey. They gloried in the belief that they were hosts of Allah, destined for the conversion of His elect and the destruction of His enemies. The cry of religion thus disguised or gilded every lower motive. The vast plunder of Syria and Al-'Irak was accepted as but the earnest of a greater destiny yet in store. Once maddened by the taste of blood, the lust of spoil, and capture without stint of female slaves, into a wild and irresistible fanaticism, the armies of Arabia swept their enemies everywhere before them. Checked towards the north by the strongholds of Asia Minor and the Bosphorus, the surging wave spread to the east and to the west with incredible rapidity, till in a few short years it had engulfed in common ruin the earliest seats of Christian and the faith of Zoroaster."[16]

Muslim Conquest Outside Arabia

During Abu Bakr's caliphate, the rebellion was quelled, and Arabs were brought under effective Muslim control. The area under Muslim control was extended during his caliphate up to the boundaries of Syria and Iraq. Abu Bakr nominated Umar as his successor after his two years' caliphate; who remained caliph for ten years. Romans were defeated at Yermuk after great slaughter. He removed Khalid, son of Walid from the chief command, and appointed Abu Obaydah in his place. Obaydah captured Syrian cities of Damascus, Hema (Epiphanis), Kinnisrin (Chalcis), Aleppo etc., and reached near Antioch, the capital of Roman East, and rival of Constantinople.

Another army was sent to Palestine under Omar bin As (Omar, son of As). Capitulation of Jerusalem was brought by that army after a siege of some duration in presence of caliph Umar. An expedition in Egypt made the country free from Byzantines. The Romans of the country took shelter in Alexandria, which also fell in the hands of the Muslims. Egypt, up to the border of Abyssinia towards the south and to the west up to the border of Libya came under Arab rule.

The defeat of Persia at Nehawand was a great occasion for the Arabs. The defeat of that great power brought huge resources to the Muslims. That victory, the Arabs termed the 'Victory of the victories' (*Fathu'l Fatuh*). Defeating a great power was a landmark in the history of the Arab Imperialism. Prior to the defeat of Iran, a peace treaty was concluded with them, but that treaty did not work, and in the war, which followed after a year, Iran was defeated by the Arabs.

Muawiya came to power after the first Arabian civil war; in 655 AD. (AH 34), Muslim fleet under Muawiya scored victory over the army led by Emperor Constance II at Phoenix (modern Finike). Situation, however, changed, and in 658 truce; Muawiya agreed to pay annual tribute to the Emperor Constance II. The truce was, anyway, nothing but stratagem; regular predatory raids against the Christian kingdom continued. With the changed situation, hostility against Caesar were restarted; the army of Islam reached its capital city. Military campaign of 669 AD (49 AH) under Yazid, son of Muawiya, and the killer of Husain, the grandson of Muhammad, and his family members, succeeded in reaching the high triple wall of Constantinople. Yazid fought with much fervour, fortitude and ferocity, and earned the title of 'Hero of the Arabs' (*Fateh al-*

Arab). Constantinople could, however, be won centuries later, only by the Turks, and not by the Arabs. The capital of Islamic Empire shifted from Medina to Damascus in Syria during the caliphate of Muawiya.

Musa, son of Nasir (Musa ibn Nasir) conquered the north coast of Africa up to the Atlantic. He was son of a Christian captive, captured by Arab general Khalid, son of Walid (Khalid bin Walid). He appointed Tariq, a freed man of barber origin as his lieutenant. Tariq crossed Mediterranean Sea, entered Spain in 711 AD, with an army of 7,000 men, mostly of barber origin. Here, it needs mention that the barbers were of the Semitic origin, and the cousins of the Arabs. Although converted to Christianity, they were not romanized, and were soon converted to Islam. Tariq's army, supplemented to 12000 by now, met the armies of King Roderick at the mouth of the Barbate River on July 19, 711. Although only on a marauding mission, Tariq's army defeated him, and occupied half of Spain within a year. The victory glorified the name of Tariq for the historically brilliant achievement with an army of barbers. But it aroused the jealousy of Musa. History, anyway, immortalized his name; the Rock, where he landed, became known as Jabal-al-Tariq, the corrupt form of which is Gibraltar. The expectation of untold plunder on one hand, and the promised entry into paradise, in case of fiasco, on the other, aroused the enthusiasm of the barber invaders; they were beyond measure and felt crazy for the battle. On the other side, the political enemies of the king, headed by Bishop Oppas, were there, the defeat of the half-hearted Visgothic army was ensured. Roderick, anyway vanished after the defeat, and nobody knew about his whereabouts after that.

Although Tariq planted the Arab flag on European soil, he received unexpected reception from Musa, the Arab governor. Tariq's success aroused the jealousy of Musa. He raised the army of 10,000 Arabs, hurriedly went to Spain in June 712, met Tariq in Toledo, and charged him for insubordination. Rather halting in the early stages, as ordered, and limiting his activities only to the marauding activities, he acted further, charged Musa. Musa spanked and reviled Tariq publicly; he scourged him mercilessly, and put him in chains as an ignominious prisoner. Musa, then proceeded to complete the conquest of Spain, and succeeded in the endeavour. Strangely, Tariq continued to serve such arrogant master during the campaign. Unfortunately, Musa was also charged with the same allegations, and summoned to Damascus by al-Walid, the caliph. Musa proceeded for Damascus with a huge train of spoils; and when he reached Tiberias (Palestine), he received a secret message from Suleman, brother and heir apparent of the caliph, that the caliph was seriously ill, and he should delay his arrival to Damascus. In reality, Suleman wanted to claim the glory of victory and booty for his own reign, but that did not happen, as al-Walid recovered temporarily. Al-Walid, after receiving extravagant plunder, which included luster of females and male beauties, received Musa favorably; he was rewarded with imperial praises and courtesies in a well-decorated Mosque. The booty which he brought, included four hundred Gothic nobles fully dressed in gold coronets and girdles, as a sign of the Divine blessings, thirty thousand most delicate European women, the superb table said to be of the King Solomon, apart from enormous wealth.

Although dazzle of the plunder made al-Walid satisfied, exactly the opposite happened with his successor Suleman, who brought him before a partial judge, who found Musa guilty of vanity and falsehood. He was publicly whipped, forced to stand in front of the palace gate a whole day in the blazing sun. Ultimately, he begged to be allowed to go to Mecca as a pilgrim, which was granted. But, his entire property was confiscated. Musa was a zealous Muslim, he remembered the *Hadis*, according to which , the Prophet said that the Arabs would subjugate Constantinople, and wanted to do it. Musa, the winner of Africa and Spain for the Arabs and the Islam, lived as a beggar in a remote village of Wady-al-Qura, in al-Hijaz.

After Musa, al-Hurr, his successor al-Samah, son of Malik al-Khawlani won Septimania and Narbonne, and then was killed in a battle. Abd-al-Rahman, son of Abdullah al-Ghafiqi, the Amir over Spain, was able to advance through Western Pyrenees in the year 732. Thus the Islamic Arab Empire, in the Centenary year of the death of Prophet Muhammad, became greater than the Roman Empire.

The expansion of the Arab Empire continued eastward towards India and northwards towards Central Asia also.

The boundary of Arab Islamic Empire touched India after the defeat of Iran in 643, almost a year before the death of Caliph Umar. Umar sent an expedition to India to pillage Thana in 636-37. Next two Caliphs, Usman and Ali, also sent expeditions, which failed. Thus, all the four 'pious' Caliphs of Islam failed to see any part of India conquered. In the expedition in 712, Muhammad bin Qasim (Muhammad, son of Qasim) succeeded in conquering Sindh. Islam, however, took 560 year after the death of its Prophet to enter Delhi. Numerous Arab attacks on India, bin Qasim's attack, via all the three existing routes, were disastrous for the Arabs, and most of the attacking army personal perished. Here, it may be interesting to peruse the results of the Arab attacks elsewhere.. Iran, Syria and Egypt were conquered by the Arabs within nine years of the death of Muhammad. Within eighteen years of his death, the boundary of the

Arab empire touched Hindu Kush and Oxus River. The whole of North Africa was conquered between 640 and 709; and Spain, the farthest place in the then Arab empire, in 711. A fringe of Indian territory, the Sindh, was captured eighty years after the death of the Prophet.

Khurasan, Balkh and Merv, the fringe areas of the Central Asia, were conquered just after the conquest of Iran. In 662, Abdullah, son of Emir, succeeded in conquering Khurasan, and he was made governor there.. Initially raids and conquests were initiated from there also. In Central Asia Qutayb conquered Kashgar in 715 AD; Nasr Ibn-Sayyar – recaptured these areas during 738-40. In 751, Arabs occupied Al-Shash (Tashkent).

Factors Causing Success

Important factors, helping the rapid spread of Islam, and extensive expansion of Arab Islamic Empire, were the following:

i. Resource Mobilization;
ii. Creation of War Machinery: Mobilization of Men and Material;
iii. Geographical and Demographic factors;
iv. Historical factors;
v. Strategic inputs.

Resource Mobilization

Gradual increase in human and material resource mobilization was the prime factor responsible for the rapid and extensive expansion of the Arab Islamic State. Initially, there was extreme dearth of men and material. Many *ahadis* show the pathetic situation of the Prophet and his men due to resource crunch. A Hadis, given hereafter, makes the situation clear. The narrator says: "We went in the company of the Prophet for a *Ghazwa* and we were six persons having one camel which we rode in rotation. So (due to excessive walking) our feet became thin and my feet became thin and my nail dropped, and we used to wrap our feet with pieces of cloth, and for this reason, the Ghazwa was named Dhat-ur-Riqa as we wrapped our feet with rags."[17] As against this pathetic situation, only few years after that, in the Battle of Honein, during AH VIII (28 January, 630), there were 12,000 men with him; there was only one camel during the raid mentioned above, and not even one in the Battle of Badr, whereas 24,000 camels were captured in the above mentioned single battle. And, mind it, that was apart from 40,000 sheep and goats, 4,000 ounces of silver and 6,000 prisoners captured in that battle.[18]

A man has natural weakness for material gain. The religious sanction of plunder; making it holy booty, encouraged the people for Jehad. The religious sanction of plunder was beneficial for Islam in many ways. The Jehadis were no more ordinary warriors; they became the warriors of Allah, the *mujahids*. Added to the help of the angels, as they believed to happen during the Battle of Badr, they were doubly benefited—this-worldly booty and other-worldly paradise. The Islamic State was not only free from paying its soldiers, but they earned and gave *khums* to the State.

Islamic War Machinery

Prophet Muhammad was the first person in Arabia to understand and popularize the need of horses in war, which was needed for enhanced mobility of the warriors. He gave three shares of the booty to the cavalry, and only one to the foot soldier. Needless to say, it had the desired result. He used the State funds for purchasing men and materials for the war, and popularized archery and swordsmanship. Continuous engagement of the Muslims in raids and battles made them efficient soldiers.

Muhammad was quick to adopt innovations, as he did during the siege of At-Taif. The Beni Daus, a tribe residing one or two days south of Medina, were famous for the use of testudo and catapults. He adopted their technique and used it during the above mentioned siege.[19]

The revenue of the State tremendously increased after the capture of foreign lands. Umar established a civil list of all Arabs; made them partners in the earnings of the State. Diwan or civil list of Umar fixed payment even to a newborn baby from the State exchequer. Obviously, making every Arab citizen a beneficiary of the State earnings enhanced the smooth working of the Arab State and the efficient working of its war machinery.[20]

Geographical and Demographic Factors

The geography and sparse population of the Arabian peninsula, and the neighbouring countries helped in rapid growth of the Islamic empire. It was easy to attack and capture sparsely populated settlements of Arabia. That was the reason, that Prophet Muhammad and his companions could capture entire Arabia within ten years; only 150 persons died during the entire period. By making defeated people sharers in the benefits of war, the entire Arabia fought, against the sparsely populated regions, and won them. The estimated populations of the conquered countries during mid-seventh century, according to Colon Clarke was: Egypt – three million, rest of the North Africa – two million, Asia Minor,

Syria and Cyprus – eleven million; other countries of South-West Asia – eleven million.[21] Moreover, these countries had very small fighting forces in seventh and eighth centuries enabling the invading Arabs to overrun and Islamise them.[22]

Historical Factor

Eight hundred years of war, between the Persian and Byzantine empires since the time of Alexander, made the two empires hollow from within; their resources were depleted. It was the resource crunch and stress of warfare, which led to the neglect of the upkeep of the Marib Dam in Yemen, which ultimately caused its destruction, leading to the desertification of the area and northward migration of the Quraysh and other tribes. Similarly, Persian-built irrigation system of the Iraqi plains between the Euphrates and the Tigris rivers were deteriorating a century later. Due to lack of money, the troops had been withdrawn from the Byzantine province of Syria, leaving many fortresses, in the long north-south line of defense, unused, and therefore, eroded by sand and dust. The Byzantine Syria of Prophet Muhammad's days, it needs mention, included today's Syria, Lebanone, Israel and Palestine.

The neglected and dilapidated Byzantine forts gave shelter, some times to the solitary monks, as Ibn Ishaq has written about monk Bahira, and, some time to Bedouin hordes during the winter. Pre-Islamic Arab folklore has numerous mention of the same. Muhammad had seen these from his experienced eyes, and he must have fathomed the reality about the inner strength of the Byzantine and Persian empires, and hence the ahadis about the defeat of these empires by the Arabs. An extra reason of the inner weakness of the Persian Empire was its wars with Central Asian nomads. Anyway, the Arab army defeated Iran, and was able to grab parts of the Byzantine Empire in no time. The huge resources acquired due to war gains made onward journey of Arab Empire smooth and easier.

Strategic Input

i. Prophet Muhammad himself admitted that he was helped by terror.[23] The very first holy booty the Prophet got was due to terror.[24] As discussed elsewhere, he was benefited by divine help; Allah helped him in Battle of Badr by terrorizing his enemies. Many of his critics were slaughtered on his prompting, which generated terror in the society, which helped conversion to Islam and defeat of his enemies.[25]

ii. Prophet Muhammad adopted changed strategy in war, based on deceit and lies. The ahadis say: "Fighting is art of deceit;"[26] "Lie is permitted in war;"[27] "War is deceit."[28]

iii. Inculcating belief in supernatural aid among his followers, enabled them to fight with renewed vigour.[29]

iv. Elements of Surprise: The Prophet used to surprise his enemies, and defeat them by unconventional acts, such as, war during the prohibited months, burning plantations and houses, etc.[30]

v. Treaties were made and broken for strategic gains, if necessary.[31]

vi. Readiness to kill near and dear ones for the cause of *umma* was the accepted norm.[32] Islamic calendar starts from *hijr*, which symbolized 'breaking of the old kinship' based on blood relationship' and beginning of the 'kinship' based on faith.' This changed the behavioural pattern of the Muslims. When a person fighting with Ali, knew him to be his friend's son, he declared: "I would not kill you;" Ali said, "I will do so."[33] and declined to fight him. But Ali insisted on fighting. Umar killed his maternal uncle;[34] wanted Ali to kill his brother. Islam had rent all bonds asunder.[35]

vii. Prophet Muhammad adopted the technique of siege of the fortified settlements for terrorization and forcing the enemies to surrender.

viii. Marauding missions were conducted for defeating the enemy and the war gains. Repeated marauding missions ensured weakening of the strong enemy and the plunder. Muhammad had to attack at-Taif twice; the object was plunder and weakening the enemy. Mahmud of Ghazni attacked India seventeen times.

ix. Islam generated strong enemy consciousness (*Shatru-bodh.*)

x. Prophet's unwavering steadfastness helped in rapid growth of Islam.

An Islamic Empire building was not possible without the pragmatism and strategic inputs by the Prophet Muhammad.

Arabization

Arab conquest in the foreign lands initiated the process of Arabization. Apart from Islamization, acute changes in the way of life, culture and language took place. Encyclopaedia Americana writes about the changes in Syria: "The advent of Islam radically altered the Syrian way of life and gave the country the new look which it has maintained to the present day. Gradually Arabic replaced Aramaic as the vernacular and Islam supplanted Christianity, When in 661 the seat of the caliphate shifted from Medina to the Damascus, Syria loomed as the leading Muslim country in the world.[36] Here, it needs mention that Syriac and Arabic differ considerably. Encyclopedia further writes: "Structurally, Syriac is almost identical with the earlier Aramaic, agreeing with it phonetically, morphologically, lexically, and syntactically, in contrast to Hebrew and Arabic. It differs from its parent Aramaic only where Greek has affected it. In addition to the rather ambiguous Semitic system of "perfect" (completed) and "imperfect" (incomplete) aspects of verbal action, Syriac developed, under the influence of Greek, a more precise system of real tenses, achieved by the use of parts of the verb *be* as auxiliary verbs."[37]

The seventh century was critical for the Syrians. The Persian War, culminating in the fall of Jerusalem (614) and Alexandria (615-616), so seriously crippled the West that there was scarcely a noteworthy man of letters during the period. The Arab invasion and conquest of Syria followed almost immediately (633-638) and Syriac language began a slow decline. As the use of Arabic increased, that of Syriac diminished until by the eleventh century Arabic was dominant.[38]

Arabic was imposed on Iran after the Arab rule. Encyclopedia Americana writes: "The Arab invasion of 641 AD imposed Arabic upon Iran, except where heretical groups persisted in preservation of the old literature in secret. A colony of Persians who refused to accept Islam migrated to India taking their religious books with them, and thus preserved a mass of literature which probably would have been lost in Iran. These Parsis still utilize the Avestic or Pahlavi for their ritualistic devotions."[39] It further writes: "The religious influence of Islam, with its preference for Arabic as a divinely revealed eternal tongue, weighed heavily on Persian literature. Arabic was a sign of erudition, wherefore writers too frequently rivaled each other in their effort to use Arabic words, phrases, and idioms. During the eighteenth and early nineteenth centuries, Persian became a little more than a vehicle for connecting Arabic words. Many compound words appeared—half-Arabic, half-Persian."[40] Here, it needs mention that Alexander "allowed most of the literature to be destroyed, and Greek was substituted as the official language during the four centuries of Parthian rule. These kings considered themselves philhellenes and suppressed official expressions in Iranian terma"[41] Of course, there have been upsurge of Iranian nationalism also from time to time, when certain changes were visible.

Inferior Status of Non-Arab Converts

Vanquished Spaniards converted to Islam, called muladies, had inferior status. The same was the case with barbers.[42] Not only Arab Muslims, but even Turks, Iranian, and other Muslims coming from the West Asia or Central Asia considered Indian Muslims to be inferior. Even Indian Muslims were not free from this malady; they considered *ajlafs*, among them, and Julahas, among Muslim castes to be the lowest.

Elements of Colonialism

The analysis of the Arab Empire formation shows that it had all the elements of colonization.[43]

Break-up of the Arab Empire

The Arab Islamic Empire did not remain the part of the Islamic caliphate for long. After the defeat of Roderick, Spain remained subject to the caliphate of Damascus only upto 756, when an Ommiad prince Abd-er-Rahman I (r. 756-788), fleeing from the Abbasids, founded an independent emirate in Cordoba. Although the emirate expanded and entire Spain came under its fold. Abd-er-Rahman III (r. 912-961) converted into a caliphate, which, undermined by continual discord, broke up into petty kingdoms early in the eleventh century.[44]

References

1. Muir, Sir William, *The Life of Mahomet*, p. 508; hereafter Muir.
2. Ibid, p. 507.
3. Ibid, p. 508.
4. *Ibn-E-Majah*, Vol. 2, p. 177.
5. Ibid, p. 169.
6. Ibid, p. 168.
7. *Sahih Al-Bukhari*, Vol. IV:178.
8. Ibid: IV:179.
9. Ibid, Vol. IV: 267.
10. *Ibn-e-Majah,* Vol. 2, p. 172.
11. Ibid, p. 178.
12. Ibid, p. 172.
13. Ibn Ishaq, *Sirat Rasuk Allah*, p. 466; hereafter Ibn Ishaq.
14. Muir, 122-123; 123 note 1.
15. Qur'an 30:1ff.
16. Muir, pp. 508-509.
17. *Sahih Bukhari*, *Hadis* 5:450(B).
18. Ibid, *Hadis* 5:450(B).
19. Muir, pp. 418-19.
20. *Tarikh Tabari*, Vol. II, pp. 476-79; .Ram Swarup, *Understanding Islam through Hadis*, p. 27 note.
21. Colin Clarke, *Population Growth and Land*, p. 64; Quoted by K.S. Lal in his *Muslim State in India*, p. 16; hereafter Lal.

22. K.S. Lal, op. cit, p. 16.
23. *Sahih Muslim. Hadis* 1968; note 731.
24. Ibn Ishaq, p. 437.
25. Muir, pp. 284, 314; Margoliouth, p. 309; 1bn1shaq; pp. 438, 461.
26. Ibn-e-Majah, Vol. 2, p. 182.
27. SM 6303-6305.
28. SB 4:262; 4:267; 4:268.
29. Margoliouth, p. 401.
30. Ibn Ishaq p.485; Margo 400; Mill p. 297 n. 1; SB 614.
31. Margo pp. 350-51; Bukhari Ch. 4. pp. 563-64.
32. Muir, p. 297.
33. Ibn Ishaq, pp. 455-56.
34. Ram Swarup, p. 168.
35. Muir, pp. 229-30.
36. Encyclopaedia Americana, Vol. 26, p. 190.
37. Ibid, p. 193.
38. Ibid, p. 195.
39. Ibid, Vol. 15, p. 306.
40. Ibid, p. 307.
41. Ibid, p. 306.
42. Ibid, p. 306.
43. Lal, pp.13; 67-68.
44. Encyclopedia Americana, Vol. 25, p. 360j.

Islamic Economy

The state and status of the traditional economy has been discussed briefly in various chapters of the book. The nature, in most cases, restricted the economic activity to animal husbandry in the desert and nomadic way of life. The sedentary people of the fertile valleys, such as Madina, Khaybar and Ta'if relied on horticulture and agriculture. Mecca relied on temple-linked economy, limited manufacturing and trade. But, Islam introduced new elements in the economic life of the Arabs, which needs to be discussed in brief.

New sources of income were added to the traditional ones after the introduction of Islam in Arabia. Initially, when the Meccan Muslims migrated to Medina, they suffered due to extreme poverty.[1] They relied on donations/ help received from rich Muslims, mainly the Madinan Muslim converts, *Ansars*, or the helpers. Thus, donation for helping the poor formed part of the Muslim religious obligation, known as *Zakat*. Later on *Zakat* became a tax imposed by the Muslim State, and every Muslim was supposed to pay 2.5 per cent of his wealth as *Zakat*. Later on spoils of war or the war booty became the main source of income. The tax imposed on the *dhimmis* or *zimmis*, known as *jizya*, became the third source of income of an Islamic State. We have discussed *Zakat* and *Jizya* in separate chapters in this book, and discussed about war booty (*Male ghanimat*) in this chapter.

Islamic State Funds

The Islamic State, during the last days of the Prophet, was funded by the following sources.

i. Zakat collection from the Muslims;
ii. Spoils of War;
iii. One-fifth share of the booty (*khums*);
iv. *Fai'*; and
v. *Jizya*

We have discussed *Zakat* and *Jizya* in separate chapters. The remaining two new introductions in the economy need further elaboration.

Spoils of War

War booty became the main source of income of the umma, i.e., the Islamic community, after the adoption of the 'profession of sword.' The plundering of the infidels and the polytheists was made lawful by Islam. A *Hadis* says: "The spoils of war were not lawful for any people before us. This is because Allah saw our weakness and humility and made them lawful for us."[2] Yet, according to another *Hadis*, Muhammad said: "while I was asleep I was brought the keys of the treasures of the earth."[3] This wealth, Abu Huraira added, the followers of the Apostle "are busy in getting them."[4] Abu Huraira, it needs mention, survived the Apostle twenty-five years, and was witness to the flow of wealth to the Muslims by plundering of infidels and polytheists.

The Qur'an said, "Eat ye the spoils of war, it is lawful and pure."[5] Sura Anfal, or 'Spoils of War' (Sura 8) came down after the Battle of Badr. With regard to the Muslims quarreling about the spoils of war,[6] the Qur'an said: 'They ask thee concerning (things taken as) spoils of war. Say, "(Such) spoils are at the disposal of Allah and the Apostle; so fear Allah, and keep straight the relations between yourselves. Obey Allah and His Apostle, if ye do believe."'[7]

Kind of the Booty

The booty, according to Islam, is of the following three kinds:

i. When non-Muslims surrender without resistance and war, the entire spoils belong to Allah and his Apostle. The spoils, acquired thus, were to be used by the Apostle for his family and the needy Muslims. That was called *fai.'* The Qur'an says: "Whatever gains Allah has turned over to his Apostle from the inhabitants of the village belong to Allah, the Apostle, the kinsfolk, orphans, the needy, the traveler in need—this is so that they do not just circulate among those of you who are rich—so accept whatever the Apostle gives you, and abstain from whatever he forbids you. Be mindful of Allah; Allah is severe in punishment."[8]

ii. The spoils, acquired after war, were to be distributed among the Apostle and the Muslim participants in the war/raid. In this case, one-fifth of the booty belonged to Allah and His Apostle, and the remaining part was distributed among the participants. The Qur'an says: "Know that of that which you seize as spoils (*Male ghanimah*), a fifth-part (*khums*) belong to Allah, to His Apostle, his family, the orphans, the poor, the traveler ..."[9] The *Hadis* says: "If you come to a township which has surrendered without a formal war and you stay therein, you have a share (in the form of an award) in (the properties obtained from) it. If a town disobeys Allah and the Apostle (and fights against the Muslims) one-fifth of the booty seized therefrom is for Allah and His Apostle and the rest is for you."[10]

iii. In case a Muslim kills an infidel then the properties of the slain infidel becomes the exclusive property of the killer. Abu Qatada, according to a *Hadis*, killed a non-Muslim and received his property.[11] A Muslim killing an infidel spy received the belongings of the infidel along with his usual share of booty.[12]

War Booty: The Gift of Allah

As Qur'an says, the war booty is the gift of Allah. It says: "And he made you heirs of their lands, their houses and their goods, and of a land which ye had not frequented (before). And Allah has power over all things."[13] Judaic-Christian God also provides such gifts, as we find in the Old Testament of the Bible.[14] It details Jehovah's instruction to the Moses and Eleazar, as to how to divide the plunder,[15] the list of the captured items by the soldiers, and the respective shares,[16] and the reporting of the same to Moses.[17] Thus, Biblical and Quranic traditions, practically did not differ in this matter.

Divine Punishment for Theft and Misappropriation of War Booty

A check against misappropriation of war booty was essential for maintaining unity within *ummah*, and therefore, divine punishment was ordained against the theft or misappropriation of the same. The Qur'an says: "And whosoever deceives his companions as regard to booty, he shall bring forth on the Day of Resurrection that which he took illegally.[18]

Sahih Bukhari says: "The person stealing anything from the booty, he shall carry that on his neck, and the Prophet will refuge to intercede for him to Allah."[19]

According to a *Hadis*, a slave of Prophet Muhammad died in a holy war, and thus earned a place in the Paradise as a martyr. The Prophet, however, "saw him in the Fire for the garment or cloak that he had stolen from the booty." Some people, hearing it, became highly perturbed, and one of them, who had presumably pilfered or committed theft, came to the Prophet "with a lace or two laces and said: Messenger of Allah, I found them on the day of Khaibar (Khaybar; name of the battle). The Holy Prophet remarked: This is a lace of fire or two laces of fire."[20]

Items of Plunder

The items of plunder included the following:

1. The land and the buildings, left behind by the Jews of Medina and Khaybar, made the life of the Muslim emigrants comfortable and happy. The landed property acquired was considered more valuable than the other property.[21]
2. Livestock: The Muslims used to capture large number of camels, sheep, goats, etc. as booty. Umar tells about one expedition: "The Prophet sent an expedition to Nejd and I was among the troops. They got a large number of camels as booty. Eleven or twelve camels came to the lot of every fighter and each of them also got an extra camel."[22]
3. Other items: The other items, apart from land and livestock, included jewelry, clothes, arms, foodstuff, etc. Muir writes about the items plundered at Khaybar: "Khaybar was a fertile and prosperous region, and plunder there was also rich beyond expectation. It included vast stores of dates, oil, honey and barley, flocks of sheep and herds of camel, and a very large spoil in treasure and jewels. As usual, a fifth was set apart for the apostle and the remaining four-fifths were sold by outcry, the proceeds, divided into 1800 shares, were distributed as per rules."[23]
4. The Slaves: A large number of slaves were captured during the expeditions. Ibn Ishaq writes about the sale of the captured Jews as slaves by the Prophet: He writes: "Then the apostle sent Sa'd b. Zayd al-Ansari, brother of b. 'Abdu'l Ashhal, with some of the captive women of B. Qurayza to Nejd and he sold them for horses and weapons."[24] Indian history written by Muslim historians is full of the capture of the Hindus in thousands during Islamic period. Slavery was institutionalized by Islam[25]

In the battle of Badr, Quraysh were captured along with war booty. The captured persons were tied for ransom,[26] Meccans paid ransom and got their redemption.[27] According to a *Hadis*, the payment of the ransom of a *Mushkirun* (polytheist, idolaters, pagans) was essential. The Prophet said: "Do not leave a single Dirham thereof."[28] Only few of the Badr prisoners, such as An-Nadr and Okba, were beheaded;[29] others were freed on payment of ransom by their relatives and family men.[30] Prophet Muhammad was, however, reprimanded for the same.[31] The Qur'an said: "It is not fitting for a prophet to take captive before he has thoroughly subdued the land. Ye look for the temporal goods of this world; but Allah looketh to the hereafter: And Allah is Exalted and Wise. Had it not been for a previous ordainment from Allah, a severe penalty would have reached you for (the ransom) that ye took. But now enjoy what ye took in war, lawful and good: But fear Allah; for Allah is oft-forgiving, Most Merciful."[32]

Though men were killed afterwards, the killing of children and women was prohibited, who were captured, enslaved and sold.[33]

Saving Women and Children was Beneficial for Jehad

As already mentioned, the women and children of the infidels and Jews could be sold and men and materials—arms and horses—, for promoting Jehad, could be procured. Otherwise also, they formed important economic assets as slaves and concubines, who eventually became Muslims. Margoliouth writes about the reaction of Prophet Muhammad towards the acts of killings, and killers of the women and children of the infidels: 'Khalid, son of Al-Walid, whose savagery had already won a rebuke from the Prophet, earned a fresh one by thinking it his duty to kill these amazons: an act which was totally against the idea of gallantry; just as he found it necessary to rebuke others who had thought their duty to slaughter the children of the unbelievers. "What are the best of you," he asked: "but children of un-believers?"'[34] The remarks of Margoliouth needs to be judged by what Qur'an and Hadis said in such cases, and I have not found Prophet's opinion about gallantry.

Immigrants Pay Back the Ansars

With the flow of booty, and expulsion and slaughter of Jewish communities, discussed elsewhere, Prophet Muhammad started returning whatever the *Ansars* gave to him earlier.[35] Other emigrants also became rich enough to pay back the *ansars* for their help and gifts given earlier.[36]

Use of State Funds

The resources at the disposal of Prophet Muhammad, in reality, the funds of the Islamic state, were mainly used for the purchase of men (payment for firming up in faith), and materials for jehad—arms and horses. This was apart from the expenditure for the maintenance of Prophet's family. Generous treatment and giving gifts for firming up in faith was thought to be necessary.[37] That was the reason that more booty was given to new converts.[38] Prophet Muhammad, vide a *Hadis* of *Sahih Bukhari*, said: "I give to Quraysh people in order to attract their hearts and let them adhere to Islam, for they are near to their life of ignorance."[39] In another Hadis, Prophet said: "I give (at times material gifts) to persons who were quite recently in the state of unbelief, so that I may incline them to truth."[40] It was impeccable behaviour, in perfect accord with the Quranic teaching[41] to gain hearts (*mullafa qulubhum*).

When the properties of Banu Nazir, the exiled Jewish tribe of Medina were confiscated, Prophet Muhammad distributed some of them among his Quraysh followers, to the exclusion of *ansars*, and kept a large part for his family's upkeep. According to a *Hadis*, "Umar said: 'The Properties abandoned by Banu Nazir were the ones which Allah bestowed upon His Apostle for which no expedition was taken either with cavalry or camel. These properties were particularly meant for the Holy Prophet. He would meet the annual expenditure of his family from the income thereof, and would spend what remained for purchasing horses and weapons as preparation of *Jihad*'"[42] In the line of this thinking, "when the Messenger of Allah conquered Hunain and distributed the booty, he bestowed upon those whose hearts it was inclined to win.[43] Even his enemies, who accepted Islam, such as Abu Sufyan, Safwan, Uyaina, Aqra and Alqama, received hundred camels each.[44] On being pointed out about the favour shown to new converts, he replied: "He may be a Muslim. I often bestow something on a person, whereas some one else is dearer to me than he, because of the fear that he (the former) may fall headlong into the fire."[45] This clearly indicates that he feared that new converts needed material incentive to prevent them from lapsing into unbelief.

After the distribution of the plundered items to the neo-converts, the *ansars* had the feeling that the Prophet is favouring his kinsmen. While distributing land plots and booty, at Khaibar, the loyal Companions of Al-Hudeibiya, were dully rewarded, and their feelings assuaged.[46]

The fundings by Prophet Muhammad for firming up faith continued lifelong. When deputations of ten men came to Prophet Muhammad from Khaulan during AH 10, and informed him that they were Muslims, then they were well received, by him, and when they departed after few days, then each of them were given twelve and half ounces of silver as reward.[47] Similar treatment was given to a delegation of 19 men from Banu Hanifa, who were given five ounces of silver each as gift.[48]

Distribution of Booty

Ibn Ishaq writes about the distribution of the booty after the massacre of Banu Qurayza: "Then the apostle divided the property, wives and children of B. Qurayza among the Muslims, and he made known on that day the shares of horse and men, and took out the fifth. A horseman got three shares, two for the horse and one for his rider. A man without a horse got one share. On the day of B. Qurayza, there were thirty-six horses. It was the first booty on which lots were cast and the fifth were taken. According to its precedent and what the apostle did the divisions were made, and it remained the custom for raids."[49] Ibn Ishaq further discusses about the distribution of booty, and about its Quranic sanction.[50] The companions of the Prophet, such as Umar, also distributed the booty.[51]

Lure of Plunder

The lure of plunder was the main motivating force for the *jehad.* The slaughter of the enemy terrorized them; Allah gave the Jehadis land, dwellings and the properties.[52] 'By modern standard the Booty acquired from the Battle of Badr may look trivial but by the then prevailing economic conditions of Arabia, its psychological effects, and the part played in building the Arab Empire, it was simply terrific; the loot consisted of 115 camels, 14 horses, a great store of vestments and carpets, articles of fine leather, with much equipage and armour.'[53] In anyway, that battle brought the break through. The number of participants in raids and battles continued to increase due to charm of booty, and paradise in afterlife. Men in need used to request the Prophet to send them with raiding parties. There were cases when non-Muslims also wanted to participate, but Prophet Muhammad did not allow them to do so.

A Muslim wanted help from the Prophet to enable him to pay dowry. The Prophet said: "We have nothing which we should give you. There is a possibility that we may send you to an expedition where you may get booty." The man was afterwards sent on an expedition marching against the Banu Abs.[54]

Rich Plunder

Initially only few Muslims, and that too, only Meccan refugees, participated in the raids; that was often without success. But with greater intelligence and authentic information gathering, success in plunder, effective participation increased. During AH 3, Zeid was dispatched by Muhammad with a raiding party to attack the caravan party of the Quraysh. The leaders fled. The booty was valued at 100,000. After giving Prophets fifth, each soldier got 800 as the share. Zeid became a favourite commander after this raid.[55] The plunder during attack on Bani al-Mustalik during December, 625 AD (AH 5) was 200 families, 2,000 camels, and 5,000 sheep and goats, besides much household goods, which was divided in the usual way.[56] The plunder of Hunain, where the Hawazin brought their families and belongings to the battlefield, was really rich and more.[57]

After the defeat, they got converted to Islam, and wanted the booty back. They were then given the choice to select one, either their families or the goods. Obviously, their choice was the family. But new converts did not like it. Margoliouth writes: "Obviously they could not have both; and being given the choice preferred their women and children; there being some question whether the Muslims would consent to part with this valuable half of the plunder; the more so, as in order to quiet the conscience of those who hesitated to violate the married women (whose husbands had not been killed), the Prophet had, on divine authority, declared that *marriage is annulled by captivity*. The older followers of the Prophet readily consented to sacrifice their slaves and concubines; the newer converts, anxious to taste the blessings of the religion they had adopted, kept a tighter hold on their prizes; which however they were induced to give up on the promise of a large share in the next booty which the Prophet could secure."[58]

The quantum of plunder enormously increased as the raids and wars, leading to the capture of new regions outside Arabia, such as Iran, and Sindh in India, spread. The pillage of Muhammad bin Qasim, the first Muslim predator, invading India in 710 AD, amounted to 600 million dirhams in addition to several thousand slaves. It was a fantastic plunder, which reduced the Sindh province to penury. Bin Qasim forced the Brahmins to beg in the streets for displaying the displeasure of Allah against those who served the cause of idolatry.[59]

Quarrel for Booty

As charm of plunder attracted many, it facilitated Jehad. But it was also a cause of intra-Islamic discord. The motive of material gain was an important reason of intra-Islamic discord. Ibn Ishaq has written about the quarrel between the Muslims for the booty just after the Battle of Badr. He quotes a narrator: "I asked Ubada, son of al-Samitabout the chapter of al-Unfal and he said that it came down concerning those who took part in the battle of Badr when they quarreled about the booty and showed their evil nature. Allah took it out of their hands and gave it to the apostle, and he divided it equally among the Muslims."[60]

On the occasion of the capture of Hunain, as Ibn Ishaq writes, the Prophet was mobbed by the Muslims; they asked: "Divide our spoil of camels and herds among us." They surrounded him and continued to demand "until they forced him back against a tree and his mantle was torn from him." He cried: "Give me back my mantle; I swear by Allah that if I had as many sheep as the trees of Tilham I would distribute them among you. You have not found me niggardly or cowardly or false."[61] *Sahih Bukhari* also mentions about such incidents.[62] In one such case, a person said: "By Allah, in this distribution justice has not been observed, nor has Allah's pleasure been aimed at."[63]

Thus, although, the spoils of war were most welcome, the occasions of the distribution of the same were rarely easy sailing. The act, being petty rough, had to be settled by the Prophet, and even he was once accused of concealing spoils.[64] *Sahih Bukhari* has also mentioned about such incidents. Anas, son of Malik, narrated: "When Allah bestowed His Messenger with the properties of Hawazin tribe as *Fai'* (booty), he started giving to some Quraysh men even up to one hundred camels each, whereupon some *Ansari* men said about Alla's Messenger: "May Allah forgive his Messenger! He is giving to (men of) Quraysh and leaves us, inspite of the fact that our swords are still dropping blood (of the infidels)'"[65]

Notes and References

1. See the chapter on "Poverty and Riches."
2. *Sahih Muslim, Hadis* 4327.
3. Ibid, *Hadis* 1058.
4. Ibid, *Hadis* 1063.
5. Qur'an 8: 69.
6. Ibn Ishaq, *Sirat Rasul Allah*, English translation by A. Guillaume, p. 321; hereafter Ibn Ishaq.
7. Qur'an 8:1.
8. Qur'an 59: 6-7.
9. Qur'an 8:41.
10. *Sahih Muslim, Hadis* 4346.
11. Ibid, *Hadis* 4340.
12. *Sahih Bukhari, Hadis* 4:286.
13. Qur'an 33:26.
14. Bible, Numbers, 31:25-54.
15. Plundering non-believers has also the sanction of Judaeo-Christian scripture, the Old Testament. Some examples from the same need mention: According to the Bible, Jehovah said to Moses: "You and Eleazar, together with the other leaders of the community, are to count everything that has been captured, including the prisoners and the animals. Divide what was taken into two equal parts, one part for the soldiers and other part for the rest of the community. From the part that given to the rest of the people, take one out of fifty

prisoners and the same proportion of the cattle, donkeys, sheep, and goats. Give them to the Levites, who are in charge of Jehovah's Tent." Moses and Eleazar faithfully followed Jehovah in this case.

16. The captured items included 675,000 sheep and goats, 72,000 cattle, 61,000 donkeys, and 32,000 virgins. The share of the soldiers was 337,500 sheep and goats, including 675 as Jehovah's tax; 36,000 cattle, which included 72 as Jehovah's tax; 30,500 donkeys, including 61 as the tax of Jehovah, and 16,000 virgins, which included 32 virgins as Jehovah's tax.
The soldiers received their share, as mentioned above, and Jehovah's share was given to Eleazar, as commanded by Jehovah, The community received the same share as soldiers, and one out of every 50 of the same was taken out and was given to Levites, as instructed by Jehovah.

17. After distribution of the cattle-wealth and virgins, the officers went to Moses and handed over 200 kg of gold ornaments—armlets, bracelets, rings, earring and necklaces—which each of them had plundered. Moses and Eleazar took that gold to the tent, so that Jehovah would protect the people of Israel. Non-officers kept their loot with them.

18. Qur'an 3:161.

19. *Sahih Bukhari*, *Hadis* 4:307.

20. *Sahih Muslim*, *Hadis* 210.

21. Ibid, *Hadis* 4006.

22. Ibid,, *ahadis* 4330; *Sahih Bukhari*, *Hadis* 4:362.

23. Muir, *The Life of Mahomet*, p. 380; hereafter Muir.

24. Ibn Ishaq, p. 466; *Hughes, Dictionary of Islam*, p. 600.

25. K.S. Lal, *Theory and Practice of Islamic State in India*, pp. 147-52, 344-45.

26. Ibn Ishaq, p. 309.

27. Ibid, p. 311.

28. *Sahih Bukhari*, *Hadis* 4:284.

29. Muir pp. 229-30.

30. Ibid. p. 231.

31. Ibid.

32. Qur'an 8:67-69.

33. *Sahih Bukhari, Hadis* 4:257; *Sahih Muslim*, *ahadis* 4319/4323; Ram Swarup, *Understanding Islam through Hadis*, p. 100; hereafter Ram Swarup.

34. Margoliouth, *Mohammed and the Rise of Islam*, p. 400; hereafter Margoliouth.

35. *Sahih Muslim*, *Hadis* 4376.

36. Ibid, *Hadis* 4376.
37. Muir, p. 438.
38. Margoliouth, pp. 407-9.
39. *Sahih Bukhari*, *Hadis* 4:374.
40. *Sahih Muslim*, *Hadis* 2303.
41. Qur'an 9:60.
42. *Sahih Muslim*, *Hadis* 4347.
43. Ibid, *Hadis* 2313.
44. Ibid, *ahadis* 2303-2314.
45. Ibid, *Hadis* 2300.
46. Muir, pp. 380-81.
47. *Tabqat-e-Ibn-Sa'd*, Vol. II, p. 100; cited by Sita Ram Goel, *India's Secularism: New Name for National Subversion*, pp. 92-93.
48. *Tabqat*, pp. 91-92.
49. Ibn Ishaq, p. 466.
50. Ibid, pp. 466-68.
51. Ram Swarup, pp. 188-89.
52. Quran 33:26-27; Ram Swarup, p. 102.
53. Anwar Shaikh, *Islam: Sex and Violence*, p. 131; hereafter Anwar Shaikh.
54. *Sahih Muslim*, *Hadis* 3315.
55. Muir, p. 245.
56. Muir, p. 296.
57. Margoliouth, pp. 406-407.
58. Ibid, pp. 406-407.
59. Anwar Shaikh, pp. 164-65.
60. Ibn Ishaq, p. 307.
61. Ibid, p. 594.
62. Tirmizi, Vol. II, *Hadis* 868; Ram Swarup, pp. 102-103.
63. *Sahih Bukhari*, *ahadis* 4:376; 4:377.
64. Ibid, *Hadis* 4:378.
65. *Sahih Bukhari*, *Hadis* 4:375.

Islam and the People of the Book

Islam and the 'People of the Book'

People of the Book

The people following the Semitic tradition of Abraham, especially of the 'Old Testament of the Bible' – the Jews and the Christians – are called the 'People of the Book' in Qur'an. The earliest portions of the Qur'an gives evidence of the extreme respect with which "Knowledge of the Book" was regarded by the Arabs, who did not have it.[1] The first encounter of Prophet Muhammad with the 'People of the Book' used to be in the fair of Ukaz, near Mecca, where Jews used to come from north from the great palm oases of Medina and Khaybar, and Christians coming from south from Yemen and cathedral city of Najran.[2] Thus the two religions – Judaism and Christianity—were not unknown to him. Moreover, his exposure and experience as a caravan man was also considerable.

Commonality of Islam, Judaism and Christianity

As we know, the three Semitic religions – Judaism, Christianity and Islam – have much in common. The Qur'an would honour the Prophets and great figures of the Old Testament – Adam, Abraham, Joseph, Moses, Solomon and Elijah. Arabians and Jews spoke of the God as al-Lah, the high one. The Qur'an often used the honorific *ar-Rahman*, the merciful; the newly completed Babylonian Talmud used *Rahmana*. Both Jews and Muslims claimed to be the common descendants of Abraham, the first *hanif*. Thus, the Jews and Muslims were at best, the cousins. As Jews were the original upholders of *Din Ibrahim*, the tradition of Ibrahim, and the Islam is of the same tradition, Muhammad expected not only the assent, but the enthusiastic support of the Jews.[3]

As Qur'an says, the Muslims, Jews and the Christians follow the same religion; all three communities follow the religion of Abraham, they have common prophets. It says: "They say, 'Become Jews or Christians, and you will be rightly guided.' Say (Prophet), 'No, (ours is) the religion of Abraham, the upright, who did not worship any god besides God.' So (you believers), say,

'We believe in God and what was sent down to us and what was sent down to Abraham, Ishmael, Isaac, Jacob, and the Tribes, and what was given to Moses, Jesus, and all the prophets by their Lord. We make no distinction between any of them, and we devote ourselves to Him.'"[4]

And again, the God of the Muslims, Jews and the Christians, according to Qur'an, is also the same. The Qur'an says: "Say (Prophet) (to the Jews and Christians), 'How can you argue with us about God when He is our Lord and your Lord. … Or are you saying that Abraham, Ishmael, Isaac, Jacob, and Tribes were Jews and Christians?'"[5]

Biblical Themes and the Prophets in Qur'an

There is extreme respect of Bible in Qur'an.[6] The Qur'an has numerous references of the Biblical themes and prophets. The first Medina *suras* of Qur'an, like the closing *suras* at Mecca, abound in Jewish fables and legends, based upon the Old Testament and rabbinical traditions; thus Jews are most prominently addressed in them. As Muir writes: "The marvelous interposition of the Almighty in behalf of his people of old are recounted with the object of stirring up the neighbouring Jewish tribes to gratitude, and of inciting them to publish unreservedly the evidence which their Scripture contained in substantiation of his claim."[7] The second sura of Qur'an (*The Cow* or *The Heifer*) tells about Allah, His angels, Adam, Moses, all what happened between him and the Allah, Abraham, Ishmael, Jacob, Isaac, Aaron, David, and Jesus, son of Mary. It also referred to Satan and King Talut.

Biblical themes and the mention of the prophets are spread throughout the Qur'an. A brief reference of some of them shall make the point clear. Sura 3 (*The Family of 'Imran*) has the story of Zachariya, Mary, and Jesus;[8] as mentioned, Jesus was unfathered, Adam was created without father. Sura 4 (*Women*) talks of the tension between Muslims in Medina and some of the People of the Book;[9] It has general discussion of war, and warns the Muslims to be cautious and to defend the weak and the helpless.[10] The fifth chapter of the Qur'an discusses that Allah has also taken pledges from the Jews and the Christians; it also deals with what they did to these pledges, and their relationship with the Muslims.[11] Suras 12 (*Joseph*), 14 (*Abraham*), and 19 (*Mary*) have mostly the Biblical themes. In Sura 18 (*The Cave*), we have Moses[12] and Dhu 'l Qarnayn.[13] The latter (also written Dhu'l Karnain) appear to be the Biblical hero Alexander.[14] In Sura 20 (*Ta Ha*), lengthy account of Moses is given so that to encourage Prophet Muhammad; Adam is mentioned in Sura 21 (*The Prophets*); There is also the listing of the prophets in the same.[15] Sura 26 has verses about Moses and Abraham, and Sura 27 refers to Solomon and queen Sheba. A verse of Sura 28 centres on the story of Moses.[16] In Sura 29, the reference is brought to earlier prophets and the punishment brought on those who denied them.

Believers, Disbelievers and the Hypocrites

The earlier verses of the second Sura divide people into believers, disbelievers and the hypocrites. About the disbelievers, it says: "As for those who disbelieve, it makes no difference whether you warn them or not; they will not believe. Allah has sealed their hearts and their ears, and their eyes are covered. They will have great torment."[17] About the hypocrites, it says: "Some people say, 'We believe in Allah and the Last Day,' when really they do not believe. They seek to deceive Allah and the believers, but they only deceive themselves, though they do not realize it. There is a disease in their hearts, which Allah has added to. Agonizing torment awaits them for their persistent lying."[18]

It further said: "Neither those People of the Book who disbelieve nor the idolaters would like anything good to be sent down to you from your Lord, but Allah chooses for His grace whoever He will. His bounty has no limits."[19]

Quranic Appeal to the 'People of the Book' and Others

The Qur'an also appealed directly to the "People of the Book," and instructed Muhammad to say: "We believe in that which has been revealed to us and that which was revealed to you. Our God and your God is one." The Qur'an instructed the believers not to argue with the Jews "except fairly and politely." Rather, they should say: "People of the Book, let us come to an agreement that we will worship none but God, that we will associate no partner with him, and that none of us shall set up mortals as deities alongside God." And so that not to exclude Christians, the further verses appear: "Believers, Jews, Christians, Zoroastrians, whoever believe in God and the Day of Judgment and does what is right, all shall be rewarded by God … We believe in God and what was revealed to us, in that which was revealed to Abraham and Ishmael, to Isaac and Jacob and the tribes, and in that which God gave to Moses and Jesus and the Prophets. We discriminate against none of them."[20] It further said: "Say, People of the Book, do not overstep the bounds of truth in your religion and do not follow the whims of those who went astray before you – that they led many others astray and themselves continue to stray from the evil path."[21]

Appeal to the Children of Israel to Accept Quranic Message

The first hundred verses of the second Sura of the Qur'an tell us about the appeal to the 'Children of Israel,' i.e. Jews, to believe in the Quranic revelations; it also referred to the hypocrites of both Aus and Khazraj communities of Medina, as well as the Jewish rabbis.

Many verses of the second Sura of the Qur'an remind the 'Children of Israel' to remember how Allah blessed them in various ways; he said: "Children of Israel, remember how I blessed you. Honour your pledge to Me and I will honour My pledge to you. I am the One you should fear."[22] Allah wanted them to believe the message of Qur'an. He said: "Believe in the message I have sent down confirming what you already possess. Do not be first to reject it, and do not sell My messages for a small price; be mindful of me. Do not mix truth with falsehood, or hide the truth when you know it."[23] Allah reminded them to remember how he blessed them and favoured them over others; He wanted them to remember that He saved them from Pharaoh's people, and gave Moses the Scripture. Allah told the Jews to remember whatever He said or did to them and to Moses.[24]

Jews and Christians Claimed Paradise Exclusively for Themselves

The Qur'an says: "Even after the truth has become clear to them, many of the People of the Book wish they could turn you back to disbelief after you have believed, out of their selfish envy. … They also say, 'No one will enter Paradise unless he is a Jew or a Christian."[25] The Qur'an further says: "They say, 'Become Jews or Christians, and you will be rightly guided.'"[26] Thus, the 'People of the Book' continued with their pre-Islamic claims.

Jews and Christians Differ on the Basics

Jews and the Christians differed on the basics and blamed each other for lack of knowledge. The Qur'an says: "The Jews say, 'The Christians have no ground whatsoever to stand on,' and the Christians say, 'The Jews have no ground whatsoever to stand on,' though they both read the scripture, and those who have no knowledge say the same; Allah will judge between them on the Day of Resurrection concerning their differences."[27]

The difference between the Christians and the Muslims also existed on basics, such as, the Son-ship of Jesus Christ. The Qur'an does not accept that God has any son or daughter; it therefore, always addresses Jesus Christ as 'Jesus, the son of Mary,' and not as the 'Son of God.' The Qur'an says, 'They have asserted, 'God has a child.'[28] This applied both to the claims of Christians, and the pagan Arabs, according to whom, Uzza, Al-Lat and Manat were daughters of Allah.

The Jews Resist Conversion

The problem was what Lesley Hazleton writes that "Medina's Jews saw no more reason to accept Muhammad as a prophet than they had Jesus. They believed that the days of prophecy had ended twelve centuries before, with the Babylonian exile. There could be no more prophets. So just as the Quraish had declared that they could not abandon the tradition of their fathers so the Jews were determined to stand firm in the tradition of theirs. In almost two years, hardly any had accepted Islam, and this appeared to confound Muhammad."[29]

The Quranic appeal to the 'People of the Book' continued: "People of the book, why do you deny God's revelations when you know they are true? Why do you confound the true with the false, and knowingly conceal the truth?" However, all these had no impact on the Jews; they stubbornly resisted every attempt of the Prophet to convert them to Islam. Of course, Jews like 'Abdullah son of Salam, accepted Islam. There was yet another such Jew, named Mukhayriq, about whom the Prophet used to say: "Mukhayriq is the best of the Jews." But these few Jews were the exceptions.[30]

Disbelievers Among the Jews Declared Enemies

The scripture, which came down from God through Prophet Muhammad, according to Qur'an, confirmed whatever messages the Jews had received earlier. According to the Qur'an, 'even knowing it to be true, they disbelieved it.' In such a case, "God rejects those who disbelieve."[31]

Ultimately, contrary to what Muhammad expected, the Jews did not accept the Quranic message, and Allah declared them to be His enemy. The Qur'an says: "Say (Prophet), 'If anyone is an enemy of Gabriel – who by Allah's leave brought down the Qur'an to your heart, confirming previous scriptures, as a guide and good news for the faithful – if anyone is an enemy of God, His angels and His messengers, of Gabriel and Michael, then God is certainly an enemy of such disbelievers. For we have sent down clear messages to you and only those who defy (God) would refuse to believe them. How it is that whenever they make a covenant or a pledge, some of them throw it away? In fact most of them do not believe."[32]

Change of Qibla

The Jews' rejection of Islam led to hardening of the attitude of Prophet

Muhammad towards them. As one of the initial and major steps to differentiate between the two communities, the change of *qibla*, the direction of prayer, was made. Earlier, the Muslims prayed Allah facing the temple of Jerusalem, now following a revelation, the direction of prayer was changed towards the Kaaba. The Qur'an says: "Foolish people will say, 'What has turned them away from the prayer direction they used to face?' Say, 'East and West belong to God. He guides whoever He will to the right way.'"[33] And again, "Turn your face in the direction of the Sacred Mosque; wherever you (believers) may be, turn your face to it."[34]

Pagan Stand Towards Islam

Most of the pagan Arabs continued to follow their religion till the last days of the Prophet Muhammad. Qur'an reveals their stand thus: "But when it is said to them, 'Follow the message that God has sent down,' they answer, 'We follow the ways of our fathers.' What! Even though their fathers understood nothing and were not guided? Calling to disbelievers is like a herdsman calling to things that hear nothing but a shout and a cry: they are deaf, dumb, and blind, and they understand nothing."[35]

Ruthlessness Towards the Pagans

Prophet Muhammad's attitude towards the pagans was considerably more ruthless. The Qur'an's prescription about them is worth pondering. It says: "Kill them wherever you encounter them, and drive them out from where they drove you out, for persecution is more serious than killing. Do not fight them at the Sacred Mosque unless they fight you there. If they do fight you, kill them—this is what such disbelievers deserve—but if they stop, then God is most forgiving and merciful. Fight them until there is no persecution, and worship is devoted to Allah."[36]

Relationship with Jews and Christians

The third Sura of the Quran 'first documents the tension that arose between the Muslims and certain of the Jews and Christians,'[37] and then[38] closes by emphasizing the unity of faith and conduct between the Muslims and some of the People of the Book, explaining that these will have their reward from God.[39]

Prophet Muhammad tried to bring Jews and Christians to Islamic fold, but he could not succeed. Only few Jews accepted Islam; the same was the case with the Christians; only nominal Christians accepted Islam.[40] As a result, there was change in the attitude of Muhammad towards them; the Quranic voice began to change. Lesley Hazleton has aptly summarized the situation. She writes:

"In Mecca, the Quranic voice had been quite accepting of challenges to its teaching. 'We have sent down this scripture to you, messenger, with the truth for the people,'" it had said: "Whoever follows its guidance does so to his own benefit. Whoever strays away from it does so at his own peril; you are not in charge of them." Yet now Muhammad seemed to feel a special responsibility for the Jews. Their lack of interest seemed impossible, the result surely of sheer stubbornness; but the more he tried to convince them, the more they resisted, and in response the tone of the Quranic voice began to change, reflecting his exasperation.[41]

As Lesley Hazleton writes: "the Prophet's exasperation followed the change in Quranic language: "People of the Book! why do you deny God's revelations when you know they are true?" It said: "Why do you confound the true with the false, and knowingly conceal the truth?" Soon the Jews were no longer addressed directly but referred to only in the third person; no longer "we" but "they." Some of them were "upright and honorable," the voice conceded, but others had "made of their religion a sport and a pastime," as had the Meccans. Couldn't they see that they were betraying their own faith? That the Qur'an was not a denial of the Judaic message but a renewal of it?[42]

Hazleton further writes: "But the Jewish tribes saw no need for renewal, let alone for an outsider telling them that they weren't good enough Jews. Their rabbis rejected the Quranic appeal, leading ibn-Ishaq to devote several pages to scenes in which they argued vehemently with Muhammad, "stirring up trouble" by insisting that his versions of the biblical tales were wrong. It's unlikely that these arguments ever took place, however."[43]

Radically Different Biblical Tales in the Near-East: Differences Between Prophet and the Rabbis

One of the reasons of conflict between Muhammad and the Jewish rabbis was that the biblical tales of the two differed radically. As Lesley Hazleton writes: "While details of the biblical stories as told in the Quran certainly differ from those now accepted in the West as canonical, they were current throughout the Middle East of the time. In fact radically different versions of many of the biblical tales can still be heard today throughout the region, where what seems "wrong" to Western ears is accepted as part of the lore of the Eastern churches."[44] Under such circumstances, it was natural that the two differed in their dialogue, as Ibn-Ishaq details in his book.[45] Here, a fact needing mention is that even in the Qur'anic text, the differences appeared so soon after the death of the Prophet, as we have discussed elsewhere in the book, and the first three caliphs had to take steps towards rectification, and Uthman, the third caliph, had to circulate standard text of the Qur'an. The reason for the differences in the text might have been due to the fault of the persons recording the Suras; and some of them might have forgotten to take note of the superseded or forgotten Suras about which the Quran says: "Any revelation We cause to be superseded or forgotten, We replace with something better or similar. Do you (Prophet) not know that Allah has power over everything?"[46]

Parting of Way Between Muhammad and the People of the Book

When repeated attempts to convert the 'People of the Book' to Islam failed, there was parting of the ways between the two. The ouster and destruction of the Jews followed; the existence of Christianity was obliterated from the face of Arabia. This aspect has been discussed elsewhere in the book. The changes were noticeable in reduction of the status of Jews and the Christians, reversal of their customs, and ultimately their removal from Arabia.

Reduction of the Status of the People of the Book

Ultimately the People of the Book were reduced to the status of *Dhimmis/ Zimmis* (*al-Zimma*; people of the Covenant or obligation); they became second class citizens, and had to pay *Jizya*,[47] for which there was provision in the Qur'an[48] and the Hadis.[49]

It is generally accepted that the *Zimmis* originated from 'Umar,[50] but they were already there at the time of the Prophet. As Ram Swarup writes:[51] "Some Ahadis on the "merit" of Moses reveal an interesting fact: the *Zimmis* did not originate with 'Umar but were already there at the time of the Prophet. The Jews were already second-class citizens and were treated roughly by the believer-hoodlums in Muhammad's own day. For example, a Jew was selling goods; when an *ansar* offered a price that was not acceptable to him, a dispute arose. During the dispute, the Jew said: "By allah, who chose Moses amongst mankind." The ansar gave him a blow on the face, chiding him for invoking Moses when "Allah's Messenger is living with us." The Jew went to Muhammad, narrated the whole story, and supplicated him saying: "Abu'l Qasim, I am a *Zimmi* (thus need your protection) by a covenant." Muhammad chided the ansar and told him: "Don't make distinction amongst the Prophets of Allah."[52]

The blood-price was reduced to half, and in one case one-third, for the Jews and the Christians.[53] The testimony of Jews, Christians, and unbelievers is not considered in a strictly Islamic court.[54] The Muslims were prohibited to use the utensils of the Jews and Christians for taking food. The Hadis said: "If you are in the land of the People of the Book (Jews and Christians) do not eat from their utensils. But if it can not be avoided, then wash them before using them."[55]

Sectarian Attitude Towards the People of the Book

Muslims were prohibited from greeting the Jews and the Christians first. The Hadis said: "Do not greet the Jews and the Christians before they greet you and when you meet any one of them on the roads force him to go to the narrowest part of it."[56] This is just the opposite of the behaviour to be shown to a fellow Muslim[57] Of course, the normal advice was that 'when the People of the Book (Jews and Christians) offer salutation to a Muslim, he should say: "The same to you."[58] The Hadis mentions about some Jews making a pun and greeting Muslims by saying as-sam-u-alaikum ("death be upon you") instead of the usual as-salam-u-alaikum ("peace be upon you"), Muhammad taught his followers to respond by saying: "Let it be upon you,"[59] and he used to respond accordingly.

One of the six "rights of a Muslim over another Muslim"[60] is that the fellow Muslims should "follow his bier," when he dies.[61] A Muslim should also offer a prayer of mercy for a fellow Muslim. But this courtesy is denied to non-Muslims. Allah forbids doing the same to non-Muslims.[62] Muhammad was himself keeping away from their funerals. The case of Mukhayriq, a learned Jewish priest, whom Muhammad himself called as "the best of the Jews," may be cited here. He recognized Muhammad as the promised prophet, bestowed seven gardens on him, which, according to some tradition, were part of the war booty seized from the Jews of Medina. He fought alongside Muhammad on the day of Uhud, even when that was a *sabath*, and died in that battle. Muhammad neither attended his funeral, nor prayed for him, though his corpse was allowed to be buried near that of the Muslims.[63]

Pronouncing Curse on Jews and Christians

Prophet Muhammad cursed Jews and the Christians for taking the graves of their Apostles as places of worship.[64] As reported by Ayesha, when the Prophet "was about to breathe his last … he uncovered his face and said in this very state: 'Let there be curse upon the Jews and the Christians that they have taken the graves of their Apostles as places of worship.'"[65]

Hell for the Jews and the Christians

Not only the unbelievers, but even the People of the Book, according to Hadis, are to go to hell. On the day of resurrection, the Christians will be summoned by the God, and asked, "What did you worship?" They will reply, "Jesus, the son of Allah," then Allah will tell them, "You tell a lie; Allah did not take for himself either a spouse or a son." Then they will be asked what they want. They will say: "Thirsty we are, O our Lord! Quench our thirst." They will be given a certain direction, and Allah will ask: "Why don't you go there to drink water?" When they go there, they will find that they have been misguided; the water is no more than a mirage, and it is really hell. Then they will "fall into the fire" and perish.[66] There are several other *ahadis* pointing to the fact that not only the Jews and Christians go to hell, but even they substitute the sinful Muslims and go there. "He who amongst the community of Jews and Christians hears about me, but does not affirm his belief in that with which I have been sent and dies in this state of disbelief, he shall be put as one of the denizens of Hell-Fire," Muhammad tells.[67]

Jews and Christians as Proxies in the Hell

According to a Hadis, Allah visits the sins of the believers on the unbelievers. The Prophet said: "When it will be the Day of Resurrection, Allah would deliver to every Muslim a Jew or a Christian and say: That is your rescue from Hell-fire."[68] In yet another Hadis, Muhammad tells us: "There would come people amongst the Muslims on the day of Resurrection with as heavy sins as a mountain, and Allah would forgive them and he would place in their stead Jews and the Christians."[69] Thus, Jews and Christians act as proxies for even the sinful Muslims, and go to hell.

According to a third Hadis, Muhammad promises his followers that on the day of reckoning, Allah will tell the Muslims: "I concealed them (your sins) for you in the world. And today I forgive them." But as for the unbelievers, their sins will be exposed before the whole world and "there should be general announcement about them before all creation," and it will be advertised that they "told lies about Allah."[70]

According to a Hadis, a person is advised to conceal his fault and perform morning and evening prayers. As reported by Abdulla, a person came to Allah's apostle and said: "Allah's Messenger, I sported with a woman in the outskirts of Madina, and I have committed an offence short of fornication. Here I am (before you), kindly deliver verdict about me which you deem fit."' Umar said: Allah concealed our faults. You had better conceal it yourself also. Allah's

Apostle, however, gave no reply to him. The man stood up and went away and Allah's Apostle sent a person after him to call him and he recited this verse: "And observe prayer at the ends of the day and in the first hours of the night. Surely good deeds take away evil deeds. That is a reminder for the mindful."[71] A person amongst the people said: "Allah's Apostle, does it concern this man only?" Thereupon he (the Holy Prophet) said: "No but the people at large," Muhammad said reassuringly."[72]

Solving the Space-crunch in the Heaven

According to the note given by the English translator of the *Sahih Muslim*, the problem of providing adequate space for the Muslims in heaven is solved by throwing Jews and Christians into the hell. It says: "Space in paradise would be provided by Christians and Jews being thrown into Hell-fire."[73]

Reversal of the Jewish Customs

Prophet Muhammad, after his disenchantment from the Jews, tried to bring a change wherever Muslims followed the common ones with them. The same was the case with many Christian and pagan customs. Sunday and Saturday were especially important for the Christians and the Jews; it was Friday for the Muslims. The prayer-direction (qibla) was already changed. The approach 'to take meal a little before dawn'[74] and to 'hasten the breaking of the fast'[75] distinguished the Muslims from the Jews and the Christians. Distinct from other religious fastings, there is no uninterrupted fasting (*saum visal*) in Islam, as Muhammad forbade it.[76] When Abu Kuhafa, the father of Abu Bakr, and a veteran old man of one hundred years, with his head and beard white like hyssop, met Muhammad on the day of the conquest of Mecca, the Prophet told him to change the hair 'with something but avoid black.' But why this change or dying at all? Asked the old man. "The Jews and Christians do not dye their hair, so oppose them."[77] In case of hair parting, Muhammad followed Jewish pattern, but later on reverted to the pattern of the polytheists.[78] The numerous cases of such changes, especially for distinct Islamic identity formation have been discussed in the book.

Prophet Muhammad did not like Muslims to follow the path of Jews and the Christians. But in spite of his warnings, as Ram Swarup observes: "Muhammad is still apprehensive about his followers and feels that they will take to the path of the Jews and the Christians." "You would tread the same path as was trodden by those before you inch by inch and step and step so much so that if they had entered into the hole of the lizard you would follow them in this also," he remonstrates with the believers.[79]

Notes and References

1. Margoliouth, *Mohammed and the Rise of Islam*, New Delhi, Reprint, 1985; p. 41. (Hereafter; Margoliouth).
2. Lesley Hazleton, *The First Muslim*, London, 2013; p. 47; (Hereafter, Hazleton).
3. Ibid, p. 187.
4. Qur'an, 2: 135-36.
5. Qur'an, 2: 139-40.
6. Margoliouth, p. 41.
7. Muir, Sir William, *The Life of Mahomet from Original Sources*, New Delhi, Reprint, 2002; p. 325; (Hereafter, Muir).
8. Qur'an, 3: 35-64.
9. Qur'an, 4: 44, 61.
10. Qur'an, 4: 71-76.
11. Qur'an, 5: 13-86.
12. Qur'an, 18: 60-82.
13. Qur'an, 18: 83-99.
14. Margoliouth, p. 146.
15. Qur'an, 21: 48-91.
16. Qur'an, 28:25.
17. Qur'an, 2:6,7.
18. Qur'an, 2: 8-10.
19. Qur'an, 2: 105.
20. Hazleton, p. 188; quotes from Qur'an.
21. Qur'an, 5:77.
22. Qur'an, 2: 40.
23. Qur'an, 2: 41-42.
24. Qur'an, 2:58-88.
25. Qur'an, 2: 109, 111.
26. Qur'an, 2:135.
27. Qur'an, 2:113.
28. Qur'an, 2: 116.
29. Hazleton, p. 188.
30. Ibn Ishaq, *The Life of Muhammad*, A translation of Ibn Ishaq's *Sirat Rasul Allah* from Arabic to English by A. Guillaume; Oxford University Press, Karachi, 1996; pp. 240-41.
31. Qur'an, 2:89.

32. Qur'an, 2:100.
33. Qur'an, 2: 143.
34. Qur'an, 2: 144.
35. Qur'an, 2: 170-71.
36. Qur'an, 2:191-93.
37. Qur'an, 3: 65-85, 98-101.
38. Qur'an, 3: 199.
39. Introductory Note; The Qur'an, English translation by M.A.S. Abdel Haleem; Oxford, 2010.
40. Margoliouth, pp. 438-439.
41. Hazleton, pp. 188-89.
42. Ibid, p.189.
43. Ibid.
44. Ibid.
45. Ibn Ishaq, pp. 239-240; 247-70.
46. Qur'an, 2:106.
47. Ram Swarup, *Understanding Islam through Hadis*, Voice of India, New Delhi, 2001, p. 105. (Hereafter, Ram Swarup).
48. Qur'an, 9:29.
49. *Sahih Muslim, Hadis* 3762.
50. Muir, pp. 381-82.
51. Ram Swarup, p. 161.
52. *Sahih Muslim, ahadis* 5853-5854.
53. Ram Swarup, pp. 87-88.
54. Ibid, p. 96.
55. *Sahih Muslim, Hadis* 4743.
56. Ibid, *Hadis* 5389.
57. Ibid, *ahadis* 6210; 5379.
58. Ibid, No. 5380.
59. Ibid, No. 5380-5388.
60. The six rights of a Muslim over other Muslims are: 'When you meet him, offer him greetings; when he invites you to a feast accept it; when he seeks your counsel give him; and when he sneezes and says: 'All praise to Allah,' you say, 'May Allah show mercy to you;' and when he falls ill visit him; and when he dies follow his bier' (Sahih Muslim, Hadis No. 5379).
61. *Sahih Muslim, Hadis* 5379.
62. Qur'an, 9:84.
63. Ram Swarup, p. 192.

64. Ibid, p. 29.
65. *Sahih Muslim* , *Hadis* 1082.
66. Ibid, 352; RS, 8-9.
67. Ibid, p. 284.
68. Ibid, 6665.
69. Ibid, 6668.
70. Ibid, 6669.
71. Qur'an, 11:115.
72. *Sahih Muslim*, *Hadis* 6658; the same theme is repeated in *ahadis* 6655-6657, 6659-6661 also.
73. Ibid, Note 2967 of the translator.
74. Ibid, *Hadis* 2412.
75. Ibid, *Hadis* 2417.
76. Ibid, *ahadis* 2426-2435.
77. Ibid, *Hadis* 5245.
78. Ibid, *Hadis* 5768; Ram Swarup, p. 157.
79. Ram Swarup, p. 194.

Islam and the Jews

When Prophet Muhammad migrated to Medina, there were two Arabian tribes—Aus and Khazraj—in the city, and three Jewish tribes in its neighbourhood. Out of the three Jewish tribes, Banu Qaynuqa were the allies of Khazraj, and the remaining two Jewish tribes—al-Nadir and Qurayza—were allies of Aus tribe.[1] Muhammad, as Muir writes: 'had acknowledged the divine authority of Jewish religion, and had even rested his claim, in an important degree, upon the evidence of their Scriptures and the testimony of their learned men. One of the objects nearest to his heart was a federal union with the Jews. His feasts, his fasts and ceremonies were, up tc this time, framed in close correspondence with Jewish customs. His very Kibla (also written as Qibla), the Holy of holies to which he and his people turned five times a day while they prostrated themselves in prayer, was Jerusalem. No concession, in fact, short of the abandonment of his claim to the prophetic office, was too great to gain the Jews over to his cause."[2]

Jews: The Quranic References

The Quranic references about the Jews, and also Christians, abound. About thirty new Suras of Qur'an appeared during the last thee years of the Prophet's stay at Mecca. Many of these Suras were very long and even new passages were added to these afterwards during his stay at Medina. Many *ayats* of these Suras deal with biblical themes refering to the prophets, and throw light on the relations of Islam with Judaism and Christianity.[3] The revelations during early years of *Hijr*, like the closing ones at Medina, abound in Jewish fable and legend, based upon the Old Testament and rabbinical tradition, and thus most prominently address the Jews. The Suras recount the 'marvelous interpositions of the Almighty in behalf of his people of old,' the object being the 'stirring up the neighbouring Jewish tribes to gratitude, and of inciting them to publish unreservedly the evidence which their Scriptures contained in substantiation of his claims.[4] In the second Sura of the Qur'an, more than 100 ayats[5] are addressed to the Children of Israel. In the revelations, and other ones, there is a call on Jews to bear evidence in favour of the revelations of Qur'an, and the Prophet: Some of such Ayats are given in previous chapter.[6]

It goes on reminding them about their deliverance from Pharaoh, the happenings with Moses, and all that, and also warn them of the consequences of the disbelief. An Ayat assures the believers of the rewards, and not to fear.[7]

Ibn Ishaq has written about the Jews mentioning Gabriel to be their enemy.[8] The Quran also says about the same:

"Say (Prophet), 'If anyone is an enemy of Gabriel—who by God's leave brought down the Qur'an to your heart, confirming previous scriptures, as a guide and good news for the faithful—if anyone is an enemy of God, His angels and his messengers, of Gabriel and Michael, then God is certainly the enemy of such disbelievers."[9]

About the wishful thinking and claim of exclusive entry of Jews and Christians to the paradise by them, the, Qur'an had a revealation.[10]

Ibn Ishaq has written about the conflicting debate/dispute between Christians and Jews.[11] The Qur'an also writes about the same.[12]

Believing Jews

Although most of the Jews did not convert to Islam, few did, and the apostle called a Jew, named Mukhayriq, to be the best of the Jews.[13] Muhammad very much wanted the conversion of Jews to Islam. According to Sahih Bukhari, the Prophet said: "Had only ten Jews (amongst their chiefs) believed me, all the Jews would definitely have believed me.[14] Initially, Muhammad was hopeful; both Jews and Muslims had common prophets, being common descendants of Abraham, Jews and Muslims were cousins.[15] Jews were in good terms with Muhammad.[16] They willingly signed arbitration agreement with Muhammad. But, like pagans, they resisted conversion to Islam. They believed that there could be no more prophets after the Babylonian exile twelve centuries earlier. Therefore, accepting Muhammad as their prophet did not arise.[17]

Hostility Between Muhammad and Jews

As discussed earlier, the relationship between Muhammad and Jews was not hostile during the earlier phase of Muhammad's migration to Medina. Gradually, the hostility developed between them. There was a revelation that Jews and Christians shall never be pleased.[18] Ultimately, Jewish-Muslim conflict developed[19] Earlier, due to tie of mutual protection and alliance, some Muslims remained friends with the Jews.[20] But a revelation prohibited such friendship. It said: "O you who believe, do not choose those outside your community as intimate friends. They will spare no pain to corrupt you longing for your ruin. From their mouths hatred has already shown itself and what their breasts conceal is greater. We had made the signs plain to you if you will understand. Behold you love them but they love not you and you believe in the book—all of it."[21]

The antagonism between Muhammad and the Jews developed due to the following reasons:

(i) The Jews refused to recognized Muhammad as a Prophet;

(ii) The Jewish rabbis used to annoy Muhammad by asking inconvenient questions.

(iii) The strong and expanding Islam was not prepared to accept any other creed in Arabia.

(iv) Expulsion/destruction of Jews was the political need for Muhammad.

(v) The unsympathetic behaviour of the Medinan Jews towards poverty-stricken Meccan refugees left the latter bitter towards the former.

(vi) Expulsion and destruction of Jews made the resources available to support the Muslim migrants of Medina, and the initial funding for the creation of the Islamic War Machinery.

Prophet and the Jewish Rabbis

The factor responsible for Muhammad's antagonism for the Jews, apart from the Jew's non-acceptance of his Prophethood, was that the Jewish rabbis used to ask questions and annoy him. Ibn Ishaq had written: "It was the Jewish rabbies who used to annoy the apostle with questions and introduce confusion so as to confound the truth with falsity. The Qur'an used to come down in reference to these questions of theirs, though some of the questions about what was allowed and forbidden came from the Muslims themselves."[22]

According to Ibn Ishaq, the Jewish rabbis showed hostility to the apostle. He writes: "About this time Jewish rabbis showed hostility to the apostle in envy, hatred and malice, because Allah had chosen His apostle from the Arabs. They were joined by men from al-Aus and al-Khazraj who had obstinately clung to their heathen religion. They were hypocrites; clinging to the polytheism of their fathers denying the resurrection; yet when Islam appeared and their people flocked to it they were compelled to pretend to accept it to save their lives. But in secret they were hypocrites whose inclination was towards the Jews because they considered the apostle a liar and strove against Islam."[23]

Ibn Ishaq also lists the names of the Jewish rabbies, calling them 'the rancorous opponents of the apostle and his Companions, the men who asked questions, and stirred up trouble against Islam to try to extinguish it;' they belonged to the three Jewish communities of Madina – Nadir, (B. al-Nadir), B. Qaynuqa and B. Qurayza (B. = Banu means descendants of) and some others. The two Jews, mentioned above, who embraced Islam and sympathized with the Prophet, were excluded from the list. Labid, son of A'sam of Zurayk community (B. Zurayk) was blamed 'who bewitched the apostle of Allah so that he could not come to his wives.'[24]

Ibn Ishaq has detailed an incident involving Abu Bakr and a learned Jewish rabbi, Finhas. Abu Bakr found Finhas and another rabbi Ashya in a school in company of many people gathered around them. Abu Bakr told Finhas 'to fear Allah and become a Muslim because he knew that Muhammad was the apostle of Allah who had brought the truth from Him and that they would find it written in Torah and the Gospel. Finhas replied: 'We are not poor compared to Allah but He is poor compared to us. We do not humble ourselves to Him as He Humbles himself to us; we are independent of Him while he needs us. Were He independent of us He would not ask us to lend Him our money as your master pretends, prohibiting you to take interest, and allowing us to. Had He been independent of us He would not have given us interest.''[25]

Being angry on such remark, Abu Bakr hit Finhas hard in the face, and said: 'Were it not for the treaty between us I would cut off your head, you enemy of Allah!' Finhas immediately went to the apostle and complained, 'Look, Muhammad, at what your Companion has done.' On enquiry, Abu Bakr said: "The enemy of Allah spoke blasphemy. He alleged that Allah was poor and that they were rich and I was so angry that I hit his face." Finhas contradicted his statement and denied that he had said so; a revelation refuting Finhas said, "Allah has heard the speech of those who say: "Allah is poor and we are rich." We shall write what they say and their killing the prophets wrongfully and we shall say, 'Taste the punishment of burning.'[26]

Political Angle

There was another angle also, which was political, which needed tackling. It was the intra-Medinan political angle. A section of the Ansars were known as hypocrites. Ibn Ubayy, a Khazraj, was a hypocrite, who had 'reservations about Muhammad's increasing political role,' which Muhammad did not like.[27] Umer, at one stage, even wanted to kill ibn Ubayy.[28] At least one Jewish tribe was allied to ibn Ubayy. Muhammad did not like the fact that the Jews were joined by Ansari hypocrites.[29] The expulsion of all two thousand of Banu Qaynuqa was, of course, the most ruthless act. It exhibited power and authority of Muhammad and helplessness of Ibn Ubayy.

Muhammad's Resolve to Expel Jews from Arabia

As Sahih Muslim says: Muhammad declared to Umar: "I will expel Jews and Christians from Arabian Peninsula and will not leave any but Muslims."[30] And he did it in his lifetime at least from Medina. His expulsion plan began with the Jews of Medina, and he expelled them ruthlessly one after another. The first to be expelled from Medina were Banu Nazir, and then Banu Qaynuqa. The fate of the last group, which will be discussed elsewhere, was most tragic one.

Reversal of the qibla,[31] the direction of prayer, changes in many Jewish customs and traditions, which the Muslims followed earlier, brought social and religious distancing; distinct Islamic identity started taking shape; Jews started figuring less and less in the revelations. Christians started replacing Jews as God's chosen people; the phenomena were, however, a short-lived one, as the Christians themselves vanished very soon from the Arabic scene.[32]

References

1. Ibn Ishaq, *Sirat Rasul Allah*, p. 253. Hereafter Ibn Ishaq.
2. Muir, Sir William, *The Life of Mahomet*, p. 183. Hereafter Muir.
3. Ibid, p. 143.
4. Ibid, p. 325.
5. Qur'an 2:40 to 2:146.
6. Qur'an 2:40-42.
7. Qur'an 2:63.
8. Ibn Ishaq, p. 255.
9. Qur'an: 2:98.
10. Qur'an 2: 111.
11. Ibn Ishaq, p. 258.
12. Qur'an 2:113.
13. Ibn Ishaq, p. 384.
14. *Sahih Bukhari, Hadis* no. 1598, p. 754; Original Bukhari 5:277.
15. Lesley Hazleton, *The First Muslim*, p. 187; hereafter Hazleton.
16. Ibn Ishaq, p. 262.
17. Hazleton, p. 188.
18. Qur'an 2:120.
19 Hazleton, pp. 187-94.
20. Ibn Ishaq, p. 262.
21. Qur'an 3:114.
22. Ibn Ishaq, p. 239.

23. Ibid.
24. Ibid, pp. 239-40.
25. Ibid, p. 263.
26. Qur'an 3: 177.
27. Hazleton, p. 191.
28. Ibid, p. 212.
29. Muir, p. 242.
30. *Sahih Muslim, Hadis* 4366.
31. Muir, p.189; Hazleton, p. 195; Ibn Ishaq, pp. 258-59.
32. Ram Swarup, *Understanding Islam through Hadis*, p. 62.

Islam and Christianity in Arabia

Semitic Religions: Islam, Christianity, and Judaism

Islam, Christianity, and Judaism, all three are Semitic religions. Their relationship has already been discussed in the chapter on *Islam and the People of the Book*. Adam, Moses, Abraham, Jesus and other biblical prophets have made repeated mentions in Qur'an. One also finds that there is extreme respect for knowledge of the book in Qur'an[1] Numerous Quranic revelations refer to the Christians[2] and Jews. All three religions are monotheistic and prophetic.

Christianity in Arabia

Christianity, for all practical purposes, was a fringe phenomenon in Arabia. Christian Ghasanide dynasty of the house of Jafnah, ruled in Golan, in Palaestina Secunda in the northern fringe up to about the beginning of 583 AD. There was presence of Christianity in southern Arabia also. But only Najran remained an island of Christianity at the time of the birth of Prophet Muhammad. The penetration of Christianity in some Southern and North Arabian states, had taken place, where certain tribes were wholly or partly Christians. But, as Margoliouth sums up, Christianity "was seed sown on stony ground, whose product has no power of resistance when the heat came: it perished without leaving a tree, when Islam appeared. A strange fact: these Christian Arabs had bishops and priests and churches, and even heresies of their own; yet we cannot to this day make out from authorities whether the Christian Scriptures were ever rendered into the vernacular of those converts, or whether only the priests had religious books, and these in a language which they must go abroad to learn. The last is most likely to have been the case, and to have been one of the causes of the unresisting collapse of Arabian Christianity."[3]

Muhammad's Contact with Christianity

Muhammad's contact with Christianity was not very deep and intimate. But, he must have gathered considerable information about that religion during his journey to Syria, or by hearing the sermons of the Christian priests, or from Waraqa, who had the fragments of the Gospels with him. Of course, Mecca had Christian slaves, and it is probable that they may have been the source of the knowledge of the basics of the Christianity in Medina.

Commonality Between Islam and Christianity

The Christian Missionary scholars studied Islam, mostly with a view to convert them to Christianity, and they found that there was much in common between it and their own faith. Ram Swarup has summed up the commonality between the two:[4]

"Both were Judaic in origin and orientation, and both had common prophets. The biblical prophets including Jesus, are highly honoured in the Quran. Both shared a common God and a common line of prophets, and both believed in the revelation from the same God. In fact, the prophet of Islam claimed that he communicated with the same God who communicated with Moses and Jesus, and that he was merely reviving the old religion of Ibrahim, the common patriarch of them all. In this revival, he expected the Jews and the Christians to play their part and enlist under his banner. He felt that he was sent to the 'People of the Book" as much as to the Arabs. "O ye People of the Book! Our apostle has come to you to explain to you much of what you have hidden of the Book." Allah told them."[5]

Diverse Biblical Lore in the Middle East

A point needing mention is that biblical stories told in the Qur'an differed from those told in the West. As was the case, even radically different biblical tales were in currency in the near east, and the lore of Eastern churches differed from that told in Qur'an. Hazleton writes: "While details of the Biblical stories as told in the Qur'an certainly differed from those now accepted in the West as canonical, they were current throughout the Middle East of the time. In fact radically different versions of many of the biblical tales can still be heard today throughout the region, where what seems "wrong" to Western ears is accepted as part of the lore of the Eastern churches."[6]

Hope on Christian Support

Although, there was disenchantment with the people of the Book, especially the Jews, who, by and large, disappointed Muhammad, but regarding Christians, his hope still lingered, and he believed that they may ultimately accept Islam. Ram Swarup writes:[7] "By and large, they disappointed him. However, the Prophet still kept his hope, particularly in the Christians. In one occasion, Allah assured him that though the Jews and the idolaters are "the strongest in enmity" towards him, but those who called themselves Christians, "you will find the nearest in love… (and) when they hear what has been revealed to the Prophet, you will see their eyes gush with tears at what they recognize as truth therein."[8] Was it that Christians were replacing Jews as Allah's chosen people? It needs mention that a *Hadis* of Sahih Bukhari mentions that Muhammad was nearest to Jesus among the prophets. It says: "I am the nearest of all the people to the son of Maryam (Mary), and all the Prophets are paternal brothers, and there has been no Prophet between me and him (i.e. 'Iesa; Jesus).[9] The next Hadis also says the same.

The above mentioned Quranic revelation shows Muhammad's optimism; he still hoped, as mentioned above, to convert Christians. The "Arabs who had been nominally Christians became nominally or actually Muslims," as Margoliouth says.[10]

Hope Belied

The realization came to Muhammad that the Jews and the Christians would not become Muslims. A revelation came accordingly. It said:

"The Jews and the Christians will never be pleased with you unless you follow their ways. Say, 'Allah's guidance is the only true guidance.' If you were to follow their desires after the knowledge has come to you, you would find no one to protect you from Allah or help you."[11]

The Quranic revelations and the *ahadis* pointed towards the differences between Islamic and Christian beliefs.

Basic Theological Differences

Islam had basic theological differences with Christianity. Qur'an and *Hadis*, both did not accept the divinity, trinity and son-ship of Jesus. He was called, as is in the above mentioned *Sura* and *Hadis*, as 'son of Maryam.' **Jesus of Qur'an was different from that of the Bible.** He was not the son of God, but that of Mary, and a prophet.[12]

Intercessory Power Only to Muhammad

According to a *Hadis*, only Muhammad has the intercessory power with Allah, and not with Abraham, Moses and Jesus. For this purpose, people approach Adam, who directs them to go to Ibrahim, Ibrahim to Moses, Moses to Jesus, and Jesus expressing his inability to intercede with Allah, directs them to go to Muhammad.[13] According to many *ahadis,*[14] Muhammad has the special intercessory power; as "no Apostle amongst Apostles has been testified as I have been testified," Muhammad said.[15] As per the *Hadis*, Muhammad "would have the largest following on the Day of Resurrection;"[16] "seventy thousand persons of his *Ummah* would enter Paradise without rendering an account,"[17] and Muslims "would constitute half the inhabitants of Paradise."[18]

Divinity and Son-ship of Jesus Denied

The Quran and the *Hadis* always addressed Jesus as the 'son of Mary,' and thus denied his son-ship of Allah. His divinity was also not accepted, as the following *Hadis* indicates.

"Do not exaggerate in praising me as the Christian praised the son of Maryam (Mary) for I am only a slave. So, call me the slave of Allah and his messenger."[19]

The Qur'an further rejects that Jesus was the son of Allah. It said:

"The Jews said, 'Ezra is the son of God,' and the Christians said, 'The Messiah is the son of God;' they said this with their own mouth, repeating what the earlier disbelievers had said, May God thwart them!"[20]

Qur'an does not accept the rabbis and the monks as well as Jesus, as the partners of God. It says: "They take their rabbis and their monks as lords beside God, as well as Christ, the son of Mary. But they were commanded to serve only one God: there is no God but Him; He is far above whatever they set up as His partners!"[21]

And as the Jews and Christians ascribe partners to God, fight against them is commanded: "Fight those of the People of the Book who do not (truly) believe in God and the Last Day, who do not forbid what God and His Messenger have forbidden, who do not obey the rule of justice, until they pay the tax promptly and agree to submit.[22]

Christians Sent to Hell for Worshipping Jesus, as the Son of Allah

According to a *Hadis*, the Christians will be summoned and asked by the Allah on the Day of Resurrection, "What did you worship?" They will reply, "Jesus, the son of Allah," Allah will tell them, "You tell a lie, Allah did not take for Himself either a spouse or a son." After that they will go to hell and perish.[23]

Supersession of Christianity by Islam

A Hadis mentions about the second coming of Jesus, according to which Jesus is turned into a crusader (*mujahid*). It says: "The son of Mary will soon descend among you as a just judge. He will break crosses, kill swine, and abolish *Jizya*," The translator of the Hadis explains it: "Cross is a symbol of Christianity, Jesus will break the symbol after the advent of Muhammad. Islam is the *din* of Allah and no religion is acceptable to him. Similarly, the flesh of the swine is a favorite dish of the Christians. Jesus will sweep out of existence this dirty and loathsome animal. The whole of the human race would accept Islam and there would be no *zimmis* left, and thus *Jizya* would be automatically abolished."[24] As the note further says: "the *Shari'ah* of all the earlier prophets stands abrogated with the advent of Muhammad's Apostleship. Jesus, regarded as a Just Judge, will, therefore, judge according to the law of Islam."[25]

The following *Hadis* also tells the same:

"How will you be when the son of Maryam (i.e., Iesa, Jesus) descends amongst you, and he will judge people (by the law of Qur'an and not by the law of the Gospel)?"[26]

The Last Years of the Prophet: Receiving Embassies, Sending Delegates

Prophet Muhammad, during the last years of his life A.H. IX and X, received several embassies of submission at Medina from different communities and regions of Arabia, and sent delegates to several other places with letters asking them to become Muslims. On one such occasion, When Mo'adh was sent on such a delegation to Southern Arabia, Muhammad asked him, before his departure, as to how he would adjudicate causes; 'By the book,' was his reply. *But if not in the Book?* 'Then by the precedent.' *But if there be no precedent?* 'Then I will diligently frame my own judgment; and I shall not fail therein.' Muhammad was happy with the reply. He clapped Mo'adh on the breast and said: 'Praise be to God, who hath fulfilled in the messenger sent forth by his Apostle, that which is well pleasing to the Apostle of the Lord!'[27]

Apart from the reliance on his own judgment, Mo'adh was advised to maintain politeness in dealing with new persons; he was to make no mention of Muhammad's prophethood. Mo'adh was sent forth to Southern Arabia with a band of collectors and teachers. Prophet Muhammad advised Mo'adh: 'Deal gently with the people, and be not harsh. Scare them not, but rather cheer. Thou wilt meet with Jews and Christians who will ask thee: What is the key of Paradise? Reply: 'Verily the key of Paradise is to testify that there is no God but the Lord alone. With him there is no partner.'[28]

Prophet Muhammad knew where to be polite and where to be harsh. Usually, the policy was to meet the situation with full strength. He followed what Qur'an said: "It is necessary that the whole body of believers should go forth to war. If certain number from every party go not forth to war, it is that they may give themselves to study in religion, and may admonish their people when they return unto them (from the wars), so that they may take heed unto their ways."[29]

Conversion at Distant Places

The Prophet was well-known in Arabia during the last couple of years of his life. He could build up effective and strong war machinery. Jihad was winning converts, and filling its coffers enormously. And now a stage had reached when the delegations/embassies were coming to him to declare their willing acceptance of the new religion; the country was rapidly becoming Muslim. One of the deputations, which came to Muhammad was from the Christians of Nejran.[30] Oman was converted in AH VIII (February 530). At first, they refused on the plea that they may become poor by paying tithe, but agreed soon after. Embassies came from south and east during AH IX and X.[31]

Conversion of Christians to Islam

A legate, like many others, was sent by Muhammad to Christian Himyarite princes in the Yemen. In a letter carried by him, "Muhammad expressed his belief in Moses and Jesus, but denied the trinity and divinity of Christ." The Himyarites accepted Islam. Praising the alacrity of their faith, he sent a curious letter setting forth the legal demands of Islam; he commended the tithe collections to their favour.[32] Among many other Christian communities converted to Islam was Beni Hanifa, inhabiting Al-Yemama, who desired to demolish its church.[33]

Demolition of Church and Mosque Construction After Purification of its Site

When Beni Hanifa were returning from Medina, "the Prophet gave them a vessel with some water in it remaining over from his ablutions, and said to them: 'When ye reach your country, break down your church, sprinkle its site from this water, and in place of it build up a Mosque.' These commands they carried into effect, and abandoned Christianity without compunction."[34]

As in the above mentioned case, the curious instruction given to a Christian envoy is worth quoting: "He was to be specially careful in his purification and prayers on reaching the country. He was to take Prophet's dispatch in his right hand and place it in the right hand of the prince. He was to recite Sura xciii and then call upon them to submit, saying that he was able to refute every argument and book they could adduce against Islam. Then he was to repeat the passage in Sura xlii, in which it is asserted that there is no real controversy between Muhammad and Christians"[35]

Christians not to Baptize their Children

A deputation of sixteen men from Beni Taghlib came to Medina and met Prophet Muhammad. Some of the members of the deputation were Muslims and others Christians, who wore crosses of gold. 'The Prophet made terms with them, stipulating that they might themselves continue in the profession of their religion, but that they should not baptize their children into the Christian faith.'[36]

Muhammad and the Church of Nejran

The Church of Nejran was an ancient one, located in the centre of Arabia. In a dispatch, it was assured that there will be no interference in the affairs of that church. It said: 'The pledge of God and his Prophet' (such are the terms of another Rescript) 'is given that no Bishop shall be removed from his bishopric, nor any monk from his monastery, nor any priest from his priesthood; their authority and rights shall not be interfered with, nor anything that is customary amongst them;—so long as they conduct themselves peaceably and uprightly. They shall not be oppressed, neither shall they themselves oppress.'[37] An embassy of the Church of Nejran also visited Medina, which finds reference in Qur'an.[38]

Christianity Allowed to Exist on Sufferance

The overall perusal of the facts clearly shows that 'the conditions upon which Prophet Muhammad permitted Christianity were those of sufferance. Muir observes: "Christianity, indeed, was less obnoxious to him than Judaism, because he did not experience from it such persevering and active hostility. Their clergy and monks are even spoken of in expressions of comparative praise."[39] Here, it needs mention that the Qur'an writes about the Jews and the Christians, the same as Muhammad experienced; it says: "You (Prophet) are sure to find that most hostile to the believers are the Jews and those who associate other deities with God; you are sure to find that the closest in affection towards the believers are those who say: 'We are Christians,' for there are among them people devoted to learning and ascetics. These people are not given to arrogance."[40] But, not the less, as Muir writes: "the object of Muhammad was entirely to *supersede* Christianity as well as Judaism."[41]

Christianity Withered Away from Arabia

Ultimately, the Christianity, like Judaism and Paganism, withered away from Arabia. Muir sums up: "It is no wonder that Christianity, which never had obtained in Arabia a firm and satisfactory footing, now threatened, and, where her adherents remained faithful, reduced to tribute, her distinctive rite prohibited wherever the professors were passive and careless, her churches demolished and their sites purified before they could be used again for worship by the Muslim converts;—it is no wonder that Christianity, thus, at the closing stage of the Prophet's mission, insulted and trampled under foot, should have languished, and soon altogether disappeared."[42]

References

1. Margoliouth, *Mohammed and the Rise of Islam*, p. 41. Hereafter, Margoliouth.
2. Muir, *The Life of Mahomet*, pp. 143-163. Hereafter, Muir.
3. Margoliouth, pp. 35-36.
4. Ram Swarup, *Introduction to the Reprint*; Muir, The Life of the Mahomet, p.3.
5. Quran 5.18.
6. Hazleton, Lesley, *The First Muslims*, p. 189. Hereafter, Hazleton ?
7. Ram Swarup, as in entry 4.
8. Quran 5.85, 86.
9. *Sahih Bukhari*, Hadis 1436, p.680; Original Bukhari, *Hadis* no. 4:651.
10. Margoliouth, p. 438.
11. Qur'an 2:120.
12. Qur'an 19: 1ff; Muir 456.
13. *Sahih Muslim*, *Hadis* 377.
14. Ibid, *Hadis* 381-396.
15. Ibid, *Hadis* 383.
16. Ibid, *Hadis* 382.
17. Ibid, *Hadis* 418.
18. Ibid, *Hadis* 427.
19. *Sahih Bukhari, Hadis* 1439, pp. 680-681; Original Bukhari, *Hadis* 4:654.
20. Qur'an 9:30.
21. Qur'an 9:31.
22. Qur'an 9:29.
23. *Sahih Muslim, Hadis* 352.
24. Ibid, Notes 289-290.

25. Ibid, Note 288.
26. *Sahih Bukhari, Hadis* 1440, p. 681; original Bukhari 4:658.
27. Muir, p. 464, note 1.
28. Muir, p. 463.
29. Qur'an 9, 123.
30. Ibn Ishaq, *Sirat Rasul Allah*, pp. 270-276.
31. Muir, pp. 455-456.
32. Ibid, p. 456; p. 456 note 1.
33. Muir, pp. 457-458.
34. Muir, p.458.
35. Muir, p. 456, note 1.
36. Ibid.
37. Ibid.
38. Qur'an 3:52ff.
39. Muir, p. 460.
40. Qur'an 5:82.
41. Muir, pp. 460-61.
42. Ibid, p. 461.

Destruction of the Jews

As discussed earlier, Prophet Muhammad wanted the Jews to accept his message. The failure in his attempt to do so led to antagonism between them. Ultimately, he resolved to get rid of them. He declared to Umar: "I will expel Jews and Christians from Arabian Peninsula and will not leave any but Muslims;"[1] and he did it in his lifetime at least from Medina. The expulsion plan began with the Jews of Medina, and he executed it ruthlessly one after another. The first to be expelled from Medina were Banu Nazir, and then Banu Qaynuqa. The fate of the last group, as discussed in the next chapter, was the most tragic one.

Asking Jews to Accept Islam, and be Safe

Prophet Muhammad went to the Jews along with his followers and told them to accept Islam to be safe. Abu Huraira, narrator of a Hadis says: "We were sitting in the mosque when the Messenger of Allah came and said: Let us go to the Jews. We went out with him until we came to them. The Messenger of Allah called out to them: O yee assembly of Jews. Accept Islam and you will be safe." On receiving unsatisfactory reply, he told them: "You should know that the earth belongs to Allah and his apostle, and I wish that I should expel you from this land."[2]

The expulsion plan of the Jews started after the Battle of Badr. Beni Qainuka (Banu also written as Beni, or B; meaning dynasty, descendants; Qaynuqa written variously as Qaynuqa, Kainuka, Kaynuka) were the first to be exiled followed by the exile of Banu an-Nadir in AH 4. Then, after the Battle of the Ditch, during AH 5, Banu Qoreiza (Qurayza, Quraiza) were massacred. Khaybar, being sixty miles to the north, towards Damascus was to suffer later on.

Banu Qaynuqa Exiled

The apostle assembled the Qaynuqa Jews in the market and addressed them: 'O Jews lest Allah bring upon you the vengeance that He brought upon Quraysh and become Muslims. You know that I am a prophet who has been sent—you will find that in your scriptures and Allah's covenant with you.' The Qaynuqas replied: 'O Muhammad you seem to think that we are your people. Do not deceive yourself you encountered a people with no knowledge of war and got the better of them; for by Allah if we fight you, you will find that we are real men!'[3] A Quranic revelation followed, which said:

"Neither their possessions nor their children will be any use to the disbelievers against Allah. The disbelievers will be fuel for the Fire. … (Prophet), say to the disbelievers, 'You will be defeated and driven together into Hell, a foul resting place. Thou have already seen a sign in the two armies that met in battle, one fighting for Allah's cause and other made up of disbelievers. With their own eyes (the former) saw (the latter) to be twice their number, but Allah helps whoever He will. There truly is a lesson in this for all with eyes to see."[4] It clearly pointed to the fact that the Quraysh army had double strength, yet it was defeated.

The situation for the Jews of Medina was already grave. The murder of the critic poets, committed by expressed authority of the Prophet, which we have fully discussed, needless to say, terrorized the Jews. Muir writes: "These lawless and sanguinary acts alarmed all that party at Medina which still regarded the strangers and the new faith with suspicion and dislike. And above all, terror crept over the hearts of all the Jews. There was good reason for it."[5]

An incident in the market place, in the mean time, worsened the situation, and the Bani Qaynuka, goldsmiths by profession, had to bear the brunt of the Prophet's displeasure. The treaty between Prophet Muhammad and them, as alleged, was already broken; how it happened, however, is not certain. Muir has detailed the incident which afforded the pretext for attack. He writes: "A Muslim woman visited their market place, and at a goldsmith's shop, waiting for some ornaments, sat down. A silly neighbour unperceived, pinned her skirt behind to the upper dress. When she arose, the awkward exposure excited laughter, and she screamed with shame. A Muslim, apprised of the affront, slew the offending Jew. The brethren of the Jew, in their turn, fell upon the Muslim and killed him. The family of the murdered Muslim appealed to the converts of Medina, who espoused their cause. Though bound by a friendly treaty, Muhammad made no attempt to compose the quarrel, or single out the guilty. Forthwith he marshaled his followers, and, placing the great white banner, which had waved the field of Badr but a month before, in the hands of Hamza, marched forth to attack the offending tribe. Their settlement, sufficiently fortified to resist assault, was invested, and a strict blockade maintained. This happened within one month from the battle of Badr."[6]

Qaynuqa expected interference in their behalf from their long time allies, Abdulla, son of Obayy and the Khazraj, but none dared to stir. Closely besieged for fifteen days, and despairing of the looked for aid, they surrendered at discretion; started coming out one by one from their stronghold. As they came out, their hands were tied behind their backs, and preparations were made for execution. Ultimately, Abdallah, "fallen as he was from his high estate, could not endure to see his faithful allies led thus away to be massacred in cold blood." He had to interfere to save them. Muir writes: "Approaching Muhammad, he begged for mercy; but Muhammad turned his face away. Abdallah persisted in suit, and seizing the Prophet by the arm, as he stood armed in his coat of mail, reiterated the petition. 'Let me alone!' cried Muhammad; but Abdallah did not relax his hold. The marks of anger mantled in the Prophet's face, and again he exclaimed loudly: 'Wretch, let me go!' 'Ney!' said Abdallah, 'I will not let thee go until thou hast compassion on my friends; 300 soldiers armed in mail, and 400 unequipped—they defended me on the fields of Hadaik and Bo'ath from every foe. Will you cut them down in one day, O Muhammad? As for me, I am one verily that feareth the vicissitudes of fortune.' Abdallah was yet too strong for Muhammad with safety to neglect the appeal so urgently preferred. 'Let them go!' the Prophet said, reluctantly; 'the Lord curse them, and him too!' So Muhammad released them and commanded that they should be sent into exile."[7]

Whereas Abdallah interfered, espoused their cause, and saved the life of Qaynukas, another person, "Ubada, son of al-Samit, who had the same alliance with them as had Abdallah, went to the apostle and renounced all responsibility for them in favour of Allah and the apostle, saying: 'O apostle of Allah, I take Allah and his apostle and believers as my friends, and I renounce my agreement and friendship with these unbelievers.'"[8] The revelation came down concerning Abdallah and Ubada: "Those who turn for protection to Allah, His Messenger, and the believers (are Allah's party): Allah's party is sure to triumph. You who believe, do not take as allies those who ridicule your religion and make fun of it—whether people who were given the Scripture before you, or disbelievers—and be mindful of Allah if you are true believers. When you make the call to prayer, they ridicule it and make fun of it; this is because they are people who do not reason."[9]

The exiled Qaynuqa were led forth some distance by one of the Khazarite leaders, Obada; then they proceeded to the Jewish settlement of Wadi al-Kora, received carriage facilities, and then reached Adhri'at, on the confines of Syria.

Attack Justified by Heavenly Message

The Jews could visualize now the things to come. Muir writes: "The Jews might now see clearly the designs of Muhammad. It was no petty question of affronted female. Blood had, no doubt, been shed in the quarrel; but it was shed equally on both sides. And, had there not been relentless enmity, and predetermination to root out the Israelites, the difference might easily had been composed. Moreover, Muhammad was bound by treaty to deal justly and amiably with the tribe: the murderer alone was 'liable to retaliation.' Indeed, of such minor importance was the quarrel, that some biographers do not mention it at all, but justify the attack by a heavenly message revealing Jewish treachery."[10]

Deportation of Banu An-Nadir

Banu An-Nadir were exiled during 4 AH. It all started with the demand of the share of blood wit from them, which Prophet Muhammad wanted to pay to B. Amir, a Chief of Nejd, with whom the Prophet had an agreement of friendship, for the murder of his two men. Ibn Ishaq has detailed 'how the murder took place,'[11] and the happenings regarding the deportation of the Nadir. He writes: "When the apostle came to them about the blood wit they said that of course they would contribute in the way he wished; but they took counsel with one another apart, saying, 'You will never get such a chance again. Who will go to the top of the house and drop a rock on him (T. so as to kill him)[12] and get rid us of him?' The apostle was sitting by the wall of one of their houses at the time. Amr, b. Jihash b.Ka'b volunteered to do this and went up to throw down the rock. As the apostle was with a number of his companions among whom were Abu Bakr, 'Umar and 'Ali, news came to him from heaven about what these people intended, so he got up (T. and said to his companions, 'Don't go away until I come to you') and he went back to Medina. When his companions had waited long for the Prophet, they got up to search for him and met a man coming from Medina and asked him about him. He said that he had seen him entering Medina, and they went off, and when they found him he told them of the treachery which the Jews meditated against him. The apostle ordered them to prepare for war and to march against them. Then he went off with the men until he came upon them."[13]

The translator of *Sirat Rasul Allah*, A. Guillaume, in his footnote brings to notice certain inconsistencies about the treachery angle of the statement given above. He writes: "I think it is clear that another story has been attached to this incident. Obviously if the Prophet had overheard their designs there was no need of a supernatural communication from heaven. Further, it should be noted that in this later story the apostle is called 'the prophet.' This is the term which I.I. uses most sparingly, though it is fairly frequently employed by his editor I.H."[14] Margoliouth's remark on this aspect of the conspiracy is also worth quoting. He writes: "We know not, having no Jewish account of the matter, whether this bold design was really contemplated; but since the Prophet had a fixed idea that the Jews always wanted to murder him—an idea which owed its origin to the accusation of "killing the Prophets" launched against them by the Founder of Christianity—he may have sincerely believed such an attempt was meditated. He therefore rushed back to Medina, asserting that he was escaping from a treacherous assault, and summoned his followers to besiege the Banu Nadir."[15]

Ibn Ishaq writes about the further developments: "The Jews took refuge in their forts and the apostle ordered that the palm trees should be cut down and burnt, and they called out to him, 'Muhammad, you have prohibited wanton destruction and blamed those guilty of it. Why then are you cutting down and burning our palm-trees?'" Abdullah and other from Khazraj community, who assured them, saying: "Stand firm and protect yourself, for we will not betray you. If you are attacked we will fight with you and if you are turned out, we will go with you.' Accordingly they waited for the help they had promised, but they did nothing and Allah cast terror into their hearts. They asked the apostle to deport them and to spare their lives on condition that they could retain all their property which they could carry on their camels, except their armour, and he agreed. So they loaded their camels with what they could carry. Men were destroying their houses down to the lintel of the door which they put upon the back of their camels and went off with it. Some went to Khaybar and some to Syria."[16] Among the chiefs, who went to Khaybar, were Sallam, son of Abu'l Huqayq, Kinan, son of al-Rabi and Huyayy, son of Akhtab. When they got there the inhabitants became subject to them.[17]

Margoliouth writes about the Prophet's order to attack the Nadir: "The followers were quite ready. Of the fighting ability of the Jews, and of the energy of their partisans in Medina, they had ample experience; there was not the least chance of any resistance to an energetic attack. One account indeed informs us that Muhammad sent messenger offering them eight days in which to remove their possessions, and that this proposal would have been accepted immediately had not the unfortunate Abdallah Ibn Ubayy urgently advised them to resist, and promised them assistance in the event of their doing so. The Banu Kuraizah, to whom an appeal was made on behalf of their brethren, flatly refused to break with Muhammad. This act of cowardice prepares us to feelless sympathy with them for the fate that afterwards befell them."[18]

The Nadir carried off the women and children and property with tambourines and pipes and singing girls playing behind them with such pomp and splendour as had never been seen in any tribe in their days.[19]

The fortresses, land, palm cultivation, and whatever was left behind came in the exclusive share of the Prophet as no war was fought for acquiring the same. The Quranic revelation, coming down after their deportation, confirmed the same.[20] The fortresses occupied by the Nadir were probably no worse than the others at Madina; and legend, if not history, recorded how the fortress of Yathrib had held out against Yemenite King Tubba' and forced him to raise a siege.[21] The Quranic Shura, which came down, declared 'cuting down of palm trees' by Allah's leave,[22] the deportation due to panic created by Allah into their hearts,[23] and the role of the hypocrites.[24]

Notes and Reference

1. *Sahih Muslim, Hadis* 4366.
2. Ibid, *Hadis* 4363.
3. Ibn Ishaq, *Sirat Rasul Allah*, p.363.
4. Qur'an 3:10, 12, 13.
5. Muir, The Life of Mohomet. Here after Muir, p. 240.
6. Ibid, p. 241.
7. Ibid, p. 242.
8. Ibn Ishaq, p. 363.
9. Qur'an 5:57-59.
10. Muir, p. 242.
11. Ibn Ishaq, pp. 433-435.
12. The remark, given under bracket, seems to be taken from the writings of at-Tabari, where he differs from Ibn Ishaq.
13. Ibn Ishaq, p. 437.
14. Ibid, footnote 1.
15. Margoliouth, Mohammed and the Rise of Islam. Hereafter Margoliouth, p. 314.
16. Ibn Ishaq, p. 437.

17. Ibid, p. 438.
18. Margoliouth, pp. 314-15.
19. Ibn Ishaq, p. 438.
20. Qur'an 59:7,8.
21. Margoliouth, p. 315.
22. Qur'an 59:5.
23. Qur'an 59:2.
24. Qur'an 59: 11-13.

The Massacre of Banu Qurayza

Gruesome Fate of Banu Qurayza

A Qur'anic verse put Allah's seal on the fate of Banu Qurayza. It said: "He brought those People of the Book who supported them down from their strongholds and put panic into their hearts. Some of them you (believers) killed and some you took captive. He passed on to you their land, their houses, their possessions, and a land where you had not set foot. God has power over everything."[1]

According to Ibn Ishaq, Gabriel came to the apostle at the time of the noon prayer, "wearing an embroidered turban and riding on a mule with a saddle covered with a piece of brocade. He asked the apostle if he had abandoned fighting and when he said that he had, he said that the angels had not yet laid aside their arms and that he has just come from pursuing the enemy. 'Allah commands you, Muhammad, to go to B. Qurayza. I am about to go to them to shake their stronghold.'"[2]

According to another Hadis, Ayesha said: "the Prophet had hardly laid his arms after returning from the Battle of the Ditch when Gabriel appeared and told him: "You have laid down arms. By Allah, we haven't laid down ours. So march against them." "Where?" asked the Prophet. Then Gabriel pointed to the Banu Qurayza. So the Messenger of Allah fought against them … they surrendered … those of them who could fight (were) killed, their women and children taken prisoners and their properties distributed among Muslims."[3]

"Commanded by Allah through Gabriel, Prophet Muhammad went to the fort of Qurayza, the place where they had gathered, and told them: "O ye brothers of monkeys and swines, we have arrived, Allah has disgraced you and has brought His vengeance upon you." The Jews replied, 'O Abu'l-Qasim, you are not a barbarous man.' He besieged them for twenty-five nights until they were sore pressed and "Allah cast terror into their hearts." Surrendering unconditionally, they were taken captive."[4]

As Prophet Muhammad received the command of Gabriel to fight against the Qurayza, just back from the battlefield, he had just washed dust of his half face; the action began. "Instantly Bilal made proclamation throughout the town;—immediate march was ordered; all were to be present at evening prayer in the camp pitched before the fortress, two or three miles south-east of Medina. The great banner standing yet unfurled in the mosque, was placed in the hands of Ali. Muhammad mounted his ass, and the army (as before 3,000 strong, with 36 horses) followed. The fortress was at once invested, and a discharge of archery kept up steadily, but without effect. One man, approaching incautiously near, was killed by a Jewess casting down millstone from the walls."[5]

Allah Cast Terror in Qurayza's Heart

There are numerous cases, such as during the Battle of Badr, when Allah cast terror in the hearts of the enemies of Prophet Muhammad. In this case also, as Ibn Ishaq writes, the "apostle besieged them for twenty-five nights until they were sore pressed and Allah cast terror in their hearts."[6] When Dihya, son of Khalifa al-Kalbi, passed upon a white mule with a saddle covered with a piece of brocade, the apostle said, "That was Gabriel who has been sent to B. Qurayza to shake their castles and strike terror to their hearts."[7]

Three Alternatives Suggested

The Qurayza, under siege, were "soon reduced to great distress," and, as Muir writes, "they sought to capitulate on condition of quitting the neighbourhood even empty-handed. But Muhammad, having no longer other Jewish neighbours to alarm or alienate, was bent on severe measures, and refused. In this extremity, the Beni Koreiza appealed to their ancient friendship with the Aus, and services rendered to them in bygone days."[8]

As there was a realization that "the apostle would not leave them until he had made an end of them," Ka'b, son of Asad, suggested three alternative ways to deal with the situation. Ibn Ishaq writes: "Ka'b b. Asad said to them: 'O Jews, you can see what has happened to you; I offer you three alternatives. Take which you please.' (i) We will follow this man and accept him as true, for by Allah it has become plain to you that he is a prophet who has been sent and that it is he that you find mentioned in your scripture; and then your lives, your property, your women and children will be saved, They said, 'We will never abandon the laws of the Torah and never change it for another.' He said: "Then if you won't accept this suggestion (ii) let us kill our wives and children and send men with their swords drawn to Muhammad and his companions leaving no encumbrances behind us, until God decides between us and Muhammad. If we perish, we perish, and we shall not leave children behind us to cause us anxiety. If we conquer we can acquire other wives and children.' They said: 'Should we kill these poor creatures? What should be the good of life when they were dead?' He said: "Then if you will not accept this suggestion (iii) tonight is the eve of Sabbath and it may well be that Muhammad and his companions will feel secure from us then, so come down, perhaps we can take Muhammad and his companions by surprise.' They said: 'Are we to profane our sabbath and do on the Sabbath what those before us of whom you will know did and were turned into apes?' He answered: 'Not a single man among you from the day of your birth has ever passed a night resolved to do what he knows ought to be done.'"[9]

Qurayza Hoping for the Support of Aus

As discussed elsewhere in detail, Banu Qurayza were the allies of the Aus tribe; the other two Jewish tribes of Medina, whose release was secured by Abdallah, were the allies of Khazraj. Naturally, Qurayza were hoping the intervention of their allies, the Aus, in their favour. The Qurayza, were, moreover desperate. They begged Prophet Muhammad to allow them to meet Abu Lubab, an ally of Aus tribe, who "came, and, overcome by the wailing of the children and the cries of the women, had no heart to speak; but symbolically drawing his hand across his throat, intimated that they must fight to the last, as death was all they had to hope for."[10]

Qurayza

The Qurayza submitted to Muhammad on the assurance of their allies, the Aus, who started asking for the same treatment to them as the other two Jewish tribes. Ibn Ishaq writes:

"In the morning they submitted to the apostle's judgment and al-Aus leapt up and said, 'O Apostle, they are our allies, not allies of Khazraj, and you know how you recently treated the allies of our brethren.' … the apostle said: 'Will you be satisfied, O Aus, if one of your own number pronounces judgment on them?' When they agreed he said that Sa'd b. Mu'adh was the man. … When Sa'd reached the apostle and the Muslims the apostle told them to get up to greet their leader. The muhajirs of Quraysh thought that the apostle meant the Ansar, while the latter thought that he meant everyone, so they got up and said 'O Abu Amr, the apostle has entrusted to you the affair of your allies that you may give judgment concerning them.' Sa'd asked, 'Do you covenant by Allah that you accept the judgment I pronounce on them?' They said Yes, and he said, 'And is it incumbent on the one who is here?' (looking) in the direction of the apostle not mentioning him out of respect, and the apostle answered Yes. Sa'd said: 'Then I give judgment that the men should be killed, the property divided, and the women and children taken as captives.'"[11]

Massacre of the Qurayza

Muir summarizes the pathetic massacre scenario of Qurayza: "No sooner was the sentence passed and ratified then the camp broke up and the people wended their way back to Medina. The captives, still under charge of Muhammad, were dragged roughly along; one alone was treated with tenderness and care,—it was Reihana the beautiful Jewess, set apart for Muhammad. The men were shut up in a yard, separate from women and children; they were supplied with dates and spent in prayer the hours of darkness, repeating passages from their Scriptures and exhorting one another to faith and constancy. During the night trenches sufficient to contain the dead bodies of the men were dug across the marketplace of the city. In the morning, Muhammad, himself a spectator of the tragedy, commanded the male captives to be brought forth in companies of five or six at a time. Each company as it came up was made to sit down in a row on the brink of the trench destined for its grave, there beheaded, and bodies cast therein. And so with company after company till all were slain. One woman alone was put to death; it was she who threw the millstone from the battlements. When she heard that her husband had been slain, she loudly avowed what she had done, and demanded of Muhammad that she might share her husband's fate;—a petition which, perhaps in more mercy than was meant, he granted; and she met her death with a cheerful countenance. This heroine's smile, as she stepped fearless to her death, Ayesha tells us, haunted her ever after. For Az-Zabir, an aged Jew, who had saved some of the Aus in the battle of Bo'ath, Thabit ibn Keis interceded and procured a pardon, including the freedom of her family and restoration of his property. 'But what hath become of all our chiefs,—of Ka'b, of Huyei, of Azzal, the son of Samuel?' asked the old man. As one after another he named the leading chiefs of his tribe, he received the same reply;—they had all been put to death already. 'Then of what use is life to me any longer? Leave me not in the tyrant's power who hath slain all that are dear to me. Slay me also; I entreat thee, that I may join them in their home. Here, take my sword, it is sharp; strike high and hard. Thabit refused, and gave him over to another who, under Ali's orders, beheaded that aged man, but attended to his last request in obtaining freedom for his family. When told of his dying words, Muhammad answered: '*Yea, he shall join them in their home,—the fire of Hell!*'" The butchery, beginning in the morning, continued throughout the day, and till evening by torchlight, drenching the market place with human blood.[12]

Victims Remained in Dark

The Qurayza remained in dark about what was happening when the massacre continued. When the men were taken out in batches to the Apostle, they asked Ka'b what he thought would be done with them. Ka'b replied: 'Will you never understand? Don't you see the summoner never stops and those who are taken away never return? By Allah it is death.1' "This went on until the Apostle made an end of them"[13]

Utilization of the Local Conflicts

As the Qurayza were the allies of the Aus, they were not well liked by the Banu Khazraj. Therefore, when Muhammad ordered the Jews beheaded, the "Khazraj began to cut off their heads with great satisfaction. The apostle saw that the faces of Khazraj showed pleasure, but there was no such indication on the part of the Aus, and he suspected that that was because of the alliance that had existed between them and Banu Qurayza. When there were only twelve of them left he gave them over to Aus, assigning one Jew to every two of Aus, saying, 'Let so and so strike him and so and so finish him.'"[14]

Abu Lubab Meets Muhammad

Abu Lubab, as discussed above, advised the Jews that war is the only way out. But he had after thought after coming back. Muir writes about the further developments: "On retiring he felt that he had been too plain and honest in his advice; for 'War,' as the Prophet had said: 'was a game of deception.' Therefore he went to Muhammad, and, confessing his guilt, said: 'I repent; for verily I have dealt treacherously with the Lord, and with his Prophet.' Muhammad vouchsafed no reply; and Abu Lubaba, the more strongly to mark his contrition, went straightaway to the Mosque and bound himself to one of the posts. In this position he remained for several days, till at last Muhammad relented, and sent to pardon and release him. The 'Pillar of repentance' is still pointed out to the pious pilgrim."[15] This case, and the following one, clearly shows that the followers of Muhammad must become new men with new conscience.

The Judgment of Sa'd

As Sa'd was brought to deliver his judgment, the Aus said, 'Deal kindly with your friends, for the apostle has made you empire for that very purpose.' On their persistence, he said: 'The time has come for Sa'd in the cause of Allah, not to care for any man's censure.' 'Some of the people who were there went back to the quarter of B. 'Abdu'l-Ashal and announced to them the death of B. Qurayza before Sa'd got to them, because of what they have heard him say."[16]

Sa'd suffered from the injury inflicted by the arrow at the battle of the Trench. He was carried from the battlefield on the advice of Muhammad to a tent belonging to a woman of Aslam called Rufayda, pitched inside his mosque ground on the advice of Muhammad.[17]

Sa'd was a large and corpulent person, but his bier was very light; on this someone remarked, 'We have never heard of a corpus lighter in the bier than that of Sa'd; know ye why this is? It is because of his judgment against the Bani Qurayza.' Muhammad, 'hearing the rash remark, turned aside its point by a mysterious explanation which was eagerly caught up by his followers: "The angels are carrying the bier.' he said, therefore it is light in your hands. Verily the throne on high doth vibrate for Sa'd, and the portals of heaven are opened, and he is attended by seventy thousand angels that never trod the earth before ...'[18]

Ibn Ishaq writes that Gabriel came to the apostle when Sa'd was taken in the middle of the night wearing an embroidered turban and said: 'O Muhammad, who is this dead man for whom the doors of heaven have been opened and at whom the throne shook?' The apostle got up quickly dragging his garment as he went to Sa'd and found him already dead.'[19] The tale of Sa'd is surrounded with many such supernatural associations.[20]

Sa'd, after his injury in the battle of the Trench developed bitter hate for the Qurayza, which Muhammad knew; and when he was made the empire, he gave the bloody judgment. Muir writes: "Sa'd still suffered from the injury inflicted by the arrow at the trench. ... His wound had begun apparently to heal. But the sense of injury still rankled in his heart; and Muhammad, no doubt knew the bitter hate into which his former friendship had been turned by the treachery of the Beni Koreiza."[21] A note by Muir says: "On his being wounded Sa'd is said to have cursed the Beni Koreiza and prayed: 'O Lord! Suffer me not to die until my heart hath had its revenge against them.'"[22]

Banu Qurayza were not a party in the battle of trench; it was fought between the Quraysh and the Muslims; and yet they are labelled as treacherous. It is strange and tells a lot about the affairs of the then Medina.

Notes and References

1. Qur'an 33:26-27.
2. Ibn Ishaq, *Sirat Rasul Allah*, p. 461. Hereafter, Ibn Ishaq.
3. *Sahih Muslim*, *Hadis* 4370.
4. Ibn Ishaq, p. 461.
5. Muir, The Life of Mahomet, p. 315. Hereafter, Muir.
6. Ibn Ishaq, p. 461.
7. Ibid.
8. Muir, p. 315.
9. Ibn Ishaq, pp. 461-62.
10. Muir, p. 315.
11. Ibn Ishaq, pp. 463-64.
12. Muir, pp.318-19.
13. Ibn Ishaq, p. 464.
14. Ibn Ishaq, p. 752; Ibn Hisham's note no. 580.
15. Muir, pp. 315-16.
16. Ibn Ishaq, p. 463.
17. Ibid.
18. Muir, p. 324.
19. Ibn Ishaq, p. 468.
20. Muir, p. 323 note 2.
21. Ibid, pp. 316-17.
22. Ibid, Muir, p. 317 note 1.

Pillars of Islam

Prayer in Islam

Prayer: A Pillar of Islam

Allah and His Messenger, prayer (*salat*), *zakat*, fasting (*Ramzan*) and pilgrimage (*hajj*) are sometimes called the "five pillars" of Islam; there are other important beliefs and institutions also, including Paradise, Hell, Doomsday or day of judgement, *jihad* (holy war against non-believers) *jizya* (the poll tax imposed on non-believers), *ghanimah* (war booty) and *khums* (the holy one-fifth), which are not less important.[1] In a statement about his mission, Prophet Muhammad said: "I have been commanded to fight against people till they testify that there is no god but Allah, that Muhammad is the Messenger of Allah, and they establish prayer, and pay Zakat and if they do it, their blood and property are guaranteed protection on my behalf.[2] The prayer is an essential part of Islam, and a pious Muslim is supposed to pray five times a day.

Qur'an Enjoins Muslims to Pray

Several verses of Qur'an enjoin the Muslims to pray Allah; Allah says:

"(Prophet), recite what had been revealed to you of the Scripture; keep up the prayer: prayer restraints outrageous and non-acceptable behaviour. Remembering Allah is better: Allah knows everything you are doing."[3]

"Seek help with steadfastness and prayer—though this is hard indeed for anyone but the humble,"[4]

"What drove you to the Scorching Fire?' and they will answer, 'We did not pray;"[5]

"bow down in worship and draw close."[6]

"I am Allah; there is no god but Me and keep up the prayer so that you remember Me."[7]

Coverage of the Prayer in the Hadis

There is the detailed coverage of the prayer in the *Hadis*. The fourth book of the *Sahih Muslim is* the "Book of Prayer" (*Salat*), which is the longest book with 1,398 *ahadis* divided into 203 chapters. *Sahih Bukhari* has the chapters on prayer divided into books, such as "The Book of *Wudu* (Ablution)," "The Book of *Tayyamum,*" "The Book of *Salat,*" "The Book of Shortened Prayers (*At-Taqsir*)," "The Book of *Tahajjud* (Prayer)."

The diverse coverage of the tradition in *Hadis* related to the bodily purity, *azan* (the call to prayer), postures like bowing, prostrating and rising, the number and times of the different prayers, *imam* in the system of prayers, the merits of prayers at different times, the prayer relating to the dead, the prayer for rain, the prayer for the protection against calamities, etc.

Gabriel Shows How to Pray

There is provision of five times prayer in Islam. The apostle was ordered to pray, writes Ibn Ishaq, and so he prayed. And as Ayesha said: "When the prayer was first laid on the apostle it was with two prostrations for every prayer: 'then Allah raised it to four prostrations at home while in a journey the former ordinance of two prostrations held.' At first Gabriel came and performed prayer, and then Khadija followed the Prophet in its performance. Ibn Ishaq writes: 'A learned person told me that when prayer was laid on the apostle Gabriel came to him while he was on the heights of Mecca and dug a hole for him with his heel in the side of the valley from which a fountain gushed forth, and Gabriel performed the ritual ablution as the apostle watched him. This was in order to show him how to purify himself before prayer. Then the apostle performed the ritual ablution as he has seen Gabriel do it. Then Gabriel said a prayer with him while the apostle prayed with his prayer. Then Gabriel left him. The apostle came to Khadija and performed the ritual for her as Gabriel had done for him, and she copied him. Then he prayed with her as Gabriel had prayed with him, and she prayed his prayer."[8]

Gabriel also came to the apostle at different hours of the day for the prayer. Referring to a tradition, Ibn Ishaq writes: "When prayer was laid upon, the apostle Gabriel came to him and prayed the noon prayer when the sun declined. Then he prayed the evening prayer when his shadow equalled his own length. Then he prayed the sunset prayer when the sun set. Then he prayed the last night prayer when the twilight disappeared. Then he prayed with him the morning prayer when the dawn rose.' Gabriel came for the prayer at different times till the next day."[9]

Evolution of the Ceremony of *Salat*

The Islamic prayer, the ceremony called *salat*, gradually evolved, and there is scant information about the same. Margoliouth writes: "Of the evolution of the Mohammedan ceremony called *salat*, the name of which was borrowed from either the Jewish or the Christian name for prayer, we possess little detailed knowledge. In the form afterwards stereotyped the Jewish practice of standing erect, the Christian of prostration, and a third of inclination (the back horizontal of with the hands on the knees) were combined; and certain formulae were prescribed. "We used at first," said a convert, "not knowing what to say when we prayed, to salute Allah, Gabriel, and Michael; the Prophet presently taught us another formula instead. A prayer corresponding to the *Pater Noster* was composed probably at a later time: it contains polemical references to some sects not specified." As will be seen, the *salat* was afterwards employed as a military drill: at the first it was ascetic in character, the devotee "tying a cord to his chest.'""[10]

The division of time for performing *salat* was a later development, but purity of body for the prayer was an accepted norm in the Southern Arabia. Margoliouth further writes: "That the division of the day into periods for the purpose of performing *salat* five times was an innovation of the Meccan period is asserted by the tradition; and the details of the purity legislation appear to have been still later. Yet the theory that Allah should be approached only by persons in a state of purity was known in South Arabia before Mohammad's time, whence it is probable that his earliest converts were instructed therein; and indeed the washing of the garments which marked convention belongs to the same range of ideas."[11]

Prayer in Submission Mode

The *salat* had the recitation of prayer part; but it also had the posture in complete submission mode, a classic posture of one of the captive before a conqueror. This shocked abu-Talib, who happened to observe the salat. Hazleton writes: "These young people were not only reciting the Quranic verses; abu Talib had come on them in the act of prayer. He had seen them bowing down low in Islam, that supple word whose associated meanings in Arabic ripple out to include peace and wholeness, but which means above all submission. True, it was not a forced submission but a willed and willing acceptance. Yet the posture of prayer—forehead on the ground, arms outstretched, rump high in the air—was the classic one of captive before conqueror, still visible today on ancient Assyrian victory steles, whose prisoners do precisely this at the feet of the victorious king. It was the posture of utter surrender to the mercy and grace of a far greater power, and thus a clear statement, felt in muscle and bone, of the literal meaning of Islam. So abu-Talib had been shocked as so many others would be. To a man of honour in a society that prided itself, as it were, on pride, nothing could be more un-Arabian."[12]

Posture During Prayer

Muslim prayer is not carried on in one tranquil posture, sitting or standing; it is accompanied by many body movements. These have been codified, as we find in the ahadis, on the basis of the practice and precepts of Prophet Muhammad.[13] A narrator saw the Prophet "raising the hands opposite the shoulders at the time of beginning the prayer and before bowing down and after coming back to the erect position after bowing, but he did not raise them between two prostrations."[14] Another narrator saw "his hands lifted opposite to ears." He also saw that Prophet Muhammad "then wrapped his hands in his cloth and placed his right hand over his left hand. After that, when he was about to bow down, he brought out his hands from the cloths, and lifted them. … And when prostrated, he prostrated between the two palms."[15]

Prophet Muhammad was commanded by Allah that "he should prostrate on the seven bones and he was forbidden to fold back the hair and the clothing." The seven bones are: "The hands, the knees, and the extremities of the fe. and the forehead."[16] He, however, asked his followers to "observe moderation in prostration" and not to stretch out (their) forearms on the ground like a dog.[17] There was the practice of putting one's hands together, palm to palm, and to put them between one's thighs; but that practice was abrogated and the followers were "commanded to place them (the hands) on the knees."[18] Mus'ab, son of Sa'd, narrated, I offered Salat beside my father and approximated both my hands and placed them between the knees. My father told me not to do so and said: "We used to do the same but we were forbidden (by the Prophet) to do so and were ordered to place the hands on knees.[19] Looking up towards the sky during Salat is forbidden, as the eyes would be snatched by doing so.[20] Similarly, if one looks hither and thither during the prayer, then the Satan takes away a portion of the prayer.[21]

Linkages Between Salat and the Bodily Exercises

Margoliouth, while discussing the results of the Battle of Badr, points out the linkages between Salat and the bodily exercises. He writes: "Of the battle that followed we have no clear or detailed account: but we know at least some of the factors which brought about the result. The discipline of the *salat* or "prayer," in which the Moslems were arranged in rows, and had to perform after a leader certain bodily exercises, and falling out of line was threatened with divine punishment, had served as rough sort of drill, and Mohammed before the battle discharged the duty of making the troops fall into line. The Meccan general, 'Utbah, son of Rabiah, was struck with their appearance: they were kneeling on their knees, silent as though they were dumb, and stretching out their tongues like snakes."[22]

Lustration Preliminary to the Prayer

By the time five times prayer was prescribed, lustration had become preliminary to prayer. Of course, the time of its prescription, as Muir writes, is uncertain. He writes: "It may have been at Mecca; but, however that may be, it was evidently borrowed from the Jews, with whose teaching the ordinances established by Mohammad respecting ceremonial impurity and ablutions very closely correspond.[23]

Different Hadis collections have detailed coverage about ablution and other aspects of body purification. *Sahih Bukhari* has 'The Book of Wudu (Ablution)', 'The Book of Ghusl', 'The Book of Menses' and 'The Book of Tayammum', which cover up various aspects of prayer related body purity. *Sahih Muslim* has 'Kitab Al-Taharah' (The Book of Purification) and 'Kitab Al-Haid' (The Book of Menstruation), dealing with bodily purity aspect of the prayer. According to Sahih Bukhari, 'No Salat (prayer) is accepted without ablution (i.e. to remove the small Hadath by ablution or the big Hadath by taking bath).' Hadath, in Arabic, is passing urine, stool or wind.[24] In this context, a statement of Prophet Muhammad, addressed to Abu Hurraira, that 'A Muslim never becomes *Najas* (impure)[25] seems to be interesting. The Qur'an, of course, declares 'those who ascribe partners to Allah' to be truly unclean, and debarred them from coming near the Sacred Mosque.[26] If there is no water for ablution and bath, one may use clean soil in place of water; rub it in his hand, body and face; blow it and perform the prayer. The process is called *Tayammum*.[27]

Use of Earth for Prayer and Purification

As narrated by Jabir, son of Abdullah, Prophet Muhammad mentioned about five things which were not given to anyone before him, and one of them was the earth. He said about the same: "The earth has been made for me (and for my followers) a place for offering *Salat* (prayer) and a thing to purify (perform *Tayammum*), therefore anyone of my followers can offer *Salat* wherever he is, at the time of a *Salat*."[28]

Prayer on Different Occasions

There is provision for the prayer on different occasions and for different purposes. During a war, one group prays while the other one fights.[29] There were prayer for rain, prayers for protection against windstorms or terrible dark clouds, prayers to be recited at the time of a solar eclipse.[30]

The Prophet was highly afraid of the windstorm and the dark cloud. "Whenever wind was stormy," Ayesha tells, the Apostle of Allah used to say: O Allah! I ask Thee for what is good in it, and the good which it contains, and the good of that which it was sent for. I seek refuge with Thee for what is evil in it, what evil it contains, and the evil of that what it was sent for."[31] To those who were dying, the Prophet exhorted to recite, 'There is no god but Allah.'[32]

When Abu Salama died, his wife, Umm Salama reported the matter to Prophet Muhammad, who advised her to recite, 'O Allah! Forgive me and him (Abu Salama) and give me a better substitute than he.' She did accordingly, and said: 'So I said this, and Allah gave me in exchange Muhammad, who is better for me than him (Abu Salama).'[33]

Things Permissible (*Halal*) and Forbidden (*Haram*) during Prayer

There are numerous ahadis indicating the permissible and forbidden things during prayer. Some such ahadis are given here. Wearing shoes, while praying, is permissible,[34] but not the clothes with designs and markings.[35] "When the supper is brought and prayer begins, one should first take the food."[36] Spitting in front of him, while praying, was forbidden, 'for Allah is in front of him when he is engaged in prayer.'[37] But according to another Hadis, while spitting towards the front or right side was forbidden, it was permitted to do so towards the left or below the left foot.[38]

While eating onion or garlic was not forbidden (was not haram), but the Prophet found their odours "repugnant"[39] It was, however, forbidden to go to the mosque after eating them, "for the angels are harmed by the same things as men."[40]

Friday Prayer

Friday is a special day for the Muslims. Muslims essentially congregate on that day for prayer. "On it (Friday) Adam was created, on it he was made to enter Paradise, on it he was expelled from heaven.[41] An episode, showing the casualness during prayer in the initial days needs mention. On a Friday, when the Prophet was delivering a sermon, a caravan with merchandise from Syria arrived; the people left the Prophet and flocked towards the caravan. After the incident, the verse revealed was: "And when they see merchandise or sport, they break away to it and leave you standing."[42]

Places Where Prayer is Prohibited

Allah's Messenger prohibited prayer at seven places, which were: "At a dung hill, in a slaughterhouse, in a graveyard, in the middle of the road, in a bathroom, and in the watering places where camels drink and sit, and upon the roof of the house of Allah.[43] He further said: "Observe prayer in the folds of the sheep, but not in the folds of the camels."[44]

Invoking Curse for Worship at Graves

According to a Hadis: "Allah's Messenger invoked curse upon those women who are accustomed to visit graves and upon those who use them as the places of worship and those who light lamps (upon them as a mark of respect to them)"[45]

The Prophet cursed Jews and the Christians for taking the graves of their Apostles as places of worship.[46] When the Prophet "was about to breathe his last, he uncovered his face and said in that very state: 'Let there be curse upon the Jews and the Christians that they have taken the graves of their Apostles as places of worship.'[47]

Recitation of Qur'an is Essential for Salat to be Valid

Recitation of the Qur'an (Surat Al-Fayiha) is essential for Imam and believers during Salat,[48] and the Salat becomes invalid without that.[49] Other Hadis say: "If you recite Surat Al-Fatiha only it is sufficient, but if you recite something else in addition, that would be better."[50]

In yet another Hadis, the prophet said: "When you stand for Salat (prayer) say Takbir and then recite from the Qur'an (of what you know by heart) and then bow till you feel at ease. Then you raise your head and stand up straight, then prostrate till you feel at ease during your prostration, then sit with calmness till you feel at ease (do not hurry) and do the same in all your Salat (prayer)."[51] It further says: "Say Takbir while going on prostration."[52] During Salat, one is 'to stand straight with calmness on raising the head from bowing,'[53] and to 'say Takbir on raising from the two prostrations.'[54] Sitting for a while between two prostrations,[55] sitting straight during prayer[56] and standing straight is essential for Salat.

Azan/Adhan

Azan, as an institution, was introduced in Medina to maintain the fixed time of prayer; the use of human voice for the same was preferred to make the Muslim practice different from that of the Jews, Christians and the Fire-worshipers. The Jews and Christians used horn and bell respectively for the purpose. Loud-throated Bilal, and 'Abdullah, son of Umm Maktum, who became blind later on, were the first *mu'azzin* (callers).[57] Umar was the first to suggest the use of human voice for *azan*, and Allah's Messenger ordered Bilal to get up and pronounce *Adhan* for *As-Salat* (the prayer).[58] According to Hadis, there can be two callers of adhan/azan in a mosque.[59] The person, who hears the adhan should respond like it, invoke blessings upon the apostle and then beg for him the *Wasila; al-Wasila* is a rank in Paradise fitting for only one of Allah's servants.[60]

Hadis pronounces effectivity of Azan. It says, 'When Satan hears the call to prayer, he runs away to a distance like that of Rauha' … 'It is at a distance of thirty-six miles from Medina.'[61] Another Hadis says, 'Whenever *Adhan* is proclaimed, Satan runs back vehemently.'[62] *Adhan* also became great indicator, as the Prophet refrained from attacking people living in *dar al-kufr* on hearing *adhan* from them.[63]

Group Prayer Led by the Imam

Muslim prayer, which is mostly a group prayer, should be led by an imam, and even "when there are three persons, one of them should lead them."[64]

Prophet Muhammad exhorts his followers to follow their imam; he says: "When he prostrates, you should also prostrate, when he rises up, you should also rise up."[65] Persons led in prayer are required to keep pace with the imam and are forbidden to recite so loudly as to compete with him. When a follower once did it, Prophet Muhammad told him: "I feel as if (you were) disputing with me … and taking out from my tongue what I was reciting."[66] The Muslims are forbidden to bow and prostrate themselves ahead of the imam; the Hadis says: "Does the man who lifts his head before the imam not fear that Allah may change his face into that of ass?"[67]

On valid reason, the imam is authorized to appoint his deputy, as Prophet Muhammad appointed Abu Bakr during his last illness.[68]

The Pulpit

The spot where the Prophet used to stand in the Great Mosque at public prayers, the branch of a date tree was planted as a post for him to hold by. When the Qibla was changed, the post was taken up from the northern end and fixed near the southern wall. In the process of time, as he grew old, he begane to feel fatigued throughout the long Friday prayer. Then, during consultantation, one of his followers suggested to make a pulpit, as the churches had, and now there is pulpit in every mosque, The pulpit acquired sanctity afterwards.[69]

References

1. Ram Swarup, *Understanding Islam through Hadis*, p.2.
2. *Sahih Muslim, Hadis* 71.
3. Qur'an 29:45.
4. Qur'an 2:45.
5. Qur'an 74:42-43.
6. Qur'an 96:19.
7. Qur'an 20:14.
8 Ibn Ishaq, *Sirat Rasul Allah*, p. 112.
9. Ibid, pp. 112-13.
10. Margoliouth, *Mohammed and the Rise of Islam*, pp. 102-103.
11. Ibid, p. 103.
12. Hazleton, *The First Muslim*, pp. 99-100.
13. Ram Swarup, op. cit., p. 25.
14. *Sahih Muslim*, *Hadis* 758.
15. Ibid, p. 792.
16. Ibid, *Hadis* 991; *Sahih Bukhari, Hadis* 1:774.
17. *Sahih Muslim, Hadis* 997.
18. Ibid, *ahadis* 1086-1092.
19. *Sahih Bukhari, Hadis* 1:756.
20. Ibid, *Hadis* 1:717.
21. Ibid, *Hadis* 1:718.
22. Margoliouth, op. cit., pp. 258-59.
23. Muir, Sir William, *The Life of Mahomet*, pp. 187-88.
24. *Sahih Bukhari*, 1:137.
25. *Sahih Bukhari*, *Hadis* 1:281.
26. Qur'an 9:28.
27. *Sahih Bukhari, ahadis* 1:330-334.
28. Ibid, *Hadis* 340.
29. *Sahih Muslim, ahadis* 1824-1831.
30. Ibid, *ahadis* 1966-1972.

31. Ibid, *Hadis*1962.
32. Ibid, *Hadis* 1996.
33. Ibid, *Hadis* 2002.
34. Ibid, *ahadis* 1129-1130.
35. Ibid, *ahadis* 1131-1133.
36. Ibid, *Hadis* 1134.
37. Ibid, *Hadis* 1116.
38. Ibid, *Hadis* 1118.
39. Ibid, *Hadis* 1149.
40. Ibid, *Hadis* 1145.
41. Ibid, *Hadis* 1856.
42. Ibid, *Hadis* 1877; Qur'an 62:11.
43. *Mishkat-ul-Masabih, Hadis* 738; also by Tirmidhi and Ibn Majah.
44. Ibid, *Hadis* 739; also by Tirmidhi.
45. Ibid, *Hadis* 740; also by Abu Dawud, Tirmidhi and Nasa'i.
46. Ram Swarup, op. cit., p. 29.
47. *Sahih Muslim, Hadis* 1082.
48. *Sahih Bukhari, Hadis* 1:722.
49. Ibid, *Hadis* 1:723.
50. *Sahih Bukhari, Hadis* 1:739.
51. Ibid, *Hadis* 1:724.
52. Ibid, *Hadis* 1:768.
53. Ibid, *Hadis* 1:765.
54. Ibid, *Hadis* 1:788.
55. Ibid, *Hadis* 1:784.
56. Ibid, *Hadis* 1:786.
57. *Sahih Muslim, ahadis* 735, 737, 741.
58. *Sahih Bukhari, Hadis* 1:578.
59. *Sahih Muslim, ahadis* 741, 743, 743.
60. Ibid, *ahadis*, 747, 748.
61. Ibid, *Hadis* 751.
62. Ibid, *Hadis* 755.
63. Ibid, *Hadis* 745; Sahih Bukhari, Hadis 1:584.
64. Ibid, *Hadis* 1417.
65. Ibid, *Hadis* 817.
66. Ibid, *Hadis* 783 .
67. Ibid, *Hadis* 860.
68. Ibid, *ahadis* 832-844.
69. Muir 194-99.

Zakat (Sadaqa)

Zakat: The Second Pillar of Islam

Of the five pillars or fundamentals of Islam, *Zakat* (*Zakat*) occupies second position. The word is derived from *Zaka*, which means "it (a plant) grew." The second derivation carries the sense of purification; *Zakat* purifies, as Qur'an says:

"In order to cleanse and purify them (Prophet), take alms out of their property and pray for them—"[1]

The Qur'an further says:

"The most pious one will be spared this—who gives his wealth away as self-purification, not to return favour to anyone.[2]

There is numerous mention of *Zakat* in the Qur'an and *Hadis*. In Qur'an, it finds mention at eighty-two places. Fifth book of *Sahih Muslim* is *Kitab Al-Zakat*. *The Book of Zakat* and *The Book of Sadaqat-ul-Fitr* has the *ahadis* related to *Zakat*.

In the Qur'an and *Hadis*, the other term used, apart from *Zakat* is the *Sadaqa*, which is derived from *sidq*, meaning 'truth.'[3] *Sadaqa* is a general term and *Zakat* is a specific kind of *Sadaqa*. Arabic term *Sadaqa* is used for whatever is given in charity, whereas the collection of *Zakat* follows certain rules and regulations. It is obligatory for the Muslim to pay *Zakat*,[4] whereas, 'giving in charity' for the poor is purely a voluntary act. It is to be paid at the rate of 2.5 per cent of one's wealth.

Charity and Alms Needed for the Migrants

Meccan Muslims, migrating to Medina, suffered due to extreme poverty, straitened means and want; many of them needed charity and alms. This was especially so during the festivals. As festival, Id al-Fitr, or 'Breaking of the fast' arrived during the very second year of *Hijr* (A.H. II, February 624 AD), Prophet Muhammad, after the rigours of Ramadan fast was over, instructed the Muslim about its observation. Muir writes:

"As soon as the new moon of the following month was seen (and it is still eagerly looked for every year throughout the Muslim world) the restriction was to cease, the next day being celebrated as a festival, called Id al-Fitr, or 'Breaking of the fast.' A day or two previously, Mohammad assembled the people, and instructed them in the ceremonies to be observed on the occasion. Early in the morning, they were to bring together offerings for the poor; each one, young or old, bond or free, male or female, a measure of dates, of barley, or of raisins, or a smaller measure of wheat. 'See' said he: 'that ye give plenty to the poor this day, so that they need not to go about and beg.' Having thus presented their alms, all wcnt forth with the Prophet, ...The service over, they returned to their homes, after which Mohammad, having made a feast at the Mosque, distributed the alms of his followers amongst the poor."[5] This happened during the observation of the festival for the first time before the imposition of regular almsgiving, or *Zakat*.[6]

Charity: A Common Jewish-Christian Practice

The collection of *Zakat* (tithe) was a Jewish and Christian practice also. The two names of Jewish derivation for tithe and voluntary almsgiving are *Zakat* and *Sadakat* respectively, of which the former signifies 'purification,' the latter 'righteousness.'[7] The Bible also refers to the same, as given bellow:

"Instead give alms from what you have and, look, everything will be clean for you.[8]

Bible further says: "Be careful not to parade your uprightness in public to attract attention; otherwise you will lose all reward from your Father in heaven. So when you give alms, do not have it trumpeted before you; this is what the hypocrites do in the synagogues and in the streets to win human admiration.[9] An *ahadi* also points towards the same. According to that, among those whom Allah gives protection is one "who gives charity and conceal it so that the right hand does not know what the left has given.[10]

Charity Among Pagans

Feeding the poor and needy during draught and famine, freeing slaves, which were acts of charity, have been discussed in the book. The Arabs used to take their camels to a pond every six or seven days, milk them there, and distribute the milk among the needy.[11] Prophet's response to such generosity was positive, but he wanted that the charity should begin at home, and many *ahadis* point towards this.[12] Two ahadis point towards the need of 'beginning of spending for one's own self, then one's family and then for relatives.[13] Some others deal with the excellence of spending and giving *Sadaqa* to relatives, to wife, to children, and parents even if they are polytheists.'[14]

Deeper Aspects

Certain *ahadis* point towards the deeper aspects of charity.[15] According to them, the people who can not pay in money can pay in piety and good acts. "Administration of justice between two men," "assisting a man to ride upon his beast, or helping him load his luggage upon it," "a good word" and "every step that you take towards prayer" and "removing harmful things from the pathway" are *Sadaqa*.[16] "In every declaration of the glorification of Allah (i.e., saying *Subhan Allah*), is also *Sadaqa*.[17]

Urging, Pleading and Divine Threat

A narrator says: "We were commanded to give charity though we were coolies."[18] Another Hadis says: "If anyone gives *Sadaqa* the equivalent of one date ... the Lord would accept it with His Right Hand."[19] According to another *Hadis*: "There is never a day wherein servants (of Allah) get up at morn, but are not visited by two angels. One of them says: O Allah, give him more who spends, and other says: O Allah, bring destruction to one who withholds."[20] Thus, the blessing and curse go hand in hand.

The divine punishment for not paying the *Zakat* is more severe and gruesome: "If any owner of gold or silver does not pay what is due to him, when the Day of Resurrection would come, plates of fire would be beaten out for him; these then would be heated in the Fire of Hell and his sides, forehead and his back would be cauterized with them. And when these cool down, the process is repeated during a day the extent of which would be fifty thousand years." And a owner of camel, who defaults, "a sandy plain would be set for him, as extensive as possible," and his camels "will trample him with their hoofs and bite him with their mouths ... during a day the extent of which would be fifty thousand years." The cows and sheep of the Zakat-defaulting owner will, likewise, "gore him with their horns and trample him with their hoofs."[21]

Exemption and Incentives

The *Hadis* provides for the lower limit on which *Zakat* is not to be paid. Accordingly, "No *Sadaqa* (*Zakat*) is payable on five *wasqs* of dates or grain (1 *wasq* = about 425 pounds), on less than five camel heads and on less than five *uqiyas* of silver (1 *uqiya* = about 10 tolas, or ¼ pound)."[22] "No *Sadaqa* is due from a Muslim on his slave or horse."[23] Also, "The horse which is used for riding in *jihad* is exempted from payment of *zakat*."[24]

Diversified Use of the Tithe

Initially, the tithe was used only for meeting the needs of Muslim poor; but with the growth of the Islamic state, and organized collection, the quantum of the tithe gradually increased. Naturally, the purpose of the collected tithe was also diversified. But, it angered those who wanted it exclusively for them and criticized the Prophet. A revelation subsequently followed, which says:

"Some of them find fault with you (Prophet) regarding the distribution of alms; they are content if they are given a share, but angry if not."[25]

The Qur'an further said about other uses of the tithe:

"If only they could be content with what Allah and His Messenger have given them, and say, Allah is enough for us—He will give us His bounty and so will His Messenger—to Allah alone we turn in hope. Alms are meant only for the poor, the needy, those who administer them, those whose hearts need winning over, to free slaves and help those in debt, for Allah's cause, and for travellers in need. This is ordained by Allah; Allah is all knowing and wise."[26]

Thus, according to the above Quranic Sura, the *Zakat* funds are meant not only for the traditional recipients of charity—the poor and the paupers (*fuqra* and *miskin*), for the persons in bondage and debt, and for the travellers—, but also for those collecting and administering the fund, i.e. the "bureaucracy." The other purposes for the use of the fund are "the service of Allah" (*fisabili'llah*) and for "gaining over (or reconciling or inclining) the hearts (*muallafa qulubuhum*)" to Islam. These phrases are frequently used in Islamic literature. Ram Swarup has elaborated them; he writes:

"In the technical vocabulary of Islam, the first phrase, "in the service, or way, of Allah" means religious warfare, or *Jihad. Zakat* funds are to be spent on buying arms, equipment and horses. The second phrase, "gaining over, or reconciling, hearts," means "bribe" in unadorned language. The faith of new converts should be strengthened with the help of generous "gifts," and that of adversaries should be subverted by the same means. This was an important limb of the Prophet's religious offensive and diplomacy, and as the above cited Quranic verse shows, it had for the Prophet, as it still has for his followers, a heavenly sanction."[27]

The Prophet tried to win over the leading chiefs of Mecca and of the Bedawi tribes by a princely liberality by giving them presents from his share of the booty after the battle of Honen, where even he was mobbed on account of the booty.[28] Muir writes about the presents made by the Prophet, and the purpose of the same: "He took the early opportunity of making good his promise, and at the same time of gaining, by a princely liberality, the hearts of the leading chiefs of Mecca and of the Bedawi tribes. To the most powerful he presented each one hundred camels. Among them we find Abu Sufyan, with his two sons, Yazid and Mu'awiya, Hakim ibn Hisam, Safwan, Huweitib, Oyeina, and others who but a few weeks before were his deadly enemies. To the lesser chiefs he gave fifty camels each. And so liberal was he that in some cases where discontent was expressed, the gift was without doubt doubled."[29]

Wining Over the Hearts to Islam

Such liberal largesses to the new and doubtful converts, no doubt, caused discontent among his older veterans, to which the Prophet had his reply. Muir writes: "Although taken from the Prophet's Fifth, these largesses to new and doubtful converts gave umbrage to his veteran followers. Thus one complained that such Bedawi chieftains as Al-Akra' and 'Oyeina received each one hundred camels, while a faithful believer like Jo'eil got nothing at all. 'And what of that?' replied the Prophet; 'I swear that Jo'eil is the best man that ever stepped on earth, were it filled never so full of Al-Akra's and 'Oyeinas; but I wished to gain over the hearts of these men to Islam, while Jo'eil hath no need of any such inducement.'[30]

Discontent on such occasions, and in such a case, were natural. A Bedawi follower, watching the proceeding, openly impugned its equity. Muhammad became angry, and said: 'Out upon thee! If justice and equity be not with me, where ye will find them?' The Prophet, however, was most concerned due to the murmurs of the citizens of Medina, talking among themselves that "Truly, he hath now joined his own people and forsaken us." Sa'd, son of 'Obada, being highly concerned due to seriousness of the discontent, represented it to the Prophet, who effectively handled the situation. The Quranic revelation cited above, confirmed the stand taken by Prophet Muhammad.[31]

Sadaqa not for Prophet's Family

Prophet Muhammad denied *Sadaqa* for him and his family. He said: "*Sadaqa* is not permissible for us."[32] The gift was, however, accepted by him. The Prophet accepted a piece of meat, sent by Barira, wife of the freed slave of his wife, as a gift, which she had sent as *Sadaqa*. He said: "That is a *Sadaqa* for her and a gift for us,"[33] It may, however, be an exceptional case. He, in anyway, did not need to depend on charity after the ouster of Banu Nazir from Medina, whose property were appropriated by Prophet Muhammad for himself and his family, and flow of *Khums*, the one-fifth share of the war booty to him. He was very strict in observing the restriction. Muir writes:

"*While he accepted presents, he refused anything that had been offered as tithe* (*Sadaka*); neither would he allow any one of his family to accept what was brought in tithe; 'for,' said he 'tithes (or alms) are the impurities of mankind' (i.e., that which cleanses their impurity). His scruples were so strong, that he would not eat even a date picked up on the road, lest per chance it might have dropped from a tithe load. One day, little Al-Hasan was playing by his grandfather when a basketful of dates was brought in; on inquiry, Muhammad found that they were tithe, and ordered them to be taken away and given to the poor Refugees. But Al-Hasan, having taken one to play with, had already put it in his mouth; the Prophet, seeing this, opened the boy's mouth, and pulled it out, saying, 'the family of Muhammad may not eat of the tithes.'[34]

Another case of the denial of *Sadaqa* to the family members of the Prophets is worth mentioning. Two young men of his family, 'Abd al-Muttalib and Fazl, son of 'Abbas, wanted to become collectors of *Zakat* to earn means of marrying. The Prophet declined to accept their request. He said: "It does not become the family of Muhammad to accept *Sadaqa* for they are the impurities of the people." He, however, arranged marriage for both and told his treasurer: "Pay so much *Mahr* (dowry) on behalf of both of them from the *khums*."[35] As we know, *khums* was the one-fifth share of the war booty for Allah and the Prophet.

Indiscriminate Charity

According to a Hadis, charity should be indiscriminate. A man gives charity, with praise to Allah, first to an adulteress, then to a rich man, then to a thief. The angel came to him and said: "Your charity has been accepted." This was because his charity might become the means whereby the adulteress "might restrain herself from fornication, the rich man might perhaps learn a lesson and spend from what Allah has given him, and the thief might thereby refrain from committing theft." These wonderful results were possible because the charity given was accompanied by "praise to Allah."[36]

From Charity to Tax

Initially, the followers of Prophet Muhammad were needy; they depended a great deal on the goodwill and charity of the people of Medina. Needless to say, that this situation necessitated the rhetoric of the old Arabian practice of charity. Moreover, in the beginning, there was no universal fellowship as such for a brother in distress. Situation, however, changed, as Prophet Muhammad, and, naturally, Islam gathered power and strength. And subsequently, the nature of *Zakat* changed from voluntary charitable contribution to the 'Poor Tax,' enforced by the new Islamic State.

Payment Resented

There was general resentment against the payment of *Zakat*, especially among the Muslims outside Medina, as the benefits of fund flow hardly reached them. As the Bedouins disliked it, one of them complained to the Prophet that the "collectors of Sadaqa come to us and treat us unjustly." The reply of Allah's Messenger was: "Please your collectors."[37] Even Qur'an eloquently witnesses to the same. It says: "Some of the desert Arabs look upon their payments as a fine, and they wait a turn of fortune against you, but against them shall a turn of evil fortune be; for Allah both hears and knows."[38]

A point needing mention here is that the payment was refused even by the persons like Khalid, son of Walid (who became a famous Muslim General later on) and 'Abbas, the uncle of the Prophet. When Umar, who was appointed collector, reported to Muhammad that they had refused to pay the tax, Muhammad replied: "You are unjust to Khalid, for he reserved the armours and weapons for the sake of Allah; and as for Abbas, I shall be responsible. … Umar, bear in mind, the uncle of a person is like his father."[39]

In the ninth year of the Hijr, after the Mecca was conquered, and Islamic State became strong, the collection of the tax was vigorously pursued; tax-collectors were appointed and sent out in different directions for the realization of the tax from Kilab, Ghifar, Aslam, Fazar, and several other tribes. As a section of the tribe of Banu Tamin refused to pay, Prophet Muhammad had to send a punitive force consisting of fifty horsemen. They took the tribe by surprise; they brought back fifty men, women and children to Medina, who had to be ransomed. The tax-collection became, somehow smoother after that.[40]

Refusal to Pay Tax After Prophet's Death

When some tribes, after the death of Prophet Muhammad refused to pay the tax, Umar advised the Caliph Abu Bakr to show tolerance, the Caliph said, "By Allah, I would definitely wage war against them who dissociate prayer from Zakat."[41] Ultimately, the rebellious sections had to be re-conquered. With the growing Islamic imperialism, the Arab tribes were immensely benefited due to enormous flow of war booty, and such rebellions became the matters of past and forgotten.

References

1. Qur'an 9:103.
2. Qur'an 92:17-19.
3. *Sahih Muslim*, p.561; Introductory Note.
4. *Sahih al-Bukhari, Hadis* 2:478.
5. Muir, *The Life of Mahomet*, pp. 193-94.
6. Ibid, p. 193 note 2.
7. Ibid, p. 432 note.
8. Bible (The New Jerusalem Bible; Doubleday, New York), Luke 11:41.
9. Bible Matthew 6:1.
10. *Sahih Muslim*, Hadis 2248.
11. Ibid, Translator's note 1329.
12. Ibid, *ahadis* 2183-2195.
13. Ibid, *ahadis* 2183-84.
14. Ibid, *ahadis* 2185-95.
15. Ibid, *ahadis* 2197-2204.
16. Ibid, *Hadis* 2204.
17. Ibid, *Hadis* 2198.
18. Ibid, *Hadis* 2223.
19. Ibid, *Hadis* 2211.
20. Ibid, *Hadis* 2205; *Sahih Al-Bukhari*, *Hadis* 2:522.
21. Ibid, *Hadis* 2161.
22. Ibid, *Hadis* 2134; *Sahih Al-Bukhari*, *Hadis* 2:487.
23. Ibid, *Hadis* 2144; *Sahih Al-Bukhari*, *Hadis* 2:542.
24. Ibid, *Hadis* 1313.
25. Qur'an 9:58.
26. Qur'an 9:59-60.
27. Ram Swarup, *Understanding Islam through Hadis*, p. 34.
28. Muir, op. cit., pp. 421-22.
29. Ibid, p. 422.
30. Ibid.
31. Ibid, pp. 422-23.
32. *Sahih Muslim*, *Hadis* 2340.
33. Ibid, *ahadis*, 2349-51; 2355.
34. Muir, op. cit., p. 526.
35. *Sahih Muslim*, *Hadis* 2347.
36. Ibid, *Hadis* 2230.

37. Ibid, *Hadis* 2168.
38. Qur'an 9:98.
39. *Sahih Muslim*, *Hadis* 2148.
40. Muir, op. cit., p. 432; Margoliouth, *Mohammed and the Rise of Islam*, pp. 412-13; Ram Swarup, op. cit., p. 35.
41. *Sahih Muslim*, Introductory Note of 'Kitab Al-Zakat,' p. 561.

The Pilgrimage (*Hajj*)

The Pilgrimage (*Hajj*) to Mecca is an obligation to be fulfilled in the lifetime of a Muslim, provided he is in good health, financially capable to meet the expenses involved, and has enough means to sustain the living of other members of his family during his absence. Ka'ba, the sacred temple of Mecca, was the centre of pagan worship and pilgrimage. It had the idols of 360 pagan gods and goddesses. The mode of worship was pagan. The economy of Mecca, to a great extent, was linked up with the pilgrimage centred around the sacred temple. It, however, became the centre of Islamic worship and pilgrimage after the conquest of Mecca by Prophet Muhammad.

The pilgrimage of Mecca is of two kinds, namely, the 'Lesser Pilgrimage' (*'Omra; 'Umra*) and the 'Greater Pilgrimage' (*Hajj*). The 'Lesser pilgrimage,' as Muir writes: "include passing to and fro with hasty steps seven times between the eminences of the Safa and the Merwa. This may be performed with merit at any season of the year, but especially in the sacred month of Rejeb. Before entering the holy territory, the votary assumes the pilgrim garb, and at the conclusion of the ceremonies shaves his head and pares his nails."[1]

The Greater Pilgrimage

The 'Greater pilgrimage,' according to Muir, "can be performed only in the holy month Dhu'l-Hijja. In addition to the ceremonies of the lesser, it embraces the tour of 'Arafat, a small granite hill in the mountains, ten or twelve miles east of Mecca. The pilgrims, starting from Mecca on the 8th of the month, stay the following day at 'Arafat, and having ascended the hill, hasten back the same evening three or four miles to Al-Muzdelifa. Next day returning halfway to Mecca, they stay at Mina, where they spend two or three succeeding days. Small stones are cast by the pilgrims at certain objects at the Mina valley, and the pilgrimage is concluded by the sacrifice of victims there."[2]

Lesser Pilgrimage by Prophet Muhammad

Prophet Muhammad, in the sixth year of the Hijra, started out from Medina to Mecca for the lesser pilgrimage (*'omra, 'umrah* ceremony). It was his first journey to Mecca after leaving that city. Fifteen hundred men, including some armed ones, accompanied him. He had appealed to the desert Arabs to accompany him in the pilgrimage. Their response, however, was lukewarm, as no booty was promised, and they thought, as the Qur'an puts it, that "the Apostle and the believers would never return to their families."[3] Anyway, the number accompanying him, which was hardly a band of pilgrims, may not be considered to be less.

The Meccans objected to Prophet's entry in Mecca; they entered into a treaty with him, called the Treaty of Hodeibiya. Prophet Muhammad regarded it as a victory for himself, and as the further developments revealed it was really so.

The Fulfilled Pilgrimage

Prophet Muhammad along with the Muslims who had returned a year earlier went for Hajj during the month of Dhu'l-Qa'da in AH 7 for the fulfilled pilgrimage. "Muhammad and his Companions are in destitution, want and privation," said the Quraysh among themselves. They gathered at the door of the assembly house to look at him and his Companions. When the Apostle entered the mosque, he threw the end of his cloak over his left shoulder leaving his right upper arm free, and said: "Allah have mercy on a man who shows them today that he is strong." After that "he kissed the stone, and went out trotting as did his Companions until when the temple concealed him from them and he had kissed the southern corner he walked to kiss the black stone. Then he trotted similarly three circuits and walked the rest."[4] He stayed in Mecca for three days during this pilgrimage and married Maymuna when he was *haram*. After three days, Quraysh told him to vacate Mecca and he did it accordingly.[5]

The Farewell Pilgrimage (*Hajj*)

Prophet Muhammad, two years later, in March 632 AD undertook another pilgrimage, called the "Farewell Pilgrimage of the Apostle," as it turned out to be his last. Unlike the earlier one, the number of pilgrims accompanying the Prophet was very large. "Messengers were sent to all parts of Arabia inviting people to join him in this great Pilgrimage." The response to join him was great. "As the caravan moved on, the number of participants swelled," and it reached more than 130,000, according to a narrator.[6] Actually, the Prophet's power was supreme and unrivalled in Arabia after the conquest of the Mecca, and his invitation to join him was taken in right earnest by the Bedouin tribes; in reality, it was also, in a way, a call to submission, which they understood and acted accordingly.

After the victory of Mecca, and the farewell pilgrimage by the Apostle, the *hajj* was declared one of the five fundamentals, or pillars, of Islam. Sanctity of Ka'ba, sacred months, sacrificial animals, all this, were accepted, as Qur'an said: "Sacred House—a means of support for people, and the Sacred Months, the sacrificial animals including the garlanded, all this."[7]

Rituals Related to Hajj

The pilgrim, after reaching at a certain place, puts on the garment of a pilgrim, and thereafter enters the state of *ihram* (prohibiting), becomes a *muhrim*. The pilgrim's robe, which a *muhrim* wears, has two seamless wrappers. After that certain things are prohibited for him till he completes the worship at Mecca.

The pilgrim after putting on the dress, should proceed towards Mecca singing the pilgrim's song, "*Talbiyah, Labbaika! Allahumma!*" ("I stand up for thy service, O Allah") The pilgrim, after reaching Mecca, performs ablution in the Masjid'l Haram, kisses the Black Stone (*al-hajaru'l-aswad*), and then makes seven circuits round the Ka'ba (*tawaf*). Prophet Muhammad himself circumambulated "on the back of his riding camel … so that people should see him, and he should be conspicuous."[8] That was also the reason that he touched the Corner (Black Stone) with a stick. "I saw Allah's Messenger circumambulating the House, and touching the Corner with a stick that he had with him, and then kissng the stick," said a narrator.[9]

The pilgrim's run from the top of Mount as-Safa to the summit of Mount al-Marwah the two "Signs of Allah," according to the Qur'an,[10] is yet another important ceremony. "Allah does not complete the *Hajj* of a person or his *'Umra* if he does not observe *Sa'I* (i.e., run between al-Safa and al-Marwa)"[11]

The casting of the pebbles (*ramu'r-rijam*) is yet another important rite. The pilgrim throws seven pebbles at Jamrat al-'Aqaba (also known as *Shaitanuu'l Kabir*, the Great Devil) on the tenth day, also the "Say of Sacrifice," while chanting, "In the name of Allah, the Almighty, I do this, and in hatred of the Devil and his shame." Several *ahadis* deal with the size, days and timings of the pebbles, and the number of the pebbles. Accordingly, small pebbles should be pelted;[12] the best time for stone throwing is after sunrise on the Day of Sacrifice, on the 11th, 12th and 13th of *Dhu'l Hijja,*[13] when the sun had declined. The number of stones should be odd (seven).[14]

The last part of the *hajj* is the sacrifice of the animals. The Prophet himself brought one hundred camels, marked by his own hands for sacrifice, led in solemn order. Others, who did not bring the victims, performed only the 'lesser pilgrimage.'[15]

The Muslim pilgrims did all that day what Prophet Muhammad did during his 'Farewell Pilgrimage.' After reaching Sarif during his journey from Medina to Mecca, he ordered all who did not bring victims, i.e., sacrificial animals, to remove their pilgrim garments. Ayesha was weeping, as she had her menses, and said that she may not do the pilgrimage. The Prophet told her, "Don't say that, for you can do all that the pilgrims do except go round the temple."[16] *Sahih Bukhari* also says that "A menstruating women can perform all the ceremonies of *Hajj* except *Tawaf* of the Ka'ba.[17] *Tawaf*, in Arabic, is the circumambulation.

The number of the sacrificial camels brought by the Prophet was the maximum—one hundred—during the farewell pilgrimage in 10 AH; during his *'umrah* pilgrimage in 6 AH, the number was seventy, and on a similar pilgrimage, next year, it was sixty. During the last pilgrimage, he "went to the place of sacrifice, and sacrificed sixty-three camels with his own hands. Then he gave remaining number to 'Ali who sacrificed them. … He then commanded that a piece of flesh from each animal sacrificed should be put in a pot, and when it was cooked, both of them ('Ali and Muhammad) took some meat out of it and drank its soup.[18] The place of sacrifice was Mina. He said to his followers, "I have sacrificed the animals here, and the whole of Mina is place of sacrifice, so sacrifice your animals at your places.[19] The seven persons are permitted to join in a sacrifice.[20] If it is not possible for a person to go for the pilgrimage, he or she may send a sacrificial animal to al-Haram and earn merit. Ayesha says: "I wove the garland for the sacrificial animals for the Allah's Messenger with my own hands, and then he marked them, and garlanded them, and then sent them to the House, and stayed at Medina and nothing was forbidden to him which was lawful for him before."[21] The Prophet allowed a woman of Khatham tribe to perform Hajj on behalf of her old and weak father.[22]

On the second day at Mina, Prophet Muhammad gave parting exhortation. Next to that, he recited the passage of the Qur'an abolishing intercalary year.[23] After that, looking up to heaven, he said: '*O Lord! I have delivered my message and discharged my Ministry.*' 'Yea, verily thou hast,' cried the people. '*O Lord!I beseech The bear Thou witness unto it,*' said he, and dismissed the great assembly. All this provided the model for future generation of Muslims to follow during *Hajj*.

Prophet Muhammad, after three day's stay at Mina, came back to Mecca; he then went straightway to the Ka'ba, performed the seven circuits of it on a camel, visited the nearby well of Zemzem, called for a pitcher of its water, drank part of its contents. After that, rinsing his mouth with the rest of the water, 'he deired that what remained in the pitcher should be thrown back into the well. After this, taking off his shoes, he ascended the doorway of the holy Temple, and prayed within its walls.'[24]

'Having now ended all the ceremonies, and being fatigued with the journey,' Muir writes: 'he (the Prophet) stopped at the house of one who kept date-water for the pilgrims to drink, and desired the beverage to be furnished to him. The son of Al-'Abbas, who accompanied him, interposed: 'The hands of the passersby,' he said, 'have been in this all day, and fouled it: come into my father's house, where we have some that is clean and pure for thee.' But the Prophet, refusing to drink of any other, quenched his thurst upon the spot. The Prophet's drinking of the *Nabidh* (water in which dates or raisins have been steeped), it needs mention, was not the part of the pilgrimage, but pious Muslims even do that during the pilgrimage. Lastly, the Prophet returned to Medina after three days stay at Mecca.

Taboos for a Muhrim

During the state of *ihram*, he is forbidden to "put on a shirt or a turban, or trouser or cap;" The use of perfume is not disallowed before or after the state of *ihram*, but it is prohibited during that period. Ayesha said: "I applied perfume to the Messenger of Allah as he became free from *ihram* and as he entered upon it."[25] In another *Hadis*, she said that she applied "The best of perfume."[26] Hunting is also prohibited for a *muhrim.* The Prophet declined the offer of the flesh of wild ass by someone, saying: "If we are not in a state of *ihram*, we would have accepted it from you.[27] The flesh of the animal killed by a non-*muhrim* is, however, accepted by a *muhrim*. The leg of a wild ass, killed by a non-*muhrim*, was presented to him. "The Messenger of Allah took it and ate it."[28] In spite of the prohibition on hunting, a *muhrim* is allowed to kill four vicious beasts, which are "kite, crow, rat and voracious dog," and, of course, a snake should "be killed with disgrace."[29]

A *muhrim* should wash the perfume thrice off, as it is taboo for him.[30]

References

1. Muir, Sir William, *The Life of Mahomet*, p. ci. (Hearafter, Muir).
2. Ibid.
3. Qur'an.
4. Ibn Ishaq, *Sirat Rasul Allah*, pp. 530-31. (Hereafter, Ibn Ishaq).
5. Ibid, p. 531.
6. Ram Swarup, *Understanding Islam through Hadis*, p. 50. (Hereafter Ram Swarup).
7. Quran 5:97.
8. *Sahih Muslim*, *Hadis* 2919.
9. Ibid, *Hadis* 2921.
10. Qur'an 2:158.
11. *Sahih Muslim*, 2923.
12. *Ibid*, *Hadis* 2979.
13. Ibid, *Hadis* 2980.
14. Ibid, *Hadis* 2982.
15. Muir, pp. 468-69.
16. Ibn Ishaq, p. 649.
17. *Sahih Bukhari*, *Hadis* 2:713.
18. *Sahih Muslim*, *Hadis* 2803.
19. Ibid, *Hadis* 2805.
20. Ibid, *ahadis* 3024-3031.
21. Ibid, *Hadis* 3036.
22. *Sahih Bukhari*, *Hadis* 2:589.
23. Qur'an 9:36-37.
24. Muir, p. 474.
25. *Sahih Muslim*, *Hadis* 2683.
26. Ibid, *Hadis* 2685.
27. Ibid, *Hadis* 2704.
28. Ibid, *Hadis* 2714.
29. Ibid, *Hadis* 2717.
30. *Sahih Bukhari*, *Hadis* 2:610. (B)

Islamic Jihad

Jihad: Fight in the Way of Allah

'Jihad' (or Jehad) is an Arabic word; it literally means endeavour or striving. It is the highest ordained duty of a Muslim; it is a divinely ordained duty in the name of Allah and in the way of Allah. Many authorities count it as one of the pillars of Islam. It is a binding contract between Allah and the believers that whatever the latter posses, including his life belongs to Allah in return for paradise. Qur'an says: "God has bought from the faithfuls their selves and their belongings against the gift of paradise; they fight in the way of Allah; they kill and get killed; that is a promise binding on Allah."[1]

Jihad is central to Islam; it is a religious duty of a Muslim state. Islam divides the earth between the 'territories under Islam' (*Dar al-Islam*) and the 'territory of war' (*Dar al-Harb*), and the latter must be won by war, which is *jihad*. The Islamic warriors, the *jihadis*, are called *mujahids*. The Muslim converts used to migrate (*Hijra*) to Medina, but after the capture of Mecca, when the power of Muhammad was fully vindicated, *Jihad*, rather than *Hijra*, became necessary. Muhammad said: "There is no *Hijra* now, but only Jihad and sincerity of purpose; when you are asked to set out (on an expedition undertaken for the cause of Islam) you should (readily) do so."[2]

Jihad is defined by *The Dictionary of Islam* as: "A religious war with those who are unbelievers in the mission of Muhammad (the Prophet). It is an incumbent religious duty, established in the Qur'an and the Traditions (i.e., the Hadis or the 'Acts of Muhammad') as a divine institution, and enjoined especially for the purpose of advancing Islam and of repelling evil from Muslims." *The Dictionary of Islam* has further noted: "The duty of religious war (which all commentators agree is a duty extending to all times) is laid down in the Qur'an in the following verses, and it is remarkable that all the verses occur in the al-Madinah Surahs, being those given after Muhammad had established himself as a paramount ruler, and was in a position to dictate terms to his enemies." Some Meccan

Surahs, though hinting towards any compromise, came down when Prophet Muhammad felt besieged and weak, stood abrogated after the coming down of Sura 9:5,6.

Some Islamic scholars write in *The Dictionary of Islam* about the same: "Sufi writers say that there are two Jihads: *al-Jihadu'l Akbar*, or the 'greater warfare,' which is against one's own lusts; and *al-jihadu;l Asghar*, or the 'lesser Jihad' against infidels." It, however, needs mention, that these later days Sufi innovations had no scriptural sanction of Islam. Moreover, the Sufis' Jihad against the infidels was never less violent in any way than the war by other *mujahids*.

Changing Voice of Qur'an and Beginning of Jihad

Islam, in the beginning, was a secret society. Muhammad forbade Abu Dhar (Al-Giffar) from disclosing others about his conversion to Islam.[3] There are similar such cases. Margoliouth writes in detail about the same.[4] The second phase was when it talked the language of "your religion to you, mine to me." The third one was the phase of Jihad.

Qur'an says that "there is no compulsion in religion" (*La ikrahfi'l din*),[5] but the language of Qur'an changes after the Second Aqaba, when Prophet Muhammad and Islam got strengthened due to the pledge of the Medinan Ansars. Even when the meeting concluded and Satanic voice was heard, and, an Ansar said: 'By Allah, if you wish it we will fall on the people of Mina tomorrow with our swords,' Prophet Muhammad's reply was, 'We have not been commanded to do that."[6]

The situation gradually changed, Allah commanded Muhammad to fight. Ibn Ishaq writes: 'When Allah gave permission to his apostle to fight, the second Aqaba contained conditions involving war which were not in the first act of fealty. Now they bound themselves to war against all and sundry for Allah and his apostle, while he promised them for faithful service thus the reward of paradise.'[7]

The Qur'an ordained fighting; it said: "Fighting has been ordained for you, though it is hard for you. You may dislike something although it is good for you, or like something although it is bad for you: Allah knows and you do not. They ask you (Prophet) about fighting in the sacred month. Say, 'Fighting in that month is a great offence, but to bar others from the Allah's path, to disbelieve Him, prevent access to the Sacred Mosque, and expel its people are still greater offences in Allah's eyes. Persecution is worse than killing.[8]

The command to take up arms was given initially, as a measure of retaliation. The Qur'an says: "Those who have been attacked are permitted to take up arms because they have been wronged—Allah has the power to help them—those who have been driven unjustly from their homes only for saying: 'Our Lord is Allah.'[9] Clearly, the command to fight was against the Quraysh, but the Jihad continued unabated against the others during the lifetime of the Prophet, and after, where there was no provocation. The jihad became a lifelong process. Muslims, digging trench around Medina, and carrying the earth on their backs, said: "We are those who have given the *Bai'a* (pledge) to Muhammad that we will carry on *Jihad* as long as we live."[10]

Qur'an, initially, asks the believer to fight, but it also advises restraint and caution. Later on, when Muslims develop confidence the voice of restraint is not heard. Qur'an says: "Fight in Allah's cause against those who fight you, but do not overstep the limits. Kill them wherever you encounter them, and drive them out from where they drove you out, for persecution is more serious than killing. Do not fight them at the Sacred Mosque unless they fight you there. If they do fight you, kill them—this is what these disbelievers deserve—but if they stop, then Allah is most forgiving and merciful. Fight them until there is no more persecution, and worship is devoted to Allah. If they cease hostilities, there can be no further hostility, except towards aggressors. A sacred month for a Sacred month: violation of sanctity (calls for) fair retribution. So if anyone commits aggression against you, attack him as he attacked you, but be mindful of Allah, and know that He is with those who are mindful of Him.[11]

After this, one finds the warlike spirit of Qur'an;[12] participation of Muhammad in raids and battle increased, and he personally participated in twenty-seven of them (according to At-Tabari, in twenty-six).[13]

In the battle of Badr, the prisoners were taken for ransom, and the Prophet was warned for that, only because, it was pre-ordained. The Qur'an says: "Had it not been for a previous ordainment from Allah, a severe penalty would have reached you for the (ransom) ye took.[14] The new command was: "It is not for any Prophet to have prisoners until he makes wide slaughter …"[15] He is advised to resist the desire for the transient goods,[16] but war booty is made lawful for him.[17]

Attitude Towards Monasteries, Churches, etc.

A Quranic verse writes about Allah protecting monasteries, churches, synagogues, and mosques. It says: "If Allah did not repel some people by means of others, many monasteries, churches, synagogues, and mosques, where Allah's name is much invoked, would have been destroyed."[18] All, one can say in this case, is that there is nothing in Islamic literature, which throws light on the destruction of these Semitic institutions of worship by the pagans, and their protection by the Muslims.

Belief in Enhanced Capacities of the Muslims

One encounters a belief in many Muslim-related accounts that a Muslim soldier has ten times capacity to that of others. In Qur'an, we find something like that. It says: "Prophet, urge your believers to fight: if there are twenty of you who are steadfast, they will overcome two hundred, and a hundred of you, if steadfast, will overcome a thousand of the disbelievers, for they are people who do not understand. But Allah has lighted your burden for now, knowing that there is weakness in you—a steadfast hundred of you will defeat two hundred and a steadfast thousand of you will defeat two thousand, by Allah's permission: Allah is with the steadfast."[19]

Targets: Unbelievers, the Satan's Party

The party, against which Jihad is to be fought, is Satan's party, which is certainly to lose. Qur'an writes: "Satan has gained control over them and made them forget Allah. They are on Satan's side, and Satan's side will be the losers; those who oppose Allah and His Messenger will be among the most humiliated. Allah has written, 'I shall certainly win, I and My messengers.'"[20] Thus, the Qur'an divides people into Mumins (Muslims, believers; Allah'a party) and Kafirs (infidels, non-believers; Satan's party). The un-believers are the worst of beasts in Allah's sight; they are ungrateful;[21] and Allah is their enemy;[22] they plot against Allah, and He plots against them.[23]

'To unbelievers,' as Qur'an says, 'Allah rejects them.'[24] According to Qur'an, 'The unbelievers schemed against Allah, and Allah schemed against unbelievers, and Allah is the best schemer.'[25] Similarly, about the hypocrites, the Qur'an writes: "The hypocrites seek to beguile Allah, but it is Allah who beguiles them.[26]

Qur'an makes it clear that the target of Jehad are the unbelievers; it is against those who have no belief in Allah and his messenger, the persons who do not forbid what Allah have forbidden; the fight is also to be against the People of the Book – Jews and Christians—, who do not practise the true religion, i.e., Islam, till they pay Jizya and are humbled. The Qur'an says: "Fight those who believe not in Allah and the Last Day, and do not forbid what Allah and His Messenger have forbidden — such men as practise not the religion of truth, being of those who have been given Book –until they pay the tribute out of hand and have been humbled."[27]

Several *ahadis* also say the same. A Hadith from Sahih Muslim says: "I (Muhammad) have been commanded to fight against people, till they testify to the fact that there is no God but Allah, and believe in me (Muhammad) as the Messenger from the Lord) ... and when they do it their blood and riches are guaranteed protection on my behalf except where it is justified by law."[28] The Qur'an says, "When the (four) forbidden months are over, wherever you encounter the idolaters, kill them, sieze them, besiege them, wait for them at every lookout post; but if they repent, maintain the prayer, and pay the prescribed alms, let them go on their way, ..."[29]

The linkages of Jihad with war against the enemies of Allah and His Messenger necessitated swordsmanship. "Paradise lies under the shades of swords," as the Hadis says, points towards the same.[30]

Reward: Jihad Entitles one to Paradise

Even if one briefly participates in Jihad, his reward is the paradise. The Prophet said: "If a man participates in a jihad for only as long as it takes to milk a she-camel, he becomes entitled to paradise."[31]

Even the endeavour to travel for jihad is praised thus: "He who travels to participate in a jihad, the dust he encounters in the process, shall become fragrance for him on the Day of Judgment.[32]

According to a *Hadis*, a person, killed in jihad, is not only dressed in radiant robes of faith, and married to *houris*, but even acquires the power of intercession. The Prophet said: "A martyr (in Jihad) is dressed in radiant robes of faith; he is married to houris and is allowed by Allah to intercede for seventy men."[33] The power of intercession, it needs mention authorizes one to recommend entry into paradise, which Allah surely grants.

"Allah has undertaken to look after the affairs of one who goes out to fight in His way believing in Him and affirming the truth of His Apostles. He is committed to His care and He will either admit him to Paradise or bring him back to his home with a reward of booty."[34] The body of a *mujahid* will not decay. The *Hadis* says: "Every wound received by a Muslim in the Way of Allah will appear on the Day of Judgment in the same condition as it was when it was inflicted. ... and the colour (of its discharge) will be the colour of blood, but its smell would be smell of musk.[35]

Qur'an advises going for Jihad.[36]

A point, needing mention is that the Prophet chided those who desisted from participation in raids;[37] and the Qur'an also does so.[38]

Reward Even for the Facilitators of Jehad

There is reward, according to *Hadis*, not only for the participants, but even for the facilitators of the Jehad. Muhammad said: "Whatever one spends to facilitate jihad, Allah shall give him a reward which will exceed his contribution 700 times."[39] According to another *Hadis*, the Prophet said: "Whatever one spends to facilitate Jihad, Allah shall give him a reward which will exceed his contribution 700 times."[40] Not only joining the Jehad, or facilitating it, is meritorious act, but even the effort to go to join the same is an act of merit.

Superiority of Jihad Even Over Prayer

According to a Hadis, "Acting as Allah's soldier for one night in a battlefield is superior to saying prayers at home for 2000 years.[41]

The Charm of Paradise Promoted Jihad

The uncontrollable charm of the paradise, and the *hurries* there, prompt the jihadis to sacrifice their life for the religious war. A man, who was eating dates, asked Prophet Muhammad: "Where shall I be if I am killed in Jihad?" "In paradise," replied the Prophet. The man threw away the dates, and fought until he was killed.[42] Thus, "motivated by force of belief, Omeir threw the dates, he was eating, joined war and was killed."

Merits of Martyrdom

Martyrdom, or even getting injured, or for that matter even the endeavour of moving towards the battlefield is a meritorious act in Islam. Therefore, the Qur'an says: "Do not say that those who are killed in God's cause are dead; they are alive, though you do not realize it."[43]

This-worldly Reward of Jihad

The lust for booty provides material incentive for jihad. By simply killing, the killer acquires the property of the killed. Muhammad said: "He who murders another, property of the murdered becomes the property of the murderer.[44]

Motivation for War

The Arabs/Muslims were motivated for Jihad, which was war against the Pagans, Jews and the Christians, due to the combination of, mainly, three factors, (i) fear of hell, (ii) charm of heaven, and (iii) the war-booty.

The Prophet motivated them to fight without caring for their lives. He said: "The superior jihad is the one in which both the crusader and his horse are wounded."[45]

Creation of War Machinery

For effectively meeting the objectives of Jihad, Muhammad did everything to promote archery,[46] swordsmanship and horses.[47] Anyone, "Who learnt archery and then gave it up is not from us or he has been guilty of disobedience of Allah's apostle," the hadis said.[48] He mobilized resources for purchasing arms and men;[49] he advised Muslims to purchase arms and horses for Allah's cause out of the one's family savings.[50] To promote the use of horses in Jihad, the Prophet allowed one share of booty to a warrior and two shares for a horse.[51]

War Strategy

The most important factor for the success of Islam and its rapid spread was the strategic planning of the Prophet. Apart from the thinking as to how to conduct war,[52] strategic ability of concealing his plans;[53] introduction of the element of surprise, such as war during sacred months; he changed the very concept of war in Arabia. He said: "Fighting is (art of) deceit."[54] Cutting down vineyards, burning houses and plants, etc. were parts of his strategy.[55] By combining paradise and this-worldly reward, i.e., booty, it was easy for him to convince Muslims that 'death was believers' gift,' and 'dying abroad is martyrdom.'

Benefits of Jihad to the Muslims

The motive for Jihad comes from the promised paradise by Allah; it provides worldly benefit as war-booty. The Jihad works for the conversion of *Dar-ul-Harb* into *Dar-ul-Islam* and infidels into Muslims.

Perpetual War

The ideology of Jihad, the permanent perpetual war, till entire world becomes *dar-ul-Islam*, is the guiding ideology developed by the Prophet of Islam. Any place, where there is *kufr* (worship of other gods; literarily, ungratefulness) and idolatry is the zone of war, i.e., *dar-ul-herb* (the war zone). A point to be specially noted here is, that Islamic year begins from the *Hijr*, rather than from the beginning of revelations. The *hijr* symbolized severing traditional kinship linkages, and establishment of new links; the links based on Islamic *Umma*. Once the raids and wars began, it continued throughout the life of Prophet Muhammad.

These forays, raids, and battles were of two kinds; some were led by Prophet Muhammad himself, and the others by the lieutenants appointed by him. The first category, i.e., the military expedition led by the *rasul* or the *imam* himself, is known as the *Ghazwat*. On the other hand, the one led by an appointed lieutenant was called *Sariya*. The number of military expeditions, conducted during Muhammad's stay in Medina, was eighty-two; this averaged two during every three months. Again, out of the eighty-two expeditions, twenty-six were the *Ghazwat* in which Prophet Muhammad himself participated; the remaining fifty-six were the *Sariya*.[56]

According to another tradition, Prophet Muhammad led nineteen military expeditions, out of which the narrator Zaid, son of Arqam, himself participated in seventeen expeditions.[57] According to another tradition, the number of the expeditions led by the Prophet was twenty-one and the narrator, Jabir, son of Abdullah, himself participated in nineteen.[58] Yet another narrator said that he participated in seven military expeditions led by Muhammad, and nine led by his lieutenants, including Abu Bakr and Usama, son of Zaid.[59]

Some military expeditions have special significance in Islamic history. As for example, the Battle of Badr[60] changed the course of Islamic history. Other important battles were the Battle of Hunain[61], Battle of Ta'if[62], Battle of the Ditch[63], Battle of Uhud[64], Battle of Khaibar[65] and the conquest of Mecca[66]

Promoting the Use of Horses

The horses enhance the mobility of the soldiers and winability in war. Realising the fact, Muhammad took effective steps to promote the use of horses as a part of the war machinery. Muhammad used the resources at his disposal for acquiring arms, men and horses, required for an effective war machienery. Muir writes: "Yet from costly paraphernalia, such as pleased the childish taste of other monarchs, he abstained to the end; he rejected a proposal of Omar that he should purchase a silken robe in which to receive deputations; neither when his resources were slender nor when they were swollen were they ever wasted on jewels or mosaics or cloth of gold. They were employed in purchasing arms and men."[67]

After the massacre of the Jewish tribe of Banu Quraiza of Medina, the booty was divided into four categories—land, chattels, cattle and slaves; Muhammad, as usual, took a fifth of each. From his share of a thousand captives (besides little children, who were counted with their mothers), "Muhammad made certain presents to his friends, of female slaves and servants; and then sent the rest of the women and children to be sold among the Bedouin tribes of Nejd, in exchange for horses and arms; for he kept steadily in view the advantage of raising around him a body of effective horses." As arms and horses were essential for the strong army build-up for Islamic empire, he used every resource including exchange of slaves for the same.

Advice to learn Archery and Horse-riding and the use of Sword The Prophet, according to a *Hadis*, advised to learn archery and horse-riding to the Muslims. He said:

> "O people, learn archery and horse riding
> Beware ! archery means power
> He who learns archery, and thereafter, gave it up
> He disobeyed me."[68]

The Prophet advised the Muslims to learn archery, as it was effective in winning war. He linked it with Muslim heritage, and said: "O Children of Ishmael, learn archery because Ishmael was an archer."[69]

Not only archery, but swordsmanship was equally important act in the eye of the Prophet. The *Hadis* says: "Paradise lies under the shade of the swords."[70]

Changing Perspective of Jihad

The beginning of Jihad was to fight against those who were responsible for the migration of the Muslims to Medina. But it did not stop just after that. The perspective changed. After the Muslims gained strength, and the flow of the booty increased, the People of the Book also became the target of Jihad. Provocation was not necessary, the raids and war continued. Gradually, the entire Arabia came under Islamic Rule. With the expanding vision of the Muslim Arab Imperialism, the neighbouring countries came under the war zone, and were also captured.

References

1. Qur'an, 9:110.
2. *Sahih Muslim*, *Hadis* 4597.
3. *Sahih Al-Bukhari*, *Hadis* 4:725.
4. Margoliouth, *Mohammed and the Rise of Islam,* pp. 83-117. Hereafter Margoliouth.
5. Qur'an 2:256.
6. Ibn Ishaq, *Sirat Rasul Allah*, p. 205. Hereafter Ibn Ishaq.
7. Ibid, p. 208.
8. Qur'an 2:216-17.
9. Qur'an 22:39-40.
10. *Sahih Al-Bukhari*, *Hadis* 4:88.
11. Qur'an 2:190-95.
12. Muir, Sir William, *The Life of Mahomet*, p. 338. Hereafter, Muir.

13. Ibn Ishaq, pp. 659-60.
14. Qur'an 8:68.
15. Qur'an 8:67.
16. Ibid.
17. Qur'an 8:68.
18. Qur'an 22:40.
19. Qur'an 8:65-66.
20. Qur'an 58:20-21.
21. Qur'an 8:55.
22. Qur'an 2:98.
23. Qur'an 86:15.
24. Qur'an 2:161.
25. Qur'an 3:54.
26. Qur'an 4:142.
27. Qur'an: 9: 29.
28. *Sahih Muslim*, 1:31.
29. Qur'an 9:5.
30. *Sahih Bukhari*, 4:73; *Sahih Muslim*, *Hadis* 4314.
31. *Ibn-E-Majah*, Vol. 2, p. 173.
32. Ibid, p. 167.
33. Ibid, p. 174.
34. *Sahih Muslim*, *Hadis* 4626.
35. Ibid, *Hadis* 4630.
36. Qur'an 4:95-96.
37. Muir, pp. 444-448.
38. Qur'an 9: 38f, 41, 47, 82, 85.
39. *Tirmzi*, Vol. 1, p. 697.
40. Ibid, p.697.
41. Ibid, p. 166.
42. *Sahih Muslim*, *Hadis* 4678.
43. Qur'an 2:154.
44. *Ibn-E-Majah*, Vol. 2, p. 183.
45. Ibid, p. 173.
46. *Sahih Muslim*, *ahadis* 4610-11.
47. Qur'an 8:60; *Sahih Muslim*, *ahadis* 4711-14; *Sahih Al-Bukhari*, 4:105, Margoliouth, p. 53 .
48. *Sahih Muslim*, *Hadis* 4714.
49. Margoliouth, 217.

[50]. *Sahih Al-Bukhar*, *Hadis* 4:153.
[51]. Ibid, 4:115.
[52]. Ibn Ishaq, pp. 325, 327; Quran, Sura Anfal.
[53]. Muir, p. 439.
[54]. *Sahih Al-Bukhari*, *Hadis* 4:267-68.; *Ibn-e-Majah*, Vol. 2, p. 182.
[55]. *Sahih Al-Bukhari*, *Hadis* 4:262.
[56]. *Sahih Muslim*. note 2283.
[57]. Ibid, *ahadis* 4464, 4465.
[58]. Ibid, *Hadis* 4466.
[59]. Ibid, *Hadis* 4469.
[60]. Ibid, *Hadis* 4394.
[61]. Ibid, *Hadis* 4385-92.
[62]. Ibid, *Hadis* 4393.
[63]. Ibid, *Hadis* 4412.
[64]. Ibid, *ahadis* 4413-4419.
[65]. Ibid, *ahadis* 4437-4441.
[66]. Ibid, ahadis 4395-4396.
[67]. Margoliouth, p. 217.
[68]. Ibn-e-Majah, Vol 2, p. 178.
[69]. Ibn-e-Majah, Vol. 2, p. 178.
[70]. Al-Bukhari, Vol. 4, *Hadis* 73.

Theology and Related Topics

The Faith (Iman)

Numerous *ahadis* throw light on the Islamic belief system. According to them Islam is faith (i.e., belief; *iman*) in Allah, faith in Muhammad as His apostle, faith in His Book, in His angels, in the resurrection, in the hereafter, and in the payment of the *zakat* (poor-tax), and the observation of *Ramzan* (fast) and *Hajj* (pilgrimage to Mecca).

The very first *Hadis* of the 431 *ahadis* (traditions) of *Kitab al-Iman* (Book of Faith) of the *Sahih* Muslims discusses questions regarding belief. Someone, coming from great distance, yet without any sign of fatigue, meets Muhammad and asks: "Muhammad, inform me about al-Islam." The Messenger of Allah replies: "Al-Islam implies that you testify that there is no god (*ilah*) but Allah and that Muhammad is the Messenger of Allah, and you establish prayer, pay *Zakat*, observe the fast of *Ramzan* (*Ramadan*) and perform pilgrimage." After that, when the stranger left, Muhammad told Umar: "He was Gabriel. He came to you in order to instruct you in matters of religion."[1] This Hadis, narrated by Umar, is repeated in other *ahadis* also through different chain of narrators.[2]

Sahih Bukhari, in a *Hadis* says the same: "Narrated Ibn-Umar, Allah's Messenger said: Islam is based in five (principles):

1. To testify that *La ilaha ill-Allah wa anna Muhammad-ar-Rasul Allah* (none has the right to be worshipped but Allah and Muhammad is the Messenger of Allah).
2. *Iqamat-as-Salat* (to offer the (compulsory congregational) *Salat* (prayer) dutifully and perfectly.
3. To pay *Zakat*.
4. To perform *Hajj* (pilgrimage to Mecca).
5. To observe *Saum* (fast, according to Islamic teaching) during the month of Ramadan.[3]

Shahada: The Confession of a Muslim

The confession of a Muslim, called *Shahada*, says: "*La ilaha ill-Allah Muhammad-ur-Rasul-Allah*, which means, 'there is no god, but Allah, and Muhammad is the Messenger of Allah.' It has two basic beliefs of Islam, which are, (i) *Tauhid* (oneness of Allah; Islamic monotheism) and (ii) the Prophethood of Muhammad. The very first principle of the above mentioned *ahadis* also says the same.

Other Aspects

Ahadis also discusses many other beliefs of the Muslims. According to a *Hadis*, "One who avoids harming the Muslims with his tongue or hands" is "a very good Muslim," and his "Islam is the best."[4] Yet another *Hadis* says, "None of you will have faith till he likes for his (Muslim) brother what he likes for himself."[5]

To love the Messenger (Muhammad) is a part of faith. A *Hadis* says: "By Him in Whose hands my life is, none of you will have faith till he loves me more than his children[6] Muhammad defines the religion (al-din) as "sincerity and well-wishing." On being enquired, "Sincerity and well-wishing for whom?" he replied, "For Allah, His Book, His Messenger and for the leaders and general Muslims."[7] Jarir, son of Abdullah, reported that he "pledged allegiance to the Apostle of Allah on sincerity and well-wishing for every Muslim."[8] *Umma* is a very important factor in Islam. Islamic morality operates in the framework of *Umma* only. For the disbelievers, there is different yardstick of morality. To steal anything, even a very small and insignificant thing, from the war booty is sinful and leads one to hell-fire, but plundering infidels is allowed.

References

1. *Sahih Muslim, Hadis* 1.
2. Ibid, *ahadis* 2-21.
3. *Sahih Bukhari, Hadis.* 1:7.
4. Ibid, *ahadis* 1:9; 1:10.
5. Ibid, *Hadis* 1:12.
6. Ibid, ahadis 1:13; 1:14.
7. Sahih Muslim, *Hadis* 98.
8. Ibid, *Hadis* 102.

Islamic Concept of the Divine

The first half of the *Kalimah* uses the word 'Allah' for the supreme, and the only Islamic divinity. It is a composite Arabic word meaning; 'The God' (*Al* = the, *Lah* = God). Allah was the supreme Pagan deity of Arabia. They believed in numerous other deities also; these deities played subordinate roles to Allah, and were partners of that Supreme Deity. There were 360 of them in Ka'ba itself, whose images/statues were destroyed by Muhammad when he captured Mecca. According to Pagan belief system, three deities—al-Lat, al-Uzza and Manat—were the daughters of Allah. Islam denied the existence of any other divinity, it does not believe in any other God, but Allah. This basic theological doctrine of Unity of Allah (*al-Tawhid*) is enshrined in Quran's chapter, *Al-Tawhid.*

"Say, He is Allah the One, Allah the eternal, he begot no one nor was He begotten. No one is comparable to him."[1]

The above mentioned *Sura* of the Qur'an, although very brief, was equal to one-third of the Qur'an, as stated by Prophet Muhammad. This is, because, it says about the most fundamental cardinal belief of Islam. The other one is the Prophethood of Muhammad, The *Kalamah,* or *Shahadah* combines the two; which says: 'There is no god but Allah, and Muhammad is his Messenger (*La illah-ill'allah Muhammadu'r Rasula'llah*).

There are ninety-nine attributes of Allah (beautiful names of Allah, *Asmau'l-Hasan*), some of which are: *ar-Rahman* (the benefactor), *ar-Rahim* (the Merciful), *al-Wakil* (the Protector), *Gaffar, Gaffur* (the Constant Forgiver), *al-Hayyu'l-Qayyum* (One and only living One and Subsisting), *al-Haqq* (the Real truth), *al Qadin* (the ancient), *al-Qadir* (the Almighty), *al-Aim* (the Omniscient), *al-Mudrik* (the Perceiving), *al-Murid* (the Will), *al-Mutakallim* (the Orator), *al-Sadiq* (the truth), *al-Azim* (the Sublime), *al-Hakim* (the Wise), *al-Aziz* (the Omnipotent), *al-Sami* (the Hearer), *al-Basir* (the Seer),*ash-Shahid* (the Witness) and *al-Wakil*.(the Protector).[2]

Ram Swarup, while discussing the names of Gods, writes about God's names in Islam, "Islam too admits God's Names though it denies His Forms. But the admission receives a certain narrowing at the hands of the more orthodox and faithful. For a Name to be valid, it must be confirmed by the Qur'an. God is *Ash-Shafi*, the healer, but not *At-Tabib*, the physician, for the Qur'an does not use the latter epithet. Similarly, Arabic *Allah* is to be preferred to the Persian *Khuda,* though both may mean the same thing. Naturally, in this kind of approach, there is no place for names like Jupiter, Brahma, or Ishvara, for they derive from the languages of the *kafirs* (infidels).[3]

The Jews, likewise, have many names of God. Ram Swarup writes: "The God of the Jews has many names. He is *Bore Olam* (creator of the world), *Kedosh Israel* (Holy One of Israel), *Ho-Malkom* (The Omnipresent Place), *El Elion* (the Most High One), *En Sof* (the Infinite One). But according to Jewish mysticism, God has also a secret name which should not even be uttered. Therefore, the Jews simply call it "the Great Name," or "the Great, Precious Name," or Just "the Name." This name was considered so secret that it was told only to the initiates and the pious and that too in whispers so that it was not overheard to the laity.[4]

About that most secret name, he further writes: "The most secret name was rendered by four letters YHWH. But as a result of this secrecy, no one knows how it was pronounced. Its present rendering 'Jehovah' appeared for the first time as late as in 1516 in Christian texts and is regarded as simply incorrect by competent authorities. When the religious men referred to this most secret Name, they used substitutes and even the substitutes were substituted. For example, they said *Adoshem* in place of *Adonai* and *Elokhim* in the place of *Elohim*.[5]

Allah, the Islamic God, is One; He makes His will, His command, known through his apostle; and Muhammad is his apostle. In reality, the commonality between Islam, Christianity and Judaism extends to many dimensions. Each of these three religions has (i) one God, (ii) revealed book, (iii) prophets, and (iv) two humanities—humanities of believers and unbelievers.

Semitic Linkages

Islam recognizes that Allah, the Islamic God, and the God of the Jews and the Christians, is the same.[6] Perusal of the Islamic literature and Judaic-Christian literature takes us further. We find that, not only the Islamic God, Allah and the Judaic-Christian God, Yahweh, the God of the Old Testament, is the same, but their traits are also the same. The believers, the Muslims, are Allah's party, and non-believers are Satan's party,[7] and the un-believers are Allah's enemy.[8] The Bible speaks the same language. According to the Old Testament of the Bible, Yahweh chooses a people "above all people."[9] He says: "I shall be gracious to whom I will be gracious and I take pity on those on whom I take pity."[10]

Allah has made the war-booty lawful;[11] Judaic-Christian God has done the same. Yahweh brings the chosen people to the Promised Land with the commands, "Thou shall consume all the people, which the Lord thy God shall deliver unto thee; thy eyes shall have no pity upon them. … (thou) shall smite them, and utterly destroy them. … shall destroy their altar, and break down their images, and cast down their groves. … for thou are an holy people unto the Lord thy God."[12]

Yahweh's command was to smash the cultic stones, and not to bow before them; He said: "My angels will precede you and lead you to the home of the Amorites, the Hittites, the Perizzites, the Cannaanites, the Hivites and the Jebusites, whom I shall exterminate. You will not bow down to their gods or worship them or observe their rites, but throw them down and smash their cultic stones."[13] Allah's command was to break down the images, and the Prophet got it done accordingly.[14] Allah allowed Prophet Muhammad to destroy the groves.[15]

Allah,[16] his angel Gabriel[17] and the Prophet terrorized the enemies. Yahweh did the same. Yahweh said: "I shall send terror of myself ahead of you; I shall throw all the people you encounter into confusion, and make all your enemies take to their heels. I shall send hornets ahead of you to drive Hivite, Cannaanite and Hittite out before you."[18]

Many 'One' God's in Semitic Religions

Semitic God, the God of the Jews, Christians and the Muslims is one, and the same. At the same time, Allah, Who 'begot no one,' and the Christian God, Who had a begotten a son, can not be the same. Semitic God is formless, yet He created man in His form. Semitic God has human-like passion—violent rage, favouritism for the believers, scheming against unbelievers, etc.

Notes and References

1. Qur'an 112:1-4.
2. Saiyed Jafar Reza, *The Essence of Islam*, New Delhi (2012), p. 28.
3. Ram Swarup, *The Word as Revelation: Names of Gods*, New Delhi (2001); pp. 122-23.
4. Ibid, p. 122.

5. Ibid, p. 122 Note.
6. Qur'an, 2: 139-40.
7. Qur'an 58:20-21.
8. Qur'an 2:98.
9. Bible, *Old Testament*, Deut. 10.15.
10. Ibid, Ex 33:19-2.
11. Qur'an 8: 69; *Sahih Muslim*, *Hadis* 4327.
12. Bible, *Old Testament*, Deut. Chapter 7.
13. Ibid, Exodus 23:23-24.
14. Margoliouth, *Mohammed and the Rise of Islam*, p. 390; Muir, *The Life of Mahomet*, pp. 451, 453.
15. *Sahih Al-Bukhari*, *Hadis* 4:262.
16. Qur'an 33:26-27; 8:12.
17. Ibn Ishaq, *Sirat Rasul Allah*, p. 461.
18. Bible, *Old Testament*, Exodus 23: 27-28.

Islamic Prophetism

Prophetism: A Semitic Institution

In Semitic religions, God makes himself known through a favoured individual, his messenger or apostle. Prophet Muhammad was the apostle, the *Rasul* of Allah, the Islamic God. The Jews and the Christians also had their prophets, whom the Qur'an duly recognizes; the Muslims pray the same God, whom Jews and Christians pray. The Qur'an said, 'Say: 'We believe in God and in that which has been revealed to us; in what was revealed to Abraham, Ishmael, Issac, Jacob, and the tribes of Israel; to Moses and Jesus and the other prophets." And, "All this is written in earlier scriptures, the scriptures of Abraham and Moses."

Relationship with Other Prophets

The Qur'an[1] and *Hadis* discuss about other prophets, especially about Moses, Abraham and Jesus. About his relationship with Jesus, Prophet Muhammad says: "Prophets are brothers in faith, having different mothers. There religion is, however, one and there is no apostle between us (between Jesus and himself)."[2] *Sahih Muslim* discusses merits of the prophets. Similarly, *Sahih Bukhari* has '*The Book of the Stories of the Prophets.*'

According to a *Hadis*, a dispute rose between an *ansar* and a Jew. During the dispute, the Jew said: "By Allah, Who chose Moses amongst mankind." The *ansar* gave him a blow on his face, chiding him for invoking Moses when "Allah's Messenger is living with us." The Jew went to Muhammad, narrated the whole story; he then supplicated him, saying: "Abu'l-Qasim, I am a Zimmi (thus need your protection) by covenant. Muhammad chided the *ansar* and told him: "Don't make distinction amongst the Prophets of Allah."[3]

The Last Prophet *(Khtimun nabiyin)*

According to a Hadis, Prophet Muhammad said: "My example and the example of the other Prophets is that of a man who has built a house completely and excellently except for a place of one brick. When the people entered the house, they wondered at its beauty and said, 'But for the place of this brick (how splendid the house will be)!'"[4] He further said: "So I am that brick, and I am the end (last) of the Prophets.[5]

There was a protuberance on the back of Prophet Muhammad, and the physical sign was taken as the seal of Prophethood.[6]

Abrogation of the Laws of Earlier Prophets

Not only Muhammad is the last Prophet, but even the laws of all the earlier Prophets stand abrogated after his apostleship.[7] In his next coming, Jesus is almost turned as a *mujahid.*[8]

A Hadis[9], which reminds us, rather brings nearer to the Biblical saying of St. Mathew—which says: "Whosoever shall smite thee on the right cheek, turn to him the other also."[10]—says: "when anyone of you fights his brother, he should spare his face." The face should be avoided, as Prophet Muhammad explained, because, "Allah created Adam in his own image.[11] In case of the Biblical advice, it needs mention that it formed the advice of Gnostic Christianity, and not of the Pauline Christianity.

A similar Hadis, advises a man, going to a bazaar or a mosque with arrows, to take care of their "pointed heads so that these might not do any harm to a Muslim."[12] Here, of course, it may be mentioned that the Prophet did not kill his deadliest enemy also if he became a Muslim.

Intercessory Power

No other Prophet has the intercessory power on the Day of Judgment,[13] except Prophet Muhammad;[14] he has the special intercessory power among the Prophets,[15] which he acquired by reserving his prayer to Allah for the same. The Prophet writes: "There is for every Apostle a prayer which is granted, but every prophet showed haste in his prayer. I have, however, reserved my prayer for the intercession of my Ummah on the Day of Resurrection."[16] The translator of Sahih Muslim, in his note says: "The Apostles are dear to Allah and their prayers are often granted. But with every Apostle there is one request which may be called decisive with regard to his Ummah, and with it is decided their fate; for example, Noah in a state of distress uttered: 'My Lord! Leave not any one of the disbelievers in the land,'[17] Muhammad reserved his prayer for the Day of Resurrection and he would use it for the salvation of the believers."[18] It needs mention that the Prophet also used to curse his enemies on several occasions:

"O Allah! Trample severely Muzar and curse them a famine … O Allah! Curse Lihyan, Ri'l Zakwan, Usayya, for they disobeyed Allah and his Messenger."[19]

Special Gift to Prophet Muhammad

Prophet Muhammad, apart from being the seal of prophethood (last Prophet) and having special intercessionary power, was given five things which were not given to others. He, as mentioned in *Sahih Al-Bukhari*, claimed that he was given the following five things, which were not given to anyone else before him:

1. Allah made him victorious by awe, (by His frightening Muhammad's enemies) for a distance of one month's journey.
2. The earth has been made for him (and for his followers) a place for offering *Salat* (prayer) and a thing to purify (perform *Tayammun*), therefore anyone of my followers can offer *Salat* (prayer) wherever he is, at the time of the *Salat* (prayer).
3. The booty has been made *Halal* (lawful) to him yet it was not lawful to anyone else before him.
4. He had been given the right of intercession (on the day of Resurrection).
5. Every prophet used to be sent to his nation only, but he was sent to all mankind.[20]

Increasing Empowerment

The first Qur'anic revelation, which Prophet Muhammad had through the angel Gabriel, was at the age of forty. It was a terrifying experience for him, and he was not sure as to what was happening to him. Ibn Ishaq has written about the same, which has been discussed elsewhere. At first, he thought himself to be a poet; he detested it, and even wanted to end his life. After that, he gradually believed himself to be the Prophet and got confident. Initial revelations declared him to be just a mortal, like other mortals, which subjected him to resurrection. As the Qur'an says, the Prophet does not know as to what shall happen to him and to others, and he is simply a warner:

> "And I know not what
> shall be done with me or with you,
> I shall follow what is revealed to me;
> I am only a clear warner."[21]

Allah confirms Muhammad's humanity in no uncertain terms; the Qur'an says:

> "Know you therefore that
> there is no god but Allah,

and ask forgiveness for your sins,
and for the believers, men and women."[22]

As Qur'an says, Muhammad was not responsible for guiding people:

"Thou (Muhammad) art not responsible for guiding them,
but God guides whomsoever He will."[23]

Qur'an further says:

"Your Lord has the most knowledge about all of you: if He pleases He will have mercy on you, and if He pleases He will punish you. (Prophet), We did not send you to take charge of them.[24]

"So keep to the right course as you have been commanded, together with those who have turned to Allah with you. Do not overstep the limits, for He sees everything you do. Do not rely on those who do evil, or the Fire may touch you, and then you will have no one to protect you from Allah, nor you will be helped."[25]

It is clear from the Qur'anic *ayats*, given below that Allah wanted the same from Muhammad and other believers, and did not distinguish between the two:

"Set not up with Allah another God,
Or thou will be cast into hell, reproached and rejected."[26]

"We are enough for you against all those who ridicule your message, who set up another god beside Allah—they will come to know."[27]

Status Change

But there is status change leading to perceptional change. As the strength of Prophet Muhammad, and that of Islam, increases, we find his name associated with the name of Allah. The following *ayats* of Qur'an and many more, confirm the same:

"Betray not Allah and His Messenger,"[28]

"It is not for any believer, man or women,
when Allah and his Messenger have decreed a matter,
to have a choice in the affair,

Whosoever disobeys Allah and His Messenger has gone astray into clear error."[29]

The Qur'an declares Prophet's nearness to the believers than even to their selves:

"The Prophet is nearer to the believers,
than their selves."[30]

Initially, as we find in Quran, the status of Prophet Muhammad is that of a warner, and he does not know as to what will happen to him. After that, however, we find his name associated with Allah; the Qur'an frequently uses the dual name "Allah and his messenger." Every Muslim takes his name as the 'Rasul of Allah' in every prayer. Allah and angels invoke blessings upon the Prophet.[31] The Qur'an says: "Allah and His angels bless the Prophet so, you who believe, bless him too and give him greetings of peace."[32]

Prophet Knows the Best

There were occasions when Muslims disapproved the permission granted by the Prophet. He said: "What has happened to the people to whom there was conveyed on my behalf a matter for which I granted permission and they disapproved it and avoided it? By Allah I have the best knowledge amongst them."[33] A verdict of the dispute between an *ansar* and Zubair, the cousin (father's sister's son) of the Prophet, was disputed by the *ansar*, who openly said that the Prophet favoured Zubair. The Prophet's colour changed, and a revelation followed: "Nay, by the Lord, they will not really believe until they make thee a judge of what is in dispute among them, and find in this no dislike of what thou decidest and submit with full submission."[34] Disputing the decision of the Prophet, anyway, might have happened in early days only.

The Prophet, after migration to Medina, prohibited artificial pollination of the palm-date, which adversely affected the yield. When he came to know about the fact, he said: "If there is any use of it, then they should do it, for that was just a personal opinion of mine; but when I say to you anything on behalf of Allah, then do accept it, for I do not attribute lie to Allah.[35] It should be a matter of enquiry whether such a decision of the Prophet, withdrawing his own decision, had any effect on the voice of *itjehad*.

Prophet's Things Became Blessed

Prophet's things, hair, shoes, etc. became blessed things for the Muslims. When he "got his hair cut by the barber, his companions came round him and they eagerly wanted that no hair should fall but in the hand of a person."[36]

Notes and References

1. Qur'an, Sura 2; and other Suras also.
2. *Sahih Muslim*, *Hadis* 5836.
3. Ibid, *ahadis* 5853-5854.
4. *Sahih Bukhari*, *Hadis* 4:734.
5. Ibid, *Hadis* 4:735; *Sahih Muslim*, *ahadis* 5673-5676.

6. *Sahih Muslim, ahadis* 5790, 5793.
7. *Sahih Muslim*, note 288-290, Ram Swarup, *Understanding Islam through Hadis*, p. 12.
8. *Sahih Muslim*, *Hadis* 287.
9. Ibid, *Hadis* 6325.
10. Bible, Mathew 5:39.
11. *Sahih Muslim*, *Hadis* 2872.
12. Ibid, *Hadis* 6332.
13. Ibid, *Hadis* 1058.
14. Ibid, *Hadis* 377.
15. Ibid, *ahadis* 381-396.
16. Ibid *Hadis* 389.
17. Qur'an 71:26.
18. *Sahih Muslim*, Note 412.
19. Ibid, 1428.
20. *Sahih Bukhari*, *Hadis* 1:331; *Summarized Sahih Al-Bukhari*, *hadith* 224; p. 151.
21. Qur'an 46:9.
22. Qur'an 47:19.
23. Qur'an 2: 272.
24. Qur'an 17: 54.
25. Qur'an 11: 112-13.
26. Qur'an 17: 39.
27. Qur'an 15: 95-96.
28. Qur'an 8:27.
29. Qur'an 33:36.
30. Qur'an 33:6.
31. Muir, *The Life of Mahomet*, pp. 331-32.
32. Qur'an 33:56.
33. *Sahih Muslim, Hadis* 5814.
34. Qur'an 4:65; Qur'an 4:65; *Sahih Muslim, Hadis* 5817.
35. Ibid, *Hadis* 5830.
36. Ibid, *Hadis* 5750.

Rival Prophethood Claims

During the last days of Prophet Muhammad, three persons started claiming prophethood in Arabia. They were Toleiha, chief of the Beni Asad, and a warrior of note and influence in Nejd; Museilima, and Al-Aswad, the 'Veiled Prophet' of the Yemen. These, rival prophethood claims, seem to be the result of the success of Prophet Muhammad. Another factor, responsible for the same, seems to be that the institution of prophethood, was of Jewish origin; Jews, themselves used to claim that their prophet is to come soon, and Muhammad claimed to be the same prophet, and the Arabs, mentioned above, basing on their magical powers, forwarded rival claims to be prophets. The incidence of such claims were made, and Muhammad's supreme authority challenged, 'till near the close of his life,' and beginning of Abu Bakr's caliphate, during the beginning of AH XI (April-May 632 AD), and crushed.[1]

Factors Responsible

Two factors were responsible for such claims. The pretenders were tempted 'to follow in the steps of Muhammad arising from his marvelous success,' thinking that, if 'one were bold enough to assert that he had received a divine commission like that of Muhammad, why should the claim not be crowned with similar success?' Another factor was that the moment was propitious for such pretentious claims. Muir writes: "The Bedawi tribes and distant people who had but lately succumbed to the new religion, began to find its rites irksome and its restraints unpalatable. How deep and general was the discontent, is evident from the rebellion which throughout Arabia followed immediately on the Prophet's death, … Muhammad was now well stricken in years, and strangers might perceive in him the marks of advancing infirmity. His death could not be far distant. No provision had been made for a successor nor for the permanent maintenance at Medina of a supreme control over the Peninsula."[2]

Stabilizing Factors

The energies and passions of the Arabs roused by foreign conquest,[3] their this-worldly interest due to constant flow of booty and its sharing, well organized leadership and war machinery, were the important uniting factors. Of course, Islam, the ideology, and the belief of Muhammad being the seal of prophethood was the greatest uniting factor, acting against any rebellion, and the claims of the fake prophets.

Toleiha's Rebellion Crushed.

Toleiha, while journeying with his tribe, overpowered by thirst in the desert, pointed towards a place, where water would be found. 'The discovery confirmed the claims to inspiration, or at least to divination, already made. Prophet Muhammad, after receiving his prophetic claims, wanted him to be crushed, and after, his death, Khalid, crushed his rebellion. He, however, survived as a brave soldier of Islam afterwards.[4]

Museilima Claims to be a Prophet

A man of small stature, insignificant in presence, and ready and powerful in speech, Museilima 'followed the example of Muhammad,' He 'gave forth verses, professed to have been received from heaven, and he pretended also to work miracles. After the rumour of his claim of prophethood reached Prophet Muhammad, the latter summoned him to submit to Islam. Moseilima replied that 'he too was a Prophet like Muhammad himself': 'I demand therefore that thou divide the earth with me; as for Koreish, they are the people that have no respect for justice.' After the letter was read before him, "Muhammad turned with indignation to the two envoys who volunteered to urge their master's claim. *'By the Lord!' he exclaimed, 'if it were not that Ambassadors are secure, and their lives inviolate, I would have beheaded both of you!'* Then he indited the following answer: 'Thine epistle, with its lies and its fabrications against the Lord, hath been read to me. Verily the earth is the Lord's, and He causeth such of His servants as He pleaseth to inherit the same. Peace be to him that followeth true Direction!'"[5] Museilima was killed in the battle of Al-Yemama during the caliphate of Abu Bakr; With its 'Gardrn of death,' it was a perilous day for Islam.[6]

Ibn Ishaq writes how Jubayr, the young Abyssinian, expert in the use of javelin, and killer of Hamza, killed Museilima. He writes what Zubayr himself said: "When the Muslims went out against Musaylima, the false prophet, lord of the Yamama, I accompanied them, and I took the javelin with which I had killed

Hamza, and when the armies met I saw Musaylima standing with a sword in his hand, but I did not recognize him. I made ready for him and so did one of the Ansar from the other side, both of us intending to kill him. I poised my javelin until I was sure that it would hit the mark, and launched it at him, and it pierced him, and the Ansari rushed at him and smote him with his sword, so your Lord knows best which of us killed him. If I killed him, then I have killed the best man after the apostle and I have also killed the worst man..."[7]

Al-Aswad Rebelled and Crushed

Al-Aswad, the 'Veiled Prophet' of the Yemen, a prince of wealth and influence in the South, assumed the garb of a magician; he gave out that he was in communication with the unseen world. Initially, he prosecuted his claims secretly, gained over the chieftains in the neighbourhood with the distribution of power upon the death of Badhan, the Persian governor, and then openly raised the standard of rebellion, and drove out the Muslim officers during the close of the AH 10. The Muslim officers fled to the nearest friendly country.[8]

Al-Aswad moved to Najran, which rose in his favour; suddenly fell upon San'a, where he killed Badhan's son, Shehr, and married his wife, the army of Shehr fled and Al-Aswad 'established himself in undisputed authority.' Fanned by the sudden success, the insurrection spread like wildfire, the greater part of the Peninsula lying between the provinces of Al Bahrein, At-Taif, and the coast, very soon came under the control of the usurper, who, however, could not keep his commanders happy, as he began to slight them. "The agents of Muhammad," Muir writes: "opened up secret negotiations with them; and, favoured by the tyrant's wife, who detested him, and burned to avenge her late husband's death, plotted his assassination. The usurper was slain, according to tradition, on the very night preceding the death of Muhammad. The insurrection ceased; and peace would immediately have been restored had not the tiding that the Prophet had passed away again thrown the province into confusion." The campaign to bring the situation back was undertaken during caliphate of Abu Bakr.[9]

Prophet Muhammad's Strange Encounter with Ibn Saiyyad

Sahih Bukhari says: Umar set out with the Prophet with a group of people to Ibn Saiyad till they saw him playing with the boys near the hillocks of Maghala. Ibn Saiyyad at that time was nearing his puberty and did not notice (us) until the Prophet stroked him with his hand and said to him: "Do you testify that I am Allah's Messenger." Ibn Saiyyad looked at him and said: "I testify that you are the Messenger of illiterate." Then Ibn Saiyad asked the Prophet: "Do you testify that I am Allah's Messenger?"

The Prophet refuted it and said: "I believe in Allah and his Messenger." Then he said (to Ibn Sayyad), "What do you think?" Ibn Sayyad answered: "The true people and liars visit me." The Prophet said: "You have been confused as to this matter." Then the Prophet said to him, "I have kept some thing (in my mind) for you, (can you tell me that?)" …" According to translator's note, Ibn Sayyad could not correctly say what the Prophet thought as he was just a soothsayer predicting things with the help of the devil. Anyway, Prophet after hearing him, said: "Let you be in ignominy. You can not cross your limits." On that Umar said: "O Allah's Messenger! Allow me to chop his head off." The Prophet said: "If he is he (i.e., *Dajjal*), then you can not overpower him, and if he is not, then there is no use of murdering him. Bukhari mentions a second visit of the Prophet also to Ibn Sayyad.[10] *Sahih Muslim* also writes about the same with slight change.[11] It needs mention that *Dajjal,* finding mention in many *ahadis,* is a kind of antichrist, blind in the left eye and red in complexion, with the word kafir inscribed on his forehead. He, "would be followed by seventy thousand Jews of Isfahan wearing Persian Shawls."[12] Muhammad, according to another *Hadis* said: "Hasten to do good deeds before six things happen: the rising of the sun in the West, the smoke, the Dajjal …"[13]

A point, before concluding, needing mention is that Muhammad was always afraid of intra-Islamic fight,[14] and his strategy was that the disrupter of unity should be killed.[15]

References

1. Muir, Sir William, *The Life of Mahomet*, pp. 476-79; hereafter, Muir.
2. Ibid, p. 477.
3. Ibid.
4. Ibid.
5. Ibid, pp. 477-78.
6. Ibid, p. 478.
7. Ibn Ishaq, *Sirat Rasul Allah*, English translation by A. Guillaume, p. 377.
8. Muir, p. 478.
9. Ibid, p. 479.
10. *Sahih Bukhari*, *Hadis* 2:437.
11. *Sahih Muslim*, *ahadis* 6990-7004.
12. *Sahih Muslim*, *Hadis* 7034.
13. *Sahih Muslim*, *Hadis* 7039.
14. *Sahih Bukhari*, *Hadis* 2:428.
15. Ram Swarup, *Understanding Islam through Hadis*, pp. 122-23; *Sahih Muslim*, *ahadis* 4565, 4567.

Life After Death in Islam

Life of a Muslim after death passes through three phases:

i. The dead body is put to rest in the grave;
ii. One remains in the grave till, on the Day of Judgment, the dead resurrect;
iii. Then the Prophet intercedes and Allah sends them to heaven or hell. Once sent to heaven or hell, they spend their lives there in eternity.[1]

Unbelievers Punished Even in Their Graves

As per the Islamic belief, sufferings of the dead ones begin after they resurrect on the Day of Judgment, and are reckoned for being sent to hell. The unbelievers, however, are tormented even in their graves.[2] The same is the case with the Jews.[3] The corpses of the unbelievers of Mecca, after the battle of Badr, were left unattended and then thrown in the well of Badr.[4] Even the soul of the believers, when taken out by two angels, smell sweet, and that of the unbelievers smell foul.[5] The ahadis mention that the Prophet used to make the supplications not only against the trial of the Hell-Fire, but even from the trial and torment of the grave.[6]

The Reckoning on the Day of Judgment

Belief on the Day of Resurrection is an essential part of Islam. As mentioned in Sahih Muslim, "The people would be assembled on the Day of Resurrection barefooted, naked and uncircumcised." On that statement, 'A'isha asked: "Allah's Messenger, will the male and the female be together on the Day and would they be looking at one another?" The Prophet replied: "'A'isha, the matter would be too serious for them to look to one another."[7]

Ahadis also mention about easy and hard reckoning[8] An easy reckoning, 'is not the actual reckoning, but only the presentation of one's deeds to Him. He who is thoroughly examined in reckoning is put to torment.'[9] The Qur'an also mentions about an easy reckoning.[10]

Coming of the Last Day

Belief in the Day of Judgment, also known as the Last Day, is an essential part of the Islamic belief system. Prophet Muhammad believed that the Last Hour is approaching soon. Pointing towards an Ansar boy, he said: "If this young boy lives, he may not grow very old till (he would see) the Last Hour coming to you.[11] Again, the coming of the Last Hour will be sudden and swift.[12] Keeping the approaching hour in mind, the Prophet used to prepare Muslims for the same. He said: "Hasten to do good deeds before six things happen: (the appearance of) the Dajjal, the smoke, the beast of the earth, the rising of the sun from the west, the general turmoil (leading to large-scale massacre) and death of masses and individuals."[13] "The Dajjal would be followed by seventy thousand Jews of Isfahan wearing Persian shawls."[14] "The people would run away from the Dajjal seeking shelter in the mountains," and (Arabs) would be small in number.[15]

Many other ahadis also mention about the signs of the last hour. "The last hour would not come unless the Muslims will fight against the Jews and Muslims would kill them and until the Jews would hide themselves behind a stone or a tree and a stone or a tree would say: Muslim, or the servant of Allah, there is a Jew behind me; come and kill him." Only *gharqad*, a very thorny tree, which is painful to touch, will be loyal to the Jews, and will not reveal their identity, "for it is the tree of the Jew."[16] Many signs would precede the great turmoil, "which would emerge like the mounting waves of the ocean."[17] "The Last Hour would not come unless the Euphrates would uncover a treasure of gold."[18] It will not come "until fire emits from the earth of Hijaz which would illuminate the necks of the camels of Busra."[19] It will not come "until the people have (again) taken to the worship of Lat and Uzza."[20] The "Ka'ba would be destroyed by an Abyssinian having two small shanks" before the Last Hour comes.[21] Before the Last Hour, *jizya* will stop coming and the people of Iraq will "not send their *qafiz* and *dirhims* (their measures of foodstuffs and their money)."[22]

The note of the translator of the *Sahih Muslim* informs about certain characteristics of Dajjal, which are: (a) He would be blind of left eye and his right eye would be floating like a grape; (b) His complexion would be red; (c) 'Kafir' would be inscribed on his head; (d) He would not be able to get into Medina; (e) Medina would rock thrice on his appearance; (f) He would kill a pious man and then bring him back to life; and (g) He would appear near the Last Hour and would be killed by Christ.[23] Here, it needs mention that the Companions of the Prophet believed Ibn Sayyad[24] to be Dajjal, who also claimed to be the prophet.[25]

The Paradise (*al-janna*; 'the garden) and the Hell

The Paradise and Hell go together in the Prophet's eschatology. In many places, when the paradise is mentioned as a reward for the believer, there is mention of the hell after that for the unbeliever. When the Qur'an mentions about the reward of heaven for the believers, saying that "Allah will admit those who obey Him and His Messenger in Garden graced with flowing stream, and there they will stay—that is the supreme triumph!,"[26] the very next *Sura* pronounces hell for the non-believers. It says: "But those who disobey Allah and His Messenger and overstep His limits will be consigned to the Fire, and there they will stay—a humiliating torment awaits them!"[27] In the Qur'an, the words "Paradise" (*jannat*) and "Hell" (*jahanam*) come 64 and 76 times respectively. *An-Nar*, "the Fire," the Qur'an's pet name for Hell, appears 121 times.[28]

It is natural that a garden and the flowing stream may be the most desired and desirable thing for the desert-dwelling Arabs. Likewise, extreme heat and fire may be the most undesired thing for them. Under such circumstances, it is understandable why the "Garden graced with flowing stream,"[29] or simply Garden,[30] have become synonymous to heaven, and likewise Fire has become synonymous to hell in Islam.

The Quranic paradise provides everything which an Arab desires; on the other hand the hell has everything, which despairs them. The Qur'an says: "Here is a picture of the Garden promised to the pious: rivers of water forever pure, rivers of milk forever fresh, rivers of wine, a delight for those who drink, rivers of honey clarified and pure, (all) flow in it; there they will find fruit of every kind; and there they will find forgiveness from their Lord. How can this be compared to the fate of those stuck in the Fire, given boiling water to drink that tears their bowels?"[31]

Life in the Paradise

At one place, the picture emerges: it has two gardens with shading branches, a pair of flowing springs, every kind of fruit in pairs for the one sitting on couches upholstered with brocade, and fruits of both gardens within his easy reach. And then, there will be maidens, like rubies and brilliant pearls, restraining their glances untouched before by man or jinn. And then, there are two other gardens below these two, both of deepest green, with a pair of gushing springs, and with fruits—date palms and pomegranate trees. Again, there are good-natured, dark-eyed, beautiful maidens, untouched beforehand by man or jinn, sheltered in pavilions. 'They will all sit on green cushions and fine carpets.'[32] For food, "they will have any fruits or meat they may desire."[33] They will be "reclining on raised thrones; and shades of the Garden will come low over them; the bunches of fruits will hang low. And amongst them will be passed round vessels of silver and goblets of crystal; they will drink of a cup of wine mixed with *Zanjabil* (ginger), and there would be a fountain called *Salsbil*. And around them will be youths of perpetual freshness (*viludanum mukhaladun*), youths of such beauty that you would think them scattered pearls; upon them will be green garments of fine silk and heavy brocade, and they will be adorned with bracelets of silver."[34]

Qur'an further says about the persons living in paradise: "Those who are mindful of Allah are in Garden and in bliss rejoicing in their Lord's gifts. He has saved them from the torment of the Blaze, 'Eat and drink with healthy enjoyment as healthy reward for what you have done.' They are comfortably seated on couches arranged in rows. We pair them with beautiful eyed maidens; We unite the believers with their offspring who followed them in faith—Who do not deny them any of the rewards for their deeds: each person is in pledge for his own deeds."[35] "Devoted Youth like "hidden pearls" wait on them."[36]

Paradise According to Hadis

Ahadis provide more details about the Paradise and its inhabitants. The Prophet informs about the height of the inhabitants of Paradise and, incidentally, the height of Adam and even of Allah. Thus, even the immeasurable is measured. Allah, the Exalted and Glorious, created Adam in his own image with His length of sixty cubits, …So he who would get into Paradise would get in the form of Adam, his length being sixty cubits." He adds that the people who came after Adam "continued to diminish in size up to this day"[37] Likewise, the inhabitants of the Paradise will have very big habitation; which will be a "tent of a single hollowed pearl, the breadth of which would be sixty miles from all sides."[38] According to yet another *Hadis*, "In Paradise, there is a tree under the shadow of which a rider of a fine and swift-footed horse would travel for a hundred years without covering the distance completely."[39] According to Sahih Bukhari, "Paradise has one hundred grades which Allah has reserved for the Mujahidun who fight in his cause, and the distance between each of the two grades is like the distance between the heaven and the earth."[40]

The life in paradise differs from that of this world in other respects also. As for example, only two spouses are allowed to the believers in the paradise, as against four here.[41] Whereas the inhabitants of the Paradise will eat and drink, but they will "neither pass water, nor void excrement, nor will they suffer from catarrh, nor will they spit.[42] "Their combs would be made of gold and the fuel of their braziers would be aloes and their sweat would be musk and their form would be form of a single person according to the length of their father sixty cubit tall."[43] As the whole catabolic process will change, "They will belch and sweat (and it would be over with their food), and their sweat would be that of musk."[44]

The Paradise, having the ranking and hierarchy as we have on earth, have exclusive quarters for the apostles. The inhabitants of the lower regions of Paradise "will look to the upper apartment of Paradise as you see the planets in the sky."[45] The ranking in Paradise and one earth will be the same. The apostle said: "The first group of my Ummah to get into Paradise would be like a full moon in the night. Then those who would be next to them; they would be like the most significantly glittering stars ... then after them others in ranks."[46]

In Islam, deeds alone are not enough for attaining salvation. Muhammad said: "None amongst you would attain salvation purely because of his deeds."[47] He advised: "observe moderation" in your doings, but if you fail, "try to do as much as you can do and be happy for none would be able to get into Paradise because of his deeds alone."[48] Here, it needs mention that intercessory power of the last prophet is the important factor in attainment of Paradise in Islam.

A Hadis expressing greater pleasure of seeing others denied Paradise than the pleasure of seeing even one's own self rewarded shows the attitude of the Paradise-dwellers. It says: "Why should we not be pleased, O Lord, when Thou hast given us what Thou hast not given to any of Thy creation?"[49]

The Paradise promises houries with swelling bosoms, retiring glances; houries "unfailing and unforbidden, on lofty sofas and of a rare creation, forever virgins, beloved and equal in age."[50] Sahih Bukhari writes about the houries thus: "If a woman (a hourie etc.) from Paradise appeared to the people of the earth, she would fill the space between heaven and the earth with light and pleasant scent and her headcover is better than the world and whatever is in it."[51] The attraction of Paradise lies in the fact that whatever is denied here on earth is promised there, such as silk dresses, wine, golden vessels, women, houries, etc.[52] A point needing mention here is that 'houries' were revealed during Meccan period, and "in all the voluminous revelations of the ten years following the Hijra—women are only twice referred to as one of the rewards in Paradise; and on both the occasions in these simple words,—*and to them there shall be therein pure wives*."[53] The Muir's remark in this case is worth noting:

"It is remarkable that the notices in the Kor'an of this voluptuous Paradise are almost entirely confined to a time when, whatever the tendency of his desires, Mohammad was living a chaste and temperate life with a wife three score years of age."[54]

The note on the observation throws a question as to the reason of the repressed picture of the sensual Paradise, which is: "Was it that satiety had then left no longings unfulfilled; or that closer contact with Judaism had repressed the picture of a sensual Paradise such as had been drawn at Mecca?"[55]

Charm of Paradise

The charm of paradise has been highly tempting for the Muslims. This continues to be even today. A believer, while on the way to the Battle of Uhud, asked Muhammad: "Messenger of Allah, where shall I be if I am killed in the battle." He replied: "In paradise." The man was eating dates at that time; he threw away the dates which he had in his hand, fought and was killed.[56]

The Quranic Hell

We find the treatment of Hell both in the Quran and the Hadis, but it is more detailed in the former. The Hell of the Qur'an is equally material as its heaven. It expresses itself throughout in material framework, such as the "flames and the scalding water."[57] Muir describes it thus: "The drink of the lost is described as boiling water and filthy corruption. When cast into the pit, they hear it roar wildly like the braying of an ass. 'Hell boileth over, it almost bursteth with fury: the smoke, rising in three columns, affordeth neither shade nor protection, but casteth forth great sparks like castles, or as it were yellow camels.'"[58]

Though the Hell is reserved for the non-believers, even Muslims shall have to go there.[59] Of course, it may be a temporary stay, and least oppressive Hell, called *Jahanam*; it is indeed a purgatory for the Muslims. However, different regions of Hell, depending on the degree of oppressiveness is perceived. The real torments are, however, reserved for the unbelievers, infidels and polytheists of different hues and degrees. Starting from the blazing fire of *Laza*, which leaves nothing unconsumed, for the Christians; and still more intense fire of *Hutamah* for the Jews, *Sa'ir* is reserved for the Sabians, *Saqar* for the Magi, *Jahim* for idolaters, and *Hawiyah* for the hypocrites.[60] All in the Hell do not suffer equally. "There would be among them those to whom Fire will reach up to their ankles, to some up to their knees, to some up to their waists, and to some up to their collar-bones."[61]

The Qur'an asks to fear the Fire whose fuel is Men and Stones, and which is preapared for those who reject Faith.[62] It sends unbelievers to the hell-fire, which "permits nothing to endure, nor leaves anything alone."[63] Qur'an promises a sorry plight for all kinds of the unbelievers—Jews, Christians, polytheists, idolaters, hypocrites. It says: Has the tidings reached thee of the Overwhelming Event? Some faces that Day will be humiliated, toiling, weary, ... No food will there be for them but a bitter zari which will neither nourish nor satisfy hunger."[64] Of course, the Qur'an mentions about such other foods also.[65] According to Hadis, the hunger of Hell is inexhaustible. "The sinners would be thrown therein and it would continue to say: Is there anything more?"[66]

The heat in Hell is more intense than the same on earth. The fire on earth is only "one-seventieth part of the Fire of Hell.[67] Moreover, the stones will hurtle down on the inmates of Hell.[68]

References

1. *Sahih Muslim, Hadis* 6829.
2. Ibid, *Hadis* 6859.
3. Ibid, *Hadis* 6861.
4. Ibid, *Hadis* 6869-70.
5. Ibid, *Hadis* 6867.
6. Ibid, *ahadis* 6534-35.
7. Ibid, *Hadis* 6844.
8. Ibid, *ahadis* 6871-74.
9. Ibid, *Hadis* 6871.
10. Qur'an 84:8.
11. *Sahih Muslim, ahadis* 7051, 7052, 7053.
12. Ibid, *Hadis* 7054.
13. Ibid, *Hadis*7039, 7040.
14. Ibid, 7034.
15. Ibid, 7035.
16. Ibid, 6985.
17. Ibid, 6914.
18. Ibid, 6920.
19. Ibid, 6935.
20. Ibid, 6945.
21. Ibid, 6951.

[22.] Ibid, 6961.
[23.] *Sahih Muslim*, Translator's Note 3061.
[24.] Ibid, 6990-7004.
[25.] Ram Swarup, *Understanding Islam through Hadis*, p. 213.
[26.] Qur'an 4:14.
[27.] Ibid 4:14.
[28.] Ram Swarup, op. cit., p. 201.
[29.] Qur'an 2:25; 4:13; 10:9-10, 66:8.
[30.] Qur'an 9:111.
[31.] Qur'an 47:15.
[32.] Qur'an 47:15.
[33.] Qur'an 56:20-21.
[34.] Qur'an 76:13:21.
[35.] Qur'an 52:17-21.
[36.] Qur'an 52:24.
[37.] *Sahih Muslim*, *Hadis* 6809.
[38.] Ibid, *Hadis* 6805.
[39.] Ibid, *Hadis* 6784.
[40.] *Sahih Bukhari*, 4:48.
[41.] *Sahih Muslim*, *Hadis* 6797.
[42.] Ibid, *Hadis* 6795.
[43.] Ibid, *Hadis* 6796.
[44.] Ibid, 6798.
[45.] Ibid, *Hadis* 6788.
[46.] Ibid, *Hadis* 6796.
[47.] Ibid, *Hadis* 6760.
[48.] Ibid, *Hadis* 6770.
[49.] Ibid, *Hadis* 6787.
[50.] Qur'an 56: 33-40; 78:32-34.
[51.] *Sahih Bukhari* 4:53.
[52.] Ram Swarup, op. cit., p. 204.
[53.] Muir, p.76, note 2.
[54.] Ibid, p. 76.
[55.] Ibid, p. 76, note 2.
[56.] *Sahih Muslim*, *Hadis* 4678.
[57.] Qur'an 55:44.
[58.] Muir, op. cit., p. 77.
[59.] Qur'an 19:71.

60. RS, pp. 209-10.
61. *Sahih Muslim, Hadis* 6816.
62. Qur'an 2:24.
63. Qur'an 74:28.
64. Qur'an 88:1-7.
65. Qur'an 56:52; 17:60; 44:43-46.
66. *Sahih Muslim, Hadis* 6825.
67. Ibid, *Hadis* 6811.
68. Ibid, *Hadis*, 6813; Ram Swarup, op. cit., p. 206.

Purification

Bodily purification is essential for prayer in Islam by ablution (*wuzu*) or bath (*ghusl*) depending on whether the impurity (*hadath*; it is passing urine, stool or wind) is small or big.[1] *A Hadis* says about the superiority of ablution. According to that, the Messenger of Allah said: "On the Day of Resurrection my followers will be called *Al-Ghurr-ul-Muhajjalun* from the traces of ablution and whoever can increase the area of radiance should do so (i.e., by performing ablution) in the most perfect manner."[2] Thus, Prophet Muhammad emphasizes the need of the purity of body. He said: "Cleanliness is half of faith."[3] We find some broad injunctions on purification in Qur'an[4], but, the *Hadis*, as expected, deals the subject in minute details in the *ahadis* of "Book of Purification" (*Kitab Al-Taharah*). The 'Book of Purification' deals with the matters such as ablution, defecation, abstersion, and even very minute acts of purification such as 'cleaning the teeth (*miswak*)'[5] and 'cleansing the nose.'[6]

The *Hadis* and Muslim *fiqh* provide details about the cleanliness, which is outer and bodily, and does not deal with inner purity. Ram Swarup has written:

"It relates not to inner purity but to certain acts of cleanliness, physical and ritualistic, that must be performed before reciting the statutory daily prayers. The main topics discussed in Muslim *fiqh* (canon law) under this heading are: (1) *wuzu*, minor ablution of the limbs of the body, prescribed before each of the five daily prayers and omitted only if the worshipper is sure that he has not been polluted in any way since the last ablution; (2) *ghusl*, the major, total ablution of the whole body after the following acts which make a person *junub*, or impure: coitus (*jima*), nocturnal pollution (*ihtilam*), menses (*hayz*) and childbirth (*nifas*); (3) *tayammum*, the minor purification, with dust in place of water; (4) *fitra*, literally "nature," but interpreted by customs of the previous, including acts like the use of toothpick (*miswak*), cleansing the nose and mouth with water (*istinshaq*), and abstersion (*istinja*) with water or dry earth or a piece of stone after evacuation or urination; (5) *tathir*, the purification of objects which have become ritualistically unclean.[7]

The Five Essential Acts (*Fitra*)

There are five acts natural to man and proper to Islam, according to the *ahadis*, which are, circumcision, shaving the pubes, cutting the nails, plucking the hair under the arm-pits and clipping the moustache.[8] Clipping the moustache and allowing the beard to grow, however, was done according to the instruction of Muhammad for distinct facial look of the Muslims, and to bring a difference from what the polytheists and the fire-worshippers did.[9]

Islam provides for detailed pollution rules, which has ritual significance, covering all aspects of life, including cleaning the soiled clothes, food and ablution, pollution related to menstruation, etc.

A point needing mention, however, is that there were exceptions also to these rules and regulations. Tirmizi has written in a *Hadis*, narrated by Abu Sa'id about one such exception. According to that *Hadis*, Muhammad told Ali: "O Ali! It is not lawful for anyone except me and thee to go to mosque in a state of sexual defilement."[10]

References

1. *Sahih Bukhari, Hadis* 1:137.
2. Ibid, *Hadis*, no. 1:138.
3. *Sahih Muslim, Hadis* 432.
4. Qur'an 4:43; 5:6.
5. *Sahih Muslim, Hadis* 487.
6. Ibid, *Hadis* 462.
7. Ram Swarup, *Understanding Islam through Hadis,*, p. 13; hereafter Ram Swarup.
8. *Sahih Muslim, ahadis* 495-503.
9. Ibid, *Hadis* 500.
10. Tirmizi, Vol. II, Hadis 1584; quoted by Ram Swarup, p. 22.

Fasting (*As-Saum*) in Islam

The fasting, in one form or the other was a common religious practice in Arabia among all the communities, including the pagans, who observed fast on *Ashor*, the tenth day of Muharram. Many of the practices, such as fasting, were adopted by Prophet Muhammad from the Jews. The Prophet, a few months after his arrival in Medina during AH 2, September 623, saw the Jews keeping the great Fast of the atonement, which he readily adopted for his own people. Before that, 'fasting does not appear to have been a prescribed ordinance of Islam.' "It was established," as Muir writes: "at a period when it was the object of Muhammad to bring his religion in harmony with Jewish rites and ceremonies. But when he had cast off Judaism and its customs, this fast was to be superseded by another. Accordingly about a year and a half later, the divine command was promulgated and the following month of Ramadan (or Ramzan)[1] was to be observed thenceforward as an annual fast. Although the new ordinance was expressly ordained as similar in principal to that of the Jews, yet, its term and mode of its observance were entirely different. At first the Muslims (following the Jews, who fasted for four-and-twenty hours from sunset to sunset) thought themselves bound to abstain from all enjoyments night and day throughout the month, Mohammad checked this ascetic spirit. His followers were to fast rigorously by day, but since sunset till dawn they might eat and drink and indulge in all pleasures that were otherwise lawful"[2]

The fasting (*Saum*, *As-Saum*, or *Roza*, *Rozah*) is one of the foremost religious obligations of the Muslims. Period of Fasting (Saum) is the entire month of Ramadhan (Ramzan). It begins when one sees the crescent of Ramadan, and continues upto seeing the crescent of Shawwal. If crescent is not visible then fast continues for thirty days,[3] as a month may be of 29 or of 30 days. Therefore, if crescent not visible due to cloudy weather or any reason, then naturally, the fast is observed for 30 days.[4] Mary or observe as-Saum,[5] keeping in mind whether the month of Ramadhan will be of 29 or 30 days in any particular year, the Prophet said: "We are an illiterare nation, we neither write, nor know accounts. The month is like this and this, i.e., some times of 29 days and sometimes of thirty days."[6]

Fasting Prescribed by Allah

Allah prescribes fasting for the believers. He provides the relief in its observation in case of the illness or journey of the believer. Qur'an says: "You who believe, fasting is prescribed for you, as it was prescribed for those before you so that you may be mindful of Allah. Fast for a specific number of days, but if one of you is ill, or on a journey, then on other days later. For those who can fast only with extreme difficulty, there is a way to compensate—feed a needy person. But if any one does good of his own accord, it is better for him, and fasting is better for you, if you only you knew."[7]

Qur'an further says: "It was in the month of Ramadan that the Qur'an was revealed as guidance for mankind, clear messages giving guidance and distinguishing between right and wrong. So anyone of you who sees in that month should fast, and anyone who is ill or on a journey should make up for the lost days by fasting on other days later. Allah wants ease for you not hardship. He wants you to complete the prescribed period and glorify Him for having guided you, so that you may be thankful."[8]

The Merits of Fasting

There are multiple merits of fasting. The Messenger of Allah said: "*Saum* (fasting) is a shield (or a screen or a shelter from the hell-fire). So the person observing *Saum* (fast) should avoid sexual relation with his wife and should not behave foolishly and impudently, and if somebody fights with him or abuses him, he should say to him twice, 'I am observing Saum'" The Prophet added, "By Him in whose Hands my soul is, the smell coming out from the mouth of a person observing *Saum* is better with Allah than the smell of musk. (Allah says about the fasting person), He has left his food, drink and desires for my sake. The *Saum* is for me So, I will reward for it and the reward of good deeds is multiplied ten times."[9]

"On the Day of Resurrection, there will be a gate of heaven, called *Rayyan* (*Ar-Raiyan*), exclusively for those who observe fast, and when the last of them would enter heaven, it would be closed and no one would enter it."[10]

A person, who combines fast with *Jihad*, his recompense will be immense. "Every servant of Allah who observes fast for a day in the way of Allah, Allah would remove, because of this day, his face from the Fire of Hell to the extent of seventy years' distance."[11]

Other Benefits

According to a tradition, narrated by Alqama, Abdullah said: "We were in the company of the Prophet and he said: 'He who can afford to marry should marry, because it will help to lower his gaze (from looking at forbidden things and other women), and save his private parts (from committing illegal sexual acts etc.) and he who can not afford to marry is advised to observe *As-Saum* (the fast), as *Saum* will diminish his sexual power. It is clear that the mechanism suggested for self-control, in this case, is by weakening the body through control of diet, rather than by mental or spiritual exercise.'"[12]

Fasting Optional under Certain Circumstances

In many cases, the fasting is optional. As for example, during journey, one may or may not observe fast. On a question, 'Should I observe fast while traveling?' The Prophet replied: "You may observe *Saum* (fast) if you wish, or you may not observe *Saum* (fast) if you wish."[13] If one observes *Saum* for some days, and then undertakes a journey, then he may break his *Saum*.[14] The Prophet and his companions did not observe *Saum* during a journey, when it was very hot.[15] If someone dies while observing *Saum*, then his guardian, or in case of a mother dying, her son, must observe *Saum*, for the remaining days on his or her behalf. The Prophet, in such a case said: "Allah's debt has more right to be paid."[16]

Women, sometimes, abstained from fast so that to perform their duties towards their husbands unhindered. Aisha reported: "I had to complete some of the fasts of Ramzan, but I could not do it ... due to my duties to the Messenger of Allah."[17] She reported the same about some of her co-wives. "If one amongst us had to break fast (of *Ramzan* due to natural reasons, i.e., menses) during the life of messenger of Allah, she could not find it possible to complete them so long as she had been in the presence of Allah's messenger till *Sha'ban* (the eighth month)commenced."[18] Here, it needs to refer to the translator's note. He explains that every wife of Muhammad was so much devoted to him that she avoided fasting lest it should stand in her way in the performance of her duty as a wife to him.

It was, however, not only from devotion but also because of Prophet Muhammad's injunction that his wives did not fast. "No women should observe fast when her spouse is present (in the house) but with his permission. And she should not admit any *mahram* in his house, while the husband is present, but with his permission."[19] A *mahram*, it needs mention, is a near relative with whom it is lawful to marry. A woman can feel free in his presence and thus need not observe *purdah*.

In the above case, it may be relevant to mention the rationale provided by the translator for this injunction, "Such is the regard which the Islam gives to the natural instinct of man that it enjoins upon women not to observe (voluntary) fast, and not to admit even those relatives of theirs in their apartments who are mahram to them so that they may not stand in the way of the husbands to satisfy their sexual urge."[20]

If one is engaged in the "Way of Allah," i.e., in the act of *jihad*, he is going to encounter the enemy in the morning and breaking of the fast would give him strength, the Prophet allowed him to break the fast.[21]

Missed Fasts

The missed fasts could be completed later on at any time of the year. The women, who abstain from fasting during the days of menses, were required to complete the fast the following year before the commencement of the next Ramzan in the month of Sha'ban (Sha'ban)[22] There are *ahadis* on "Forbiddance to observe perpetual fast and Excellence of observing fast on alternate days."[23] Similarly, there are ahadis mentioning about the "Excellence of observing fast for three days during every month, and fasting on the day of 'Arafa and 'Ashura and Monday and Thursday."[24] Prophet advised the observance of fast for two days in the middle of the month of Sha'ban.[25]

Ashura fast, among several other fasts mentioned, observed on the tenth day of Muharram, "was the one which the Jews respected and treated as 'Id,"[26] and during the pre-Islamic days, "Quraish used to fast on this day,"[27] was made optional by the Prophet for the Muslims after his migration to Medina. An interesting fact about these fasts is that one could declare one's intention to observe them in the morning but break them without reson in the evening. One day, Prophet Muhammad asked Aisha for some food, but nothing was available. On that he said: "I am observing fast." But some food came as gift afterwards, and Aisha offered it to him. He asked: "What is it?" Aisha said: "It is *hais* (a compound of dates and clarified butter)."He said: "Bring that." So Aisha brought it and he ate it, and then said: "This observing of voluntary fasts is like a person who sets apart *Sadaqa* out of his wealth. He may spend it if he likes, or he may retain it if he so likes."[28]

Sex Permitted during Ramzan

Kissing and embracing are allowed during fast.[29] The translator of Sahih Muslim, however, elucidates: "It is one of the great favours of Allah upon humanity that He has guided us in every sector of our life through His Prophet Muhammad.

Prior to Islam, the man observing fast separated himself completely from his wives. Islam did not approve this practice."[30] Sexual intercourse, during the night of the fast, has a divine sanction. The Qur'an says: "It is made lawful for you to go to your wives on the night of the fast. [31] It has the sanction of the tradition too."[32]

The *ahadis* discuss cases when one gets up in a state of seminal emission and the dawn overtakes him without giving him time for the ordained bath; and still he should go on with his fast, although in the state of *janabah* (in which one is "unclean" and cannot perform a religious act or join in religious assemblies). Thus, even being in the state of *Junub*, there is no breaking of the fast.[33] Many other *ahadis* discuss this situation.[34]

Breaking Fast in Forgetfulness

A *Hadis* says about a person, eating or drinking forgetfully while fasting: "If somebody eats or drinks forgetfully, then he should complete his Sawm (fast), for what he has eaten or drunk, has been given to him by Allah.[35]

Expiation for the Lapse

There is provision for the atonement for the sexual intercourse during the daytime in the month of Ramzan either by freeing a slave or, failing that, by observing a two-month fast or, failing that, by feeding sixty poor men—but during the Prophet's lifetime, a poor man who violated this provision got his expiation at no cost to himself. Prophet Muhammad gave him a basket of dates and told him: "Go and give it to your family to eat."[36]

Lunar Year and the Fasting

Originally, the Arabs followed lunar year, which was changed to luni-solar one during the fifth century in imitation of the Jews by the interjection of a month at the close of every third year. This change, intended to make the season of pilgrimage correspond invariably with the autumn, when the supply of food for the vast multitude would be easily procurable, did not solve their problem, as the new system was still imperfect; the year was still short of a day and a fraction, and during the long two century, during the period of Prophet Muhammad, the pilgrimage session shifted from October to March. The shift back to the lunar system by Prophet Muhammad has resulted into the swifter swift of the period of fasting and other festivals in Islam.[37]

References

1. Written as Ramadan, Ramazan.
2. Muir, Sir William, *The Life of Mahomet*, pp. 191-92.
3. *Sahih Al-Bukhari, Ahadis* 3:124; 3:133.
4. Ibid, *Hadis* 3:131.
5. Ibid, *Hadis* 3:129.
6. Ibid, *Hadis* 3:137.
7. Qur'an 2:183-84.
8. Qur'an 2:185.
9. *Sahih Al-Bukhari, Hadis* 3:118; *Sahih Muslim, Hadis* 2568.
10. *Sahih Al-Bukhari, Hadis* 3:120; *Sahih Muslim, Hadis* 2569.
11. *Sahih Muslim, Hadis* 2570.
12. *Sahih Al-Bukhari, Hadis* 3:129.
13. *Sahih Al-Bukhari, Hadis* 3:164; *Sahih Muslim, Hadis* 2488.
14. *Sahih Al-Bukhari, Hadis* 3:165-66.
15. Ibid, *Hadis* 3:167.
16. Ibid, *Hadis* 3:173-74.
17. *Sahih Muslim, Hadis* 2549.
18. Ibid, *Hadis* 2552.
19. Ibid, *Hadis* 2238.
20. Ibid, note 387.
21. Ibid, *Hadis* 2486.
22. Ibid, *Hadis* 2552.
23. Ibid, *Ahadis* 2587-2599.
24. Ibid, *Ahadis* 2600-2606.
25. *Sahih Muslim, Ahadis* 2607-2608.
26. Ibid, *Hadis* 2522.
27. Ibid, *Hadis* 2499.
28. Ibid, *Hadis* 2573.
29. *Sahih Al-Bukhari, Hadis* 3:149; *Sahih Muslim, Ahadis* 2436-2450.
30. *Sahih Muslim*, Note 1502.
31. Qur'an 2:187.
32. *Sahih Al-Bukhari, Hadis* 3:139.
33. *Sahih Muslim, Hadis* 2454.
34. Ibid, *Ahadis* 2451-2456.
35. *Sahih Al-Bukhari, Hadis* 3:154.
36. Ibid, *hadis* 3:157; *Sahih Muslim. Hadis* 2457.
37. Muir, op. cit., p. cii.

The Epilogue

Strength and Weaknesses of Islam

A casual perusal of Islamic history clearly shows its inner strength, as well as its weaknesses. Both, solidarity and conflict is in-built in Islam. But solidarity mechanism, as we will see, has two way operations. Prophet Muhammad, in a *Hadis*, said that he was helped by the terror and the treasure given to him.[1] While these two factors—terror and *malgenimat*, the war-booty—worked within for intra-societal solidification, the same factors also worked for intra-Islamic divide.

Strength of Islam

Islam makes new man and new society. It is an excellent bridge-breaker; the new Muslims break away from their past (*Jahiliya*) and their parent society. Once converted to Islam, its greatest enemies become its pillars of strength. Take the case of Afghanistan and Pakistan, which were once the bitterest resisters of Islam, but now the Af-Pak region is the most supportive of fundamentalist Islam. Islam took less than a century to become bigger imperial entity than the erstwhile Rome. But it took five to six hundred years to break the Hindu-Buddhist barrier of Af-Pak and enter India. Ideology, however, brought the change; its one-time toughest resisters have become its strongest supporters. With the new ideology and new mindset, new men have emerged, leading to continental shift.

There are numerous cases, showing that the break of old kinship and social ties, for a new one as a member of Islamic *Umma,* brought attitudinal change, due to inner strength of Islam. Abu Na'ila, foster brother of Ka'b killed him;[2] The Muslim Muhayyisa told his pagan brother Huwayyisa that he may kill him also if the Prophet wished so.[3] The son of Abdullah ibn Ubayy, an *ansar* hypocrite, told Muhammad, "If you really want him (his father) killed, command me to do it and I will bring you his head."[4] There are other such cases also, such as, Abu Hozayfa, an emigrant to Medina, helped Hamza to kill his own father in the battle of Badr.[5] Qur'an prohibited Sa'd, son of Abi Waqqas, from obeying his parents, if they stood for polytheism.[6] Solidarity of the Hindu converts to Islam, such as Kala Pahar, Malik Kafur and Suhabhatta, for the cause of Islam, and what they did against Hindu society, is well-known and need no elaboration.

Islam, like other Semitic belief systems, gives new identity to its adherents. It gives a new identity in 'real forefathers,' rather than in the 'tribal ones;' and that identity is tenacious and strong, which, in turn, gives Islam tremendous inner strength. Lesley Hazleton is of the view "that a man orphaned before he was born would be more than willing to abandon the ways of the fathers." And, "However intentionally, Muhammad's immediate ancestors had let him down, leaving him adrift when the whole point of his culture was to be well moored. But what he was preaching now went far beyond matters of personal identity. Like that other prophet six centuries earlier and far to the north in Galilee, he was calling on his people to transcend the traditional ties of family clan, and tribe, and to unite in the renewed loyalty to the one God."[7]

"I am come to set a man at variance with his father," Jesus had said. "If any man come to me and hate not his father, and mother, and wife, and children, and brethren, and sisters, yea and his own life also, he can not be my follower." And now Muhammad was saying essentially the same. The Meccans faced losing everything "if your fathers, your sons, your brothers, your wives, your clan, the possessions you have gained, and the commerce you fear losing, the dwellings you love—if all these are dearer to you than to strive in the way of Allah." Those who accepted Islam were the true brothers and sisters, a new family that superseded the old, crossing all established boundaries to find its identity in the real forefathers: not the tribal ones, but the original founding figures of monotheism, Abraham and Moses.[8]

The point in the case of the new identity in the framework of Islam, as well as in the cases of Christianity and Judaism, which needs mention, is that whereas the new identity worked excellently against its opponents, in matters of intra-Islamic solidarity, it proved to be most fragile. The Muslims and the Christians have fought more intra-community wars than with the others. The reason of the same is that the material factor of identity formation was more important than the spiritual one.

When just after the death of Prophet Muhammad, there was rebellion in Arabia against the very faith of Islam, by a master-stroke of policy decision of giving benefit of the plunder of war to the tribal communities, not only the rebellion was brought under control, but the pace of onward journey of Islamic imperialism was highly accelerated. Needless to say that war-booty highly strengthened Islamic *Umma*, but it proved to be a double-edged sword. Muslims often quarrelled for booty,[9] and Muhammad had to pacify his followers; the Prophet had to handle dissatisfaction, and gain hearts by satisfying his followers by material incentives and sharing the gain.[10] Gaining hearts (*mullafa qulubhum*) for Islam with the help of gifts had even the Quranic sanction.[11]

The Weaknesses

As mentioned above, conflict is in-built in Islam; it started showing its face just after the death of the Prophet. As soon as Muhammad died, there were three groups, each seeking power. Ansars started their meeting to elect their leader; Ali and Abbas, who were preparing grave in the house of Ayesha, and not allowing anyone in the room, had their own design. Abu Bakr and Umar formed the third group. Umar had to threaten the Ansar, on one hand, and, Ali on the other, to secure caliphate for Abu Bakr.

Out of the first four caliphs, only Abu Bakr had a natural death; three others—Umar, Uthman and Ali—were assassinated. Out of twelve Imams, eleven did not have natural death. Except Ali, who was assassinated during Arabian Civil War, and Husain killed in Battle of Karbala, all the remaining ones were killed by poisoning.

After the Arabian Civil War, and assassination of Ali, Muawiya came to power, seat of caliphate was shifted to Baghdad from Medina. Calph Muawiya's son, Yajid got the descendants of Prophet Muhammad massacred.

Intra-Islamic Conflict and Violence

Prophet Muhammad was the best judge of human nature. He knew the internal weaknesses of man for wealth and power. According to Sahih Bukhari, he feared intra-Islamic fight.[12] Yet another *Hadis* also predicted the same. According to that *Hadis*, Muhammad asked Allah three things, and Allah granted him two only. What was not granted by Allah was his wish that there should be no bloodshed among the people of his *Ummah*. Muhammad said: "I asked my Lord three things and he has granted me two but has withheld one. I begged my Lord that my *Ummah* should not be destroyed because of famine and He granted me this. And I begged my Lord that my *Ummah* should not be destroyed by drowning (by deluge) and He granted me this. And I begged my Lord that there should be no bloodshed among the people of my *Ummah*, but he did not grant me."[13] What the *Hadis* said is confirmed by the Islamic history. Prophet Muhammad, being the best judge of the human nature, was fully aware of the human weaknesses responsible for the intra-Islamic conflicts, wars and bloodshed. The *ahadis* regarding the 'mischief of Satan in the Muslim Society and sending his detachments for the creation of turmoil, and there is a Devil attached to every person' point towards the same weaknesses of man.[14] One of the ahadis, narrated by Ayesha, the wife of the Prophet, also says the same. She said: One day Allah's Messenger came out of her (apartment) during the night and she felt jealous. "Then he came and he saw me (in what agitated state of mind) I was. He said: Ayesha, what has happened to you? Do you feel jealous? Thereupon she said: How can it be (that a woman like me) should not feel jealous in regard to a husband like you? Thereupon Allah's Messenger said: It was your devil who had come to you, and she said: Allah's Messenger, is there along with me a devil? He said: Yes. I ('Ayesha) again said: Allah's Messenger, is it with you also? He said: Yes, but my Lord has helped me against him and as such I am absolutely safe from his mischief."[15]

Yes, the basic human weaknesses are the devils with or within the individuals, and every society developed mechanism to get rid of the same. The Islam's prescription to get rid of the same is the fear of Hell-Fire. While killing unbelievers is meritorious in Islam; it wins paradise for the believers; killing a Muslim is heinous and earns the punishment of hell-fire. A Hadis says: "When two Muslims confront each other with their swords, both the slayer and the slain are doomed to Hell-Fire."[16] As discussed elsewhere, the Prophet never killed even his worst enemy or the worst critic, once he presented himself before the Prophet as a Muslims. But, inspite of the scriptural prohibitions, the Muslims continued to kill each other; the reason was lust of power and wealth. Muir has written about the lust of plunder among the Muslims.

Lust of Plunder

Lust for plunder worked against the inner unity of Islam, as there was a tendency even to kill a Muslim for the same. Muir has written: "The warlike spirit of the Suras of this period has been perhaps sufficiently illustrated in the preceding chapters. I may just refer to one passage which is peculiarly demonstrative of the lust of plunder which had been stirred up, and which (so natural was it to the Arab) the Prophet soon found it difficult to restrain within expedient bounds. Only those could be lawfully slain and plundered who were *disbelievers* in his mission; but so insatiable had the thirst for spoil become, that cases now occurred of Muslims slaying others who had made profession of the Mohammadan faith, on the pretext that they were insincere Believers. Stringent prohibition was required to guard against this abuse. Whoever trifled with the life of any one professing Islam, did so at the peril of his soul. After prescribing the penalty or penance for killing a Muslim unintentionally, the ordinance proceeds:"[17]

"If anyone kills a believer deliberately, the punishment for him is Hell, and there he will remain: Allah is angry with him, and rejects him, and has prepared a tremendous torment for him. So you who believe, be careful when you go to fight in Allah's way, and do not say to someone who offers you a greeting of peace, 'You are not a believer,' out of desire for the chance gains of this life—Allah has plenty of gains for you. You yourself were in the same position (once), but Allah was gracious to you, so be careful; Allah is fully aware of what you do."[18]

Ensuring Solidarity Within the Ummah

Prophet Muhammad was conscious of the need of maintaining solidarity of the Islamic *Ummah* for which he advised Muslims to follow single leadership. An *ahadi* says: "When you are holding to one single man as your leader, you should kill him who seeks to undermine your solidarity or disrupt your unity."[19] According to another *Hadis*, "Anyone who tries to disrupt the affairs of this *Ummah* while they are united you should strike him with the sword."[20] The next Hadis[21] also enjoins the same: "Kill him." For eliminating the root cause of conflict, the same thing is said about the Khalifas. As Muhammad said that there will be no Prophet after him, but only the Khalifas, someone asked him as what to do when there are more than one Khalifas? He said: The one to whom allegiance is sworn first has supremacy over the others.[22] It further enjoined: "When oath of allegiance has been taken for two Khaliphas, kill the one for whom the allegiance was taken later."[23] Umar, the second Khalifa, while on his deathbed, followed the above mentioned injunctions, while laying down the guiding principles for the selection of the next Khalifa. He appointed a six-member elector council and the following principles to be followed by them:

i. The person elected unanimously was to be designated as the next Khalifa.
ii. In case there was no unanimity, then the person supported by the majority was to be designated as the Khalipha, and the dissenters were to be immediately killed.
iii. In case there was equal division, then the deciding vote was to be that of 'Abdullah bin 'Umar, his own son and one of the six electors.

The perusal of the above mentioned procedure for the selection of caliph clearly by shows that the fear of internal strife was the reason for the same and even one of the topmost functionary of Islam faced the probability of being assassinated. The divide between alides and others, leading to Shia and

Sunni sects of Islam was the development, whose roots may be found only in the intra-Islamic divide based only on personality clash. The property disputes involving Fatima, and another between Ali and Abbas, are well known.

The Sufis were the Muslim mystics. The root cause of Sufism was the mystic input, as it has happened in case of the Gnostic Christianity.

References

1. *Sahih Muslim, Hadis.*
2. Muir, Sir William, *The Life of Mahomet*, p. 247; hereafter Muir.
3. Ibn Ishaq, *Sirat Rasul Allah*, p. 752; hereafter Ibn Ishaq.
4. The story is given in *Sirat Rasul Allah* of Ibn Ishaq, and repeated in Tabari.
5. Ram Swarup, *Understanding Islam through Hadis*, p. 190.
6. Qur'an 29:8; 31:15.
7. Lesley Hazleton, *The First Muslim*, p. 107, hereafter Hazleton.
8. Ibid.
9. Ibn Ishaq, p. 307.
10. *Sahih Muslim, ahadis* 2300, 2303-14, 231.
11. Qur'an 9:60.
12. *Sahih Bukhari*, *Hadis* 2:428.
13. *Sahih Muslim*, *Hadis* 6906.
14. Ibid, *ahadis* 6752-6759.
15. Ibid, *Hadis* 6759.
16. Ibid, *Hadis* 6899.
17. Muir, p. 338.
18. Qur'an 4:93-94.
19. *Sahih Muslim*, *Hadis* 4567.
20. Ibid, *Hadis* 4565.
21. Ibid, *Hadis* 4566.
22. Ibid, *Hadis* 4543.
23. Ibid, *Hadis* 4568.

Islamic Appropriation of Ka'ba and its Worship

The conquest of Mecca became the political necessity of Prophet Muhammad, and eventually he did it. But, that was not enough. The appropriation of the sacred temple of Ka'ba became equally necessary for the Islam to be readily accepted by the Arabs, and especially by the Quraysh of Mecca. A parallel of this phenomenon may be found in the adoption of eastern spiritual values by Christianity, and there by changing into Gnostic Christianity, whose traces may be found in the Gospels of Matthew and Jones as against the Pauline Christianity. Of course, this happened with a difference. Whereas Christianity tried to purge and get rid of the elements of eastern spirituality, Islam had to partially accept the Pagan Arabic elements.

Islamic Appropriation of the Temple

Prophet Muhammad did two things after the conquest of Mecca; firstly, he placed the temple in the Semitic legendary frame-work by associating the temple, and even the Arab people with Abraham; secondly, the main item of worship, the Black Stone, and partially, the Pagan mode of worship was also retained. Thus, although Islam appropriated Ka'ba, it had to compromise in doing so. The Black Stone remained the focal point of veneration, and most of the rituals related to pilgrimage continued to be Pagan. The statement of Umar, about the Black Stone of Ka'ba, makes it clear that the view point of Muslim theology, rather the whole idea of pilgrimage of Mecca and the Ka'ba is idolatrous. Umar came near the Black Stone and kissed it and said, "No doubt, I know that you are a stone and can neither harm anyone nor benefit anyone. Had I not seen Allah's Messenger kissing you I would not have kissed you."[1] Margoliouth also writes about the Muslim opposition of Ka'ba to the extent that they even wanted to destroy it. He writes: "and since Mohammed's followers prayed toward another sanctuary and no longer kissed the Black Stone, it could be inferred that he wanted to destroy the Ka'ba; and indeed till a late period in his career there were Muslims who wished for its destruction."[2] However, the practical sense of the Prophet came in its way, and an early revelation ensured the place of the Temple in Islam, and its safety. Margoliouth writes: "An early revelation seems intended to reassure the Meccans on this point; and Mohammed whose practical sense never deserted him, was careful to find a place for the Ka'ba in his system.[3]

The ceremony part was also adopted with slight modification. Circumambulation of the deity, or even the sacred region, using unstitched pair of white cloths during pilgrimage, shaving the hair, paring nails, use of water for body purification, taking bath for purity of body before prayer and pilgrimage, are the parts of ceremonial rites which Hindus still practiced and shared with Arabian Pagans. Muir writes about the retention and prevalence of the earlier Pagan ceremonies during Islamic pilgrimage. He writes: "The ceremonies of the pilgrimage thus handed down by Kosai were substantially the same as we find them in the time of Mohammad; and, with some modifications introduced by Mohammad himself, the same as practiced at the present day. The centre of them all is the Ka'ba, to visit which, to kiss the Black Stone imbedded in the eastern corner, and to make seven circuits round the sacred edifice, is at all times and seasons meritorious."[4]

Sura 22 (The Pilgrimage) threatens to punish the disbelievers, who bar others "from the sacred mosque–which we made for all people, residents and outsiders alike."[5] It further says: "We showed Abraham the site of the House, saying, 'Do not assign partner to Me. Purify My House for those who circle around it, those who stand to pray, and those who bow and prostrate themselves. Proclaim the Pilgrimage to all people. They will come to you on foot and on every kind of lean camel, emerging from every deep mountain pass to attain benefits and mention Allah's name, on specified days, over livestock He has provided for them. Feed yourself and the desperately poor from them. Then let the pilgrims perform their acts of cleansing, fulfil their vows, and circle around the Ancient House. All this (is ordained by Allah): anyone who honours the sacred ordinances of Allah will have good rewards from Allah."[6] The *Sura* refers to the sacrificial animals and the place of sacrifice near the Ancient House.[7] Incidentally, it may be mentioned that *Sahih Bukhari* mentions about the demolition of Ka'ba by *Dhus-Suwaiqatain* (One with two thin legs) from Ethiopia.[8]

After Mecca was conquered, the idols of pagan gods and goddesses were destroyed, and the entry of the pagans was banned in the temple. That necessitated Abrahmic linkages with the site and the construction of Ka'ba. Qur'an mentions such linkages.

At first, Prophet Muhammad wanted the Jews and the Christians to be his followers. Islam is an Abrahamic religion; the fundamentals of the three religions are the same. The *qibla* of Islam continued to be Jerusalem for quite some time. But, as Jews and Christians did not accept to be his followers, the inevitable change came; Mecca became the *qibla* for the Muslims. But the Muslim belief attributed both—history of Mecca and the origin of Ka'ba—both to Abraham, and the ceremonial, of course, only partially, to Biblical legend. Muir questions such linkages. He writes: "In reviewing the history of Mecca, the origin of the temple and of the local worship demands further scrutiny. Muslim belief attributes both to Abraham, and connects part of the ceremonial with Biblical legend; but the story is plainly a fable. The following considerations strengthen the conviction that Mecca and its rites can not possibly claim any such origin. *First,*—there is no trace of anything Abrahamic in the essential elements of the superstition. To kiss the Black Stone; to make the circuit of the Ka'ba, and perform other observances at Mecca, Arafat, and the vale of Mina; to keep the sacred months and to hallow the sacred territory—have no conceivable connection with Abraham, or with the ideas which his descendants, would be likely to inherit from him. Such rites originated in causes foreign to the country chiefly occupied by the children of Abraham; they were strictly local; or, in so far as based on the idolatry prevailing in the south, were imported by immigrants from the Yemen."[9]

Muir searches a second cause in the remote antiquity of Ka'ba. He writes: "*Second,*—A very high antiquity must be assigned to the main features of the religion of Mecca. Although Herodotus does not refer to the Ka'ba, yet he names one of the chief Arab divinities, ALILAT; and this is strong evidence of the worship at that early period of Al-Lat, the great idol of Mecca. He likewise alludes to the veneration of the Arabs for stones. Diodorus Siculus, writing about half a century before our era, says of Arabia washed by the Red Sea, 'there is, in this country, a temple greatly revered by the Arabs.' These words must refer to the Holy House of Mecca, for we know of no other which ever commanded such universal homage. Early *historical* tradition gives no trace of its first construction. Some authorities assert that Amalekites rebuilt the edifice, which they found in ruins, and retained it for a time under their charge. All agree that it was in existence under the Jurhum tribe (about the time of Christian era), and, and being injured by a flood of rain, was then repaired. Tradition represents the Ka'ba as from time immemorial the scene of pilgrimage from all quarters of Arabia:—from the Yemen and Hadramaut, from the shores of the Persian gulf, the deserts of Syria, and distant environs of Al-Hira and Mesopotamia, men yearly flocked to Mecca. So extensive a homage must have had its beginnings in an extremely remote age; and a similar antiquity must be ascribed to the essential concomitants of the local worship—the Ka'ba with its Black Stone, the sacred territory, and the holy months. The origin of a superstition so ancient and so universal must be looked for within the peninsula itself, and not in any foreign country."[10]

Muir bases his submission on yet another factor. He rightly traces the native religious system of Arabia, but viewing it wrongly from Christian angle. He writes: "*Third*,—The native systems of Arabia were Sabeanism, Idolatry, and Stone-worship—all closely connected with the religion of Mecca. There is reason for believing that *Sabeanism*, or the worship of the heavenly bodies, existed from an early period in Arabia. The book of Job contains historical notices of the system, and contain early names in the Himyar dynasty imply its prevalence. As late as the fourth century, we find sacrifices offered in the Yemen to the sun, moon, and stars. The seven circuits of the Ka'ba were probably emblematical of the revolutions of the planetary bodies; and we are told that a similar rite was observed in other Arabian fans. And again the practice of idolatry overspread the whole peninsula. We have authentic record of ancient idol shrines scattered in various quarters from Yemen to Duma and even as far as Al-Hira, some of them subordinate to the Ka'ba and having similar rites."[11]

Muir informs and analyses correctly about the time depth, and linkages of the Arabs before their adoption of Islam. He, however, carries all the weaknesses which Christianity and colonialism imposes on him. For him, a Semitic blind faith is sacred belief, but a similar Pagan phenomenon is superstition and gross idolatry. Muir is certainly the best Western Arabist Islamic scholar, but like most of them, never pushes the boundary of his inquiry to the east and north; actually. He should have extended the area of inquiry of the Sabeanism, idolatry and stone worship in extended continuum frame, and found that Arabs, like Indians, were worshipping the deities inside the sun, moon, stars, idols, and the stones, rather than these material items. Unfortunately, the Semitic bias, terror of their God, basic incapacity of the Christian mind, makes them thoroughly incapable of understanding the same.

Ibn Ishaq writes about 'Amr, son of Lubayy, who was the first, according to the prevailing legend, to change the religion of Ishmael to set up idols, and institute the custom of the bahira, sa'iba, wasila, and hami; and Prophet Muhammad saw him "dragging his intestine in hell."[12]

Ibn Ishaq writes about the introduction of stone worship also. He writes: "They say that the beginning of stone worship among the sons of Ishmael was when Mecca became too small for them and they wanted more room in the country. Everyone who left the town took with him a stone from the sacred area to do honour to it. Wherever they settled they set it up and walked round it as they went round the Ka'ba. This led them to worship what stones they pleased and those which made an impression on them. Thus as generations passed they forgot their primitive faith and adopted another religion for that of Abraham and Ishmael."[13] Clearly, what Ibn Ishaq writes is about the spread of stone worship, and not of its origin.

The source of population and the Pagan mode of worship—polytheism, Sabeanism, idolatry, stone worship—was Aden. But sprinkling of the population was certainly Abrahmic. The overlapping of the two traditions must have taken centuries before the birth of Islam, which needs in-depth study.

While concluding, it may be safely accepted that there are many legends related to Ka'ba; it had its existence since deep antiquity; and Islam's acceptance of Ka'ba was an unavoidable necessity for Islam. The Prophet of Islam knew that his end was coming, and he really expired soon after the "Farewell Pilgrimage."

References

1. *Sahih Bukhari*, *Hadis* 2:667.
2. Margoliouth, p. 120.
3. Ibid.
4. Muir, *The Life of Mahomet*, p. ci. Hereafter Muir.
5. Qur'an 22:25.
6. Qur'an 22:27-30.
7. Qur'an 22:33.
8. *Sahih Bukhari*, *Hadis* 2:661; 2:665.
9. Muir, p. cii.
10. Ibid, pp. cii-ciii.
11. Ibid, pp. ciii-civ.
12. Ibn Ishaq, *Sirat Rasul Allah*, p. 35. Hereafter Ibn Ishaq.
13. Ibid, pp. 35-36.

Annexures

Annexure -1

Book Review in the Pioneer, New Delhi; 16 Nov.' 13

The First Muslim

B. B. Kumar

We have numerous biographies of Prophet Muhammad written by the Muslims as well as the Western scholars, many of whom were Arabists. *Sirat Rasul Allah* by ibn-Ishaq (born in Madina around the year 704, just 72 years after the death of the prophet; death in Damascus in 767 AD) and *Tarikh al-Rasul wa-al Muluk* (*History of the Prophets and the Kings*) by Abu Jafar al-Tabari (838-923 AD) were the earliest biographers of the prophet. Their biographies were based on original Islamic sources. Ibn-Ishaq's *Sira* was expanded and annotated by ibn Hisham in the ninth century in Egypt. The English translation of the same by Alfred Guillaume, *The Life of Muhammad: A Translation of Ishaq's Sirat Rasul Allah* was published by Oxford University Press in 1955. Thirty-nine volume *The History of al-Tabari* has already been translated and published in English. His volumes on Muhammad's life drew heavily on ibn-Ishaq's biography and also on other early historians' writings which has not survived. The book under review (*The First Muslim: The Story of Muhammad* by Lesley Hazleton; Atlantic Books, London; 2013) is based on these original sources for the basic facts. Quotes and Dialogue in the book have been taken from eight different volumes of al-Tabari's work. She has used primarily the five different English-language translations the Quran, cross-referencing them with the original Arabic, apart from using many other secondary sources. The title of the book *The First Muslim* has been taken from Quran, which has appeared thrice in the same. Quran says: Muhammad, say, "I am the first Muslim."

The book under review has three parts covering orphanhood, exile and leadership of the prophet respectively. Overall, the book covers the story of Muhammad "how he accomplished his journey from powerlessness to power, from anonymity to renown, from insignificance to lasting significance." The book is the latest addition in the biographies of the Prophet of Islam. It differs in many ways, in approach, focus and objective in comparison to the other biographies.

The author takes the discourse to a higher level. She broadens the perspective; avoids value judgment and polemics. The book starts with quotes from Quran, and the writings of Ibn-Khaldun and Mahatma Gandhi. In the treatment of the subject, even Machiavelli figures.

Among the biographies of Muhammad written by the Westerners, apart from the one in hand, mention may be made of William Muir's *The Life of Mahomet*), D.S. Margoliouth's *Mohammed and the Rise of Islam*), *A.* Sprenger's *Life of Mohammed* (he also wrote *The Life and Doctrine of Mahomet from Sources hitherto for the most part Unused*), Maxime Rodinson's *Muhammad* and Washington Irving's *Life of Muhammad.* The books of Muir and Margoliouth, of course, were pioneer, authentic and excellent studies; both heavily relied on the original Islamic sources. Muir – whose biography in four volumes was published in 1861, an abridged edition in 1876, and third edition with important alterations in one volume in 1894 – was an outstanding Arabist and Islamist. He belonged to the highest rung of British officialdom in India. He was a believing Christian with missionary motivation behind the scholarly labour. Of course, in spite of such motivation and outlook, he did not compromise his scholarship. Muir opposed the biographies by the Missionary and some other writers for their factual inaccuracies, slipshod scholarship, hostile intent, unsympathetic treatment and uninhibited expression of opinion about the Prophet. He felt the difficulty which the Missionaries could face in getting the hearing of the Muslim by using epithets such as "a spurious faith" and "counterfeit Messieh." He emphasized the need of the statement of facts "based on sound, orthodox Muslim sources" while discussing the inaccuracies of Washington Irwing's *Life of Muhammad.* Muir disagreed with Sprenger, who regarded Muhammad as having a "weak and cunning mind." Here, it needs mention that Muir is richer in data, analysis and presentation on various dimensions and aspects of the life of Muhammad, including political aspect, in comparison to all others. Hazleton has focused more on psychological and political aspect.

Muir found that early traditions relating to the Prophet's nativity did not contain highly fanciful and extravagant fabricated traditions; he pointed out the same while discussing the biography of the Prophet, *Moulud Sharif* (The Enobled Nativity) written by Ghulam Imam Shahid, an Indian Muslim. Lasley Hazleton also, in the book under review (pp. 140-144), relies on early traditions documented by ibn-Ishaq and al-Tabari while discussing the Night Journey of the Prophet, about which the Quran (Sura 17) clearly refers: ("Glory be to God, who made his servant go by night from the sacred house to the far house, that we might show him some of our signs."), but dces not give the story. Ibn-Ishaq, in this case caries out a delicate balancing act "with considerable aplomb, stepping carefully between his duty as a believer and his obligation as a biographer. As Hazleton observes, it's "a wisely phrased abstention from certainty. Al-Tabari, on the other hand, "writing a century later in the new Muslim capital city of Baghdad, was wary as always of miracle tales and far more focused on politics," as is the case with the writer of the book under review. For her, the night journey, in its simplest form, is a miracle story.

Most biographies of Muhammad, except the hagiographical ones in which miracles abound, remarkably agree on facts. Of course the analysis and the way of looking at the facts differed. As in the case of the massacre of the Jewish tribe of Banu Quraiza by the Prophet after their surrender, the earliest Muslim biographers of impeccable orthodoxy celebrate the same with undisguised glee; the Christian scholars of the eighteenth century like Sprenger, Muir, Gustav, Weil and Osbon, treated the event with moral horror, which was, however, considerably subdued by the end of the century. Dr. David Samuel Margoliouth, publishing his biography in 1900, took it as a matter of fact. Maxime Rodinson, the author of *Muhammad* written in 1960s, justifies it "from a purely political point of view" According to him Muhammad had his compulsions and "the massacre was an extremely wise move".

After the massacre, as analyzed by Lesley Hazleton in *The First Muslim*, Muhammad was in full control of Madinan politics. With the annihilation of their allies, the *munafiqun* (hypocrites) were totally subdued. By undermining Ibn-Ubayy by challenging his ability to protect his allies, Muhammad demonstrated his ruthlessness, power and authority and ibn-Ubayy's lack of the same. It needs mention that The break with the Jews was already complete after the change of *Qibla* from Jerusalem to Makka, and departure of two thousand Qaynuqas (Jews) having business ties with Makka after the Market incident. With the irony – "the exiles had now in turn exiled others" – the *Muhajirun* (emigrants from Makka) became rich and were no more dependent on *Ansars* (helpers from Medina). The Prophet could further exhibit his ruthlessness and became unchallenged after getting the pithiest wordsmiths, harassing him by their satire, the poets of Arabia – Asma, Abu-Afak, ibn- Ashraf and Hassan ibn-Thabit – massacred one by one. Here, it needs mention that Madina was not free from inter-tribal conflict between Aws and Khazraj with Jews as ally, when Muhammad migrated there.

Muir, like Lesley Hazleton, used original sources, as he wanted to present his biography written from rational point of view to "thinking Mohammedans" with the fond hope that they would come to prefer Christianity to their own faith. Sayyid Ahmed, however, wrote his own biography of the Prophet in reply of Muir, and argued whether the same yardstick of rationality should not be applied in the case of biblical miracles of Moses and Jesus.

The Chinese writer, Sun Tzu wrote *The Art of War* in which he declared: "War is deception." The same strategy was adopted by Muhammad, when he declared: "Make sure they abandon each other, for war is deception." Islam emerged when two great powers – Byzantium and Iranians – "fought each other to exhaustion, creating a vast vacuum of power in the Middle East. Strategic location of Medina, 200 miles south of Macca in the trade route of Syria was disadvantageous for Macca. The battle of Badr and subsequent raids were strategically advantageous for the Muslims. Moreover, there was unprecedented flow of money from raids on the non-believers, and all who joined Islam were made partners in the same. Hazleton has ably discussed some of these factors.

Qur'an: Makki and Medinan Suras

Arabic Title	English Title	Meccan or Madini
1. *Al-Fatiha*	The Opening	
2. *Al-baqara*	The Cow, or the Heifer	Medinan.
3. *Al-'Imran*	The Family of Imran	Medinan
4. *Al-Nisa*	Woman	Medinan
5. *Al-Ma'ida*	The Feast	Medinan
6. *Al-In'am*	Livestock	Meccan
7. *Al-A'raf*	The Heights	Meccan
8. *Al-Anfal*	Battle Gains; The Spoils	Medinan
9. *Al-Tawba,* or *Baraat*	Repentance	Medinan
10. Yunus	Jonah	Meccan
11. Hud	Hud	Meccan
12. Joseph	Yusuf	Meccan
13. *Al-Ra'd*	Thunder	Medinan
14. Ibrahim	Abraham	Meccan
15. *Al-Hijr*	Al-Hijr?	Meccan
16. *Al-Nahl*	The Bee	Meccan
17. *Al-Isra'*	The Night Journey	Meccan
18. *Al-Kahf*	The Cave	Meccan
19. Maryam	Mary	Meccan
20. Ta Ha	Ta Ha	Meccan
21. *Al-Anbiya'*	The Prophets	Meccan
22. *Al-Hajj*	The Pilgrimage	Medinan
23. *Al-Mu'minun*	The Believers	Meccan
24. *Al-Nur*	Light	Medinan
25. *Al-Furqan*	The Differentiator	Meccan
26. *Al-Shu'ara'*	The Poets	Meccan
27. *Al-Naml*	The Ants	Meccan
28. *Al-Qasas*	The Story	Meccan
29. *Al-'Ankabut*	The Spider	Meccan
30. Al-Rum	The Byzantines	Meccan
31. Luqman	Luqman	Meccan

32. *Al-Sajda*	Bowing Down in Worship	Meccan
33. *Al-Ahzab*	The Joint Forces; Confederates	Medinan
34. Saba'	Sheba	Meccan
35. *Fatir*	The Creator	Meccan
36 Ya Sin	Ya Sin	Meccan
37. *Al-Saffat*	Ranged in Rows	Meccan
38. Saad	Saad	Meccan
39. *Al-Zumar*	The Throngs	Meccan
40. *Al-Ghafir*	The Forgiver	Meccan
41. *Fussilat*	Made Clear (Verses)	Meccan
42. *Al-Shura*	The Consultation	Meccan
43. *Al-Zukhruf*	The Gold Ornaments	Meccan
44. *Al-Dukhan*	The Smoke	Meccan
45. *Al-Jathiya*	Kneeling	Meccan
46. *Al-Abqaf*	The Sand Dunes	Meccan
47. Muhammad	Muhammad	Medinan
48. *Al Fath*	The Triumph	Medinan
49. *Al-Hujurat*	The Private rooms	
50. Qaaf	Qaaf	Meccan
51. *Al-Dhariyat*	Scattering (Winds)	Meccan
52. *Al-Tur*	The Mountain	Meccan
53. *Al-Nazm*	The Star	Meccan
54. *Al-Qamar*	The Moon	Meccan
55. *Al-Rahman*	The Lord of Mercy	Medinan
56. *Al-Waki'a*	That which is coming	Meccan
57. *Al-Hadid*	The Iron	Medinan
58. *Al-Mujadal*	The Dispute	Medinan
59. *Al Hashr*	The Gathering (of forces)	Medinan
60. *Al-Mumtahan*	The Woman Tested	Medinan
61. *Al-Saff*	Solid Lines	Medinan
62. *Al-Jumu'a*	The Day of Congregation	Medinan
63. *Al-Munafiqun*	The Hypocrites	Medinan
64. *Al-Taghbun*	Mutual neglect	Medinan
65. *Al-Talaq*	Divorce	Medinan
66. *Al-Tahrim*	Prohibition	Medinan
67. *Al-Mulk*	Control	Meccan
68. *Al-Qalam*	The Pen	Meccan

69. *Al-Haqqa*	The Inevitable hour	Meccan
70. *Al-Ma'arij*	The Ways of Ascent	Meccan
71. Nuh	Noah	Meccan
72. *Al-Jinn*	The Jinn	Meccan
73. *Al-Muzzammil*	Enfolded	Medinan
74. *Al-Muddaththir*	Wrapped in his Cloak	Meccan
75. *Al-Qiyama*	The Resurrection	Meccan
76. *Al-Insan*	Man	Medinan
77. *Al-Mursalat*	Sent Forth (Winds)	Meccan
78. *Al-Naba'*	The Announcement	Meccan
79. *Al-Nazi'at*	The Forceful Charges	Meccan
80. *'Abasa*	He Frowned	Meccan
81. *Al-Takwir*	The Rolling Up	Meccan
82. *Al-Infitar*	The breaking	Meccan
83. *Al-Mutaffifin*	Those Who Give Short Measure	Meccan
84. *Al-Inshiqaq*	The Cracking	Meccan
85. *Al-Buruj*	The Towering Constellations	Meccan
86. *Al-Tariq*	The Night Commet	Meccan
87. *Al-A'la*	The Most High	Meccan
88. *Al-Ghashiya*	The Overwhelming Event	Meccan
89. *A;-Fajr*	Daybreak	Meccan
90. *Al-Balad*	The City	Meccan
91. *Al-Shams*	The Sun	Meccan
92. *Al-Layl*	The Night	Meccan
93. *Al-Duba*	The Morning Brightness	Meccan
94. *Al-Sharh*	Belief	Meccan
95. *Al-Tin*	The Fig	Meccan
96. *Al-'Alaq*	The Clinging Form	Meccan
97. *Al-Qadr*	The Night of Glory	Meccan
98. *Al-Bayyina*	The Clear Evidence	Medinan
99. *Al-Zalzala*	The Earthquake	Medinan
100. *Al-;Adiyat*	The Charging Steeds	Meccan
101. *Al-Qari'a*	The Crushing Blow	Meccan
102. *Al-Takathur*	Competing for More	Meccan
103. *Al-'Asr*	The Fading Day	Meccan
104. *Al-Humaza*	The Bachbiter	Meccan
105. *Al-Fil*	The Elephant	—

106. Quraysh	Quraish	Meccan
107. *Al-Ma'un*	Common Kindnesses	Meccan
108. *Al-Kawthar*	Abundance	Meccan
109. *Al-Kafirun*	The Disbelievers	—
110. *Al-Nasr*	The Help	Medinan
111. *Al-Masad*	Palm Fibre	Meccan
112. *Al-Ikhlas*	Purity of Faith	—
113. *Al-Falaq*	Daybreak?	Meccan
114. *Al-Nas*	The People	Meccan

Islam – Early Period: A Chronology

AD 570 Birth of Muhammad (after the death of his father)
576 Death of Muhammad's mother
578 Death of Muhammad's Grandfather
595 Muhammad marries Khadija
610 First revelation of the Qur'an
615 Migration of the Muslims to Abyssinia
615 'Umar's conversion to Islam
619 Death of Khadija and Abu Talib
620 Prophet's Night Journey to Jerusalem
622 Migration (*Hijra*) to Medina; beginning of Islamic calendar
624 Battle of Badr
625 Battle of Uhud
627 Battle of Trench
628 Treaty of Hudaybiya
630 Truce broken; Capture of Mecca
630 Battle of Hunayn
631 Expedition to Tabuk
631 The Year of Embassies
632 Prophet's Farewell Pilgrimage to Mecca
632 Death of the Prophet
633 Collection of the Qur'an in one volume under the Caliphate of Abu-Bakr
645 'Uthman commissions copies of the Qur'an to be made and circulated

Some Names Used in Qur'an and Bible

Name in Quran	–	Bible
Adam	–	Adam
Ayyub	–	Job
Daud	–	David
Firaun	–	Pharaoh
Hawwa	–	Eve
Harun	–	Aaron
Ibrahim	–	Abraham
Idris	–	Enoch
Iesa	–	Jesus
Ishaque	–	Isaac
Ismail	–	Ishmael
Jibrael	–	Gabriel
Lout	–	Lot
Maryam	–	Mary
Musa	–	Moses
Saleh	–	Salih
Sulaiman	–	Solomon
Yaqub	–	Jacob
Yunus	–	Jonah, Jonas
Yusuf	–	Joseph

A Note on Arabic Personal Names

Arabians used tc have a real and an honorific name, called *Kuniya.* The honorific way of calling a person 'as father or mother of so and so' is called Kuniya. This practice is widely prevalent even in India, though, it is diminishing now-a-days. While using the honorific name, a person calls a man, 'O father of so and so,' and to a woman, he calls, 'O mother of so and so.' *Kuniya*, likewise, addresses on as 'son or daughter of so and so.' For this the term 'Abu-' is prefix for father and 'Um-' for mother. In many cases, the honorific names became so popular that real names were almost forgotten. Some examples of such names are given below:

Abu Talib - Father of Talib; he was uncle of Prophet Muhammad, and father of Ali; we find only *kuniya* is used in Islamic literature.
Abu Sufyan - Father of Sufyan.
Abu Bakr - Father of maiden (Ayesha; wife of Muhammad)
Abu Lahab - Father of Lahab (father of flames; Muhammad's uncle)
Abu Hanzal - Father of Hanzal
Abu Hodheifa - Father of Hodheifa.
Um Habiba - Mother of Habiba; she was wife of Muhammad.
Um Kulthum - Mother of Kulthum; she was wife of Muhammad.
Um Selama - Mother of Selama; wife of Muhammad.

Some times, article 'al' or simply '-l' is inserted before the name of the father or mother, as for example:

Abu'l-Qasim - Father of the Qasim (Abu-al-Qasim; Qasim was the son of Prophet Muhammad, who died during childhood.)

Such way of calling is applied to a son or daughter also. In that case, for the identity of a son, the prefix 'bin' (son of; in short 'b.') or 'Ibn' (son of) is prefixed before the name of the father by the son, and 'bint-' (daughter of) by the daughter. This custom was in such currency in Arabia that the real names of many persons were almost forgotten, or became obscure. As for example, We may take the names of Abu Bakr; whose real name was Attiq, and full name Attiq bin-Uthman or Attiq ibn Uthman (Usman). His previous name was Abdu'l Ka'bah (meaning, Ka'ba's slave), Muhammad changed it to 'Abdu'llah ibn Abi Quhafa (Abdu'llah, son of Abi Quhafa). He, however, came to be popularly known as Abu Bakr ('father of the young camel;'[1] 'father of the maiden') The word 'Siddiq,' i.e., 'truthful,' was also added to his name, due to obvious reason. His name is also Attiq ibn Uthman (Attiq, son of Uthman) Thus, the single person may have multiple names, and such thing we really find in the Islamic literature. Interesting picture emerges, if we elaborate the possible nomenclature of the single person, Abu bakr. His all possible name may be:

i. Real name – Attiq;
ii. Popular name – Abu Bakr;
iii. Another name – Abu'l Ka'bah;
iv. Changed name – Abdu'llah;
v. Name with kuniya – Attiq ibn Uthman;
vi. Name attached with *kuniya* of father – Abdu'llah ibn Abi Kuhafa;
vii. Aquired name –Siddiq

A person may have more names may *kuniya* of son, rather than that of father is used for fuller identity. Ibn Ishaq in his *Sirat Rasul Allah,* usually adds the names of grandfather, or even longer genealogy in the kuniya.

When we find a person, being referred by different names then those who do not know get confused. Difficulty, however, does not arise, whether a person is referred by his real name or *koniya*, when he is well known. The Prophet Muhammas, Umar and Ali are mostly known by their real names; similarly, Abu Bakr and Ibn Ishaq are known only by their *koniya*. They are mostly known by one name, and the people hardly know the other. Ibn Ishaq in his Sirat Rasul Allah mostly used real name joined with the *koyina*. Ibn Ishaq (son of Ishaq), is mostly known by his honorific name (*koyina*); very few knew his real name 'Muhammad' or used full name 'Muhammad Ibn Ishaq' (Muhammad, son of Ishaq). Al-Wakidi and Ibn Sa'd were the names usually popular, and used in the literature, rather than the personal name of both of them was Muhammad, or their full names 'Muhammad ibn 'Omar Al Wakidi' (Muhammad, son of 'Omar al-Wakidi) and Muhammad Ibn Sa;d (Muhammad, son of Sa'd) respectively. Al-Wakidi, of course, is neither rhis real name, nor his honorific name.

As discussed above, when a son, named Kasim (Qasim), was born to Prophet Muhammad, he acquired the name of Abu'l Kasim (Abu al-Kasim, father of Kasim, Qasim). His uncle got the name Abu Talib, when a son, Talib was born to him. Now, Abu Talib had four sons, including Ali, but he did not acquire a name such as 'Abu Ali' or 'Abu'l Ali. Thus, here also, a pattern operates. A perusal of the nomenclature makes the point clear that either only real name such as, Muhammad, Ali, Omer, Usman, or full name, such as, Ka'b Ibn Malik (Ka'b, son of Malik), Abdullah Ibn-Ubayy (Abdullah, son of Ubayy), Zeid Ibn Haritha (Zeid, son of Haritha), Abdullah Ibn Rawahah (Abdullah, son of Rawahah), or simply *kuniya* of the persons concerned, as in the case of Ibn Ubayy (Abdallah, son of Ubayy), Asma bint Marwan (Asma, daughter of Marwan) remained popular, and in currency, as we find in the literature. In some cases, such as, Ibn Subanah (son of Subannah), Um Kulthum (mother of Kulthum), Abu Kulthum (father of Kulthum), the *Kumiya* became popular. Some times, the name acquired due to historical or other reasons also became popular. As for example, the real name, 'Al-Mughira' of Abd'l Muttalib (meaning, slave of the Muttalib) was not well-known.

Many times, we find the chain of genealogy attached to the personal name of a person. In such cases, the real name of a person was not attached to only one name, but with a chain of ancestral names starting with father's name. The following examples make the point clear. Ibn Ishaq does not identify Khadija by informing that she was daughter of Khuwaylid. Rather, he writes: Khadija was daughter of Khuwaylid b. Asad b. Abd'l-'Uzza b. Qusay b. Kilab b. Murra b. Ka'b b. Lu'ay b. Ghalib b. Fihr.[2] Similarly, about her mother, he writes: "Her mother was Fatima d. Za'ida b. al-Asamm b. Rawaha b. Hajar b. 'Abd b. Ma'is b. Amir b. Luayy b. Ghalib b. Fihr. Her mother was Hala d. Abdu Manaf b. al-Harith b. 'Amr b. Munqidh b. 'Amr b. Ma'is b. 'Amir b. Lu'ayy b. Ghalib b. Fihr. Hala's mother was Qilaba d. Su'ayb b. Sa'd b. Sahm b. 'Amr b. Husays b. Ka'b b. Lu'ayy b. Ghalib b. Fahr.[3] As Ibn Ishaq is the earliest biographer of the Prophet, it is clear that he was following the Arabic tradition of those days, which required Identity not by naming father, mother, son and daughter, but the whole ancestry.[4] Thus, a person's identity provided greater genealogical information about that person in those days.

The prefixing of the article 'Al-' with the Arabic common names, or any noun, is a common Arabic practice. Of course, the names are used without the same also, or by simply using apostrophe (') before the name. It needs mention that the use of 'Al-' makes a lah (one god) Allah (Al-Lah; the God). In cases, when initial letter of a name is a letter like R, S, Sh, T or D then these letters replaces 'l' of 'al,' as we find in the cases of Ar-Rasul; As-Saji, Az-Zuhri, Ash-Shafi, ud-Din respectively..

A large number of personal names, during pre-Islamic days, used to have 'Abd-' (slave of) prefixed to the names of Arabian deities. Names, such as, Abd al-Shams (Abdul Shams; slave of the Sun), Abd al-Uzza (Abdul Uzza; slave of goddess Uzza), Abd al-Manat (Abdul Manat; slave of the goddess Manat) lost currency except Abd al-Lah (Abdallah; Abdu'llah, Abdullah; slave or servant of the God). There are numerous examples, when the Prophet himself changed the names of many individuals, finding them unsuitable. Ibn

Ishaq has written about 'Abdu 'Amr becoming 'Abdu'l-Rahman after his conversion to Islam.[5] An interesting episode related to change in name is reported by Ibn-Ishaq. A narrator related to him the statement of some authority: "Umayya b. Khalaf was a friend of mine in Mecca and my name was 'Abdu 'Amr, but I was called Abdu'l Rahman when I became a Muslim. When we used to meet in Mecca he would say, "Do you dislike the name your parents gave you" and I would say yes; and he would say, "As for me I don't know al-Rahman, so adopt a name which I can call you between ourselves. You won't reply to your original name, and I won't use one I don't know." When he said O 'Abdu 'Amr" I wouldn't answer him, and finally I said, "O Abu 'Ali, call me what you like," and he called me "'Abdu'l-Ilah" and I accepted the name from him. Here, it is interesting to note that (i) change in nomenclature created communication gap, at least during initial days of Islam; (ii) surprisingly, 'Rahman,' a very known word by the Muslims of today, was not known to a Meccan during early days of Islam; (iii) the relationship between a Meccan Pagan and a Muslim, was some how cordial during the Meccan phase.[6]

Prophet Muhammad wanted ugly personal names to be replaced with good ones. He himself changed the name of Asiya (Umar's daughter; meaning 'disobedient') to Jamila (meaning 'good and handsome'),[7] and one of his wife, Barra's name (Barra means 'pious') to Juwairiya.[8] Muhammad forbade giving four names to servants, which are Aflah ('successful'), Rabah ('profit'), Yasar ('wealth'), and Nafi ('beneficial').[9] The vilest names, according to him, are 'Malik al-Amlak' and Shahinshah, both meaning 'king of kings.'[10] The dearest names to Allah, according to him, are 'Subhan Allah' (meaning, 'Hallowed be Allah') and Hamidulillah (meaning, 'praise be to Allah')[11]

Prophet Muhammad attached great importance to omens, especially those connected with names. Margoliouth has written:

"When a man was wanted to milk a camel, he disqualified one applicant after another, till one offered whose name meant "long life." Whenever the name of a new adherent contained anything ill-omened, it was his custom to alter it; if a convert was named Rough, he called him Smooth.[12]

Margoliouth has further written about the changing the name of a Muslim convert. He writes: "The privilege of re-naming followers was one of which other prophets had availed themselves, and this Mohammad claimed wherever a proselyte was called after an idol, or title of honour were also conferred, but probably at a later time: Abu Bakr was called the 'Faithful Friend,' Zubair, 'the Apostle,' Abu Ubaidah, son of Jarrah, 'the Faithful,' Omar, 'the Saviour.' These were like the decorations conferred by the sovereign in modern times on persons who have either done some public service, or are entrusted with some important charge.[13] Thus, we find Prophet Muhammad giving good names[14] or changing bad names[15] to his followers. But bad names were also given to the enemy. We find Muhammad's bitterest enemy, Abu Hakam's name changed to Abu Jahl (father of darkness).

References

1. Muir, Sir William, *The Life of Mahomet*, p. 57 note 2; hereafter Muir.
2. Ibn Ishaq, *Sirat Rasul Allah*, p. 82; hereafter Ibn Ishaq.
3. Ibn-Ishaq, p. 82.
4. Lesley Hazleton, *The Last Prophet*, p. 105. Hereafter Hazleton.
5. Ibn Ishaq, p. 302.
6. Ibid.
7. *Sahih Muslims, Hadis*, 5332.
8. Ibid, *Hadis* 5334.
9. Ibid, *Hadis* 5327.
10. Ibid, *Hadis* 5338.
11. Ibid, *Hadis* 5329.
12. Margoliouth, D.S., *Mohammed and The Rise of Islam*, pp.61-62.
13. Ibid, p. 110.
14. *Sahih Muslim, Hadis* 1404.
15. Ibn Ishaq, p. 302.

Glossary

Abbasites (*Abbasi*) : Descendants of 'Abbas-bin-'l-Muttalib,uncle of the Prophet Muhammad. This dynasty had the caliphate for 507 years from 750 To 1257 AD

'Abd : A male slave.

'Ad : An ancient, prosperous tribe destroyed by Allah with violent destructive westerly wind due to its naughtiness and disobedience to Allah.

Ad-Dabur : Westerly wind.

Adhan : Call to prayer pronounced loudly.

Adhkhar/Idhkhir : A kind of good-smelling grass of Hijaz, Saudi Arabia.

Adl : Divine Justice.

Ahkam : 'Orders;' there are five kinds of orders according to Islamic law:

1. *Wajib* or compulsory,
2. *Mustahab* or 'order' without obligation,
3. *Muharram* or forbidden,
4. *Makruh,* 'disliked' but not forbidden,
5. *Halal* or 'legal and allowed'.

Ahlu'l Bayt or *Itrat* : Household or progeny of Prophet Muhammad.

Ahl'l- Kitab : The People of the Books; Jews and Christians.

Ahlu'r Ra;I : Persons following their own opinion in absence of a clear instruction of Allah in Qur;an or Sunnat.

Ahlu'r-Ra'i-w'al-Qiyas : Persons following hypothetical assumptions and opinion in religion.

Akhirat : Last judgment.

'Ajwa : A kind of dates; pressed soft dates.

Al-ahzab : The confederates.

Al-'Amanah : Allah's ordained duty, the trust, the moral responsibility, honesty.

Al-Aqiq : A valley, about seven kilometers west of Medina.

Al-Awamir : Snakes living in houses.

Al-Bahira : A milking she-camel, whose milk was used for the idols.

Al-Baida	:	A place between Mecca and Medina.
Al-Bait-ul-Mamur	:	Allah's House over the seventh heaven.
Al-Batsh	:	The Grasp.
Al-Fatiha	:	The first *Surah* of the Quran.
Al-Firdaus	:	The middle and the highest part of Paradise.
Al-Ghaba	:	A place near Medina (Literally, the forest).
Al-Hudaibiya	:	A place ten miles away from Mecca.
Al-Kauthar	:	A river in paradise (see Quran, Surah 108).
Al-Madina	:	Athrib; the place where the Prophet migrated from Mecca.
Al-Maghazi	:	Plural of Maghza; holy battle, battle place, deeds and virtues of *Ghazi* (warriors in Allah's cause).
Al-Maqum-al-Mahmud	:	The highest place in Paradise to be granted only to Prophet Muhammad (See Sahih Al-Bukhari, Vol. 6, Hadith no. 242).
Al-Qaswa	:	The name of the Prophet's she-camel.
Allahu-Akbar	:	Allah is the Most Great.
'Ama	:	A female slave.
'Amin	:	O Allah, accept our invocation.
Amin	:	The truthful person; trustee in Allah.
Amir	:	Commander, chief leader.
Amiru'l-Mominin	:	The leader of the faithful, caliph.
Ansar	:	Helpers; the Muslim Companions of Prophet Muhammad from Medina who received and supported the Muslim emigrants from Mecca and elsewhere.
'Anaza	:	A spear-headed stick.
Aql	:	Wisdom.
Aqli	:	Intellectual.
'Arafat	:	A place of Muslim pilgrimage about 25 kilometers towards south-east of Mecca.
Ayat	:	Evidence, proof, verses, lessons, revelations, signs, etc.
Ayat-al-Kursi	:	Verse no. 255 of *Sirat Al-Baqarah* of Qur'an.
Azan	:	Call for prayer.
Badana	:	A sacrificial animal to be offered as sacrifice by a pilgrim at the Sanctuary of Mecca; plural – *Budn*.
Badr	:	Historic battleplace, about 150 kms to the south of Medina, where the first battle was fought between the Muslims and the Kureish of Mecca.

Bai'a : A pledge; a pledge of obedience given by the Muslims to their Imam (Muslim Ruler).

Bait : House; *Baitullah* – house of Allah; *Bait-ul-Maqdis* – the famous Mosque of Jerusalem.

Bait-ul-Midras : A place in Medina; originally a Jewish centre.

Banu al-Asfar : The Byazantines.

Bu'ath : A place, two miles away from Medina, where a battle between two tribes of Medina – Al-'Aus and Al-Khazraj – took place. during pre-Islamic days.

Barid : The distance of three Farsakh (equal to 12 miles); plural – *Burud.*

Bin (b. or *Ibn*) : Son of

Bint : Daughter of

Burhan : Demonstration, evidence of fact.

Caliph or *Khaliph* : A Muslim ruler; *Imam.*

Caliphate : The Muslim state.

Daniq : A coin equivalent to one sixth of a *Dirham.*

Dar : House.

Darud-wa'l-Salam: Allah's blessing.

Dar-ul-Hurb : The region of war; a non-Muslim region or State.

Dar-ul-Islam : Islamic region or State.

Dar-ul-Qada : Court; the House of Justice.

Da'wat : Feast, propagation.

Dhimmi : Non-Muslim living under an Islamic State paying protection tax, *Jijiya.*

Dinar : A gold coin used in ancient days.

Dirham : A silver coin.

Din : Religion.

Diya : Blood money paid by the killer or his relatives; plural – *Diyat.*

Duha : Forenoon.

'Eid-al-Adha : The four days' Muslim festival starting on the tenth day of Dhul-Hijja month.

'Eid-al-Fitr : The three days' Muslim festival starting on the first day of *Shawwal* month, following the month of *Ramdan/ Ramjan*, the Month-long fasting month of the Muslims. *Fitr* means breaking the *Saum* (fast).

Eidu'l-Miladu'l-Nabi : Prophet Muhammad's birth anniversary celebration.

Fadak : A town near Medina.
Fahish : The person talking evil.
Fai : The war-booty gained without war or fighting; it, exclusively comes in the share of the Allah and the Prophet.
Fajr : Dawn, early morning before sunrise, morning Salat (prayer).
Faqih : A learned man capable of delivering religious verdict.
Fara'id : Fixed share of the relatives of a deceased.
Faraq : A measuring bowl.
Farsakh : A distance of about three miles.
Fasiq : Sinful.
Fatat : A female slave, a young lady.
Fatwa : Islamic edict.
Fidai' : Devotee, who willingly hazards his life; Plural – *Fidai'n.*
Ghazi : A mujahid, who has slaughtered infidel(s) in Jihad.
Ghazw : A holy war with the Prophet himself leading the army.
Ghazwat-ul-Khandaq: A war between the Muslims and the Makkan army, in which a trench (*Khandaq*) was dug to prevent the enemy from entering Medina.
Ghusl : Bath, taking bath.
Hadi : An Islamic spiritual guide.
Hadith : Traditions, collections of the Islamic traditions, Prophet's sayings and deeds.
Hady : A sacrificial animal.
Hais : A dish prepared from butter, dates and cheese.
Hajaru'l-Aswad : The Black Stone, believed by the Muslims to have come from the heaven.
Hajj : Pilgrimage to Mecca.
Hajjam : One who performs cupping.
Halal : Lawful.
Hanif : Islamic Monotheism.
Haram : Unlawful, forbidden by religion.
Hawazin : A Quraish tribe.
Hijra : Muhammad's migration from Mecca to Madina.
Hira : A well-known cave in a mountain near Mecca.
Houris : Very fair females of the paradise with intense black irises of their eyes and intense white scleras.

Hubal	:	A pre-Islamic deity whose idol was worshipped in Kaaba by non-Muslims.
Hudud	:	Allah's boundary line between Halal (lawful) and Haram (unlawful).
Hukm	:	A judgement, legal decision.
Hulul	:	Incarnation.
Hums	:	A community residing in Mecca.
Hunain	:	A valley between Mecca and At-Taif, where the battle took place between Prophet Muhammad and Pagan Quraish.
Iddah	:	Prescribed period for divorce and marriage, etc. (vide Quran, Surat 65).
Iftar	:	Breaking the fast.
Ihram	:	A state, such as during *'Umra* and *Hajj*, in which one is prohibited to do certain things. During *Umra* or *Hajj*, when o*ne* enters into the state of *ihram*, the first thing he should do is to express mentally and orally his intention to assume the state of ihram for performing the same, recite *Talbiya*, put on two sheets of unstitched cloths – one below the waist, called *Izar*, and the other round the upper part of the body, called *Rida'*.
Ihsan	:	The state of deeds and worship, when one considers himself if he sees Allah, or bearing in mind that Allah sees him.
Ijma	:	The only way to resolve or to agree on religious issues in In Shi'is is by the consensus of all the clergies; principles, such as *Qiyas* (analogical reasoning), *Istihsan* (lenient interpretation), *Masaelu'l-Mursala* (expedient issues) – the three elements of *Ijma* – unlike in the case of Sunnis, do not help in reaching any authentic judgment. Same is the case with Taqlid (emulation) and Ijtihad.
Ijtihad	:	The process of innovative exegesis, in points of religious law using reason and principles of jurisprudence, to arrive at judgment; exertion.
Ikhtiyar	:	One's responsibility for his/her actions; free will.
Ila	:	The oath of not approaching one's wife for certain period.
Ilhad	:	Heresy.
Iliya	:	Jerusalem.

Imam	:	One who leads others in prayer (*Salat*), the caliph.
Imamat	:	Imamate.
Iman	:	Belief, faith.
Ikamat-as-Salat	:	The performance of Salat.
Iradah	:	Will.
Irfan	:	Spiritual wisdom.
'Ismat	:	The state of being sinless and infallible.
Istihsan	:	Lenient interpretation of Shari'a.
Ithna-Ash'ari	:	Twelve Shi'is.
Jabr	:	Predeterminsm; One has no choice, but bound to do as predestined.
Jahiliyah	:	Age of ignorance.
Jidal	:	Dialectics; conclusion or arriving at the facts through scientific debate.
Jihad	:	The holy war in the cause of Allah; one of the fundamentals of Islam; to strive hard in the path of Allah; struggle.
Jinn	:	A creation of Allah from fire; man was created from mud and angels from light.
Jizya	:	An Islamic tax on non-Muslims; protection tax.
Jumu'a	:	Friday.
Junub	:	One, in a state of *Janaba*.
Jurhum	:	Name of a tribe.
Ka'ba	:	A square stone building in the great mosque of Mecca; the Muslims turn their faces towards the same during prayer.
Kafir	:	Pagan, infidel, apostat.
Khariji	:	The sect driven out of Islam; plural – *Khawarij*.
Khilafat	:	Caliphate.
Khula	:	Wife's right of separation as per religious law; dismissal.
Khumus	:	1/5 annual tax levied on net profit.
Kufa	:	A town of Iraq.
Kufr	:	Infidelity, blasphemy.
Kuniya/Kunya	:	Calling a person as a father or mother of so and so; an Arabian practice; as for example, Prophet Muhammad was called 'Abu'l Kasim (father of Kasim).
Al-Mahdi	:	Rightly guided one, 12th Imam.
Mu'azzin	:	Caller for prayer.

Muhajir	:	An emigrant, Muslim emigrants from Mecca to Madina.
Muharram	:	The first month of Arabian calendar; a Muslim festival.
Muhrim	:	A person in the state of *Ihram* for the performance of *Hajj* or *Umra*.
Muhrima	:	A female in the state of *Ihram*.
Muhsar	:	A *Muhrim*, intending to perform *Hajj* or *'Umra*, but unable to do so due to some obstacle.
Mujahid	:	A Muslim warrior, a jihadi; plural – *Mujahidin*.
Mujtahidun	:	Religious scholars only following Kuran and the *Sunna* of the Prophet.
Mukatab	:	A male or female slave binding himself or herself to pay certain ransom for freedom.
Mula'ana	:	The act of performing *Li'an* (*Li'an* is an oath taken by the wife and the husband when the husband accuses his wife committing illegal sex; Quran 24:6,7,8,9).
Mulhidun	:	Heretical.
Mumin	:	Believer (in Islam); plural – Muminin.
Munafiqun	:	Hypocrites; a section of Muslims of Medina, who, according to Kuran and Hadis, were believed to be enemies of Islam; singular – *Munafiq*.
Mushrikun	:	Idolater, polytheist, Pagan; singular – *Mushrik*.
Mut'a	:	A temporary marriage allowed in the early period of Islam, but abrogated later on.
Nabi	:	Prophet, *Rasul*, messenger of Allah; a divinely inspired person.
Namaz	:	*Salat*, prayer.
Nikah	:	Islamic Marriage
Qiblah	:	The direction towards Ka'ba, in which the Muslims face during prayer.
Qiyas	:	Verdict given by the Islamic religious scholars.
Quraish	:	The tribe to which Prophet Muhammad belonged.
Quraishi	:	A person belonging to the Quraish tribe.
Qiyamah	:	Catastrophe.
Qaza	:	Divine decree.
Qazi	:	Judge of Islamic court.
Qur'an	:	Quran, Koran, Kuran; the word of Allah.
Rabb	:	Lord, owner, the term is also used for Allah.
Rabbuka	:	Your Lord.

Ramadhan/Ramajan : The Islamic month of fasting (*Saum*).
Riba : Usury.
Rida : A piece of cloth worn around upper part of the body.
Roza : *Saum*, fast during the month of Ramjan.
Ruh : Spirit, breath.
Sabath : Religiously ordained rest in Semitic religions; Saturday and Sunday are the *Sabath* days for Jews and Christians respectively.
Sadaqa : Anything given in charity.
Sadiq : One, who is absolutely truthful.
Sahab : Companions of the Prophet.
Shahadah : Profession of Islamic faith.
Sahifa : The Book.
Salat : *Namaz*, the prayer.
Sariya : The army unit/expedition in which prophet did not participate.
Sarif : A place six miles distant from Mecca.
Sa'y : The ritual of going seven times between As-Safa and Al-Marwa Mountains in Mecca during Hajj ceremony.
Sayyid : Master, title of the descendants of Prophet Muhammad.
Sayyidi : My master.
Sham : The region comprising Syria, Palestine, Lebanon and Jordan.
Shari'a : Islamic jurisprudence, the law of Islam.
Shj'a/Shi'I : A prominent sect of Islam; followers of Imam Ali.
Shighar : Exchange marriage in which persons exchange their daughters or sisters and marry without *Mahr*.
Shirk : *Kufr*, Polytheism, worshipping others along with Allah sin.
Siddiq : First and the foremost followers of the Prophet (see Kuran V.4.69); plural – *Siddiqun*.
Subhan Allah : Allah be glorified.
Sufi : An Islamic ascetic sect.
Sultan : Monarch.
Sunni/
Ahlu'l-Sunnat-wa'l- Jama't : Sunni sect of Islam.
Sura : A chapter of Quran.
Tabarrah : Being emotional and Using abusive language for the

enemies of the Prophet and his family.

Tafsir : Exegesis or commentary of the whole or part of Koran.

Talaq : Divorce.

Tanasukh : Transmigration of soul.

Taqiyyah : Concealment of faith for self-protection if life is threatened.

Tasbih : Reciting Allah's glory on the beads of rosary.

Ṫawhid : Divine unity.

Tawaf : Circumambulation of Mecca.

Thaur : A mountain of Madina.

Tulaqa : The persons who embraced Islam on the day of the conquest of Mecca.

Tur : A mountain.

Uhud : A mountain near Madina where the battle between Muslims and Kuraysh, called *Ghazwa Uhud* was fought.

'Ulama : Islamic scholars; singular – *Alim.*

Umayyites : Descendants of Umayya,

Ummah : Islamic community.

Umm-al-Walad: A slave-woman who begets child for the master.

'Umra : A pilgrimage to Mecca during which the *Tawaf* around Ka'ba and *Sa'y* between As-Safa and Al-Marwa in is performed (see *Sahih Al-Bukhari*, Vol. 3, page 1).

'Ushr : One-tenth of the land's yield to be taxed as *Zakat* (see *Sahih Al-Bukhari*, Vol. 2, Hadith No. 560).

Usulu'd Din : Principles of Islam.

Wahy : Revelation from Allah.

Waihaka : May Allah be Merciful to you.

Wailaka : 'Woe upon you.

Wala : Relationship between freed slave and the master who freed him.

Wali : Guardian, protector, helper, supporter, friend, etc.

Walima : Marriage banquet.

Waqf : Religious endowment.

Wasay : Wills of testament.

Yakin : Absolute faith.

Yathrib : Old name of Madina.

Zakat : The poor tax paid by every Muslim.

Zakat-ur-Fitr : An obligatory Sadaqa given by the Muslims before he

		The prayer of Eid-ul-Fitr (see *Sahih al-Bukhari*, Vol. 2, *The book of Zakat-al-Fitr*).
Zam-zam	:	The sacred well inside the grand mosque (*Haram*) in Mecca.
Zanadiqa	:	Atheist.
Zuhr	:	Noon, mid-day prayer is called *Zuhr* prayer (*Salat*).

Bibliography

Qur'an

1. *The Holy Qur'an*, Translation and Commentary by A. Yusuf Ali, Islamic Propagation Centre International, Durban.
2. *The Qur'an*, English Translation and Parallel Arabic Text, English translation by M.A.S. Abdel Haleem, Oxford University Press, New York, 2010.
3. *The Holy Qur'an*, Transliteration in Roman Script with Original Arabic Text, English translation by M. Marmaduke Pickthall; Kitab Bhawan, New Delhi, 2007.
4. *Quran Majid*, with Arabic text, and Hindi translation and Devanagari transliteration by Muhammad Farukh Khan, Maktab Al Hasanat, New Delhi, 2006.
5. *The Qur'an*, The Sacred Books of thc East (in Two Vols.), edited by F. Max Muller, translated by E.H. Palmer, Delhi, Reprint (2006, 2007).
6. *The Essential KORAN*, Thomas Cleary, Harper Collins *Publishers* India, New Delhi (2011).

Hadis

1. *Sahih Muslim*, English translation with notes by Abdul Hamid Siddiqi in four volumes, Kitab Bhawan, New Delhi, 2004.
2. *Sahih Bukhari*, Summarized edition, Arabic-English, translation by Dr. Muhammad Muhsin Khan, Maktab Dar-us-Salam, Riyadh, Saudi Arabia, 1994.
3. *Mishkat-ul-Masabih*, in three vols., translated and annotated by Abdul Hameed Siddiqi, Kitab Bhawan, New Delhi, 2009.

Biography of Prophet Muhammad

1. *Sirat Rasul Allah* by Ibn Ishaq; English translation, *The Life of Muhammad* by A. Guillaume, Oxford University Press, Karachi, 1996.
2. *The Life of Mahomet*, Sir William Muir, Reprint, New Delhi, 2002.
3. *Muhammad and the Rise of Islam*, D.S. Margoliouth, Reprint, New Delhi, 1985.
4. *The First Muslim*, Lesley Hazleton, Atlantice Books, London, 2013.

Fatwas

1. *The World of Fatwas or The Shariat in Action*, Arun Shourie, HarperCollins *Publishers* India, New Delhi, 1997.
2. *Fatwa on Terrorism and Suicide Bombing*, Shaykh-ul-islam Dr. Muhammad Tahir-ul-Qadri, Hyderabad (India), London (UK), 2011.

General

1. *Tabakat-i-Nasri,* Two Vols., Malana Minhaj-ud-Din and Abu-'Umar-i-'Usmam, translation from original Persian manuscript by Major H.G Raverty, Reprint, New Delhi, 2010.
2. *The Preaching of Islam,* T.W. Arnold, Reprint, Delhi, 2006.
3. *Politics and Development of the Jamaat-e-Islami Bangladesh,* Bhuian Md. Monoar Kabir, Dhaka, 2006.
4. *Religion and Science, a Philosophical Approach,* Hamid Rezania, New Delhi, 2012.
5. *Understanding Islam,* Ram Swarup, Voice of India, Delhi,
6. *Hinduism and Monotheistic Religions,* Ram Swarup, Voice of India, New Delhi, 2009.
7. *Understanding Islam through Hadis,* Ram Swarup, Voice of India, New Delhi, 2001
8. *Tall Islam and Small Muslims*, Mumtaz Ali Khan, New Delhi, 2013.
9. *The Essence of Islam*, Saiyed Jafar Reza, New Delhi, 2012.
10. *Combining Religious Extremism in Central Asia: Problems and Perspectives*, Dusambe, Tajikistan, 2002.
11. *Theory and Practice of Muslim State in India*, K.S. Lal, New Delhi, 1999.
12. *The Legacy of Muslim Rule in India*, K.S. Lal, New Delhi, 1992.
13. *Hindu Temples, What happened to them*, Sita Ram Goel, Voice of India, New Delhi,
14. *Islam Vis-à-vis Hindu Temples*, Sita Ram Goel, New Delhi, 1993.
15. *Demolishing Myths or Mosques and Temples*, Sunil Kumar (Ed.), Gurgaon, 2008.
16. *Endangered Democracy*, Bimal Pramanik, Kolkata, 2005.
17. *Illegal Migration from Bangladesh*, B.B. Kumar (Ed.), New Delhi,
18. *India and Central Asia*, K. Santhanam and R.K. Dwivedi, New Delhi, 2004. There is some material on religious extremism in the book.
19. *A Secular Agenda*, Arun Shourie, New Delhi, 1997.
20. *Negationism in India,* Koenraad Elst, Voice of India, New Delhi, 1993.

21. *Religious Democracy of India,* Centre for Policy Studies Chennai, Chennai, 2003.
22. *Agrarian System of Mughal India,: 1556-1707,* Oxford, New Delhi, 1999.
23. *Muslim League Attack on Sikhs and Hindus in the Punjab: 1947,* New Delhi, 1991.
24. *Indo-Bangladesh Relations in the New Millenium,* The Centre for Research in Indo-Bangladesh Relations, Kolkata, 2003.
25. *Jihadis in Jammu and Kashmir,* K. Santhanam and others, IDSA, New Delhi, 2003.
26. *Bharat Vibhajan ke Gunahgar* (Hindi), Ram Manohar Lohi, New Delhi, 1906.
27. *Terrorism and the Indian Media,* Rakesh Sinha, India Policy Foundation, New Delhi, 2009.
28. *Islam and the Religious Riots: A Case Study, Riots and Wrongs,* R.N.P. Singh, India First Foundation, New Delhi, 2004.
29. *Deadly Embrace,* Bruce Riedel, HarperCollins *Publishers* India, New Delhi,2011.
30. *The Caliphate's Soldiers,* Wilson John, Amaryllis in association with Observer Research Foundation, New Delhi, 2011.
31. *Growth of Scheduled Tribes and Castes in Medieval India*, K.S. Lal, New Delhi, 1995.

Journals

1. *Islam and the Modern World*, Zakir Husain Institute of Islamic Studies, Jamia Milia Islamia, New Delhi.
2. *Russia and the Muslim World,* Bulletin of Analytical Reference information, Institute for Scientific Information in Social Sciences, Institute of Oriental Studies, Russian Academy of Sciences, Moscow.
3. *Dialogue*, Journal of Astha Bharati, Delhi.
4. *Dialogue*, Organization for Islamic Culture and Communication and Relations, Secretariat for Inter Religious Dialogue, Tehran.

Index

35